W9-AGG-782

Jossey-Bass Teacher

Jossey-Bass Teacher provides K–12 teachers with essential knowledge and tools to create a positive and lifelong impact on student learning. Trusted and experienced educational mentors offer practical classroom-tested and theory-based teaching resources for improving teaching practice in a broad range of grade levels and subject areas. From one educator to another, we want to be your first source to make every day your best day in teaching. *Jossey-Bass Teacher* resources serve two types of informational needs—essential knowledge and essential tools.

Essential knowledge resources provide the foundation, strategies, and methods from which teachers may design curriculum and instruction to challenge and excite their students. Connecting theory to practice, essential knowledge books rely on a solid research base and time-tested methods, offering the best ideas and guidance from many of the most experienced and well-respected experts in the field.

Essential tools save teachers time and effort by offering proven, ready-to-use materials for in-class use. Our publications include activities, assessments, exercises, instruments, games, ready reference, and more. They enhance an entire course of study, a weekly lesson, or a daily plan. These essential tools provide insightful, practical, and comprehensive materials on topics that matter most to K–12 teachers.

Classroom Teacher's Survival Guide

Second Edition

Classroom Teacher's Survival Guide

Practical Strategies, Management
Techniques, and Reproducibles
for New and Experienced Teachers

Second Edition

Ronald L. Partin

JOSSEY-BASS
A Wiley Imprint
www.josseybass.com

Published by Jossey-Bass
A Wiley Imprint
989 Market Street, San Francisco, CA 94103-1741   www.josseybass.com

Jossey-Bass books and products are available through most bookstores. To contact Jossey-Bass directly call our Customer Care Department within the U.S. at 800-956-7739, outside the U.S. at 317-572-3986, or fax 317-572-4002.

Jossey-Bass also publishes its books in a variety of electronic formats. Some content that appears in print may not be available in electronic books.

Some images © 2003-4 www.clipart.com

ISBN 0-7879-7253-3

Printed in the United States of America
SECOND EDITION
PB Printing   10 9 8 7 6

*Dedicated with much love and pride to
our grandchildren,*

*Braedon Long, Jacob Partin,
Brooke Partin, and Aaron Partin*

Contents

The Author

Ronald L. Partin, professor emeritus and former coordinator of the graduate guidance and counseling program at Bowling Green State University, holds a Ph.D. degree in educational psychology and counseling and has more than thirty years' experience as an educator, scholar, and consultant. As a counselor educator, he taught courses in counseling, educational consultation, group dynamics, and learning psychology. A former high school teacher and coach, Ron is in frequent demand as a speaker, trainer, and consultant. He uses his classroom experiences to teach and motivate, with his everyday examples and ready-to-implement techniques.

Ron is the author of numerous journal articles in the areas of time management, goal setting, creative problem solving, stress management, and effective teaching skills. He is the coauthor of P.R.I.D.E., a training program on effective classroom management, which over forty thousand teachers nationwide have completed. Ron is the coauthor of *The Social Studies Teacher's Survival Kit* (Prentice Hall, 1992) and author of *The Prentice Hall Directory of Online Social Studies Resources* (Prentice Hall, 1998) and *The Social Studies Teacher's Book of Lists* (Jossey-Bass, 2nd ed., 2003). He is the editor of *The Heart of Teaching* newsletter, which Performance Learning Systems distributes to teachers nationally. Ron is known for facilitating fun, interactive workshops and has been invited to present programs to over four hundred schools, businesses, and professional organizations.

Ron and his wife, Jan, are now enjoying their second adulthoods as residents amid the mountains of western North Carolina. Their twin sons are both gainfully employed and are excellent parents. Ron collects hobbies: woodworking, genealogy, golf, square dancing, bluegrass music, gardening, stained glass, and travel. His overwhelming passion continues to be helping teachers thrive in the classroom. He may be contacted at rpartin@bgnet.bgsu.edu.

Acknowledgments

The greatest source of ideas for this book are the hundreds of teachers who participated in my workshops and classes over the past thirty years. Where known, the original or published sources are credited for any ideas used. This project would have been much more difficult without the emotional support and encouragement of my wife, Jan.

The selection of clip art in this book is from a variety of electronic sources, including the following: ArtToday subscription service, DeskTop Art by Dynamic Graphics, Desk Gallery by Zedcor Corporation, Digit Art from Image Club Graphics, Metro ImageBase, Click Art from T/Maker Company, Image Club, Imagenes With Impact!, School Clip Art from Quality Computers, and Volk Clip Art from Dynamic Graphics. Special appreciation goes to Performance Learning Systems for permission to excerpt items from *The Heart of Teaching* newsletter, which I edit.

The diligent efforts of Steve Thompson, education editor; Pamela Berkman, senior production editor; and the rest of the editorial staff at Jossey-Bass are most appreciated.

About This Book

Each year 130,000 new teachers assume teaching positions in U.S. elementary, middle, and high schools. Most are filled with enthusiasm—ready to enrich their students' minds—only to be dismayed to find that not all of their students are on the edge of their seats ready to receive their inspired words of wisdom. Beginning teachers are often unprepared to cope with the overwhelming paperwork, flying spitballs, irate parents, machines that don't work, occasionally cantankerous administrators, and unpredictable challenges of the real-world classroom.

Most survive; but the first year can be a most stressful, frustrating, and painful learning process. Some teachers do not survive their rookie season; and approximately 40 percent leave the profession within the first four years, disillusioned and prematurely burned out. While colleges of education strive to adequately prepare students for what lies ahead in their first classroom assignment, general education requirements, methods courses, and state-mandated courses fill the teacher-preparation curriculum, leaving the burden of reality testing the textbook knowledge of classroom teaching to a single student-teaching experience. Most of the daily survival techniques are left to on-the-job experience. The costs of such trials by fire are high—impaired mental and physical health of the "defeated" teachers, lost learning opportunities for their students, and the lower organizational effectiveness and decreased morale of the school community.

The content of *Classroom Teacher's Survival Guide* is derived from experienced teachers' contributions of "all the things I wish I had known when I started" or "things I had to learn the hard way." This survival guide provides a smorgasbord of strategies and tips for solving the main problems teachers face: organizing and managing the classroom, achieving a working relationship with students and maintaining classroom control, working with other adults in the school community (including parents), developing competence as an effective instructor, and coping with the daily stresses of teaching. Teachers can learn from veteran educators' mistakes and successes. This treasury of survival skills is not intended as a simple cookbook but rather provides a range of practical options for teachers to adapt to fit their unique classroom situations. These ideas and strategies are to be tested and modified to fit the user's grade level and specific needs.

Much research suggests that the events of the first few weeks of school determine the teacher's success. Hence, much of the book focuses on strategies for beginning the school year. It also provides scores of practical tips, most gathered from successful classroom teachers or gleaned from research on outstanding teachers. The *Classroom Teacher's Survival Guide* provides a treasury of suggestions, tips, checklists, reproducible overhead transparency masters, posters, ready-to-use forms, letters, and activities. These will help beginning and experienced teachers save time while tapping the wealth of knowledge of successful educators.

When I wrote the first edition of this book, I had no idea what kind of reception it would receive. The positive feedback I have received, particularly from beginning teachers, has been most rewarding. The fact that a number of districts provide each beginning teacher a copy reinforces the importance of practical strategies and timesaving suggestions to augment the theoretical and philosophical foundations new teachers learned in undergraduate school.

However, change in the teacher's role and the learning environment has spread rapidly since I wrote the first edition. The standards-based, high-stakes testing movement has mushroomed. The Internet has reached into virtually every classroom in America. Demands on teachers' time have grown, along with increased responsibility and accountability. The challenges to become more effective, as well as more efficient, have probably never been greater. Incorporating suggestions from practicing teachers who have used the first volume, this edition should prove even more helpful.

—Ronald L. Partin

Classroom Teacher's
Survival Guide

Chapter One

Creating a Supportive Learning Environment

The First Day of School

The foundation for a successful school year is laid on the first day of school. Everything you do the first day sets the tone for the rest of the year. Spending time planning and organizing the first day's activities is one of the most valuable investments you can make as a teacher.

Your three primary objectives the first day of school are to get acquainted, establish your expectations, and stimulate enthusiasm and interest in what you are teaching. The best advice for the first day is "Be prepared." You want to convey to your students that you are organized, are in control, and know what you are doing. It is wise to develop a checklist of items to cover the first day.

Arranging Successful Classrooms

Before the first day of school, spend time organizing your classroom for maximum efficiency. The physical arrangement of your classroom can influence your students' behavior and learning. The placement of desks, bookshelves, pencil sharpeners, and cabinets can influence traffic flow, student interaction, noise level, attention, or disruption. The impact of the room arrangement is too important to leave to chance.

Plan the classroom learning environment before the beginning of the school year. Your goals for the class must guide your choices. Whether you wish to maximize group interaction with lots of small-group activities or lecture most of the time, the physical arrangement can help or hinder. Students get a pretty good picture of what their year is going to be like from the decor and arrangement of the classroom as they enter for the first time.

More than creating aesthetic appeal, each piece of furniture redefines a part of the classroom space, directing attention, pupil interaction, or traffic flow. Overlooking the importance of even casual rearrangements within the classroom is easy. Something as simple as the placement of a new pencil sharpener, a new bookshelf, or an area rug can have a significant impact on the learning events of your classroom.

The environment you see may be quite different from the one your students perceive, especially younger ones. When no one else is around, crouch down to the children's eye level and view your room as they see it. Waddle around the room to see how the furniture directs your attention and movement.

Draw your current classroom arrangement to scale on graph paper. Include all the furniture, windows, doors, bulletin boards, electrical plugs, cabinets, wastebasket, and pencil sharpener. Observe your class for a day, noting on your drawing the traffic patterns. Indicate any bottlenecks. Are there any areas that invite students to stop and talk? Does the present arrangement direct students through work centers or group activities? Are there dead spaces that no one ever enters? Be sure to place electrical equipment so that students cannot trip over the cords.

Arrange any special areas in the room. Some teachers have reading areas, perhaps with stuffed furniture, a rug, or pillows. Have the necessary supplies and materials sorted and organized for any learning centers, art area, writing area, labs, and so on.

Give special attention to minimizing unnecessary noise in your classroom. Where possible, use soft, quiet, sound-absorbing materials: carpeting, rubber, sponge, cardboard, and cork.

Students' Desks

The single most important decision influencing the physical classroom environment is the students' seating arrangement. Ideally, the arrangement of students' desks should not be permanent, except for large lecture halls or laboratories. The purpose of the learning activity should dictate the most favorable seating pattern. Unless furniture is bolted to the floor, it can be moved during the day as the lesson dictates. The custodial staff's ease of cleaning should play only a minor role in such decisions. What to do:

✔ If your class uses several seating arrangements regularly, teach your students how to move from one to another as quickly and quietly as possible. You may want smaller children to help each other carry desks without dragging them across the floor.

✔ Seating students in clusters or around a table facilitates group interaction. This arrangement enhances small-group discussions and cooperative learning, but it also invites chatting and socializing.

✔ Whole-class discussion is facilitated with a circular, semicircular, or open-ended rectangular seating arrangement. Traditional rows are probably least supportive of student-to-student interaction.

✔ Traditional seating in rows has endured because it is very functional for many classroom purposes. Particularly early in the year, seating students in rows enables you to observe behavior more easily and minimizes distractions. Research has shown that row seating produces higher levels of on-task behavior in elementary classrooms. The greater the distance between students, the less they distract each other. Independent seatwork, lecture, movies, and tests are activities that row seating can facilitate.

✔ Performance classes, labs, and special activities such as story time might dictate atypical seating choices or even no seats at all. The important thing is to monitor your seating pattern's effects. Don't be afraid to experiment with different arrangements to achieve different results.

✔ After a few weeks, experiment with different seating arrangements. Simply changing the seating patterns, even which direction the seats face, will influence your group's dynamics.

✔ To minimize the tendency to look primarily at the students in the front and center of a classroom, make a conscious attempt to scan the back corners, where the more disruptive students tend to cluster. It is often wise to move disruptive students to the front center, as that is the natural region of most eye contact. Interestingly, some researchers have discovered that students' test scores increase after they move to the front center. However, avoid seating two troublesome students next to each other.

✔ Give careful consideration to the direction students normally face in your chosen seating arrangement. As they will attend most to whatever is in their direct line of sight, try to arrange for students to face away from windows and doors to minimize distractions. Facing windows or bright lights creates excessive glare, causing eyestrain.

If you have several learning centers or areas in your room, separate noisy from quiet areas. Plan your seating so that you can move freely among students when providing individual assistance. Avoid seating arrangements that hide some students behind bookshelves or cabinets. Avoid creating mazes that force students into long, winding traffic patterns to reach the pencil sharpener or wastebasket.

Assigning Seats

You must decide before school begins whether to assign students to specific seats or to allow them to select their seats. Most teachers prefer to assign seats at first. It is best to announce that the initial seating assignments will be temporary. After having learned their names, established behavioral control, and taught students your desired procedures and routines, you might allow them to choose (or assign them) different seats. However, if you have several difficult students, it is best to maintain control over the seating pattern, separating troublemakers from one another and keeping them where you can easily monitor their behavior. You need not single them out or draw attention to the fact that you are putting them where you want them. Whatever seating pattern you select, always be sensitive to the special needs of hearing- or visually impaired students.

If you use printed seating charts, use a pencil to fill them in, as they will change. Keep any seating charts current in case a substitute must use them in your absence.

Another option is to tape or staple a clear transparency over the master seating chart. Names can be easily changed using an erasable marker on the transparency film.

Hot Tip for a Seating Chart

Becky Laabs, a veteran art teacher at Bowling Green City Schools (Ohio), devised a creative and handy seating chart that you can make too. On the outside of a manila folder, sketch your classroom-seating layout, with a small rectangle to represent each student's seat. Cut out small pieces of cardstock and print a different student's name on each one.

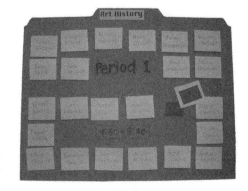

Attach each name to its appropriate spot with Velcro. Future changes in assigned seats will be easy to make, simply by switching the removable rectangles. Make a different colored folder for each class, if you have more than one.

Store daily lesson plans, papers to be returned, or other items inside the folder for easy access. The folder will prove especially valuable to any substitute teachers during the year.

Source: Reprinted with permission from *The Heart of Teaching* newsletter, Performance Learning Systems.

Note: Ron Partin is the editor of *The Heart of Teaching* newsletter, published five times a year by Performance Learning Systems. Subscriptions may be ordered at www.plsweb.com/ or by calling (800) 255-8412.

Keeping Desks Clean

Some students' desks begin to resemble an attic, hiding assorted old papers, tattered books, pencil stubs, broken crayons, pens, and miscellaneous treasures. Teachers have resorted to a range of tactics for encouraging students to keep their desks tidy, from spot checks to formal inspections with checksheets. Some choose to ignore the mess and allow students to suffer the consequences.

One strategy that many teachers adopt is to institute visits by a desk fairy, a mythical creature that visits their desks after school. If the desk is orderly, the fairy leaves a special surprise such as a certificate, sticker, or ribbon.

The Teacher's Desk

Not all teachers require a desk. If your room is crowded and you spend little time at your desk, consider removing it or replacing it with a small table and a filing cabinet. Some prefer an old-fashioned writing desk, which makes monitoring students easier. A high stool eases the burden on the feet.

If you do have a desk, the next choice is where to place it. It does not have to be at the front center of the classroom. If you do not usually sit at your desk during class, place it in a front corner or even at the back of the classroom. It is best not to place it near the door, thus inviting people to grab things off it as they leave the room or to interrupt or distract you as you work there. Make sure your desk does not block any student's view of the chalkboard.

Teachers have different perspectives on the ownership of their desks. Some prefer to define their desks as private territory, off-limits to students. They may even arrange bookshelves and filing cabinets to create barriers from others' intrusions.

Germs at Your Fingertips

A study by University of Arizona microbiologist Chuck Gerba revealed that the average desktop has four hundred times more bacteria than the average toilet seat. And the office telephone is even worse.

After collecting seven thousand bacteria samples from a variety of office building surfaces, Gerba found that bathrooms had the lowest levels of germs of all. The average keyboard had a count of three thousand bacteria per square inch, compared to the office toilet seat, which measured only fifty per square inch. His explanation: "People use disinfectant to clean that."

The telephone had the highest bacteria counts, closely followed by the desktop itself and the computer keyboard. Water fountain knobs and microwave oven door handles also harbored high levels of germs. The report concluded: "The oily grime that collects on keys and headsets becomes a breeding ground for bacteria, increasing the risk of colds and other infections spreading through an office. They get this contaminated because they're rarely cleaned."

The area where you rest your hand on your desk contains some ten million bacteria! While the research examined business offices, it is unlikely that cleaning patterns are any better in schools.

Gerba suggested that regularly cleaning the desktop greatly reduces the number of germs. Daily use of disinfecting wipes decreased the bacteria count by 99 percent.

Source: Gerba, C. (2002). *Office germ study.* Online at www.disinfectingwipes.com/. Reprinted with permission from *The Heart of Teaching* newsletter, Performance Learning Systems.

Note to the reader: This book intentionally omits the standard *http://* prefix from all Web site addresses. Most Internet browsers do not require users to type that prefix into the address bar.

Other teachers have an open-desk policy, inviting students to help themselves to staplers, tape, and other materials. Of course, a locked drawer or closet might be reserved for private belongings or confidential records. Whichever practice you adopt, communicate your expectations to your students at the beginning of the year.

Basic Classroom Supplies

Attendance forms	Old towels
Chalk	Paper
Cleaning rags	Paper clips
Clock	Paper towels
Desk calendar	Rolodex
Dictionary	Rubber bands
Disposable tissues	Rulers
Eraser	Stapler
Extension cord	Staples
Felt pens	Tape
File folders	Tardy slips
First-aid kit	Teacher's manuals for texts
Glue	Thumbtacks
Grade book	Tool kit
Hole punch	Whistle
Note cards	Yardstick

The Room Environment

✓ Be creative in arranging your room. You need not be bound by the traditional configurations, with everything arranged in a rectangle. Filing cabinets or bookshelves do not have to be placed against the walls. Placed at right angles to the wall, they create study areas or redirect traffic.

✓ Plan the traffic patterns you wish to create. Keep high-traffic areas, such as the pencil sharpener, clear of obstructions. If a student's desk is immediately in front of the pencil sharpener, a disturbance is inevitable when other students use the sharpener. Avoid patterns that create congestion by funneling many students through a small path.

✓ When working with small groups, place their chairs so that the students face away from the rest of the class. That prevents their being distracted by the rest of the class, and it allows you to monitor all students. If an aide is working with small groups, you may use a portable chalkboard to screen the small-group activity from the rest of the class.

✓ Keep the room tidy. Before allowing a class to leave the room, have students pick up litter around their desks. A cluttered and dirty environment invites further abuse. Similarly, have any graffiti removed immediately. Research has shown that graffiti's presence serves as a stimulus for more graffiti. Removal may involve some additional effort at first but saves time and damage later. Avoid creating an impression that abuse of the room is acceptable.

✓ Use posters, decorations, banners, signs, artifacts, and displays to create an inviting atmosphere. Changing them periodically to reflect the topic your class is studying is especially effective.

✓ Before school begins inspect your classroom to identify any broken, dirty, or unsightly clutter. Broken windows, hinges, desks, shades, or locks should be repaired or replaced. It may take time, but see your principal about how to get these things done. Don't give up easily if you encounter delays. Doing some smaller tasks yourself may be easier.

Your classroom's physical arrangement can minimize off-task behavior and invite learning. Experiment with changing your room setup, including the arrangement of students' desks, making it a regular part of your preparation. It pays dividends.

Greeting Your Students

On the first day, greet all students at the door with a smile and tell them where to sit. You might have a seating chart on the overhead with their names placed on their assigned seats. Some elementary teachers have name tents already at each student's desk. It is wise to direct them to begin work on a specific task as soon as they take their seats: completing a word puzzle, filling in a personal information survey, or scanning their textbook's table of contents. You are creating an expectation that learning begins as soon as your students enter the classroom, not necessarily when the bell rings.

The first day of school is likely the single most important day of the school year. Expectations are created; the foundation of routines and procedures are established; and first impressions are formed. You should be better organized and better prepared the first day than any other of the year. Recovering from a bad start will take a long time.

Post your name and room number beside your door. That will help students avoid the embarrassment of discovering ten minutes into the class that they are in the wrong room.

The first five to ten minutes of the first day's contact with your students is probably the most important segment of time the entire school year. Consider carefully what you want to accomplish these first few minutes and the most effective means of doing so. Choose your words carefully. Your goal is to create a warm yet businesslike atmosphere. You must convey that you know what you are doing, have confidence in yourself, and expect appropriate behavior and effort from your students.

Don't waste the most precious minutes of the year taking roll. That can wait. First, introduce yourself. Have your name printed on the board. Clearly and slowly pronounce it for your students and tell them how you expect to be addressed. If you have an aide in the room, introduce him or her. Spend a couple of minutes telling the class a little about yourself and your background. Share a bit of your life: family, hobbies, pets, interests, where you went to school, or experiences. If you are just beginning your teaching career, it is best not to emphasize your inexperience. Don't overdo the introduction; a couple of minutes is sufficient. Some teachers allow students to ask them questions. Other teachers construct a biographical display or bulletin board. How much you choose to share about yourself and when are matters of personal comfort and judgment.

If you are particularly skilled in some aspect of what you will be teaching, you might exhibit your skill by demonstrating something students will be learning. Show them you are a pro; it helps establish respect and credibility.

During these first few minutes, your students are sizing you up. Who are you? How will you treat them? What are the boundaries of what they can do in your classroom? It is wise to convey positive expectations and enthusiasm. You aren't going to get them very excited about your class if you don't seem too enthusiastic yourself. Put some energy into your opening. Also use your most poised, assertive body language. If possible, stand, scan the class with your eyes, and don't be afraid to smile.

Getting to Know Your Students

Spending time getting to know your students is one of the most valuable investments you can make. Establishing rapport helps build mutual respect and minimize classroom behavior problems. A deeper understanding of your students' needs, problems, and interests will enable you to plan instruction that succeeds. Here are some tips for getting to know your students:

✓ Some teachers prefer to look at each student's cumulative folder before school begins. This gives them a sense of their class's special talents and problems. Of course, this may not be feasible for high school teachers with over a hundred students.

✓ Allow some time the first day to get acquainted with your students. A fun icebreaker activity, particularly if it can relate to your subject area, can be helpful. One way to learn a bit more about your students is to call the class roll this way: instead of replying "here," have them respond by naming their favorite hobby or sport. The next day you could have them answer with their favorite song or food.

✓ The first day may be the only time you actually call the roll. The main purposes are to clarify the pronunciation of students' names and identify what they prefer to be called. One of the best ways you can show respect for your students and earn their respect and trust is to learn their names. This should be a prime objective for the first week of school. Any time you address a specific student the first week, make a special effort to use his or her name. Many effective teachers use name tags or name tents to help learn students' names.

✓ If you really want to impress your students, end the first day by having them remove their name tags or name tents. Then proceed around the room, identifying each student by name. You don't have to hit 100 percent; they will be impressed that you even tried. It doesn't take a great memory, just a focused, determined effort. If you accomplished little else that day, the year would be off to a good start. Knowing and using a student's name communicates that you regard that person as more than an anonymous face among a group of students. Some have suggested that a person's favorite word to hear is his or her own name.

✓ To help in remembering names, attempt to connect a student's name with another person of the same name. For example, if you have a student named Brett and that is also your son's name, try to visualize the two playing together. If you don't know anyone by that name, associate that person with a famous person of the same name. Visualize a new student named George with a powdered wig like George Washington's. As you make a mental connection, consciously use that student's name every time you talk to or call on him or her for the next week. Stand by the door and greet each one by name to reinforce your name awareness.

✓ Take photographs of students the first week and attach their names and cutouts of their faces on a master seating chart.

✓ If you have a printed roster the first day, be sure it is accurate. Make any corrections, but do not write your class roster in the grade book the first week. It will change. Indeed, assume that no matter when you finally write your class roll into your grade book, a new student will show up the next day!

> ### Classroom Climate Concerns
>
> Students enter a new classroom experiencing common psychological needs that can be expressed in the following questions:
>
> - Will I feel accepted?
> - Will I be safe?
> - What will be expected?
> - How comfortable will I be?
> - Will the class content be helpful to me?

✓ Make a special effort to welcome students new to the school or area. Try to pair them up with a returning student and make sure they are included in some of the student groups during lunch and recess.

✓ Some kindergarten and first-grade teachers send notes to their students inviting them to come to school in small groups a couple of days prior to the beginning of the school year. They might invite students to bring a favorite toy to share. This provides an opportunity for the teacher to get to know their students before school begins; and the students get a chance to meet their teacher and a few of the other students in a safe, inviting environment.

✓ Give students a chance to get to know you. One option is to let the group interview you for a few minutes.

Clarifying Expectations

Establishing your hopes, expectations, rules, and routines is an essential first-day goal. Explain, demonstrate, and allow time for students to practice the routines that will help get things done smoothly throughout the year. Clarify specific procedures for taking attendance, beginning work each day, turning in assignments, requesting help, going to the bathroom, and other reoccurring classroom routines. It is not essential to introduce every routine the first day, but certainly do focus on each as the need arises. (See Chapter Six for some teachers' suggestions on how to manage these routines.)

In communicating your hopes for the class, you might say something like, "I don't expect you to be perfect. I do hope you will strive for excellence and work to improve. We all will make mistakes. The important thing is to learn from those mistakes."

Tasks to Accomplish

There are several important tasks to accomplish during the first week, if not the first day. Do the following:

✓ Explain the rules. A few rules (ideally, no more than five) are preferable to a long list. Some teachers prefer to hold a class meeting, allowing students to provide input into the norms that should be enforced. Beyond giving them some influence in their school lives, it also provides practice in the process of democracy.

✓ Discuss emergency procedures. Clarify and perhaps practice the drills for fire, tornadoes, or other emergencies. Be sure everyone knows which exits to use in the event of an evacuation.

✓ Distribute books and other materials. This provides a good opportunity to practice routines for distributing materials. Be sure to have students complete the necessary records for end-of-the-year collections of signed-out materials.

✓ Assign lockers or drawers. If combination locks are provided, be sure to keep a master list for those who forget their combination.

✓ Clarify what materials and supplies students will need for your class. What items will the students be expected to bring every day? Which will they need tomorrow? Will you need to collect any fees? It is generally best to distribute a written list they can take home.

✓ Discuss your grading procedures. Many (but not all) students want to know this: "What do I have to do to get an A in this class?" or at least to pass it. Clarify what their academic responsibilities will be, what criteria you will be using to evaluate their performance, and how you will allot grades. Clarity and fairness here can eliminate a lot of arguments and protestations at the end of the term. Many effective teachers distribute a handout detailing their class expectations and grading scheme.

✓ Explain the schedule your class will typically follow. At least the first day, having the day's activities listed on the board is a good idea.

✓ In laboratory or shop classes and in elementary classrooms, a tour of the classroom will be helpful in orienting students to the various stations and features they will be using during the year.

✓ Set the tone for the year. Creating an inviting, warm class environment gets the year off to a good start.

Additional Suggestions

Arrive early the first morning, allowing ample time to tend to any last-minute details. Be available to greet students as they enter the room. You cannot do that if you are in the office waiting for the copy machine. Also students are less likely to engage in mischief if you are in the room when they arrive.

First-Day-of-School Checklist

Before School Begins

_____ Become familiar with the building.

_____ Post your name, grade level or subject, and room number beside your door.

_____ Have name tags or name tents and markers available.

_____ Write your name on the chalkboard.

_____ Have a sufficient number of textbooks available (remember the teacher's edition).

_____ Write the day's class schedule on the board.

_____ Double-check the day's school schedule (recess, lunch, class changes).

_____ Have the class roster readily accessible.

_____ Have all teaching materials ready for the first day's lesson.

_____ Know the school rules and policies.

_____ Complete the first day's lesson plans.

_____ Arrange desks in the desired pattern.

_____ Create an inviting atmosphere (bulletin boards, posters).

_____ Set up a tape or CD player and any music to play.

_____ Have "sponge" activities available.

Opening Day

_____ Greet students at the door—smile!

_____ Assign temporary seats.

_____ Begin learning students' names (check pronunciation).

_____ Take attendance.

_____ Establish rules.

_____ Get students started on learning.

_____ Specify supplies and fees that students must provide.

_____ Make any assignments for the next class.

_____ Begin training routines and procedures.

_____ Show enthusiasm for your subject!

SCHOOL RULES

=▷ no gum or sunflower seeds.

=▷ no hats.

=▷ no running in hall.

=▷ no play-fighting.

— THE Principal

Expect the unexpected. The first day is always a bit hectic. Murphy's Law will rule: anything that can go wrong will. Students will show up in the middle of the class because they have been sitting in the wrong class. There may not be enough textbooks, desks, or supplies. Strive to remain calm and flexible. Remember, students are assessing your mettle the first day. If you are easily flustered, it will undermine your credibility and respect. A true professional can handle any situation, even when things don't go as planned. Be patient.

Overplan the first day. It is better to have too much to do than to have a class of students sitting idly or for you to aimlessly wing it.

Dress your best the first day. This is part of creating a professional image and establishing credibility. It also communicates that you value your students enough that you will make a special effort to look your best for them. We also tend to be more confident when we are well groomed.

Set your standards from the very beginning. Classroom management style is very much established the first day. Be fair yet firm in enforcing your classroom rules. Once you tolerate a behavior, changing it later is difficult.

Show that you have a sense of humor. Don't try to be a stand-up comedian, but allow yourself to laugh with—not at—your students. An amusing cartoon on the door or overhead helps create a warm, inviting atmosphere.

Don't hesitate to ask your principal or colleagues questions if you don't understand something. If you are new, be sure to explore the building and meet some of your colleagues before the first day. Also read the policy manual.

Creating an Inviting School Climate

For all too many students, school has become something to avoid. Many see it as a boring, depersonalized, irrelevant institution. Fortunately, school doesn't have to be a dreaded experience. Some classrooms and schools, even in the most impoverished of environments, remain inviting and nurturing. Schools that maintain a positive school climate are marked with a high degree of cohesiveness and high level of morale, among students as well as staff. Research provides evidence that school climate is related to the level of academic achievement.

Interestingly, research reveals that students' self-esteem increases immediately on dropping out of school. The students' former environment daily communicated that they were losers, incompetent, and slower than everyone else. When they stop going to school, they suddenly escape those degrading messages and begin to accept themselves more. (Unfortunately, that gain in self-acceptance may later erode as they face the challenge of surviving in the economic world without a diploma.) Positive school climates occur when students believe they have a shared responsibility in developing and maintaining a warm and supportive environment. The following tips will help you do just that:

✓ Always remember the adage "Students do not care how much you know until they know how much you care." We earn respect only by showing respect; we gain trust by trusting. Develop a student-centered rather than subject-centered classroom.

✓ Schools are most likely to be successful when students experience a sense of ownership and belonging. Both are nurtured when students have some degree of choice and control in their daily experience. Involving students in classroom decisions, valuing student contributions, and respecting individual differences help meet these needs.

✓ Make a conscious effort to get to know the good things about your students. Publicly and privately acknowledge their achievements outside of your class.

✓ Treat all students fairly. While it is natural for teachers to enjoy teaching some students more than others, overt favoritism can create a divisive and resentful climate.

✓ Strive to be consistent in your enforcement of rules, grading, and treatment of students. While we all have our good days and bad days, students' inability to predict a teacher's expectations and responses is poisonous to an atmosphere of trust and respect.

✓ Take time to listen to your students. Not only does this convey your respect for them, but you may also receive feedback that might help you become a better teacher. Solicit their opinions about how they perceive your class. Occasionally invite them to complete open-ended sentences anonymously, such as "The thing I enjoy most about this class is . . . " or "I would enjoy this class more if . . ."

✓ Communicate your expectations clearly, both for academic tasks as well as behavioral norms. Don't make students guess what you want.

✓ Inviting teachers communicate that they expect all students to succeed. Every day, both verbally and nonverbally, inviting teachers genuinely communicate that each student is capable, unique, and valued.

✓ Provide opportunities for choice. The ability to have control over one's life is a basic human need. While many school tasks are not optional, there are ample opportunities to allow students a degree of freedom. For example, offering a choice of learning activities or homework assignments may not only give students a greater sense of freedom but may actually enhance their learning as well.

✓ Treat students decently. Treat them as you would have wished to be treated as a student, not necessarily as you were treated.

✓ Consider holding periodic classroom meetings in which students can openly discuss their views on the class procedures and climate. Of course, to succeed you must convey to your students that you are genuinely interested in their views. The best way to communicate that is to listen nonjudgmentally.

✓ Plan lessons that offer more instructional techniques than the talking head in front of the classroom. Teacher talk is still the dominant instructional mode in many of our schools. Education has become a very passive endeavor. Strive to actively involve students in meaningful learning activities. Construct lessons with ample student interaction, challenging content, and a variety of instructional approaches.

✓ Pay attention to your classroom's physical environment. The seating arrangement, wall decorations, bulletin boards, special reading areas, learning centers, and posters all contribute to your classroom's emotional tone.

✓ Always try to convey an attitude of acceptance toward all students. This does not mean you must approve of all they do; but when you must condemn an unacceptable behavior, do so without rejecting the child.

✓ Recognize, encourage, and reinforce positive behaviors and achievements. Especially express your appreciation for deeds that contribute to a positive class climate: cooperation, helpful behaviors, caring, and inclusion. Reward direction, not perfection. Acknowledge small gains.

✓ Pay attention to the students in the middle of the normal curve—those who neither lag nor excel. For the most part, the academically average student is ignored in our classrooms. Recognize and encourage their small successes and progress.

✓ Don't be afraid to smile. A gentle smile conveys warmth, acceptance, and caring. Avoid the perpetual wide, toothy pseudosmile. A genuine smile is conveyed with the eyes as well as the mouth. If smiling is not a natural behavior for you, practice in front of a mirror (privately, of course!).

✓ Avoid developing a highly competitive classroom climate. While some argue that competition prepares students for the real world, a great deal of evidence shows that it is destructive and unnecessary. Even corporate America is teaching its employees to work in cooperative teams and strive for win-win solutions to conflict.

✓ Empathize with the students who are always at the bottom of the normal curve—in academic achievement, athletic ability, popularity, or physical development. Consider ways in which you might help make them feel included and valued. Emphasize growth over perfection or being the best. No matter how hard they try, most students will never be the top of the class.

✓ Always remain sensitive to the influence you have in your students' lives. Your choice of words, disapproving nonverbal messages, harsh tonality, ignoring, or sarcasm can have long and profound effects on your students' self-esteem.

✓ Strive to catch the student being good. Too often we ignore students until they misbehave. Then we reprimand or punish them. Acknowledging what they are doing right is more important than only giving criticism of what they do wrong.

✓ Never use sarcasm or ridicule when talking to students. It accomplishes nothing permanently positive. Once used it is hard to retract and erodes the teacher-student relationship. When reprimanding a student for misbehavior, condemn the behavior, not the person.

✓ Pay attention to multicultural and gender inclusiveness in all your teaching activities. Use examples and visuals that include persons of a variety of cultural and ethnic backgrounds and of both genders. Do not tolerate bigoted behavior in your classroom.

✓ Remain sensitive to the fact that your students come from a variety of religious backgrounds. Avoid imposing your religious views on your students. Holidays, especially religious ones such as Christmas or Hanukkah, may not hold the same meaning for some of your students. Respect their freedom of religion and avoid activities that clearly endorse one particular religion to the exclusion of others (unless you teach in a parochial school).

✓ Remember the adage "Praise publicly, criticize privately." Even when reprimanding or criticizing students' behavior, do so in a style that leaves their dignity intact. If at all possible, never cause a student to lose face in front of his or her peers. It achieves nothing positive in the long run.

✓ Aim to talk with each student every day, even if it is only a smile and greeting as they leave or enter the classroom. Attempt to get to know your students better during these miniconversations. It helps build rapport as well as discover the frustrations, challenges, disappointments, and conflicts facing your students.

✓ Become an inveterate note writer. Keep a stack of notepaper. Make a commitment to recognize the good deeds of students, colleagues, custodians, secretaries, administrators, librarians, aides, parents, or volunteers. Five minutes each day spent sending a couple of thoughtful notes will pay dividends and contribute to making your school a more pleasant place.

✓ When a student is ill for any extended period of time, send a "Get Well Soon" message from the entire class. If feasible, let the group use its creative talents to create the message, perhaps on videotape or DVD.

✓ Recognize birthdays and other special occasions. The first day of school, have your students enter their birth dates on a personal information sheet. Transfer all their birth dates to your calendar. You might make birthday cards for each student. Computer software such as Print Shop makes this quick and inexpensive.

✓ In the primary grades, you might want to designate a birthday chair and extend special privileges (for example, being first in line) to the honoree. Sing "Happy Birthday."

✓ Send birthday messages to the other adults in the building as well. Secretaries and custodial staff will appreciate being included.

✓ Find special occasions to celebrate: athletic or quiz-bowl team victories, change of seasons, holidays, or individual student achievements. Let students decorate a bulletin board in recognition of the occasion.

✓ Develop the habit of saying "please" whenever you make a request of a student. Convey respect by responding with "thank you" whenever a student complies with a request, no matter how grudgingly he or she may do so. Strengthen the appreciation by also using the student's name.

✓ Don't be afraid to make learning fun. Dress-up days, field trips, skits, songs, demonstrations, and learning games can break the predictable, dull, passive approach to instruction that many students experience.

✓ Bring in a camera to take pictures of each student in your class the first week. Post the pictures along with their names on a bulletin board display. It will help you learn your students' names. Take informal shots of various learning activities throughout the year. Display these on a bulletin board for two to three weeks, and then let the students have the pictures.

✓ Develop a repertoire of anecdotes and amusing stories related to your academic content. Search for cartoons that you can incorporate into lessons.

✓ Be creative in planning your teaching activities. Challenge yourself to invent new, more interesting ways to help your students learn. Learn from successful teachers through workshops, books, and magazines. Keep an idea notebook with you at all times to jot down interesting possibilities—anecdotes, examples, quotations, anything that might be of use in one of your classes. Part of being a professional is seeking continual improvement in your skills and curriculum.

✓ Convey your own enthusiasm for the topic you are teaching. Getting your students excited about a topic will be nearly impossible if you are unenthusiastic.

✓ Publicize your students' successes to the parents and the community. Use local newspaper articles, school assemblies, school and class newsletters, local television stations, parent-teacher associations, and open houses to showcase your students' accomplishments. This has multiple beneficial effects for your students as well as the school.

Welcoming New Students

Arriving in a new school the very first day is a stressful event for most students. They may be filled with anxiety about whether they will be accepted, whether they will be academically competitive with their new classmates, and how their new teachers will treat them. Make a special effort to make new students feel welcome. Here's how:

✓ In elementary classrooms invite the rest of the class to brainstorm things they might do to make a new student feel welcome. This is especially helpful if you know ahead of time that a new student will be joining the class.

✓ Spend a few minutes getting to know a little about the student's background. Ask to meet with him or her a few minutes during the day to chat informally.

✓ Some teachers develop a brief questionnaire for new students to complete, detailing family information, interests, extracurricular activities, and past coursework.

✓ Consider pairing the new person with a reliable student buddy or guide who can teach your routines and procedures. The buddy can show the new student around the school and introduce him or her to schoolmates.

✓ Give the new student some time to get acclimated before calling a lot of attention to him or her. If the student appears shy, don't publicly make too big an issue of his or her arrival. If the student seems comfortable after a few days, you might spend a few minutes letting the student tell the class a little about his or her background, interests, and family.

✓ Consider calling the parent(s) or guardian of a new student to introduce yourself and to learn a little more about their child. Invite them to visit the school for a conference.

✓ Have several welcome folders prepared to immediately give any new students. Besides classroom and school rules and routines, include a personal note or letter welcoming the new student.

✓ To help the new student feel more comfortable with the class, find something to praise or acknowledge.

✓ Some teachers have everyone wear name tags during the week following a new student's arrival.

Humor in the Classroom

Mary Pettibone Poole's observation that "He who laughs, lasts" is probably nowhere more true than in teaching. A moderate touch of humor can nurture an inviting class climate. Bob Hope had suggested that humor serves as a welcome mat between speakers and their audiences. It is a powerful tool that can break the ice and get the listener on your side. Humor recaptures students' attention and anchors their memory, improving achievement. One classic study found students to be more creative after listening to a humorous recording. Humor can defuse tense situations, combat resistance, and reduce stress in the classroom. It provides comic relief from the serious, sometimes tedious, business of learning. Humor tends to make any experience more fun and brings a group closer together.

Laughter has been called internal jogging. It's good for the soul, the mind, and the body. As John Kennedy and Abraham Lincoln so capably demonstrated, we can be quite serious about our subject yet still infuse it with humor.

The cardinal rule for using humor in the classroom is that it must never be used to harm, humiliate, ridicule, or otherwise make fun of students. Cruel, sarcastic humor is totally inappropriate and must not be tolerated. Likewise, humor that is sexual or involves ethnic or gender slurs is taboo. If you have a doubt as to whether an anecdote, quip, or joke is appropriate, don't use it in school. The safest target of humor is you. Make a self-disparaging remark about your handwriting or stick figures drawn on the board.

Humor can be spontaneous or planned. Some people have a natural gift for finding humor in the everyday ironies and foibles in their world. Just in the normal course of daily classroom interactions, amusing predicaments will emerge on their own. A smile or chuckle on our part communicates that we are also human and can enjoy a good laugh, granting permission to our students to do the same. Good-natured kidding and puns can be forms of spontaneous humor. If you are not spontaneously witty, plan your humor by looking for cartoons, anecdotes, and quotations that you find amusing and can share with your students.

Your humorous quips or observations need not evoke knee-slapping, ripsnorting belly laughs. Lighthearted humor that brings a twinkle to the eye, a smile to the face, or a groan or chuckle serves its purpose. You're not running a comedy shop. You don't have to be hilarious to weave humor into your class presentations.

Here are more tips on using humor in your classroom:

✓ Props, such as costumes, hats, masks, or unusual objects, can inject some levity into otherwise very serious subjects. Many teachers collect unusual pencils and pens. Accumulate inexpensive toys and puzzles with which students can spend a few minutes playing before class or during breaks.

✔ Use odd or funny noisemakers to signal the class to be quiet and give you their attention.

✔ Some teachers convey their sense of humor through their dress and accessories. Colorful, funny ties, scarves, sweaters, socks, and watches are widely available.

✔ Successful teachers develop a repertoire of stories and anecdotes illustrating various aspects of the subjects they teach. Some of the tales may be naturally amusing or can be made so with a bit of exaggeration, animated gestures, or surprising twists. Begin by drawing on funny things that have happened to you.

✔ Most people who believe they are not funny argue, "I can't tell a joke. I never remember the punch line." If so, then don't try to tell jokes in class (or if you do, overrehearse it until it flows naturally). Jokes are probably overrated as a source of humor; they are the most difficult form to use successfully. Even a teacher who is a good joke teller should not overuse the technique. If you do tell a joke, make sure it is pertinent to the topic you are teaching. If it bombs, you've at least made an academic point.

✔ If a joke bombs, don't try to explain the punch line. Better to use a self-disparaging comment: "That's why I keep the day job," or "I told my writers that wouldn't work."

✔ In most classes you'll have at least one student who will be spontaneously, genuinely witty. Sometimes all you have to do is play straight man to the amateur comedian. Such a person often enjoys the attention, so take care not let it become disruptive or excessive.

✔ An easy source of humor is the comic section of the newspaper. Read it every day with an eye toward cartoons that illustrate some point related to your curriculum. Comic strips that frequently feature school and child-related topics include *Peanuts, Sally Forth, For Better or for Worse, Dennis the Menace,* and *Family Circus.* Gary Larson's *Far Side* cartoons are rich with off-the-wall quips students love; his past cartoons are still available in books. Educational journals such as *Phi Delta Kappan* and the *Chronicle of Higher Education* include cartoons related to various aspects of education. Clip these and make them into transparencies. It helps to enlarge them and add color with markers. Post some cartoons on the door, use others on tests or handouts, or post some on the bulletin board. If you are going to reproduce a cartoon for instructional use, most cartoonists will freely grant you permission. Call the local newspaper for their addresses.

✔ Quotations and proverbs are another planned source of humor. You don't have to be funny, just recognize what is. Chances are that if a quotation makes you laugh, it will also make your students laugh. Periodicals such as *Reader's Digest* are good sources for quotations. Invite students to be on the lookout for ones they find funny and relevant to your subject. You might even designate a section of a bulletin board where they might post humorous clippings. Specify that they must make some point relevant to your course.

Laughter is the shortest distance between two people.

—Victor Borge

✓ Construct your own variation of David Letterman's top-ten lists or allow your students to brainstorm their own lists. Do remind them to stay within the bounds of good taste.

✓ When a lesson isn't going well, carry on a monologue with yourself in a stage whisper. Some teachers pick up a puppet, stuffed animal, or other object and begin talking to it. Pull out a picture of the person you are studying and have a chat. Or talk to the class goldfish or hamster. You can ask it questions and then answer them yourself. Personification, treating objects as though they were people, can be funny. Give your chalkboard eraser a name and talk to it. They will chuckle. They may lock you up, but they will chuckle.

✓ When several unexpected events disrupt your class, react with humor rather than stress. "Well, it went better in rehearsal."

✓ Suddenly shifting to an accent for emphasis gets attention. Or have students try doing a routine task in a different accent than normally expected (such as reading Shakespeare or Poe in an exaggerated Southern drawl or Bronx accent).

✓ Intentionally slaughtering a foreign phrase (*mercy bow-cup* for *merci beaucoup*) can be amusing. Of course, the students need to be familiar with the phrase to recognize what you've done. It isn't essential that everyone catches it, and don't pause to wait for a laugh.

✓ Insert a touch of humor into your tests, perhaps by using the name of your principal (in a tasteful way), a local celebrity, a rival school, or alluding to a current school event.

✓ Find a humorous poem or song to celebrate a special occasion or holiday. Teach it to the class.

✓ Check bookstores and educational supply catalogs for humorous posters. Draw your own if you are artistic.

✓ A humorous song related to the topic being studied can grab students' attention and inject a touch of levity. This can be a good way to open a challenging or controversial subject.

✓ Cultivate inside jokes within your class. Some funny things just happen, without planning. They can become part of the class lore, which can be referred to from time to time throughout the year.

✓ Create a comedy file. Save in a folder or a notebook items that you might use later in your class. Include news items, cartoons, anecdotes, jokes, and quotations. As your file expands, you might categorize your items by topic.

✓ Discover your own humor style. Rather than forcing some brand of humor that is unnatural, experiment and rely on the kinds of humor that you already enjoy and use.

✓ Observe your students to see what works. Listen to them talking among themselves to discover what they think is funny.

✓ Become a student of humor. Read the daily comics, watch funny movies, read humorous books, go to comedy clubs, watch the good (though rare) situation comedies on television.

✓ One last piece of advice: don't try too hard. With experience, you'll discover what kind of humor works and how much helps but does not hinder.

For More Information

Books

Berk, R. A. (2002). *Humor as an instructional defibrillator: Evidence-based techniques in teaching and assessment.* Sterling, VA: Stylus.

Burgess, R. (2000). *Laughing lessons: 149⅔ ways to make teaching and learning fun.* Minneapolis, MN: Free Spirit.

Cornett, C. E. (2001). *Learning through laughter . . . again.* Bloomington, IN: Phi Delta Kappa Educational Foundation.

Lundberg, E. M., & Miller Thurston, C. (2002). *If they're laughing, they just might be listening: Ideas for using humor effectively in the classroom—even if you're not funny yourself.* Fort Collins, CO: Cottonwood Press.

Shade, R. A. (1996). *License to laugh: Humor in the classroom.* Englewood, CO: Teacher Ideas Press.

Internet Resources on Humor

Humor in the Classroom
www.abbottcom.com/Humor_in_the_classroom.htm

Humor in the Classroom Teacher's Zine
teacherszine.tripod.com/teacherszine/id13.html

Humor Matters
www.humormatters.com/

HumorSource
www.humorsource.com

Keeper of the Lists
www.keepersoflists.org/

SchoolJokes.com
www.schooljokes.com/

True humor springs not more from the head than from the heart; it is not contempt; its essence is love.

—Thomas Carlyle

Catalogs of Humor-Related Resources

HUMOResources
The Humor Project
480 Broadway, Suite 210
Saratoga Springs, NY 12866-2288
(518) 587-8770
www.humorproject.com

The Land of Mirth and Funny
P.O. Box 50312
Irvine, CA 92619-0312
(949) 654-4500
www.humormatters.com/lmf.htm

What on Earth
2451 Enterprise East Parkway
Twinsburg, OH 44087-2399
(800) 945-2552
www.whatonearthcatalog.com

Whole Mirth catalog
Allen Klein Publisher
1034 Page Street
San Francisco, CA 94117
(800) 788-6262

My way of joking is telling the truth. That is the funniest joke in the world.

—George Bernard Shaw

Seeking Student Feedback

Listening to your students' views will help develop an inviting classroom. The following open-ended statements can be used to stimulate feedback on how your students see the classroom's day-to-day operation. Students can occasionally anonymously write their responses to one or more of these sentence stems. They are also useful to stimulate discussion during class meetings.

- I like this class because . . .
- I would like this class better if . . .
- In this class I wish we spent more time . . .
- I like it when the teacher . . .
- The most interesting part of this class is . . .
- I feel special when the teacher . . .
- One thing I feel proud about in our school is . . .
- I would like our class to improve . . .
- When I enter our classroom I usually feel . . .
- When I leave our classroom I usually feel . . .
- I am most bored when . . .
- My favorite part of school is . . .
- I feel left out when . . .
- My favorite activity in class is . . .
- This class is most fun when . . .
- I feel challenged when . . .
- I don't like it when other students . . .

- I think I could learn better if . . .
- One thing I would like to achieve in this class is . . .
- I would like to have more choice in . . .
- I believe our teacher wants us to . . .
- I think the teacher most values me when . . .
- Every day I look forward to . . .
- I become discouraged when . . .
- I feel special when the teacher . . .
- One thing in our class I would like to see changed is . . .
- I wish we spent less time . . .
- The best teachers seem to . . .
- When I must be corrected by the teacher, I would prefer . . .

Establishing Rules

Research suggests that effective teachers are in control of their classrooms but not obsessed with the idea of control. A necessary (though not sufficient) first step in establishing standards of acceptable behavior in a classroom is to set some norms or rules of conduct. Here's how:

✓ Some teachers prefer to involve students in the rule-setting process the first day of class. The class meeting as advocated by William Glasser, founder of control theory and reality therapy, can be an effective device for involving students and gaining their commitment to the rules they set.

✓ Most effective teachers establish a few, positively stated rules, for example:

- Keep your hands to yourself.
- Ask permission before using others' things.
- Bring your materials and books to class.
- Only one person should talk at a time.
- Always be on time.
- Complete and turn in all assignments.
- Respect others' rights.

✓ The maximum number of enforceable rules seems to be around five to seven. Many classrooms function very well with only three or four rules.

✓ It is important to establish your own set of rules, based on your needs and experience, your students' maturity, and the school climate.

✓ Don't try to cover every possible unacceptable behavior; you aren't writing a penal code. On the other hand, don't be so vague that no one really knows what the rule means.

✓ Motivation to comply with rules seems highest when they are stated positively. When possible, convey what you do want to happen rather than trying to list all the possible unacceptable behaviors.

✓ It is essential the first day not to let behaviors slide that are clear violations. Enforcing a higher standard once you have tolerated a lower standard of behavior becomes very difficult. It is easier to start out a bit firm and ease up later.

✓ Early in the year, hold a class discussion on students' rights in your classroom. Solicit ideas from your students as to what is a right and which ought to be accorded all students. Examples might include the right to make mistakes or the right to express one's opinion. Focus the discussion on the responsibilities that must accompany any right (for example, the responsibility to learn from our mistakes).

✓ Construct or let a volunteer student construct a poster listing the class rules. Display it prominently to remind students of the rules. It is imperative that every student know your rules.

✓ It does little good to establish rules if you have no plan for enforcing them. Your plan should in some fashion provide encouragement and reinforcement for students complying with the rules as well as some penalty or consequence for those who choose to violate the class rules.

✓ If you find it necessary to add a new rule later in the year, do so. Dr. Harry Wong, an expert on classroom management, suggests replacing an old rule with the new one. The old one can become an unwritten rule or expectation.

✓ Of course, honor school or district rules beyond those established for your classroom (for example, restrictions on drug use, weapons in the school, attendance policies). You are responsible for knowing and enforcing these. If you don't know them, ask for a copy of the teacher or student handbook. Post these rules and assure that all students know them. You can be held legally liable if you fail to enforce them.

✓ There is no substitute for consistently and fairly enforcing your class rules. Doing so assures some predictability in the students' learning environment.

✓ Allow students to role-play scenarios in which rules might be violated. Present several hypothetical situations for small groups or volunteers to role-play. Encourage them to resolve the dilemma by practicing a behavior that does not break the rules. They learn by seeing others model appropriate responses and also by practicing responsible behaviors. Examples might include the following:

- Sandy asks to copy your homework to hand in as hers.
- Lynn trips and accidentally pushes you from behind.
- Pat slips on a wet spot and falls while returning from the pencil sharpener. Other students begin to laugh at him and call him names.
- Shoving breaks out between two students arguing over who was first in line.
- The student seated behind you pokes you with a pencil.

✓ The classroom routines and procedures you establish at the beginning of the year convey your standards and expectations. They help you get things done in an orderly manner. Such informal rules or expectations complement your formal rules.

Thirty Hot Tips for Managing Classroom Behavior

The ability to manage students' behaviors is the number one concern of beginning teachers, and it is near the top for most experienced teachers. Indeed, the ability to develop harmonious, mutually respectful relationships with students is one of the best predictors of who will survive in the teaching profession. The inability to effectively manage students' behavior accounts for more teacher dismissals than any other cause, including lack of knowledge of subject matter. Here are some tips on effective classroom management gleaned from research and observations of effective teachers:

1. Invest in relationship building from the beginning, accumulating a "psychological bank account" with your students. Remember the adage "They don't care how much you know until they know how much you care." This does not mean you should try to be their buddy. It does mean treating each student with dignity and respect. Show interest in their lives as you chat before and after class. Sure, it takes time; but much of the success of outstanding teachers, such as Jaime Escalante, the celebrated real-life model for the film *Stand and Deliver,* can be understood in terms of the caring relationship they developed with their students. It is a case of "You can pay me now or pay me later": you'll either spend time now building a mutually respectful relationship or spend it later in a classroom power struggle. If you've made regular deposits to the psychological bank account, you can make withdrawals later when you ask students to comply with your demands. They'll also be more likely to forgive your mistakes than to capitalize on them.

2. Expect some students to test you to determine the boundaries of acceptable behavior and your competency to respond. While such tests are usually minor infractions (whispering, note passing, and so on), they constitute a challenge to your classroom control. It is essential to react immediately, calmly, and appropriately to these infractions; but it is vital not to overreact.

3. Preserve your classroom momentum at all costs. *Momentum* means that every student is on task and the lesson is rolling along smoothly. Most discipline problems do not occur during periods of momentum but rather during those periods of chaos—when something has broken the lesson's momentum. These classroom interruptions may sometimes be beyond our direct control: announcements over the P.A., a knock at the door, a fire engine passing the building, or the custodian riding by the window on a power mower. However, sometimes teachers may unwittingly break their own momentum: by not having the necessary audiovisual equipment ready, by hunting for misplaced items in the middle of the lesson, or by stopping to reprimand an offending student. Note what happens when momentum is lost: the class goes from 95 or 100 percent on-task behavior to 0 percent on task. Now the teacher faces the challenge of refocusing everyone's attention and getting all students back on task. Pay special attention to making smooth, orderly transitions from one activity to another.

4. It may sound cliché, but the best way to prevent classroom misbehavior is to deliver interesting, fast-paced, organized learning experiences, particularly ones that actively engage students in the lesson. A dull lesson is an invitation to misbehave. Much student acting out is simply a reaction to boredom. While even the best, well-prepared teachers occasionally have behavioral infractions in their classroom, they are less frequent and less severe. Additionally, recapturing students' attention and getting them back on task is less difficult in a fast-paced classroom.

5. Be sure your rules and expectations are clear. Some teachers haven't given much thought to what they do want but only to what they don't want. Such negative focusing is inefficient. Don't assume students will correctly guess what you expect of them. Develop high expectations of your students, their academic performance, as well as their classroom conduct. Students will not always meet your expectations but seldom will they exceed them.

6. It is also better to have a few rather than many rules. Remember that you have to enforce them. You have a right to be in control of your classroom, but do not become obsessed with control. Rules should also be conspicuously displayed in the room.

7. Avoid causing students to lose face in front of their peers. Avoid needless public confrontations. You will almost always lose in the long run; kids can, and do, get even. Whenever possible, reprimand privately; avoid giving your perpetrator an audience.

8. Keep your eyes moving. Eye contact is your most powerful tool in maintaining classroom control. Probably 80 percent of potential classroom misbehaviors can be nipped in the bud through timely, direct eye contact. Keep your eyes moving to scan the entire room at least once every minute or less. You actually don't have direct eye contact with every single student every minute but rather focus on clusters of four or five students at a time. Hold that gaze for four or five seconds and then move on to another group. Remember that most teachers have less eye contact with students sitting in the furthest corners of the room, and that is exactly where most troublemakers choose to sit!

9. Continually monitor what is happening in your classroom. Some researchers refer to this as having eyes in the back of your head. Always know what's going on in your classroom. Avoid standing or sitting with your back to the class. For example, when working in a small group, sit so that you are facing the rest of the class. It is also difficult to monitor all of the class if you are sitting at your desk in front of the room. It is generally better to pace around the room during whole-class instruction. Effective teachers seem to develop a sixth sense in anticipating potential problems and appropriately intervening to nip them in the bud.

10. Practice the principle of escalation. This means you don't go after a fly with a baseball bat; if you have a small problem, use a small tool. If

your initial strategy doesn't work, you can always escalate to a more potent strategy. You can always go up, but you can never effectively go down to a lower-level strategy if a more confrontational one does not work. Direct eye contact might be the lowest level of challenge. If the student does not correct his or her behavior, then escalate, perhaps by moving into his or her body space, standing near his or her desk. All of this can occur while you are still teaching the rest of the class, without directing everyone's attention toward the transgressing student. You've not broken your own momentum.

11. Use the power of silence. Follow your behavioral directives with a pause while maintaining direct eye contact. Silence is power; use it constructively. After giving each behavioral directive, pause and take two slow, deep breaths. Not only does this give the student time to comply, but the breathing also helps you to remain calm. You don't want to convey either fear or hostility. If you must escalate to the next level of confrontation, pause again for two deep breaths. Say no more than is absolutely necessary. Avoid haranguing or degrading the student. You'll only fuel resentment and create sympathy for the offender among the rest of the class. You don't need to get drawn into a power struggle.

12. Don't overreact. When you lose your composure in front of the class, they, not you, are in control of your behavior. Some students will test you to discover your "hot buttons," the behaviors that cause you to lose control. Also remember that most of the things students do in our classrooms to annoy us are not evil, dastardly deeds. They are simply inappropriate, not acceptable in that situation. Of course, if a student's misbehavior is potentially harmful to others or destructive of property, then we must employ the necessary strategy to deter that behavior. This might mean getting immediate help from other adults. When you correct a student's behavior, don't dwell excessively. Nagging will only alienate the student.

13. Develop selective hearing. Learn to ignore some minor infractions, particularly when you suspect that the student's motive is to bait you into a confrontation. Of course, potentially harmful or disruptive outbursts must be handled. Even things that are ignored during class can be dealt with after class. This also is a way to buy time if you're not sure what to do about a behavior.

14. Divide and conquer. If you have two or three people who sit next to each other and frequently collude to disrupt the classroom, rearrange the classroom seating arrangement to separate the offenders. Sometimes this can be done subtly without revealing your true intent. For example, in forming groups you can count off so that the perpetrators are in different groups. As you assign groups to different areas of the room, you can assure that the troublesome ones are seated as far apart as possible.

15. Never argue with a student in front of the class. Decline to argue the issue now, but offer to discuss it privately with the student later. Public arguments inevitably lead to one of you losing face in front of the class. Either way, you lose! Students who lose face in front of their peers do get even.

16. Quiet reprimands are much more effective than loud ones. Indeed, some research suggests that loud reprimands are actually more disruptive. Avoid shouting at students! It reveals your loss of control. However, your tonality and nonverbal cues must be congruent. If your body language is too nonassertive, students will receive a mixed message that you aren't really serious.

17. When you do discuss a student's misbehavior, make it clear that you find the behavior, not the student, unacceptable. Remain firm yet compassionate. If possible, praise what they do well, but encourage improvement in their erroneous ways.

18. Understand the school's student behavior code. What disciplinary measures are to be taken for serious infractions (for example, fighting, drugs, alcohol, truancy)? What is the procedure for reporting such problems? Is in-school suspension or detention used? If so, how? How are parents involved in correcting misbehavior?

19. Early in the year, develop classroom routines. Carefully explain how students are to handle the details of daily classroom activities: taking attendance, procedures for making up missed work, distributing and collecting materials, going to the bathroom, leaving for lunch, and so on.

20. Be cautious of touching students when they are very angry. This can stimulate a violent response in some students.

21. Be aware of students' occasional concealment (for example, covering their mouths when whispering, hiding behind their desks, standing books on edge to hide other reading material). Moving about the classroom discourages such strategies.

22. Avoid branding a student a failure because of one mistake. Help your students recognize that we all make mistakes but also have a responsibility to learn from our mistakes.

23. Avoid punishing the whole class for one student's misbehavior. It is simply unfair, and the innocent students will perceive it that way. It will only turn the whole class (and probably their parents) against you.

24. Try to find acceptable means for students to receive the attention and approval they often seek through misbehavior. Provide an opportunity for them to earn the spotlight through appropriate behavior.

25. Always have a couple of "sponge" activities (for example, small-group brainstorm, word puzzle, or review game) available to use when the unexpected happens (the projector bulb burns out, a visitor comes to the door, or a student becomes ill in class) or when some students complete seatwork or tests ahead of others.

26. Don't be too quick to send students to the principal's office or to call their parents. If done too frequently, this suggests that you have a problem with classroom management. Involve others only for serious or persistent misbehavior.

27. Don't send students out into the hallway as a punishment. Aside from potential liability problems, many students find the hall a pretty exciting place to be, especially if the class is boring.

28. For persistent, serious problems with a student, use the private teacher-student conference. Explain without blaming exactly what behaviors you find inappropriate and why. Avoid verbally attacking the student, and do listen to his or her view. Push the student for a plan for correcting the behavior in the future and making a commitment to follow through with that plan.

29. If you feel overwhelmed by a student's challenging behavior, don't be afraid to consult other professionals: your principal, experienced teachers, school psychologist, or counselor. They have likely confronted the same problems. Ask several persons for a variety of opinions. Allow yourself to learn from their mistakes and successes. A secondary benefit is that they will probably be flattered that you came to them for advice.

30. There are a number of excellent nationally marketed programs on effective classroom management: Performance Learning Systems' Classroom Management course, Lee Canter's Assertive Discipline, Curwin and Mendler's Discipline with Dignity, Linda Albert's Cooperative Discipline, or Bob Wubbolding's Managing the Disruptive Classroom. If you are having difficulty managing student behavior, find one of these courses being offered locally, often for graduate credit. Ask colleagues if they have taken any of these courses and can evaluate its effectiveness.

What Do You Want?

A goal-oriented problem focus requires that teachers know what they want as well as what they don't want to have happen in their classroom. If an auto mechanic is confronted with a car that will not run, the goal is quite apparent: to get the car to start. In dealing with students, it is equally important, though not always easy, to clarify what you want to have happen. We often give students lots of information about what they should not do but very little about what we expect them to do.

An objective is incompatible with the problem behavior. It is impossible for both to occur at the same time. Hence, in focusing on any problem, it is important not only to attempt to decrease the undesirable behavior but also to emphasize what we do expect the student to do. For example:

Problem	**Objective**
Brooke is out of her seat during class.	Brooke will remain in her chair through class.
Jake doesn't do his homework.	Jake completes his homework.
Braedon hits the other kids.	Braedon keeps his hands to himself.

Remember, success in decreasing an undesirable behavior will be enhanced if you emphasize what you *do* want.

Positive Reinforcement of Good Behavior

If consumers shopping at a new department store are pleased with the service and goods received, they will likely continue to shop at that store in the future. Behaviors that have desirable consequences will likely continue. Pleasant or desirable consequences that cause a behavior to be repeated are called rewards or positive reinforcement. Note that any consequence functions as a reward only if the behavior it follows is maintained or increased.

Some might ask: "Isn't rewarding students for good behavior just a form of bribery?" Definitely not. A *bribe* is payment in kind or value for the commission of an immoral or illegal act. Hopefully, what you are asking of your students is neither immoral nor illegal. Second, a bribe is usually paid before commission of the requested action, whereas a reward should always follow the completion of the desired behavior.

The Reward Hierarchy

Rewards (positive reinforcers) can be extrinsic or intrinsic. The ideal would be for each student to enter the classroom intrinsically motivated and eager to devour the wisdom you have to share. Unfortunately, I have met few self-actualized, self-motivated third graders (or high school or college students, for that matter). My advice is to take students at the level they are and help them move to the next higher level of motivation.

A word of caution: there are few universal rewards. An incentive that may work with most students may not influence the behavior of others. For example, public praise from the teacher would serve many students as a pleasant consequence and positively motivate their behavior. However, for a small portion of students (for example, some adolescent males), public praise from a teacher may backfire, becoming a source of derision from their peers.

Students often enter the classroom with little internal motivation for the virtue of studying Shakespeare, Roman history, or quadratic equations. They might like it once we get them to give it a try, but they may well need some external incentive to entice them into taking that first step. External incentives are not inherently evil. Certainly, they can be misused and overused. Few adults disdain the paychecks they receive for their labors. People of all ages strive for appreciation and approval.

The Hierarchy of Rewards

Internal

Self

Social

External

Activities

Tangibles

It helps to view rewards as falling into a hierarchy. The reward hierarchy includes four levels of positive reinforcers. At the lowest level are *tangibles,* physical items that the recipient can hold, touch, taste. These would include stickers, posters, or food.

The next higher level are *activities,* privileges that might include computer time, recess, or being first in line. For younger students particularly, helping the teacher (for example, collecting papers or running an errand) may function as a reward.

Social rewards are next up the hierarchy. These tend to convey appreciation, recognition, or approval. Examples include praise, smiles, or pats on the back.

Intrinsic (or internal) reinforcements are at the pinnacle of the reward hierarchy. These are autonomous, arising from within.

Tips on Using Positive Reinforcement in the Classroom

✓ A teacher's goal in using positive reinforcement in the classroom should ultimately be to move students up the reward hierarchy from external motivation to internal control. It is best to use the highest level of reinforcer that will motivate a student to put forth the effort toward the desired behavior. If a student is already intrinsically motivated to do a task, don't attempt to offer lower-level reinforcers. Use social reinforcers, such as praise or a smile, if they provide sufficient encouragement for the student to maintain a behavior.

✓ Reinforce positive behaviors. A great many students go through school generally being ignored, as long as they don't step out of line. They may not be the greatest students, but they don't usually create trouble. They may receive little of the teacher's time or attention. Find ways to show recognition and appreciation of their gains, even the small ones. Reward appropriate behavior; don't ignore it. "Catch the student being good," some teachers say. This involves a different kind of attitude, a new, more positive outlook on the world.

✓ Use praise effectively. While verbal praise can be effective in encouraging positive behaviors, it is often used ineffectively. To be most constructive, praise should be specific rather than general. Rather than saying "Good job," offer specific information on what you liked about the student's work: "Excellent paragraph transitions" or "Your use of color in this picture was very unique." Also be aware that public praise does not work for everyone. It may backfire when used with some adolescents, whose peers may rib them mercilessly. However, private encouragement still might be influential with such students.

✓ Use group contracting to reward good performance, both behavioral and academic. This can be done informally (for example, "As soon as we all have put away the art supplies, we'll go out for recess") or in a more structured, formal contract. It allows the group to earn a group reward, which might be free time to play an educational game, no homework for a night, a field trip, or special treat.

✓ When you use rewards, vary them to be effective. The same reward used over and over quickly satiates, losing its value to motivate. Variety and novelty are powerful reinforcers.

Dr. Judy Cameron and Dr. David Pierce, University of Alberta professors, systematically and thoroughly reviewed the body of research on the use of praise and other rewards. Their work has debunked the myth that rewards stifle students' intrinsic motivation. For more information, see their book, *Rewards and Intrinsic Motivation: Resolving the Controversy* (Bergin & Garvey Press, 2002).

Potential Classroom Rewards

Tangible (Physical) Reinforcers

Popcorn	T-shirts
Pretzels	Bumper stickers
Fruit	Pencils
Pizza	Notebooks
Cookies	Books
Lemonade	Computer software
Posters	Music CDs
Stickers	Scented crayons
Ribbons	Plaques
Food coupons	Trophies
Trinkets	Gift certificates

Activity Reinforcers

Choose seats	Sharpen pencils
Breaks, recess	Use learning center
Lunch with teacher or principal	Independent study activity
Reserved parking space	Receive "no homework" pass
Teacher tell personal story	Work in "quiet" corner
Be first in line	Extra locker space
Hold class outdoors	Computer time
Feed the class pet	Free time to . . .
Reserved seat at sports events	Play games
Hall passes	Play sports
Parties	Cook
Display work	Watch movies or videos
Picnics	Attend concerts
Do artwork	Be on safety patrol
Field trips	Sing
Learn a magic trick	Floor hockey in gym

Teacher read a story

Early dismissal

Parties

Make videos

Preferred seating

Work with younger students

Assemblies

Take pictures

Go to library

Play musical instrument

Draw

Do puzzles

Exercise

Watch TV

Dress-up days

Play with pets

Help the Teacher

Construct bulletin boards

Pass out materials

Collect papers

Be line leader

Do research on the Internet

Design Web pages

Tutor other students

Take attendance

Design a class Web site

Photocopy materials

Help with experiments

Work in office

Arrange furniture

Clean the classroom

Run audiovisual equipment

Use the computer

Edit newsletter

Take pictures or movies

Rental Privileges as Potential Activity Reinforcers

Games

Magic markers

Hand puppets

Calculator

Chalk

Video camera

Funny hats

Tape recorders

Football

Computer software

Computer

Table toys

Computer games

Audiotapes

Sports and playground equipment

Musical instruments

Paints

Baseball mitts

Weights

Punching bag

Books

Blocks

Scented markers

Videos

Jump rope

Magazines

Colored pencils

Special hat, costume

Social Reinforcers

Grades

Smiles, nods, hugs

Certificates of merit

Winks, eye contact

Honor rolls

Stickers

Approval

Athletic letters

Peer approval

Encouragement

Positive comments on papers

Standing ovations

Applause

Positive nonverbal gestures

Compliments

Acceptance in honor societies

Drawings on papers, smiling faces

Pats on the back

Drum rolls

Awards

Check marks

Mysterious warm-fuzzy notes

Principal's signature on good papers

Being asked opinions, advice

Recognition

Name mentioned in assembly

Letter to parents

Phone call to parents

Name in paper

Honor roll

Student of the week

Work displayed

Photograph in paper

Trophies, stars

Photograph on bulletin board

Intrinsic (Internal) Reinforcers

Fun

Meeting goals

Learning (for the sake of learning)

Self-sufficiency

Philosophical humor

Relaxation, tranquility, serenity

Meaningfulness

Novelty, surprises

Self-satisfaction

Success

Enjoyment of beauty

Improvement

Openness

Having options, alternatives

Playfulness

Self-awareness

Constructive feedback

Achievement

Creative Self-Expression

Arts and crafts

Painting

Gardening

Athletics

Cooking

Poetry

Music

Dancing

Writing

Designing

Positive Referrals: Recognition That Works

The adage "The squeaky wheels get the grease" too often holds true in schools. In many schools misbehaving students get the bulk of the staff's attention. In such a climate, educators can easily overlook students' positive behaviors. To assure that didn't happen at Olympia High School in Orlando, Florida, the staff initiated the Positive Referrals Program.

Students gain special recognition when they do something positive—in or out of the classroom—that benefits the school or community. Any student, teacher, administrator, parent, or staff member may fill out a referral form reporting a student's positive behavior. The positive referral forms go to the grade-level administrator, who gives the student a certificate of recognition and calls the parents.

The program was a response to feedback from students that more recognition should be given for positive behaviors. The criteria for behaviors worthy of positive referral are open-ended to allow as many as possible to be recognized.

One student was referred for finding a wallet with $60 and returning it to the owner. The student said it was simply the right thing to do. Another student received recognition for earning a perfect score on a very difficult midterm exam.

Assistant principal David Christiansen believes that "It is a great way to recognize the little things that happen every day that help make a great environment." He reports that the students, staff, and parents have shown an overwhelmingly positive response to the program.

Source: Interview with David Christiansen, assistant principal at Olympia High School in Orlando, Florida. Reprinted with permission from *The Heart of Teaching* newsletter, Performance Learning Systems.

Helpful Resources

Alberto, P. A., & Troutman, A. C. (2003). *Applied behavior analysis for teachers* (6th ed.). Columbus, OH: Merrill.

Belvel, P. S., & Jordan, M.M.P. (2003). *Rethinking classroom management: Strategies for prevention, intervention, and problem solving.* Thousand Oaks, CA: Corwin.

Charles, C. M. (2002). *Building classroom discipline* (7th ed.). Boston: Allyn & Bacon.

Evertson, C. M., Emmer, E. T., & Worsham, M. E. (2003). *Classroom management for elementary teachers* (6th ed.). Boston: Allyn & Bacon.

Evertson, C. M., Emmer, E. T., & Worsham, M. E. (2003). *Classroom management for secondary teachers* (6th ed.). Boston: Allyn & Bacon.

Harlan, J. C., & Rowland, S. T. (2002). *Behavior management strategies for teachers: Achieving instructional effectiveness, student success, and student motivation.* Springfield, IL: Charles C. Thomas.

Jackson, L., Panyan, M. V. (2002). *Positive behavioral support in the classroom: Principles and practices.* Baltimore: P. H. Brookes.

Kerr, M., & Nelson, C. M. (2002). *Strategies for addressing behavior problems in the classroom.* Upper Saddle River, NJ: Merrill/Prentice Hall.

Martella, R. C., Nelson, J. R., & Marchand-Martella, N. E. (2003). *Managing disruptive behaviors in the schools: A schoolwide, classroom, and individualized social learning approach.* Boston: Allyn & Bacon.

Weinstein, C. S. (2003). *Secondary classroom management: Lessons from research and practice.* Boston: McGraw-Hill.

Corporal Punishment

The practices of whipping, flogging, paddling, thumping, birching, whacking, caning, and otherwise inflicting physical pain on students is embedded in the history of American education. The Puritans' writings frequently refer to the use of the rod to "beat the devil out of" misbehaving students. The use of corporal punishment is seldom discussed dispassionately; it evokes heated arguments from both its proponents and opponents.

In *Reading, Writing, and the Hickory Stick,* a thorough examination of the use of corporal punishment in schools, Irwin Hyman reviewed studies documenting the following practices:

✓ Corporal punishment occurs more frequently at the primary and intermediate levels.

✓ Boys are paddled much more frequently than girls.

✓ Minority and poor white children receive corporal punishment four to five times more frequently than middle- and upper-class white children.

✓ Corporal punishment is used least in schools in the Northeast.

✓ It is a myth that corporal punishment is used as a last resort. Studies suggest corporal punishment is frequently the first punishment for minor and nonviolent misbehaviors.

✓ There is evidence that corporal punishment is one of the causes of school vandalism.

✓ Corporal punishment is forbidden in the schools of Europe, Japan, Israel, Ireland, Russia, China, Turkey, Iceland, Puerto Rico, twenty-eight U.S. states, and many U.S. metropolitan areas. The United States and Canada remain the only industrialized nations tolerating corporal punishment in their schools.

✓ Teachers who frequently paddle tend to be authoritarian, dogmatic, relatively inexperienced, impulsive, and neurotic as compared to their peers.

✓ Generally, teachers who do not paddle were rarely, if ever, spanked or paddled as children. This modeling effect has been repeatedly demonstrated. The more teachers were hit as children, the more they tend to hit their students.

✓ Schools with high rates of corporal punishment also have high rates of suspensions and are generally more punitive in all discipline responses than are schools with low rates of corporal punishment.

Some states now restrict the use of corporal punishment, mandating that a witness be present, paddling not be done in front of other students; in some locations such punishment can take place only after a parent has granted consent. Some areas continue to permit spanking by the hand

---

Ways to Discourage Students

- Set unrealistically high standards; demand perfection.
- Focus on mistakes to motivate.
- Make pessimistic interpretations.
- Compare people.
- Dominate by being too helpful.

Source: Evans, T. D. (1996). Encouragement: The key to reforming classrooms. *Educational Leadership, 54,* 1, 81–85 but prohibit the use of paddles or other objects. Many organizations, including the National Education Association, the American Civil Liberties Union, the American Academy of Pediatrics, the National Committee on the Prevention of Child Abuse, the Association of Childhood Education International, the American Medical Association, the Children's Defense Fund, the National Association of Social Workers, and the Parent Teacher Association, have lobbied to restrict or ban the use of corporal punishment in schools. The majority of states now ban the use of corporal punishment; others restrict its use. Although reliance on corporal punishment has declined, over one million instances of corporal punishment still occur each year in the United States.

The arguments that paddling develops character or reforms errant behavior simply are not supported by any objective examination of the data. Indeed, evidence suggests that corporal punishment is counterproductive.

The Case Against Corporal Punishment

✓ Corporal punishment does not extinguish undesirable behaviors. It merely temporarily suppresses them.

✓ Physical punishment models aggression and violence as appropriate means of getting what you want.

✓ All child abuse begins as punishment. There is a relationship between how severely and frequently children experienced physical punishment and the propensity toward violence later in their lives. Researchers estimate between twenty thousand and 150,000 children each year require medical treatment as a result of corporal punishment received at school. Circulatory and nervous system problems, paralysis, broken bones, knocked-out teeth, brain damage, and post-traumatic stress disorder have all been documented in instances of school-administered corporal punishment.

✓ There is an inherent unfairness in who gets punished. Paddling is not distributed equally, even for similar offenses. Race, gender, and socioeconomic level influence whether a particular student will experience corporal punishment.

✓ Paddling in schools can lead to stress reactions, such as school phobias, nightmares, loss of appetite, bed-wetting, and nervousness.

✓ Punishing situations tend to be avoided. Schools that rely heavily on corporal punishment also experience higher rates of absenteeism, truancy, and dropping out.

✓ Paddling poisons the teacher-student relationship. It breeds mistrust. Fear is not the equivalent of respect.

✓ In instances where paddling was banned, the amount of student misbehavior did not increase. Indeed, in at least one instance, vandalism actually decreased.

✓ There is increased risk today of being sued or charged with child abuse for paddling students.

Despite overwhelming evidence that corporal punishment has detrimental effects on students, as well as teachers, and virtually no evidence that it has any long-term benefits, the practice has its supporters, including some administrators, parents, and teachers. The long-term effects cannot be justified by any short-term gains the teacher may reap from this sadistic behavior. Yet teaching remains the sole profession that is permitted to beat its clients. The beating of criminals or animals is forbidden, yet many states still legally sanction the paddling of students.

There is substantial evidence that corporal punishment is not essential to maintaining decorum and obedience in today's schools. See the earlier section Hot Tips for Managing Classroom Behavior for alternatives to the use of corporal punishment.

A teacher does best armed only with knowledge. Corporal punishment is a cruel and obsolete weapon. The battle for children's minds should not be waged on their behinds.

—**U.S.A. Today editorial, August 22, 1990**

Additional Reading on Corporal Punishment

Binggeli, N. J., Hart, S. N., & Brassard, M. R. (2001). *Psychological maltreatment of children.* Thousand Oaks, CA: Sage.

Essex, N. L. (2002). *School law and the public schools: A practical guide for educational leaders.* Boston: Allyn & Bacon.

Hinchey, P. H. (2003). Corporal punishment: Legalities, realities, and implications. *The Clearing House, 76*(3), 127–131.

Hyman, I. (1990). *Reading, writing, and the hickory stick.* Lexington, MA: Lexington Books.

Straus, M. A., & Donnelly, D. A. (2001). *Beating the devil out of them: Corporal punishment in American families and its effects on children.* New Brunswick, NJ: Transaction.

Turner, S. (2002). *Something to cry about: An argument against corporal punishment of children in Canada.* Waterloo, ON: Wilfrid Laurier University Press.

Time-outs

Sometimes students do break class rules, behaving in ways that are inappropriate, disruptive, and unacceptable. Usually such misbehaviors are not severe, but they must be discouraged. Maybe the teacher has unsuccessfully tried smaller interventions, like warning the student or correcting the unacceptable behavior, to no avail. What's a teacher to do? Many teachers have had excellent success through the use of time-out procedures.

Time-out is not painful. It doesn't hurt. Nor should it humiliate the child. It may be a bit boring. Children would generally prefer to be engaged, participating in anything but sitting quietly. Time-out involves isolating the student for a relatively brief period of time. It is not greatly unlike the cartoons of Dennis the Menace sitting in the corner in his chair.

Time-outs are also designed to allow students time to calm down and to reflect on why their behavior is inappropriate.

Dos of Using Time-outs

✔ Be sure to check with your principal on any state or local school restrictions on the use of time-outs.

✔ Generally, it is best to offer a single warning prior to resorting to a time-out.

✔ Instruct the student in a calm, nonhostile tone to go to the designated time-out area. It should ideally be an area within your classroom where you can clearly see the student but he or she cannot see the rest of the class. A chair off to the side partitioned with a bookcase or filing cabinet may be sufficient.

✔ Clearly specify the amount of time the student will be in time-out. A relatively brief amount of time is generally sufficient. The younger the child, the shorter the time. Experts typically suggest a maximum of fifteen minutes. A good rule of thumb is to assign one minute of time-out for each year of the student's age.

✔ Some teachers use a kitchen timer to keep track of the time-out so that everyone knows when the time-out is over.

✔ Any outbursts require that the time-out interval be restarted.

✔ Modify time-outs for older students. After-school detentions are a form of time-out.

✔ Time-outs should be used in conjunction with positive discipline procedures. Technically, time-out is a form of punishment.

✔ It is a good idea to document in writing any use of time-out, noting the transgression, amount of time, time-out location, and any observed consequences.

✔ Train students early in the year about time-out procedures. Clarify the behaviors that may result in time-outs.

✔ Use common sense. Putting a child in a locked or dark closet is inexcusable. One teacher was fired after he put a student in a refrigerator carton, cut holes in the sides, and encouraged the rest of the students to make faces and ridicule the student inside. You are running a classroom, not a marine boot camp.

Don'ts of Using Time-outs

Time-outs can backfire if used foolishly. Here are pitfalls to avoid:

✔ Never just send the student out into the hall. Big mistake! I know this one from experience: I spent a lot of time standing in hallways as a child, usually for talking too much. It isn't that bad a place to be, especially if the class is boring. You get to chat with everyone who comes down the hallway, make funny faces in the door window, and find other mischief.

✔ Avoid sending students to the principal's office if at all possible. Done regularly, it communicates that you can't handle your class. And often the principal isn't there, so the secretary is stuck with the problem. One of my former graduate students had one male student who started misbehaving regularly, and she would send him to the principal's office. None of the other teachers seemed to ever have problems with this lad. His motivation was unveiled when she discovered that his girlfriend was an office assistant during that class period. What we think is a punishment may not always be so.

✓ Don't harangue the child. No shouting. A time-out is more apt to succeed when the teacher uses it without condemnation, instead communicating that he or she cares but cannot accept the behavior. Avoid a public argument. Being firm but fair is the key.

✓ Avoid allowing the student to garner extra attention from the rest of the class. Ordering the student to stand along the wall (or even worse, behind the teacher) gives the student a free audience.

✓ Don't overdo it; use time-outs sparingly. Time-out rooms used in some schools are somewhat controversial, as students end up missing too much schoolwork by being out of the classroom.

✓ Time-outs do not work with all children. Particularly for shy or withdrawn children, time-outs may actually serve as a reward and generally not as a deterrent. Time-outs will not work if a time-out is more rewarding than class.

A True Story

When I was in elementary school, I had a problem: I talked too much. Actually, the way my teachers reported it on my grade cards was "Ronnie has a voice that carries," meaning that everyone else talked, but the teachers would hear me above the rest of the students.

One day my fourth-grade teacher just lost it. She ranted and shouted and then ordered: "Go up to the teachers' workroom, and don't you come out until I tell you."

As commanded, I left the classroom and climbed the six steps up to the teachers' workroom. It was a tiny space: a desk, three chairs, and a small window.

I sat quietly looking out the window. In ten minutes I was quite bored. "Come on, let me go back. I'll be quiet. This is dull."

I stirred. I paced the room. I looked out the window. I saw all the kids go home. I sat. I pouted. I saw all the teachers go home.

I don't plead innocence. I knew exactly where this was headed. "Now, let's see. You said, 'Stay there until I tell you to come out.' Hmm. We'll see!"

About five o'clock the school matriarch, a third-grade teacher, entered the room. "What are you doing in here?" she demanded. In my whiniest voice I mumbled, "My teacher made me come in."

"Go on. Go home," she uttered.

The next morning when I returned to school, my teacher said, "Now, Ronnie, you know you could have gone home, don't you?" I just sheepishly peered back up at her. That night I found out through the grapevine that my teacher had really been called on the carpet by her principal.

The moral of the story is this: if you use time-out, don't forget where you put the kid!

Bullying in School

Students bullying other students is not a new phenomenon, but the risks of allowing bullying to continue have increased. The level of violence in schools has risen, with kids behaving more aggressively at younger ages and having increased accessibility to guns.

Why Students Bully

Bullying may consist of teasing, taunting, threatening, hitting, or stealing. Students who bully others appear to have a need to feel powerful and in control. They gain satisfaction from inflicting injury and suffering on others, feel little empathy for their victims, and rationalize their actions by claiming that their victims provoked them in some way.

Research suggests that bullies are often raised in homes where physical punishment is used, parental involvement and warmth are missing, and children are encouraged to handle problems by striking back. Contrary to prevailing myths, bullies appear to have little anxiety and to possess strong self-esteem. Young bullies may grow up to be big bullies.

Students who are victims of bullying exhibit anxiety, insecurity, caution, and low self-esteem. Victims are frequently socially isolated, lacking friends or social skills. They tend to be close to their parents, who are often overprotective. Researchers estimate that seven percent of America's eighth graders stay home at least once a month to avoid bullies.

Successful Interventions

The most effective interventions involve the entire school community rather than focusing only on the perpetrators. Experts recommend the following strategies:

✓ Survey students and adults. The questionnaire helps the school community to become aware of the extent of the problem, gains support for intervention efforts, and provides baseline data for measuring the success of interventions.

✓ Conduct a parental awareness campaign during parent-teacher conference days, through school newsletters and parent organization meetings. Distribute survey results as part of this campaign.

✓ Develop rules against bullying. Role-playing exercises and related assignments can teach alternative coping skills to student bullies and their victims. Other students can learn to assist victims and discuss how everyone can work together to create a school climate where bullying is unacceptable.

✓ Employ individualized interventions with the bullies and victims; use cooperative learning activities to minimize social isolation; and increase adult supervision during recess or lunch.

✓ Teach conflict resolution. Research shows that conflict mediation programs do work. If your school doesn't have one, teach your students basic conflict resolution skills.

Sources: Bullying in Schools, ERIC Digest by Ron Banks; *The Bully-Free Classroom* by Allan L. Beane (Minneapolis: Free Spirit Publishing, 1999). Reprinted with permission from *The Heart of Teaching* newsletter, Performance Learning Systems.

"Fight, Fight!": Intervention Strategies

Student altercations are among the most stressful events for teachers, but knowing how to safely and efficiently intervene can minimize the risks of escalation to more serious violence. Chandra Hawley of Indiana University's Center for Adolescent Studies offers this advice on intervening in a fight:

✓ The teacher's top priority must be to avoid getting hurt! Immediately send a student—preferably one you know—for help: "Alice, please go to the office and ask Mr. Gomez to come immediately. Tell him there is a fight in room 122."

✓ Break up the crowd. With direct eye contact, sternly, but without screaming, direct students to leave the area. Use names of students you know. "Matt, Kelly, all of you, go directly to the cafeteria. Wait there for me."

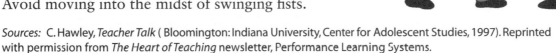

✓ After the crowd has moved away and help is coming, you can attend to the fight. Usually, one person quickly dominates the fight. Assertively address the other person, by name if you know it, "Allen, that's enough! Move back now!" If necessary, make a loud noise, such as clapping your hands. Avoid moving into the midst of swinging fists.

Sources: C. Hawley, *Teacher Talk* (Bloomington: Indiana University, Center for Adolescent Studies, 1997). Reprinted with permission from *The Heart of Teaching* newsletter, Performance Learning Systems.

Noisy Classrooms: Learning Impediment

A series of research studies by University of Florida professors Gary Siebein and Carl Crandell revealed that noisy classrooms seriously impair students' learning. Observations in forty-seven Florida elementary, middle, and high schools revealed that most had background noise levels between forty and fifty-five decibels. Most people have difficulty hearing once background noise reaches fifty decibels.

The research revealed that students seated more than twelve feet away from the teacher in noisy classrooms hear less than 5 percent of what their teachers say when addressing the whole class. The problem is compounded by the finding that between 10 percent and 30 percent of students possess some kind of moderate to mild hearing impairment. Noisy classrooms further impede the learning of students with attention deficit disorder.

Source: "Most Classrooms Are Too Noisy for Learning," *University of Florida News,* December 5, 2001.

Suggestions for Improving Classroom Acoustics

1. Close the classroom door to eliminate ambient hallway noise.

2. Keep windows closed if possible.

3. Cover hard surfaces with sound-absorbing materials (acoustic tiling, carpeting, cork, or cloth).

4. Ideally, floors should be carpeted and windows curtained.

5. If floors are not carpeted, cover chair feet with slit tennis balls.

6. Use felt or cork pads on desk lids to minimize noise from opening and closing.

7. Turn off computers and printers when not in use.

8. From the beginning of the year, set noise rules: indoor voices only, no slamming books or doors.

9. Get every student's attention before talking.

10. At the beginning of the year, establish a nonverbal cue to signal that students are to stop talking and listen.

Source: University of Florida News. Online at www.napa.ufl.edu/2001news/classnoise.htm. Reprinted with permission from *The Heart of Teaching* newsletter, Performance Learning Systems.

The Teacher as a Skilled Helper

It is not uncommon for students to turn to teachers for help in times of stress, disappointment, frustration, and loss. Almost daily every teacher has the opportunity to respond to at least one student's emotional turmoil. In the course of a year, some students in your class very likely may experience the death or disability of a family member or classmate, their parents' divorce, a parent's unemployment, the loss of pets, moving to new schools, academic failure, or rejection by classmates or sweethearts.

All compassionate teachers should have some high-yield, low-risk listening skills in their repertoire. They are high-yield skills because if they are done well, these basic counseling tools have the potential to make a large difference in students' lives. They are low risk because as long as teachers stick to these skills and don't venture off into amateur psychotherapy, no harm is likely to occur. No one has ever been hurt by being listened to, and a great many people have been helped.

The skills described here are the basic attending skills that every beginning counselor learns, often termed *active listening* skills. *Passive listening* is the kind of listening that occurs when students are staring at you during a lecture. Maybe they even occasionally nod their heads to signal that they are skill awake, but you have no idea whether they are actually hearing a word you have said. Passive listening is one-way. Active listening, on the other hand, is a two-way process; it involves a true dialogue. What one person is saying is clearly and directly related to what the other has said. The listener must actively prove that he or she has heard the speaker.

Become a good listener, and the world will beat a path to your door. Truly good listeners are all too rare; they stand out. Effective listeners have mastered the fine art of inviting people to talk about themselves, and the listener seems genuinely interested. Listening is one of the most precious gifts you can give to your students. You may be the only adult in their lives who truly takes time to listen.

Talking is sharing, but listening is caring.

—Anonymous

Becoming a skilled helper does not mean having to sit down with a student and become involved in a long tearful conversation. Every day in every classroom, students are struggling with emotional pain and conflict. One compassionate moment of listening can let the child know he or she has been heard, that you care. It may indeed take less than ten seconds. And that student may remember the brief encounter for the rest of his or her life.

What Good Listening Is Not

Good listening is not advice giving. Indeed, giving advice to others is tempting, especially when the solutions to their problems are so obvious to us. Take a moment to recall the last time someone freely offered you advice, especially if it was unsolicited. Chances are it fell on deaf ears. We tend to reject unsolicited advice, no matter what the source. Though it may not be the giver's intent, advice subtly communicates "I can run your life better than you can"—not a message most people are eager to hear.

Even if the student asks for advice, giving it is not necessarily the best thing to do. There is an old Chinese proverb: "Give me a fish and I eat for a day; teach me to fish and I eat forever." We should be more interested in teaching people how to fish, not in giving fish away. It is far more important to equip our students with the skills needed to face and solve life's challenges than to ease their short-term discomfort. When we prematurely give advice, we rob students of a valuable learning experience. Further, we, not the student, have assumed responsibility for the problem. Embedded in the use of active listening is the assumption that students can work out the solutions to their problems given support and time. (Of course, advice giving is appropriate if you are in the role of an academic adviser. We are referring here to discussion of students' personal, not academic, problems.)

Reflection of Feelings

Reflection of feelings is a powerful tool that almost every counselor uses. It appears on the surface to be a simple skill. Do not be deceived: it is very difficult to do well and genuinely. The aim is to practice reflections of feeling until they become reflexive, so that the next time you are sitting with a person in pain, you automatically respond with such a response.

The basic structure of a reflection of feeling is "You feel . . . ," filling in the blank with a feeling word that accurately reflects the feeling the student is experiencing at that moment. After you have mastered the technique, experiment with putting it into your own phrasing, such as "You seem . . . "; "It sounds like you are . . . "; or "You are . . . " The key ingredient is that you must include the feeling word in your observation. Later you might also add the source of the perceived feeling, "You feel . . . about [or because of] . . ."

Reflection of feeling is one of several perception-checking devices. They are used to verify what we think we have heard. They develop a crucial helping condition called empathy. *Empathy* (not sympathy) is the ability to communicate to other persons that you are trying to understand what it is like to be them. That is why "I know how you feel" is an inadequate response. Maybe you know; maybe you don't. Only when you test your hypothesis with a reflection of feeling ("You seem pretty discouraged") do you really prove that you heard what the student has said. You are striving for a deeper level of understanding.

The beauty of a reflection of feeling is that you gain either way. If you are accurate in your perception, the student will almost always respond, "Yes," and then will elaborate. They will almost never stop at yes, unless you have raised your tonality at the end of your observation, making your statement into a closed-ended question. If you are off in your observation, the student will almost always reply, "Well, no, it's not so much discouraged [or another feeling] as it is . . . "), giving you more accurate feedback. Either way, you gain.

Reflections of feeling are always offered tentatively. The intent is to check out what you perceive their feelings to be. The fact is that you can never know with absolute certainty what another human being is feeling. You can project how you would feel; you can guess how they feel; but you can never know with 100 percent certainty. Take the risk of checking out your perceptions.

As a skilled helper, it is important to listen more to the feelings a student expresses than the surface content. People, including students, seldom say all they mean and seldom mean all they say. It is critical to learn to listen between the lines. Sometimes a student may mean exactly the opposite of what he or she really says (for example, "I don't need your help!"). By listening to students' feelings, we help them move to a deeper level of understanding than if we focus only on the content, which tends to stay at an intellectual level. Students perceive that teachers who listen empathically by using reflections of feeling as caring more.

Listening to students' feelings prevents them from bottling up their emotions and ultimately erupting in aggressive and destructive acts. Good active listening helps defuse stress and tension.

There are very practical reasons for using reflections of feeling in working with your students. David Aspy and Flo Roebuck reported in their book *Kids Don't Learn from Teachers They Don't Like* (Human Resource Development Press, 1977) that students of teachers using such active listening skills scored higher on academic achievement tests, attendance, and measures of self-esteem. Good listening *does* make a difference.

Twenty-three More Tips for Becoming a Better Listener

1. To be a successful listener, you must be genuinely interested in what the student has to say. If you don't have time at the moment, offer to talk with the student later.

2. In a counseling role, listen nonjudgmentally, achieving what psychologist Carl Rogers terms unconditional positive regard. By the time students come to their teachers with a problem, they have probably had advice and lectures from others. They often just need someone who

cares enough to listen for a few minutes. Nothing nips trust like critical judgment and negative labeling. Beware of conveying disapproval through your tonality, leading questions, or nonverbal responses.

3. The next time you have a student sitting knee-to-knee in front of you with tears streaming down his or her cheeks, resist the urge to give advice or sugarcoated reassurance. Just take time to listen compassionately. Follow the adage "Talk a little less; listen a little more."

4. Become comfortable with silence in a counseling relationship. These pauses can create valuable reflection time for students.

5. Use a variety of listening skills. Restate a student's comment in your own words. This tends not to include the reference to feelings that are included in reflections of feeling. Good clarifying questions, used sparingly, can be most helpful in encouraging students to examine the causes and possible solutions to their problems.

> ## Comments That Do More Harm than Good
>
> What you'd better do is . . .
> What's wrong with you?
> I wish you didn't feel that way.
> Others have problems worse than yours.
> Don't worry; everything is going to turn out just fine.
> Here's what I'd do if I were you: . . .
> Why do you feel that way?
> Everyone feels that way.
> Why don't you . . . ?

6. Be sure your nonverbal messages are congruent with your verbal ones. Unless the student's culture forbids it, offer the student direct eye contact while he or she is talking. It helps establish trust and communicates interest. Leaning forward is also interpreted as an expression of concern and interest.

7. Brief responses such as "Mm-hmm" or "I see" or "Go on" are useful in communicating that you are still with the speaker. Occasional head nods also encourage the student to continue.

8. Avoid finishing others' statements. Besides being rude, it also communicates impatience and a lack of interest. More important, it's lazy listening. Sometimes you will just be wrong in your interpretation. It's also generally best not to interrupt the speakers unless they begin to ramble. Then you might inject a clarifying phrase or question.

9. Invest in building rapport with your students by listening to them when they don't have serious problems. Acknowledge and validate their positive feelings as well as the negative ones (for example, "You're really excited about making the team"; or "You must be very proud of your award").

10. Study outstanding listeners in your daily life and in the public media. Larry King and Charlie Rose are good models to observe. Note their nonverbal posture and the quality of their open-ended questions.

Never give advice unasked.

—German proverb

11. Reflective listening is also a valuable technique to employ with angry students or adults. You are not getting into the blame game. You are neither saying "You're wrong!" nor "I'm wrong." By listening to their feelings (for example, "You're pretty upset with the way your child has been treated") you are simply communicating that you are listening to them at the deepest level. It is like verbal judo. Instead of meeting force with force, you are letting their anger dissipate into the wind. Once the angry person has vented his or her feelings and you refuse to get caught up in a shouting match, the person will begin to calm down.

12. Avoid the "Have you tried . . . ?" trap. Most students will respond with "I tried that" or "It won't work because . . ." They will wait for you to suggest one more solution so that they can chop it down. It creates a no-win game.

13. *Why* questions tend to put a student on the defensive, asking them to justify their actions or feelings. It is preferable to ask *what* and *how* questions.

14. Feelings are neither good nor bad. They just exist. What counts is how we handle those emotions. Don't say, "I wish you didn't feel that way." Now the student may feel guilty about the emotions he or she is experiencing. Accept and help the students explore the feelings they are experiencing.

15. A particularly helpful question is "What would you like to have happen?" It encourages the student to focus on a goal.

16. Be cautious of projecting your own issues onto the student. If racial or sexual harassment is an issue in your life, don't assume your students are wrestling with the same issue.

17. It is often helpful to help students explore the potential long- and short-term consequences

Barriers to Effective Communication

- Advice giving
- Overuse of closed-ended questions
- Criticizing and labeling
- Becoming distracted
- Daydreaming
- Sugarcoated reassurance
- Preaching or moralizing
- Interrupting
- Fixing other people's problems
- Listening only to content, not hearing feelings
- Not attending to nonverbal cues
- Finishing another person's sentences
- Prejudging the speaker
- Jumping to conclusions
- Talking, not listening
- Asking leading questions
- Interpreting, diagnosing
- Incongruent body language

of their anticipated actions in resolving a problem. They often fail to anticipate the unintended effects of their actions.

18. Respect your students' confidentiality. Of course, you must report instances of suspected child abuse or threatened harm to another or themselves, but don't gossip with other faculty about things students tell you in private.

19. Do be aware of when a student needs professional help. Offer to go to the school psychologist's or counselor's office with the student to make an appointment. Do communicate that you are concerned but that the student needs someone else with specific training in counseling to help with the problem. A classroom teacher will seldom have the time or training to engage in long-term, in-depth counseling relationships with students.

20. Pay attention to what the student is not saying. Are any obvious pieces of information or concerns not mentioned? That does not mean you must force the issue, but do make a mental note of what the student is avoiding.

21. Conclude a helping session with a summary of the main points discussed and any action the student might be planning to deal with the issue. Try to end on a hopeful, encouraging note.

22. One of the most valuable things you can give a student is hope, an expectation that things can and will eventually get better. Some students come from deplorable home environments. You have limited power to change the world the student returns to at the end of the day, but knowing that someone genuinely cares can make a tremendous difference.

23. Keep a phone list of various support services, both within the school system and the greater community, to which you might choose to refer parents. It is much easier if you have the information readily at your grasp rather than having to hunt for it and then get back to the parent later. The kinds of information you might want to accumulate could include the following:
    - Sources of children's health services
    - Emergency food, housing, and clothing assistance
    - Sources of scholarship funds
    - Counseling services for individuals and families
    - Tutoring programs
    - Child protective services

> *Education is the ability to listen to almost anything without losing your temper or your self-confidence.*
>
> **—Robert Frost**

Teachers become significant persons in many of their students' lives. If you were to list the ten most significant persons in your life, chances are at least one teacher would be on that list. Do you think that teacher realizes how important he or she was in your life? Probably not. It is indeed a joy when former students return years later to let us know how dramatically we shaped their lives, but it is all too rare. Yet it is a certainty we must accept on faith. You never know how much impact you are having. Teachers plant seeds and do everything they can to nurture them. Sadly, we aren't always around for the harvest.

Sample Letter of Welcome to Students Before School Starts

Einstein Elementary School
203 Gibson Ave.
Hendersonville, NC 28729

(Date)

Greetings,

In less than two weeks, school will begin. As you probably know by now, I will be your fifth-grade teacher. This is my sixth year of teaching at Einstein Elementary School. I love teaching and very much enjoy the students at Einstein. I always look forward to meeting my new class each year.

I hope you have had an enjoyable summer and look forward to hearing about what you did. My family spent a week camping in a national forest. I'll be showing some of the slides in our geography class this year.

School begins at 8:00 A.M. Tuesday, September 3. You should come directly to room 78. I do expect all students to be on time every day. I think most students find my classes to be fun, although we also work hard. We do a lot of cooperative work in groups. Most nights you can expect to have thirty to forty-five minutes of homework.

I have enclosed a list of supplies you will need. The only ones you definitely need the first day are the pen, spiral notepad, and glue. The rest of the items you should have by Monday, September 9. If you or your parents have any questions, I can be reached at home at 646-3371. It will be easiest to reach me between five and nine in the evenings.

Best wishes for a most successful year!

Sincerely,

Mr. Green

Getting to Know You

Directions: Please complete the following sentences. There are no right or wrong answers.

1. During the summers I most enjoy _____
   _____

2. I wish I could _____
   _____

3. What I like to do most is _____
   _____

4. The thing I enjoy best about school is _____
   _____

5. I am happiest when _____
   _____

6. My favorite television program is _____
   _____

7. I learn best when _____
   _____

8. My favorite sports are _____
   _____

9. One thing I do well is _____
   _____

10. One thing I would like to do better is _____
    _____

11. I dislike school when _____
    _____

12. When I grow up, I hope to be _____
    _____

Get-Acquainted Bingo

Directions: Find a person who fulfills each of these categories. Collect their signatures in the appropriate boxes. Write your favorite activity, sport, or hobby in the middle box. Try to get as many different signatures as you can.

Likes to cook	Has ridden a subway	Is wearing blue socks	Knits	Is left-handed
Has ridden a horse	Owns a cat	Loves the beach	Reads	Plays a musical instrument
Has seen the Grand Canyon	Has lived on a farm	Your favorite activity	Has been to a college	Loves to dance
Is an only child	Owns red shoes	Has written a poem	Has been in a play	Likes broccoli
Enjoys fishing	Has been on television	Visited Canada	Has a 1990 coin on them	Keeps a diary or journal

Wow!

I'm excited for you.

_____

_____

_____

Keep up the good work!

Hurray!

Well done!

BRAVO!

Excellent!!

Super! *Fantastic!*

We're very proud of your
accomplishment of

_____

Best wishes for continued success.

_____   _____
Date   Teacher

Acts of Kindness Citation

_____

was found on this day to have committed one or more acts of kindness, helping make our school a friendlier, more caring community.

_____ _____
Date   Witness

Student Personal Record

Directions: Fill in the blanks.

Name _____

Street address _____

City _____

State _____ ZIP _____ Home phone _____

Parent or guardian name _____

Brothers' and sisters' names and ages _____

_____

_____

_____

What are your favorite sports, hobbies, and activities? _____

_____

_____

_____

_____

_____

_____

_____

_____

_____

_____

_____

_____

_____

Outstanding Student of the Week

awarded to

_____

for a high level of effort and performance.

_____
Date

_____
Teacher

You're on target!

Presented to_____

for outstanding progress in

_____

_____

Date _____

Congratulations to _____

for _____

_____

Problem Behavior Checklist

Directions: Indicate the frequency with which each of the following behaviors occurs in your classroom.

	Frequently	Occasionally	Rarely	Never
Hitting, fighting				
Shouting, loud talking				
Calling out				
Students talking with each other in class				
Stealing				
Cheating on tests, quizzes, homework				
Tardiness to class				
Name-calling				
Use of obscenities				
Handing in assignments late				
Not bringing necessary materials to class				
Not completing homework				
Leaving room without permission				
Wearing hats in the classroom				
Students out of their seats without permission				
Classroom vandalism				
Chewing gum in class				
Bullying others				
Weapons at school				
Violations of school dress code				
Noncompliance with teacher's requests				
Rude comments to others				
Littering				

Problem Behavior Checklist *(continued)*

	Frequently	Occasionally	Rarely	Never
Whining				
Tattling				
Abuse of books, equipment				
Incessant talking				
Truancy				
Nonparticipation, apathy				
Sexual harassment of other students				
Doing work for other classes in your class				
Playing dumb				
Excessive messiness				
Teasing other students				
Other _____				

The mind is not a vessel
to be filled but a fire to
be ignited.

-Plutarch

Documented Interventions

Student's name _____

Parents' or guardians' names _____

Parent's daytime phone _____

Teacher _____ Subject/grade _____

Intervention	Date	Comments
Discuss problem with student	_____	_____
Clarify rules	_____	_____
Change seats	_____	_____
Telephone parent or guardian	_____	_____
Parent conference	_____	_____
Peer tutoring	_____	_____
Extra help after school	_____	_____
Adapt assignments	_____	_____
Student contract	_____	_____
Time-out	_____	_____
Home/school daily or weekly notes	_____	_____
Individual conference with student	_____	_____
Refer to principal	_____	_____
Refer to counselor	_____	_____
Refer to school psychologist	_____	_____
Refer to specialist: _____	_____	_____
Conference with parent and student	_____	_____
Home visit	_____	_____
Team conference	_____	_____

Notes:

_____

_____

_____

Proficiency Notice

Date _____

To: _____

From: _____

I am most pleased to report that the performance of _____ in my class has been noteworthy and deserving of recognition. In particular, I wanted to bring to your attention the following success:

_____

_____

_____

I hope we can both encourage this progress to continue. Please feel free to contact me if you have any questions or concerns.

You're on target!

_____
Name

is to be commended for

_____

_____
Teacher

_____
Date

Let's Make A Deal!

If _____ can

_____

by _____ then the teacher will _____

Official Seal

_____
Teacher

_____
Student

_____
Date

It Adds Up

The special effort of _____

has paid dividends! For _____

you may _____

Seal of Approval

_____
Teacher

_____
Date

Certificate Of Appreciation

Presented to

_____

In recognition and gratitude for

_____

_____

_____

Outstanding Job

Presented to

_____

Your hard work greatly
improved your achievement!

_____

Thanks for your help!

It really is appreciated.

Homework Pass

Awarded to _____

for _____

This certificate entitles the above person to one free night of no homework. Turn in this pass on the day the assignment is due.

_____   _____
Date   Teacher

Hard Worker Award
To

_____

for

_____

_____
Teacher

Homework Pass

Awarded to _____

for _____

This certificate entitles the above person to one free night of no homework. Turn in this pass on the day the assignment is due.

_____

CERTIFICATE OF ACHIEVEMENT

Awarded to

_____

For demonstrating mastery of _____ .

_____
Teacher

_____
Date

Chapter Two

Creating Successful Lessons

Lesson Plans

The aim of any lesson is change—purposeful transformation. Each day you walk into a classroom, you should know exactly what you expect to accomplish and how you are going to do it. What will your students know how to do when they leave your classroom that they did not know when they entered?

Generally, too little time is spent on instructional planning. A list of assignments or textbook pages to cover is not a plan. A lesson plan is simply a sequential guide to how you plan to accomplish your instructional objectives or goals. Can you imagine a builder trying to construct a house without a blueprint? Lesson plans tell you what you will be doing and what your students will be doing.

Lesson plans also help identify the resources, including time, needed to accomplish these activities. While you may not always be able to stick to your plan, you'll be more likely to intentionally affect your students' learning if you start with a plan. Some courses will require more detailed planning than others. At least early in your teaching career, clearly written plans are essential for success. There is no one right format for these plans. Develop a format that works for you. It should be simple yet complete. Here are some practical planning tips veteran teachers have found useful:

✓ First, make a general plan for the year. It will necessarily be vague and deal with general concepts, topics, and skills. These are usually drawn from any written program of study the school is obligated to follow. Monthly plans begin to add more detail. Weekly plans should be quite specific in both objectives and instructional strategies.

✓ Try to plan at least a week in advance. The first time you must unexpectedly be absent, you and your substitute will appreciate it.

✓ Make a master lesson plan form, filling in all the details and activities that will remain the same each week. Place these in a large loose-leaf notebook. In each class's notebook, also keep any additional information needed for that class, such as rosters, form letters, phone numbers, and so on.

✓ The first step in every lesson is to focus on the goal(s) you hope to accomplish. State these in terms of how the students should be different after encountering your instruction. You are planning to intentionally change the students' knowledge, skills, or attitudes. Be specific. Also be reasonable in what you can realistically accomplish in a week or a day. It is better to teach less but do it well than to give superficial coverage to more content that students quickly forget.

✓ Don't overrely on knowledge-level objectives. Within one year students forget 80 percent of what they learn, most of that being facts they were required to memorize. Skills and attitude changes tend to have a much more permanent effect. (See p. 77 for writing instructional objectives.)

✓ Keep a notebook for each class to organize the lesson plans, handout masters, tests, quizzes, and lists of audiovisual requirements for each subject. It will save you much time next year.

✓ Some teachers prefer to develop and store their lesson plans on the computer. This makes revision much simpler. Of course, a paper copy will be needed for classroom use in most instances.

✓ First, schedule the blocks of time your students have to be out of the room. Then schedule the topics and content you are responsible for teaching. Effective teachers cover the curriculum but teach more than the written course of study. Embellish and enrich the established curriculum with your interests, talents, and creativity.

✓ In planning any lesson, develop the body of the instruction first, including specifics on what you will do and what the students will do. Then give special attention to developing a powerful and interesting opening and ending. These are often overlooked in planning, yet they are the parts students are most likely to remember. Be sure to list any equipment, supplies, and preparations that you will need to arrange before the class.

✓ Where possible, schedule challenging and new content early in the day. Generally, student attention and concentration wane in the afternoon. Ideally, save the less mentally challenging, more energizing activities for afternoon.

✓ Likewise, schedule the most demanding content on Monday, Tuesday, and Wednesday. Student productivity and enthusiasm diminish after Wednesday. Friday shouldn't be discarded, but save it for more active learning experiences and fun review opportunities. Simulations, field trips, films, guest speakers, and other special activities can keep students motivated at the end of the week.

✓ Always have several "sponge" activities available for students to work on if they complete an assignment or test early. These should have an educational purpose yet be interesting, lest students perceive them as punishments.

✓ After you teach each lesson, note on your lesson plan which parts of the lesson went well and which need to be improved. Don't rely on your memory to make those changes next year.

✓ Use colored folders to arrange each day's lesson plan and student papers. Use a different color for each class. Use the same color to identify any materials for that class.

✓ Some teachers choose to put their lesson plans on note cards, a single idea or activity on each card. That makes it easier to reshuffle the order or add and delete items in the future. (*Tip:* Punch holes in all your cards and put them on a large ring. If you drop them, they stay together.)

✓ Use checklists to help organize your lessons. For example, if you use a simulation game, develop a checklist to record any items you'll need or tasks to include.

✓ Some tasks, such as ordering films or arranging speakers, must be done well in advance. Ideally, you'll save time by ordering all films for the semester at one time. While doing such long-term planning may be difficult the first year or two, it will become easier.

✓ Try to have materials for the next day's lesson ready before you leave school. Even if you have to stay after school to copy handouts or prepare other materials, it will prove less stressful than racing in the next morning to complete your preparation. Even early morning preparation periods can't always be counted on to be free to handle those last-minute tasks. A hallmark of any professional is being prepared.

✓ Develop a card file or loose-leaf notebook to collect teaching ideas. These might include copies of ideas you find in professional magazines. At least once a month, scan your file to see if you can incorporate any of the activities into your upcoming lessons.

✓ If you see another teacher or presenter use a successful technique or strategy, brainstorm ways you might adapt the idea for one of your lessons.

✓ Visit teachers who teach the grade above or below yours to discover how your lessons fit into the larger picture.

✓ As you develop each lesson plan, include a brief note indicating the state or national content standards that the lesson addresses. These will prove valuable in assessing the degree of alignment of course content with these standards.

✓ Save a few moments at the end of each day to reflect on your day's lessons. What went well? What clearly needs to be improved? Any ideas on how to make your lesson more effective the next time? Jot these down on your lesson plan and file them in your notebook.

Beginning a Class

Students are most likely to remember the first and last things you do in a lesson. Indeed, many people believe the first three minutes of a class are the most important. An effective opening can serve several valuable purposes. It can focus students' attention on what they are about to learn. It can also arouse students' curiosity and interest in the lesson. It helps motivate them to become involved in the lesson.

The beginning sets the tone for the rest of the lesson. It creates psychological readiness to engage in learning. The opening of the lesson stimulates your students' emotions, such as puzzlement, curiosity, tension, empathy, wonderment, excitement, amusement, pride, skepticism, or fascination.

Remember that students of all ages approach any lesson with the question "What's in it for me?" If your opening addresses that question, you will have a motivated learner.

It is essential to get your students actively involved within the first two minutes of the lesson. You can accomplish this in many ways, and it need not take a big chunk of time; a three- or four-second response actively draws their attention to the lesson. Here are several strategies effective teachers successfully use to engage their students in the lesson:

✓ Learning begins before the bell rings. Use posters, door signs, music, transparencies, and other techniques to engage the students' minds, capture their attention, and arouse anticipation before the class officially begins. Many teachers have music playing as students enter to set the appropriate mood. Attention getters, such as trivia and interesting facts related to the day's topic, might be suspended from the ceiling, hung upside down, or otherwise interestingly displayed to grab students' attention.

✓ Be sure you have everyone's attention before you begin. Don't try to talk over the group noise. Convey enthusiasm for the lesson. It can be contagious. If you don't sound very interested in what you are teaching, it is improbable your students will be. Be especially cognizant of maintaining eye contact with your students during the opening. Scan the entire class to include everyone.

✓ The opening must be connected to the main lesson. Your students must be able to see that the opening is relevant to the rest of the lesson.

✓ Avoid beginning the class with routine, procedural tasks (taking attendance, collecting homework, general announcements, and so on). Remember, your students most remember the first and last things that happen in class. Later, while students are working individually or in small groups, you can unobtrusively take attendance. Get your lessons off to a good start; give them punch.

✓ Begin with a personal anecdote. A personal illustration that ties to the topic makes it more interesting. Remember, it must be relevant to the lesson you are teaching.

✓ Pose a challenging question. Give careful thought to your opening questions. You may have students respond by jotting down their answer, volunteering to share it aloud, or simply answering silently to themselves. It is often helpful to ask a question to which all students are likely to raise their hands (for example, "How many are ready for a vacation?").

✓ Present a startling statistic or fact about some aspect of the lesson. Collect interesting statistics related to your course content. As an option, make these into an overhead transparency. Have the statistic on the screen as students enter the classroom. Examples:

> The earth's population increases by eighty-six hundred people every hour.
> Two percent of American homes had electricity in 1900; 99 percent do today.
> U.S. corporations spend $9 billion each year combating spam.
> In 1910, 13 percent of the adults in the United States were high school graduates; 83 percent are today.
> Some bristlecone pine trees in California are over four thousand years old, making them the oldest living things on Earth.

✓ Open the class with an unusual, surprising behavior or event.

✓ Present an interesting, relevant problem.

✓ Start with a funny story. It can be a true incident or a fictional tale. Even better is something that really happened to you. Don't try for jokes. Most important, the story must pertain to the day's topic.

✓ Use a true/false quiz reflecting major issues or research related to the topic. Before you give students the right answers, devise ways for them to share their answers. You might tabulate their responses on the board or move their bodies to different spots on a "live" continuum to indicate how sure they are of each answer.

✓ Display interesting visuals: a cartoon, poster, or quotation. In groups or as a whole class, you might have them discuss their reaction to the visual.

✓ Use a prop—an unusual piece of equipment, artifact, collection, toy, or creature. Use a gimmick to grab your students' attention. Walk into class with a portable telephone. Carry on a conversation over the phone in which you introduce the day's topic. Add humor or a personal anecdote. Use your imagination.

✔ Use drama to let students introduce the issue or problem that will be the focus of the day's lesson.

✔ Experiment with using costumes or hats related to the topic being introduced. Pull off a shirt to reveal a T-shirt depicting a quotation or graphic related to the lesson.

✔ Make a promise ("By the end of this lesson you will be able to . . . ").

✔ Draw analogies between what students have learned previously and the new skills or content they are learning in the current lesson.

✔ On a large sheet of newsprint or butcher paper, ask groups to draw three large circles at least a foot in diameter. Label them "What I know about [the topic being studied]." Give the groups five to ten minutes to brainstorm and record anything they know about the topic under consideration. They should then label the second circle "What I hope to learn about [the topic]." Give them five minutes to list in that circle any questions they hope to have answered about the topic. The students then post all their sheets on the wall. At the end of the lesson, direct the groups to retrieve their sheets and to label the third circle "What I learned about [the topic]." Give the groups ten minutes to list everything new they learned about the subject. (*Source:* Reprinted with permission from *The Heart of Teaching* newsletter, Performance Learning Systems.)

✔ Initiate a memory dump activity. Pair students and give them the following directions: "Tell your partner everything you know about [the new topic]." Allow ninety seconds. Have students switch and repeat the process. Allow another ninety seconds. Switch and continue for sixty seconds. Switch and repeat for sixty seconds. Switch and continue for thirty seconds more. Switch a last time for thirty seconds. (*Source:* This idea was adapted from Cerylle Moffett, a consultant for the Association for Supervision and Curriculum Development.)

✔ Use a magic trick. Many good books can suggest simple tricks you can easily master. Or visit a magic shop to look for gimmicks or tricks that might fit into one of your lessons. Your banter during the trick is what ties it into your lesson. Don't let it just hang by itself.

✔ It is a sound practice to frequently build in some form of review of the previous lesson at the beginning of a lesson. However, to be effective strive to make the review segment interesting and active. Mind maps, analogies, brainstorming, role-playing, or a cooperative learning activity will generally be more effective than just telling the students what they studied previously.

✔ To maximize their impact, vary your openings. Strive to be creative and occasionally use the element of surprise. If your openings become the best part of the lesson, you have much less problem with tardiness!

Action Verbs for Writing Instructional Objectives

Effective teachers know what they are trying to accomplish in each lesson. Their instruction has a purpose or clearly focused objective. That goal may be for students to master a new skill; to change a behavior, attitude, or value; or to memorize a fact. Some research suggests that students forget within one year as much as 80 percent of what they learn in school. Most of what is lost are facts—those pieces of data learned solely through rote memory. Most likely to be retained are the skills, attitudes, and values learned in the classroom.

Objectives that remain at the knowledge level include verbs such as *memorize, list, name,* or *know.* While a degree of factual information must be retained to allow higher-level thinking, most educators recognize the value of teaching higher-level critical thinking. You are seeking to answer the question "What will my students be able to do as a result of my instruction?" Action verbs assure that you are focusing on *doing,* not merely knowing. Here are some verbs that will help you construct objectives at a higher level:

Advise	Devise	Participate
Analyze	Direct	Perform
Appraise	Discuss	Place
Arrange	Draw	Plan
Assemble	Establish	Prepare
Assign	Estimate	Process
Assist	Evaluate	Propose
Build	Execute	Provide
Calculate	Exercise	Rate
Collaborate	Explain	Recommend
Collect	Formulate	Report
Compare	Furnish	Represent
Compile	Implement	Research
Compute	Improve	Resolve
Conduct	Initiate	Review
Consolidate	Inspect	Revise
Construct	Instruct	Schedule
Contrast	Interpret	Secure
Coordinate	Investigate	Select
Criticize	Locate	Show
Debate	Maintain	Solve
Decide	Manage	Submit
Deliver	Measure	Teach
Demonstrate	Negotiate	Train
Design	Obtain	Transcribe
Determine	Operate	Verify
Develop	Organize	

Thirty-eight Hot Tips for Maintaining Interest

It is absurd to expect all students to be constantly on the edge of their seats, mesmerized by masterful instruction. Students do bring outside distractions into the classroom; divorces, deaths, infatuations, conflicts, and normal growing pains can divert the attention of even the most conscientious students. While you cannot control these outside events, you do have a significant effect on most students' learning. Some teachers have greater skill at teaching lessons that hold students' attention and that result in higher achievement than other teachers.

Probably all teachers have a few lessons that always excite and interest students. Those successful attention-holding lessons likely adhere to most of the following principles. Here are some ideas that may help gain and maintain learners' interest:

1. Learning begins before class starts. Challenge yourself to devise creative ways to capture students' attention and engage their minds the moment they enter the room. Every day plan to have something available related to the day's topic to arouse curiosity and stimulate thinking before the bell rings. Examples: a quotation on the board or overhead, a word puzzle for individuals or groups to complete, a couple of thought questions, a startling statistic, a related cartoon.

2. Get the class actively involved in the lesson's first three minutes. This might be through raising their hands in response to a question related to the day's lesson (for example, "How many have ever visited a dairy farm?"), participating in a small-group brainstorm, or writing a response. Strive to create an atmosphere of active involvement, not passive listening, early in the class period.

3. Plan carefully and fully. Lessons that are run smoothly keep students' attention and minimize interruptions. This has little to do with charisma. Lessons run smoothly because they are carefully planned and organized. Time is invested up front to assure that materials are ready, the teacher knows what to do next, and the unexpected is anticipated. This helps create a businesslike, task-oriented atmosphere.

4. Clarify the specific objective(s) for each lesson. The single most important question you can ask yourself each day is "What do I want my students to learn from this class?" Unfortunately, some teachers have no clearer notion of where they are headed than "to make it through the textbook" or "to make it to the Civil War by Christmas."

5. Share your objectives with your students. Let them know what they should get out of this lesson. Of course, you cannot tell them if you don't know yourself. With purposes clear and instruction systematic, students will more readily master that lesson.

6. Divide learning tasks into smaller subskills. Present those subskills in logical and manageable lessons. Sequence your lessons so that you aren't trying to teach skills for which students have not yet mastered necessary prerequisites. Otherwise, both you and your students will be frustrated.

7. Design lessons that encourage students to contribute their views and knowledge. Many have special talents or experiences they might enjoy sharing and from which other students can learn.

8. Make a conscious effort to connect your lesson to students' lives beyond school. Incorporate their interests as illustrations. Provide opportunities for them to apply what they are learning to daily life and the problems they face.

9. Employ visual aids—transparencies, pictures, slides, props, demonstrations, and posters. Overall, the visual is the most powerful learning modality. Maximum learning is likely to occur when the instruction is both auditory and visual and, where possible, also kinesthetic (involving doing things and motor movement).

10. Keep moving while you talk. An easy way to lose any group's interest is to become the stationary talking head in front of the room. Talking while seated is also more likely to lead to speaking in a monotone. An additional benefit of moving while teaching is that you are better able to monitor the class, nipping in the bud potentially disruptive misbehavior.

11. Generally, it is best not to start each class with housekeeping chores. The reason is that students most remember the first and last thing you do in a class period. Don't waste this valuable learning time on mundane distracting content.

12. Build a breath of fresh air or energizing activity into your lesson about every eight to ten minutes. It doesn't have to be long, but inject something that changes the pace and refocuses the students' attention. Examples include a humorous cartoon, a prop, personal illustration, sharing a response in pairs or small groups, a role-play, demonstration, visualization. Anything that actively engages their brains is likely to be helpful in refocusing attention. Provide opportunities for active involvement through exercises and activities that break up long formal presentations. When asked, most students prefer lessons in which they act out parts, build things, interview people, or carry out projects. Least favored are those classes in which they are allowed only to listen.

13. Variety is the spice of life and the secret to successful lessons! Effective teachers don't use the same teaching techniques day after day. They employ an assortment of instructional strategies. Most ineffective teachers tend to use the same few techniques for every lesson—usually lecture and worksheets.

14. Strive to develop the broadest range of teaching approaches and employ that variety. Experiment with simulations, role-playing, videotaping,

and cooperative learning. Students generally are more excited about working in groups.

15. Involve students in real-life activities that have a practical usable product. For example, in the remarkably successful Foxfire project, students interviewed their Appalachian neighbors and relatives and produced and sold books they wrote and published. Other classes have developed handbooks for teenage consumers, constructed solar walls, or set up community car pools. Hands-on activities are most successful by far in arousing student interest.

It is by surprises that experience teaches all she designed to teach us.

—Charles Sanders Pierce, Collected Papers

16. The element of surprise works wonders in building student enthusiasm and motivation. Some teachers dress up in costumes, have surprise guest speakers, or use drama to capture students' attention. (For example, students are much more excited about reading Shakespeare when they act it out using an exaggerated Southern drawl—or Bostonian accent if they are from the South!) Occasionally, do the unexpected. Allow suspense to build in anticipation as the class unfolds. Questions, storytelling, and props are especially effective in creating intrigue.

17. Use anecdotes. Personal illustrations of events from your and your students' life experiences make academic content come alive. It is essential that such stories pertain to the topic being studied. Irrelevant war stories add nothing to the lesson.

18. Try to relate new content to things the students already know. As much as possible, encourage the students to make those connections themselves. Personalize as much of your content as possible.

19. Minimize criticism and offer praise when appropriate. If students are too frequently criticized, they quickly learn to avoid volunteering their answers or opinions. There is no quicker way to squelch creativity or participation than to criticize the first couple of contributors. Use praise judiciously. Praise specific behaviors, not general characteristics. Be aware that public praise can backfire for many adolescents, whose peers may taunt them for being the teacher's pet.

20. Become aware of your voice level and speaking patterns. Tape a couple of classes and listen for your tonality, verbal tics (for example, *um, er, so*). Solicit feedback from a speech and hearing specialist as to the pitch of your voice.

21. Vary your speech pattern. Use pauses or stage whispers for emphasis. Always remember to talk to the students at the furthest corner of the room. If students must strain to hear you, you will have trouble holding their attention.

22. Make your presentations clear. Use vocabulary appropriate to your students' developmental level. Speak at a pace they can understand. If your voice tends toward the monotone, work on developing more animated

speech. Periodically record or videotape your lessons. Seeing or hearing yourself as your students do may reveal areas that need improvement.

23. Remain flexible in your teaching. Read your audience and adjust accordingly. Furrowed brows and frowns will tell you that some students did not grasp a point. Squirming, fidgeting, or daydreaming may cue you to pick up the pace or change your approach. Good planning must remain flexible. There is little sense in plowing ahead with a lesson plan that isn't working.

24. Use your sense of humor. Do not try to become a stand-up comic, but don't be afraid to laugh or add humorous remarks to your presentation. The guiding principle for using humor in the classroom is that it should be relevant to the topic under discussion. Avoid the temptation to entertain with jokes that don't have an educational point. Interesting lessons make learning fun, and a natural response to fun activities is the occasional laugh. You need not strive for a belly laugh, but when a humorous incident or anecdote presents itself, use it to your advantage.

25. Incorporate students' names in your presentations. For most people their name really is their favorite sound.

26. Use appropriate analogies, especially humorous ones.

27. Use props whenever possible. Student interest is piqued when they enter the room and see a jar of beans, a model airplane, guitar, telephone, or parrot sitting on the teacher's desk. Almost any lesson can benefit from the inclusion of one or more props. If what you need is not immediately available, try using "invisible props." Describe the needed item in detail, using gestures as though you were actually holding it in your hand.

28. A special form of prop is the collection. Campaign buttons, artifacts, insects, leaves, rocks, tools, costumes, or postcards are among items that interest students and enrich their knowledge of the academic subject. You can develop your own collections or invite parents and other community members to share theirs. It is best if they can bring their collection and talk briefly about it. Ask students questions about the items in a collection to encourage them to think about its value, purpose, and meaning.

29. Use music. Many effective teachers successfully incorporate music into their classes. Having music playing as students enter the classroom begins to set the mood for the day's class. You can let students take turns bringing their favorite tapes or CDs to play before class or during breaks or recess. Soft music playing quietly in the background during individual seatwork can be pleasant and inviting. The beat of baroque compositions seems to work best for this.

> Give me a level long enough
> And a prop strong enough,
> I can single-handed move the world.
>
> —Archimedes

30. Music related to the topic (for example, the Civil War, Ireland, China, the Roaring Twenties) can bring the topic to life and enrich students' understanding of the subject. Use sound effects recordings for emphasis of important points. Some teachers even write new lyrics for familiar tunes. The new song conveys a message related to the day's lesson or an upcoming school event. It is fairly easy to devise your own composition using a rap beat. Either you can sing it or get a group of students or even the whole class to perform. Try reading the day's assignments to a rap beat!

31. Take timely breaks. Continually monitor your students' nonverbal expression. When nodding heads and drooping eyelids suggest you are losing their attention, insert a thirty-second stretch break. It can be something as subtle as standing up as soon as they have figured out an answer or turning their chairs to face a different direction. Of course, you don't want to create chaos or disrupt the flow of your lesson. A minibreak works best if it ties into your lesson.

32. Avoid becoming too involved with one student during class discussions. The rest of the class may assume they are not a part of the discussion and turn their attention elsewhere. While being sensitive to individuals, teach to the whole class. Maintain control of the discussion. If one student is monopolizing the interaction, ask questions of others to get them involved.

33. Assume the role of a character (an old woman, Superman, George Washington, a Civil War soldier). Embellish your character with props or a costume. (Garage sales and thrift shops are good sources for inexpensive costumes.) You might teach part of the lesson as your character for a few minutes or the whole period. Or alternate between two characters, debating with yourself. Consider acting out a real historical role in the actual setting as part of your vacation. Dress in authentic costumes and have someone videotape or take slides as you reenact some historical event or journey. These can be edited and used in class (or all-school assemblies).

Mock Cell-Phone Call: Attention-Grabbing Technique

Generate student interest with a mock cell-phone conversation. Put a cell phone in your pocket and pretend that it is vibrating. Apologize to the class for taking the call during class. Then proceed to have a mock phone call with a well-informed caller.

Select a famous person (for example, a scientist, politician, or writer) who is associated with the content you are teaching. Carry on a conversation with the celebrity in which you repeat his or her part of the conversation, allowing students to hear both ends of the discussion. You'll need to give some thought to the questions you would ask and the expert caller's responses.

This strategy might be successfully used as an introduction to a new topic, as an energizer, or as a review of a lesson.

Source: Reprinted with permission from *The Heart of Teaching* newsletter, Performance Learning Systems.

34. Use quotations to make an emphatic point. Sometimes the impact of this technique can be enhanced if a brief quotation is read aloud to the class directly from the original source rather than merely from your notes.

35. Build in brief, one- to three-minute pauses for reflection or writing. Give students a question to consider. For variety you may have all students stand and share their responses with someone else.

36. End each lesson answering the *so what* question. Encourage your students to consider why this content is important. Help them connect their new content with previous knowledge and with their personal lives wherever possible.

37. If a lesson falls flat, refine it or discard it. Why intentionally bore your students? Learning isn't happening. Spend you time on something that is working.

38. Most importantly, remember that you are unlikely to get students enthusiastic about a topic or activity if you are not enthusiastic about it yourself. Conversely, if you believe what you are teaching is interesting, fun, or useful, that view might become contagious.

Seven Cardinal Rules for Effective Visuals

Good visuals have the potential to enhance attention and retention. Most learners perform better when they receive information through more than one learning modality. Slides, transparencies, multimedia projector visuals, flip charts, and posters all can be used to effectively embellish any presentation.

Any material you write on the chalkboard or whiteboard each time you teach a lesson is a good candidate for a permanent visual, such as an overhead transparency or slide. Visuals prepared in advance can also be much easier to read, more eye-catching, and faster than hand printing on the board or newsprint.

Have you ever heard a teacher or presenter say, "I know you can't read this, but . . . " as he placed a transparency on the overhead projector? Some feel that should be grounds for instant dismissal or worse. Visuals that can't be read are as useless as a parachute that doesn't open! Some simple rules will make your visuals more effective. These same principles generally apply to overhead transparencies, slides, or multimedia projectors.

1. To construct visuals that will be readable, remember the number six: no more than six lines on a visual and no more than six words on a line. Another way of gauging whether your overhead transparency is readable is to place it on the floor at your feet as you stand. If you can't read it, the print is too small.

2. With the near universal availability of computers and laser printers, there really is no excuse for poorly constructed visuals. However, resist the temptation to clutter up your visuals with too many cute graphics and all the fonts at your disposal. No more than two font styles should be used on any one visual, and sans serif fonts (such as Geneva, Arial, or Helvetica) tend to be more readable. Use type that is at least twenty-four points and preferably thirty-six points. Always avoid type-writer print (Courier) in constructing transparencies. Print them by hand if necessary. If you still doubt whether your transparencies can be read, put one on the projector and view it from the last row of your classroom.

3. It is better to put long lists on several transparencies or slides than to cram too much on one. It is more effective to use progressive exposure, where each successive visual reveals one more line of information. This can be accomplished with several slides or with a transparency covered with a sheet of paper that you pull down to reveal one line at a time.

4. Whenever possible, use graphs and charts instead of tables for your visuals. Tables are more difficult to read and understand.

5. In preparing projected visuals, use a horizontal format rather than vertical. Since most screens are horizontal rectangles, your visual will fit more neatly on the screen. When you project onto the screen, try to use the upper three-quarters of the screen. The bottom quarter tends to be difficult for some participants in the back to see.

6. Don't read your visuals aloud. It's insulting to your audience.

7. Square the projector in front of the screen to minimize the keystone image: because the distance from the projector image is farther from the top of the screen than the bottom, the image will always appear wider at the top than at the bottom. Using a screen that tilts forward about seven degrees can cure this. If your screen is bolted flat to the wall, you'll have to live with it.

Additional Tips for Using Transparencies

✓ Use colored, erasable, water-soluble pens to highlight transparencies during presentations.

✓ Arrange your transparencies in the order you will display them, and place them near the projector.

✓ After placing a transparency on the projector, step away so that you do not block any student's view.

✓ Use frames on your transparencies. This looks more professional and makes them last longer. You can make your own out of scrap cardboard. Many presenters use the transparency frames as cue cards, writing key words in large print. A quick glance as you place the transparency on the projector reminds you of points to emphasize.

✓ When you are done talking about a transparency, turn off the projector. Don't just remove the transparency, leaving a blinding and distracting white screen. Instead, hinge a five-by-eight-inch card with tape on top of the projector lens. Simply flip the card down to block the light when you are done with a transparency.

✓ Try something other than just black on white overhead transparencies. Use variety; experiment with color. Photocopiers that run black and white transparencies can also produce transparencies with color backgrounds. Or use overhead transparency markers to add some color. White on dark colored backgrounds produces very readable transparencies.

✓ When using flip charts or newsprint, experiment with using a variety of dark colors. Print large and legibly. Notes to yourself can be penciled lightly on the newsprint beforehand. Tape sheets to the wall when they are completed.

✓ Tape four pennies along one long edge of a sheet of paper to make a mask to place over transparencies and pull down, gradually revealing one line at a time. The pennies keep the paper from slipping off as you get to the bottom of the transparency.

Storyboarding

The storyboard, originally a creative tool for moviemakers, has been adapted by many businesses to stimulate creative thinking and organize projects. In designing multimedia programs (movies, videos, or Web sites), storyboards are used to describe everything that the viewer will see, hear, or experience.

Storyboards help capture and stimulate imagination and visualization. They are especially valuable in facilitating collaborative creative designs. Writers sometimes use storyboards to help them organize their novels' plots.

Although storyboards were originally done on paper, storyboarders now have the option of using computers to generate storyboards.

A four-by-four-foot sheet of corkboard (or regular blank bulletin board), push pins, felt-tip markers, and four-by-six-inch index cards are all the materials required. Some teachers use three-by-five-inch sticky notes instead of cards. This works fine if you don't intend to keep the storyboard for more than a day.

As the group brainstorms ideas, they are pinned into clusters or under specific headings on the board. Storyboards can be adapted to a variety of uses in the classroom.

Teach your students how to storyboard as a way of stimulating their creativity. To begin, present small groups of three or four students with a question to consider. As they take turns individually brainstorming ideas, they should jot down their ideas on index cards or sticky notes.

Ideas are hung in sequence on the corkboard, much like the frames of a comic strip. An alternative is to draw a large window with up to nine cells on a sheet of newsprint. Beginning at the top left block, ideas are depicted in words or drawings.

Storyboarding is also an effective device for organizing a lesson plan or other interactive presentation. It would prove especially valuable in designing an online course.

Software package Storyboard Pro is freeware available at www.atomiclearning.com/freestoryboard.shtml. Available in Macintosh or Windows versions, this software helps lay out the shooting sequence for video production. It is worth a try, especially if you have access to an electronic tablet or notepad and a whiteboard display. Another storyboarding software package, Springboard (Six Mile Creek Systems at 6sys.com/Springboard/), can only be used with an electronic pen and tablet. A big advantage of digital storyboards is the capacity to save, reproduce, and share the end product.

Interestingly, many high schools now teach storyboarding skills as part of their visual communications or digital arts courses. As part of its project-based curriculum, students in Utah's Granite School District learn storyboarding as early as the fifth grade.

For More Information

Center for Digital Storytelling. (n.d.). *Storyboarding: A recipe*. Online at www.storycenter.org/memvoice/pages/tutorial_3.html.

Fraioli, J. O. (2000). *Storyboarding 101: A crash course in professional storyboarding*. Studio City, CA: Michael Wiese Productions.

Hart, J. (1999). *The art of the storyboard: Storyboarding for film, TV, and animation*. Boston: Focal Press.

Simon, M. (2000). *Storyboards: Motion in art* (2nd ed.). Boston: Focal Press.

Review Techniques

Successful teachers allow ample time for reviewing new concepts and skills and integrating them into students' prior knowledge. The purpose of review is to clarify, reinforce, and set the stage for new content. The challenge is to make review interesting. It is probably a good idea to include a brief review each day of some content covered in the previous lesson. Here are some options that may help:

✓ Have each student draw three large balloons (or box cars, apples, or diamonds) on a sheet of paper. Ask them to write the three most important (or interesting) things they learned about the day's topic in the balloons. After a couple of minutes, invite them to share their ideas in pairs. Finally, you can solicit ideas from the whole class, providing three separate opportunities to review some aspect of the day's content.

✓ In the middle of a lesson, you can stop and ask each student to jot down one idea from the lesson he or she most wants to remember. Allow a minute for reflection, then solicit ideas from various class members.

✓ Post on the walls several sheets of newsprint, each listing a major idea or concept studied during the previous lesson. At a signal students are to move from one sheet to another, adding one fact or idea they know about each topic.

✓ Another fun way to stimulate reviews is for one student to draw on the board or newsprint a picture representing an idea related to the previous lesson. The rest of the students attempt to guess the word or topic in a Pictionary or Win, Lose, or Draw format.

✓ One of the most powerful techniques for organizing ideas and concepts is the mind map. The mind map is also a most useful note-taking device. Every student should have this tool in his or her repertoire. It can also be used in a variety of ways to stimulate reflection and review.

Mind Maps

The mind map is started by writing the key word or general topic (for example, PRESIDENTS) in a circle in the middle of a sheet of blank paper. The subtopics (for example, the WHITE HOUSE, ELECTIONS, FIRST LADIES, POLITICAL PARTIES, ASSASSINATIONS) are written on spokes drawn out from the circle. A good way to generate the subtopics is to ask students to brainstorm the main chapters they would include if they were going to write a book on the topic. Ideas and facts associated with the subtopics are drawn on shorter lines branching from the spokes containing the subtopics. Encourage students to use symbols or small pictures whenever possible. Using different colored markers or pens for the subtopics also helps stimulate creative thought.

After individual students have developed their mind maps of the topic, a useful option is to ask them to join another person and combine their two separate mind maps into one. After several minutes redirect each pair to join another pair and again

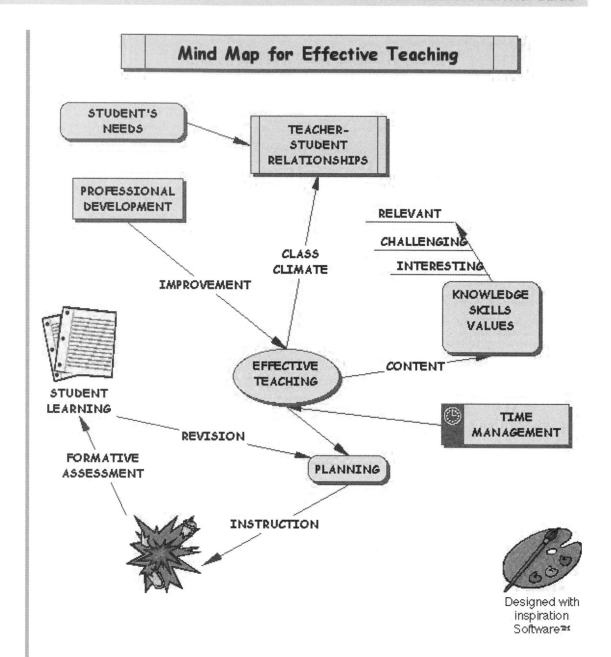

Mind Map for Effective Teaching

Designed with
inspiration
Software™

combine their mind maps into one. An option is to finally have all the students then gather around one large sheet of newsprint (or tape four regular sheets of newsprint together to form a gigantic one). Write the topic in a circle in the middle of the paper and give them the task of compiling a final mind map that includes all the ideas their individual mind maps generated.

Some teachers have employed the mind map as an assessment device. Students complete mind maps to reflect their understandings of complex concepts. All students should be taught the mind-mapping process as an aid to note taking.

For More Information

Buzan, T. (1983). *Use both sides of your brain.* New York: E. P. Dutton.

Buzan, T., & Buzan, B. (1994). *The mind map book: How to use radiant thinking to maximize your brain's untapped potential.* New York: E. P. Dutton.

Margulies, N. (1991). *Mapping inner space: Learning and teaching mind mapping.* Tucson, AZ: Zephyr Press.

Wycoff, J. (1991). *Mindmapping: Your personal guide to exploring creativity and problem-solving.* New York: Berkley Books.

Twenty Tips for Closing a Lesson

An outstanding lesson can be spoiled with a poor ending. Remember that students are most likely to remember the first and last things that happen in class. For this reason it is essential to give careful thought to each lesson's ending. A good ending allows students to connect what they learned in a lesson with their previous knowledge.

An effective closure provides students with a sense of accomplishment. It helps them reflect on what they have learned in a lesson and integrate new skills and concepts with their previous knowledge. The ending also provides an opportunity to plant seeds of curiosity for the next lesson. Each activity should be followed by some processing experience to allow students to reflect on what they have learned. The challenge is to present interesting, creative closure activities that keep students actively involved rather than serve as a cue to pack up their books. Here are twenty suggestions for providing effective closure to your lessons:

1. Make a commitment to allow time in each lesson for a proper closure. Shouting the next day's assignment to your class as students rush out the door is ineffective. Allotting five to ten minutes of each class period for closure and debriefing is a valuable investment. Think of your lesson as a gift to your students; the ending is the bow on the package. It ties the whole experience together. It adds the finishing touch to your masterpiece.

2. Have students draw three balloons on a blank sheet of paper. In each balloon they are to write one important thing they learned in today's class. Have the students then pair with another and share what they wrote. It is a subtle way of encouraging them to review and reflect on what has happened during that lesson. (Of course, don't tell them it is review or they may disengage their brains from the activity!)

3. If you began the class with a question, you might now solicit their answers. Do they think differently about the topic now than they did at the beginning? Have they reassessed any assumptions?

4. Design a guided visualization. Leave parts open-ended, such as the best solution to a problem. Process their visualizations as a small-group or whole-class activity.

5. Pair students and allow one to interview the other about what he or she learned in the day's lesson.

6. Place a cartoon related to the lesson on the overhead projector. Always read the cartoon section of the newspaper with an eye for any cartoons that might pertain to any of your lessons. Enlarge them on the photocopier and make them into transparencies. Let a student color them with colored markers.

7. Ask all students to jot down one idea from the lesson they most want to remember. Allow a minute for reflection, and then solicit ideas from various members of the class. As an alternative, you can have them share in pairs or small groups. Or you could give students topics and have them generate answers and use a *Jeopardy* format for teams to generate appropriate questions.

8. Connect this lesson with previously learned content. This might be achieved through reflective questions or as a cooperative learning activity.

9. Provide an opportunity for application. Structure an activity that encourages reality-testing a new skill or concept. Ideally, students should receive immediate feedback on their success.

10. If you have been teaching a controversial topic, have pairs of students do a forced field analysis of the topic. They draw a line down the middle of the page. On one side they list all the arguments for and on the other side all the arguments against the proposition. You might summarize their grids as one large chart on the board.

11. Use a crossword puzzle that incorporates key concepts, names, or vocabulary included in the day's lesson. You can easily create crossword puzzles with inexpensive computer software such as Crossword Construction Kit (Insight Software Solutions) or Crossword Compiler

(Anthony Lewis Software). You may let students work in pairs or alone for three minutes; then they are free to help one another.

12. Let students write themselves a letter to encourage goal setting and self-monitoring of progress. Have students complete three sentence stems on a sheet of paper: (1) One thing I am doing well and will continue to do is . . . (2) One thing I will start doing in the next month is . . . (3) One thing I will stop doing in the next month is . . . You may substitute other questions or statements related to your lesson's objectives. Students place their completed sentences in envelopes, seal them, and write their names on the outside. Collect the envelopes and return them unopened one month (or a longer time period) later.

13. Have each student write one quiz question about the topic being studied. Collect them and then ask teams of students to respond to the questions in quiz-bowl style. Teams of students compete, accumulating points by giving answers.

14. Provide one or more sentence stems on a transparency or write them on the board, for example:

> I learned . . .
> I was surprised that . . .
> I discovered . . .
> I realized . . .
> I am puzzled about . . .
> I noticed . . .
> I recognize . . .
> I now appreciate . . .

15. Give your class two to three minutes to complete any one or two of the stems. Solicit several from volunteers. Be sure to thank contributors for offering their ideas.

16. Let students draw mind maps summarizing the content from the previous lesson. After individual students have developed their mind maps of the topic, ask them to join another person and combine their two separate mind maps into one. After several minutes redirect each pair to join another pair and again combine their mind maps into one. An option is to finally have all the students gather around one large sheet of newsprint (or tape four regular sheets of newsprint together to form a gigantic one). Write the topic in a circle in the middle of the paper and

give them the task of compiling a final mind map that includes all the ideas generated on their individual mind maps.

17. Remind students of what they already know that ties into the new content they have just learned.

18. End with a teaser or promo for the next day's lesson. The "coming attractions" hook leaves students in suspense and enhances their motivation to show up next time. Be creative; borrow from television and theater promos. You might pose a couple of startling questions that the class will address next time. Post an intriguing problem or challenge. Make a promise. Exaggeration is permitted. Whatever you do, do it with enthusiasm.

19. Ask each student to write down on a blank sheet of paper one thing he or she learned about the topic today. After everyone has finished writing, instruct the students to wad up the paper and throw it across the room. Each person picks up one and reads it aloud. Assign a volunteer to collect all the papers with the wastebasket.

20. Of course, remind them if there is a test or assignment due or they need to bring special materials to the next class. It is also important to add a word of encouragement if the day's lesson has been particularly difficult for many students. Acknowledge their efforts and successes. Thank them for working so hard. You might even invite them to give themselves a standing ovation.

Putting More Pizzazz in Your Presentations

Making presentations is an inescapable part of the teaching profession: class lectures, in-service workshops, parent open houses, faculty reports, board of education updates, and community service organization speeches. The person who can give a lively, interesting stand-up presentation is in demand.

While lecturing is only one tool in your instructional kit, teacher talk is a vital part of any classroom. Even those who employ a workshop approach must clarify, give directions, help process experiences, and share information. Great speakers are not born but made—through practice, reflection, feedback, and effort. Remember that the great Greek orator Demosthenes began with a speech impediment yet strove to become a competent public speaker. Many actors and politicians overcame shyness to confidently address hundreds. With determination, you can become a better public speaker. Here are a few suggestions to help.

Voice

✓ Tape record yourself teaching a variety of different kinds of lessons. Try to listen to yourself as objectively as possible. Is your voice soft, drowned out by background noises? Is the pitch reasonably pleasing? Note the speed at which you speak. Is the pace so fast that words jumble together? Do you occasionally mumble? Do you fill gaps with *OK* or *you know*? Do you clip the end of some words (for example, *goin'* for *going*)? Is there a nasal quality to your voice?

✓ Varying the pace and pitch of your presentation voice is an effective way to avoid slipping into a monotone. A current mannerism of many young people is to continually raise the pitch at the end of each sentence, making them all sound like questions. This can be most distracting and makes the speaker sound very unsure of what he or she is saying. Equally distracting is dropping the volume at the end of each sentence.

✓ Be aware of the messages you send simply with your voice, independent of the content you are uttering. Your speaking style may communicate confidence, passion, excitement, enthusiasm, and joy; or it may convey boredom, self-doubt, or fatigue. Always remember that your students will echo your emotional tone.

✓ Is your throat sore at the end of the day? While this is not uncommon among teachers the first couple of weeks of school, if it persists it may be a sign that you are using your voice mechanism improperly. Consult with a speech therapist for training in more effective and less harmful use of your voice.

✓ When talking in front of the class, always project your voice as though you were talking to the person in the remotest corner of the room. However, speaking too loudly is also unpleasant for your listeners. Some variation in your voice level is most effective.

✓ Use pauses for impact. Slight pauses refocus students' attention. But avoid fillers, such as *um, uh,* and *er.*

Nonverbal Communication

All teachers should be students of effective nonverbal communication. A rich understanding of the nonverbal level of expression will allow you to more accurately read students' messages, to remain congruent and accurate in the messages you send, and to avoid negative or incongruent messages you might inadvertently send to others. You are continually expressing nonverbal messages to everyone around you. Indeed, research suggests that the overwhelming portion of what you communicate is expressed nonverbally, not verbally. Here are a few tips on using nonverbal communication more effectively in teaching:

✓ Avoid leaning against the lectern or grasping it with a death grip. As much as possible, move away from the lectern. It is generally best to keep moving while providing whole-class instruction, such as lecturing.

Not only does that allow you to monitor student behavior better, but also you are more likely to be animated while moving than when remaining stationary.

✓ Teaching the whole class while seated at your desk encourages you to speak in a monotone with subdued gestures, two traits that convey a lack of enthusiasm. Move about the room, but don't zip around like a gazelle. You'll wear your students out trying to follow you.

✓ Be aware of using the same gestures repeatedly. Students may begin to mimic such nonverbal tics.

✓ Strive to achieve a relaxed, natural posture while talking. Too many as well as too few gestures tend to inhibit your message.

✓ Talk facing your class; avoid talking to the chalkboard or the screen. Not only is it ineffective speaking style, but also you will be less able to monitor your students' behavior with your back to them.

✓ While there are cultural differences among different ethnic groups, generally it is best to offer eye contact with your audience. Eye contact conveys that you are interested in the listener. Keep your eyes moving around the classroom, holding your gaze on clusters of four or five students at a time for three to five seconds before moving to the next group. From ten feet away, this provides the illusion of individual eye contact, even though you aren't maintaining direct eye contact with any one of the students in the cluster. This is not a natural practice; doing it naturally takes concerted effort.

✓ When calling on a student, avoid pointing. Rather, gesture with your palm up, a more inviting message.

✓ Many see a smile as a visual hug; it conveys warmth and acceptance. The smile is likely your most powerful social reinforcer. Remember, a genuine smile is conveyed as much with the eyes as with the mouth. Practice in front of the mirror to achieve the twinkle in the eyes.

✓ Occasionally videotape a class. Turn the volume down and just observe your nonverbal behavior. Do you like what you see? Are you directing eye contact equally around the room or only teaching to the students in the front center? Do you look animated or bored? Do you project confidence and enthusiasm through your nonverbal expressions? Do you look relaxed or stiff? Do you exhibit nervous gestures, such as rattling coins in your pocket, biting your lip, rubbing your nose, twirling your hair, stroking your beard, popping the top on your Magic Marker, or playing with your watch or jewelry? These can be very distracting mannerisms. Chances are you have one or more such habits of which you are unaware. That is why videotaping is essential. The camera does not lie. Although you may be unaware of your idiosyncratic gestures, your students aren't. And likely they will begin to joke about them among themselves. One of students' favorite pastimes is mimicking their teachers' quirks. Don't make it too easy for them!

Improving Your Speaking Effectiveness

✓ Teach to a variety of sensory modalities. Employ interesting visuals to augment your lecture.

✓ Use vocabulary that all students can understand. While you may want to introduce new vocabulary as part of your lessons, be sure you define unfamiliar terms. Your goal is to help them understand, not impress them with your expansive vocabulary. Simple, direct language usually will be easier to follow.

✓ Consider joining Toastmasters International, which teaches public speaking in almost every community. It is an excellent way to improve your speaking style. Toastmasters provides outstanding training programs and valuable practice with a supportive audience.

✓ If you are not sure of the pronunciation of a new word you are introducing in your lesson, look it up in the dictionary before class. Remember, you are serving as a model; and your students may copy your mistakes.

✓ Don't let your dress upstage your message. While wild, flashy costumes may express who you are, your students may be paying more attention to your fashion statement than the content you are trying to teach.

Homework That Helps

Homework, like any other instructional technique, is only a means to an end. Its value is determined by how effectively it enhances learning. If it does not, it is busy-work and serves little constructive purpose. Many critics argue that too little homework is assigned and that learning time can be increased cheaply by requiring more homework. A recent national study emphasized that more than two-thirds of seventeen-year-olds reported spending less than one hour a night on homework. It is not surprising that the same study revealed that higher-achieving students spent more time per week on homework than their classmates and that hours of television viewing and time spent on homework were inversely related.

How much homework you should assign is a complex question. The answer depends on your students' age, abilities, and habits, as well as your instructional objectives. It is probably reasonable to expect students to spend an hour per day on homework by the end of elementary school. High school students who have study halls should be able to complete two or three hours of work per day out of class. When students have several teachers, some coordination is needed among the faculty on the homework schedule. Otherwise, some students may end up with five or six hours of homework in an evening, an unreasonable amount. Students, like teachers, need some rest and recreation. Merely assigning more homework will not guarantee learning gains. Assignments that are not completed or are done incorrectly are of little benefit. Like seatwork, homework assignments that are too difficult or misunderstood will prove counterproductive.

Activities such as reading the text usually can be done out of class, preserving class time for activities that students cannot do independently. Homework provides a valuable opportunity to practice and reinforce new skills. It also provides an opportunity to connect new knowledge and skills with the outside world. Homework also serves an assessment function, providing the teacher with information on the success of his or her teaching.

Homework can be assigned to provide remedial instruction to students who lag in skill development. When the purpose of homework is to provide remediation, giving a blanket assignment to all students is hardly justified, as students progress at different rates. Assigning homework provides the golden opportunity for individualization, although it does require advance planning. Even though reading assignments, short essay answers, and drill problems make up the bulk of homework assignments, long-range projects seem to be of greater benefit. Such projects encourage students to use higher-level cognitive skills in gathering information, analyzing data, planning sequences, and synthesizing a variety of skills. Another valuable function of homework is to allow parents an active role in their child's education.

Do not use homework as a punishment. That practice only communicates to students that homework is an unpleasant activity, something to avoid. Such negative attitudes will not benefit either the teacher or the students. The first week of school, teachers must establish a fair and consistent homework policy.

Interesting Homework

Used effectively, homework reinforces practice and synthesis of skills and concepts developed in class. When asked by his father whether he had any homework, a boy replied, "No, the teachers ran out of toner." This anecdote reveals that many teachers lack imagination in assigning homework.

Professional journals, in-service programs, and other teachers are sources for gathering ideas on worthwhile homework assignments. A bit of imagination and planning can yield high-interest assignments and help develop students' skills. Here are a few ideas that other teachers have tried successfully:

✓ Write a new myth.

✓ Conduct experiments.

✓ Do volunteer work.

✓ Use math skills to measure common objects around the home.

✓ Plan a trip; include itinerary and costs.

✓ Develop a budget.

✓ Write a computer program.

✓ Observe and record birds, traffic, or weather.

✓ Plan a week's balanced menu.

✓ Trace family trees to personalize history.

✓ Interview an older person about a historical event he or she experienced.

✓ Plan and produce a film or skit.

✓ Write new endings to old stories.

✓ Teach someone a skill.

✓ Keep a journal.

✓ Invent a game; teach it to the class.

✓ Write a handbook for consumers.

✓ Construct a Web page.

✓ Research a topic and create a bulletin board display.

✓ Interview people about their jobs.

✓ Develop a creative solution to a problem.

✓ Develop an advertising campaign to promote a product, solution, or idea.

✓ Attend a public meeting.

✓ Design an ideal house, car, school, or government.

✓ Take sides on an issue; prepare a debate.

✓ Design a costume.

✓ Draw a map of the neighborhood or yard.

✓ Develop a case study.

✓ Prepare a photo essay on a community problem.

✓ Collect specimens of rocks, leaves, and wood.

✓ Draw a political cartoon.

✓ Participate in a political campaign.

Such "fun with a purpose" assignments can greatly increase students' motivation to learn. The relevance of the skills you are teaching becomes apparent. They must not only be fun but also have a legitimate educational purpose to justify their use.

Making Assignments

The first week of school, clarify your expectations regarding homework. Will work that students do not finish in class automatically become homework? If you do not make a specific assignment for the next class, will you expect students to read in their textbooks or review previous work? The procedures for assigning homework must be taught as part of the classroom routine. Here are some practical suggestions for effectively making homework assignments:

✓ Do not compete with student noise when giving oral directions. Stop talking and wait for their attention. Otherwise, you will end up repeating the directions.

✓ Save time and stress by putting directions for assignments on the board. If you prefer, cover them with a map until you are ready to discuss them. Some teachers instruct students to immediately take their seats and copy the assignments into their

notebooks, without waiting for the bell to ring. Many teachers choose to put all assignments on handouts for distribution. This minimizes later student remarks such as "I didn't hear you" or "I didn't know you wanted it done that way." Be sure to write clearly. Save the master copy for use next year. If any problems of understanding arise in completing the assignment, make a note on the master to refine the directions next year. Avoid shouting the next day's assignment over students gathering books as they scramble for the door.

✓ Students are more likely to complete homework assignments that are highly structured and have very specific directions. In assigning major projects, displaying completed sample projects will clarify your expectations and save time answering questions. Some teachers take pictures or slides of completed products for next year's demonstration.

✓ Set up a homework center on your class Web page. Parents and students can access this site. Add supplemental materials to assist students who need additional practice.

✓ It may be helpful to reserve specific days for regular assignments. For example, on Tuesdays students are to read the next chapter in the text; Thursdays they review the drill questions at the end of the chapter. You will have fewer assignments to plan every week, and students will be less likely to forget what their assignment is.

✓ Try to be creative in designing some homework tasks that will be fun as well as educationally sound. Experiments, interviews, math games, and active assignments tend to have a higher completion rate. One technique for creating suspense in the next day's lesson is to give students an unusual assignment but not explain its purpose. For example, ask them to count the number of lightbulbs in their house or to bring in the next day an empty egg carton or a baby picture. Of course, that activity must be incorporated into the next day's lesson.

✓ Early in the year, communicate with your students' parents what role you wish them to play in helping with their child's homework. This can be done in a newsletter and again at any open houses scheduled. Some send a special sheet home to parents, titled "How to Help Your Child with Homework." Add the same information to your online homework center, if available.

The Internet and Homework

HERE'S MY ESSAY MRS. SMITH. I DIDN'T HAVE TIME TO PRINT IT OUT.

Many teachers now post their homework assignments on their school or class Web sites. Parents can pull up the site to check whether their children have homework that day. This technology also provides a valuable communication tool for improving teacher-parent relationships, encouraging parents to take an active role in the learning process. It is a good idea to post your homework policy on the Web site as well.

Seeing the assignment on a Web page, forgetful students can download directions and worksheets from home.

A few schools have begun to experiment with using personal digital assistants (PDAs) and wireless technology as learning tools. Teachers can download homework assignments and accompanying worksheets onto every student's PDA.

Collecting and Grading Homework

Students must receive feedback on their homework for it to enhance learning. Not every homework assignment must be collected and graded. Use a variety of techniques to help students check their own or each other's assignments.

Generate homework teams with one student in each team responsible for collecting everyone's work and reporting to the teacher who did not complete their assignments. On some days simply circulating the room with a clipboard and checking off that students have completed the day's assignment may be sufficient.

Some teachers give each student a "no homework" pass at the beginning of each term. A student may redeem it once when he or she does not complete a homework assignment. One option would be to allow students to turn in any unused passes at the end of the term for bonus credit.

The Homework Lottery

One strategy that teachers at all grade levels use successfully for motivating students to complete homework assignments is the lottery. The idea is relatively simple and easy to implement, yet it can encourage otherwise apathetic students to complete their work. All students who successfully complete their homework for the day put their names on small cards that they drop in a jar or box. On Friday the class holds a drawing, selecting one or more winners.

What the winners receive is quite secondary. Just the recognition of having their names drawn is rewarding for most students. Most will value a privilege, such as being first in line all week or using the tape recorder or computer. Some teachers become proficient at scrounging for freebies such as tickets, posters, coupons, and prizes. Students soon learn that the more times their names are in the jar, the greater are their chances of winning. Of course, you must ensure that the only way to get their names in the jar is to complete their homework. It may be wise to specify a criterion of correctness for work submitted if students begin handing in hurriedly completed assignments.

One prize students value is a pass good for one night of no homework. Instead of handing in homework, the holder may redeem the coupon. If the student did the assignments necessary to win the coupon, one night of missed work will not likely be irreparable.

Handling Makeup Work

Whenever possible, put directions for assignments, projects, or homework in writing, being as explicit in your directions as possible. You might also notify parents that this is the practice. This avoids possible misunderstandings as well as saving you time in giving directions to absent students. Be sure to save a copy for next year.

Every teacher faces the challenge of getting students who were absent to make up missed assignments. Over the course of the year, this task can consume huge amounts of time that might better be allocated to other duties. The first week of school, clarify the procedures you expect students to follow for making up missed assignments after an absence. There is no one right routine for accomplishing this. The most successful approach will depend on your students' age and maturity. Here are some ideas veteran teachers have found helpful in dealing with this problem:

✓ For each subject or class you teach, attach a clipboard to the wall. Each day hang copies of the next day's assignments on the clipboard. Absent students (or students who lose their copy) can pick up the assignment as needed.

✓ For projects in which students are to create a product (for example, drawing, model, report), first demonstrate what is to be done, then post directions along with a sample. Save some of the best projects to use next year as models. This helps clarify your expectations and gives students an idea of what level of work you expect.

✓ At the beginning of the year, assign each student a partner. Have them exchange phone numbers. If one partner is absent, the other is responsible for gathering assignments, handouts, or materials and helping the partner catch up when he or she returns. Ninety percent of your students will successfully handle this. You may still have to help the other 10 percent get caught up, but this saves you a huge amount of time dealing with the others.

✓ Make a large calendar with numbers one to thirty-one for the days of the month. Laminate it so it can be reused. Each day write the day's assignments. Absent students can check missed assignments quickly.

Degree of Effort and Challenge

Percentage responding "yes" in a representative sample of American teenagers:

It is important to me that I do my best in all my classes.	72 percent
The amount of work I do in school now is important to my success later in life.	66 percent
I try to take the most difficult and challenging courses I can.	51 percent
Doing homework is a priority for me. I complete it before participating in other activities.	43 percent

Source: Horatio Alger Association. *The State of Our Nation's Youth 2001–2002.* Alexandria, VA: Horatio Alger Association of Distinguished Americans, 2001.

✓ Audiotape your directions as you give them to the class. Pencil the day's date and class on the tape and file it in a box. Students who are absent that day listen to the taped directions when they return. Have a tape recorder available in a set location.

✓ If makeup work involves handouts, put the date and the student's name on them. Then, on a designated spot on the bulletin board, tack the handouts and any assignment for each student absent that day.

✓ Develop a homework form to record the exact assignments for absent students. The student's partner or another responsible student should fill out the form with the missing assignments.

✓ Keep a homework notebook. Have a separate section for each class. Each day record what work was done in class and any homework assignment with any special directions. Also include copies of any handouts needed. When students return after being absent, they are responsible for checking the homework notebook.

✓ Tape five small cardboard boxes together to make a large mailbox with five compartments. Label the dividers with the days of the school week. As you give out each day's assignment, place any leftover photocopies into that day's slot. When students return from being absent, they are responsible for gathering the necessary materials from the mailbox.

Seventeen Tips for Making Outstanding Bulletin Boards

Well-designed bulletin boards can be effective learning and motivational tools. Their value as an instructional device should not be overlooked or left to chance.

Preparing bulletin boards can be time-consuming. Enlist others' help. Occasionally allow students or parent volunteers to help create attractive bulletin boards.

Don't assume that attractive bulletin boards are for elementary classrooms only. They are just as effective with middle and high school students.

For inspiration and ideas, check Web sites and professional journals. Here are some tips for constructing great bulletin boards:

1. From a roll of colored paper, tear a piece to the approximate size of the bulletin board to make a cover. Mold this to the bulletin board by hand and temporarily pin it to the board. With a small pin or razor knife, tear or cut along edges to remove the excess paper. You are ready to place objects and letters on the board.

2. Make two to three covers for bulletin boards at once, placing one on top of the other. When it is time to change displays, simply pull off the top display, revealing the next one beneath it.

3. Rather than repeatedly correcting students for the same errors, create a bulletin board display explaining the error and the correct procedures.

4. You need not decorate every bulletin board. Use blank ones for announcements, posters, student work, newspapers, magazine articles, and so on. Use some class time to have students brainstorm ideas for bulletin boards.

5. Generate graphics and letters with computers. Special software is readily available in most schools for printing banners and posters. Use letters of various sizes. Large ones grab the students' attention and get them to read the rest.

6. Give your students time and materials to cut out bulletin board letters of various styles and sizes. Store these in envelopes for future use.

7. Project coloring book images onto large sheets of paper taped to the wall. Trace and color the images to make large characters to include in your bulletin boards.

8. Use some bulletin boards to teach or reinforce a skill or concept. Make them interactive, engaging students in tactile or kinesthetic learning.

9. Reserve one section of a bulletin board for students to use to post interesting articles, invitations, unusual quotations, pictures, cartoons, and other items of interest.

10. At the end of the school year, whenever students have some free time, let them create a bulletin board for you. It will be ready for the fall, welcoming the new class back to school. You might want to have them cover it with newspaper to protect it during the summer.

11. Develop interactive bulletin boards. Use pockets and flaps to hide answers to questions displayed on the board. Post a daily question, riddle, or puzzle for students to explore when they enter the room. Some displays might pose a question to which students write their answers or estimate in a block on the bulletin board. These are especially valuable if they relate to a topic to be studied that day.

12. Hang a clothesline across one wall of your room. Attach students' papers to the line with clothespins.

13. Velcro or flannel boards can be incorporated into manipulative boards that invite students to experiment. Bulletin boards can be dynamic, inviting students to interact and reform the display. Self-checking questions can be displayed, with answers covered by flaps.

14. Shop fabric stores after holidays to purchase inexpensive fabrics with holiday themes. These make excellent backgrounds for seasonal bulletin boards and can easily be reused for many years.

15. Think of creative materials and ideas to incorporate into unique borders. Discarded fabric, game pieces, silk flowers, ribbons, leaves, greeting cards, or photographs can all be incorporated into attractive borders.

16. Go 3-D, attaching objects to your bulletin board display. Objects such as feathers, dried flowers, discarded ties, masks, hats, and costume jewelry can all be incorporated into your bulletin boards. Strive to use multiple textures to make the bulletin boards more attractive.

17. To help maintain interest, alter some part of a bulletin board every day or once a week. Changing a featured quotation or startling statistic each day keeps the students motivated to keep looking at it. Remember, a bulletin board is more than just wall decoration. It can be a great motivational device and instructional aid.

Internet Sources for Bulletin Board Ideas

Bulletin Boards Across the World
www.gigglepotz.com/bulletin.htm

Bulletin Board Ideas
www.ilovethatteachingidea.com/ideas/subj_bulletin_boards.htm

Bulletin Boards Library
www.teachnet.com/how-to/decor/bboards/index.html

Ideas for Bulletin Boards
www.kimskorner4teachertalk.com/classmanagement/bulletinboards.html

Teacher Bulletin Boards
www.teachertools.org/bulletinboards_dynam.asp

Differentiating Instruction

One of the earliest lessons most teachers learn is that one size does not fit all. Most classes include a broad range of students with a broad range of maturity, ability, motivation, temperament, home environment, and interests.

Multiple Intelligences

Since 1905, when psychologists Alfred Binet and Theodore Simon first developed an intelligence scale for identifying those students who would most benefit from special education, schools have placed much emphasis on measuring and reporting students' levels of intelligence. It is worth noting that Binet explicitly did not intend his measure to be used to rank students by intellectual ability or even to identify their innate potential. He also did not believe intelligence to be a single quality, measurable by a number. The struggle to define and assess intelligence is probably articulated most clearly by Harvard psychologist Edward Boring's quip that intelligence is defined as what intelligence tests measure.

In the mid-1980s Howard Gardner, professor at the Harvard Graduate School of Education, popularized the concept of multiple intelligences. Gardner offered an alternative view of intelligence, defining it as "the ability to solve problems or fashion products that are valued in at least one culture" (1999, p. 33). He views intelligence as biopsychological potential.

Gardner and his followers have identified specific sections of the brain that control each of the eight intelligences he proposed:

- ✓ *Logical-mathematical:* verbal skills and sensitivity to the sounds, meanings, and rhythms of words
- ✓ *Linguistic:* possessing a mastery of language and ability to express oneself rhetorically or poetically
- ✓ *Spatial:* ability to think in images and pictures, to visualize accurately and abstractly
- ✓ *Musical:* ability to recognize and compose musical pitches, tones, and rhythms
- ✓ *Bodily-kinesthetic:* ability to control one's body movements and to handle objects skillfully
- ✓ *Intrapersonal:* possessing a high degree of self-knowledge, including awareness of one's own strengths, weaknesses, and inner feelings
- ✓ *Interpersonal:* competent in leadership skills, communication, understanding of others' feelings
- ✓ *Naturalist:* capacity to detect significant patterns in nature and distinguish and categorize items of various classes (plants, animals, chemicals)

Schools have traditionally stressed and rewarded linguistic and logical-mathematical intelligence. Many contend this narrow conception of intelligence has shortchanged those students whose talents lie in other forms of intelligence. Recognizing and nurturing the students' individual patterns of multiple intelligences allows teachers to help all students maximize their success, both in and out of school. Not all students have strong logical or linguistic intelligences. However, capitalizing on their strengths allows these students to excel in other arenas.

Tom Armstrong, author of *Multiple Intelligences in the Classroom,* suggests that knowledge of multiple intelligences provides teachers with eight unique pathways to learning, enabling them to more effectively personalize instruction. Skills can be learned and applied in a variety of modes. Attending to multiple intelligences will invariably change the teacher's role in the classroom. It must become less focused on textbooks and lectures, encouraging teachers to be more creative in designing lessons.

Gardner frowned on tests that were designed to measure a student's intelligence. However, through observation teachers can usually identify students' natural inclinations. Armstrong suggests that noting how students misbehave provides valuable clues to students' preferred intelligences. For example, students with high spatial intelligence may spend a lot of time doodling in class. Interviewing students, their parents, and previous teachers will provide insights into individuals' dominant intelligences. Finding out how students prefer to spend their free time out of school usually reveals their talents.

Gardner suggested that memory is intelligence specific. There is no such thing as a good memory or bad memory. He argues that memory will accompany one's predominant intelligences. For example, an individual with strong musical intelligence may be able to hear a composition once and play it back on a musical instrument, but that person may have a very difficult time remembering names or memorizing multiplication tables.

Armstrong suggests that by using multiple ways of teaching content, teachers encourage students to tap their strengths in accomplishing more challenging tasks. For example, a teacher might encourage that student to sing the multiplication tables at home as a memory aid.

Gardner and his colleagues have promoted nontraditional forms of assessment to evaluate student achievement. Such authentic assessments may incorporate student portfolios or demonstrations. Ongoing teacher observation and student self-evaluation are significant aspects of instruction oriented toward multiple intelligences. Gardner (1993, p. 178) concludes that "it is extremely desirable to have assessment occur in the context of students working on problems, projects, or products that genuinely engage them, that hold their interest and motivate them to do well. Such exercises may not be as easy to design as the standard multiple-choice entry, but they are far more likely to elicit a student's full repertoire of skills and to yield information that is useful for subsequent advice and placement."

Teachers determined to implement multiple intelligence strategies in their classroom face real-world obstacles. The time and energy needed to redesign instruction can be significant. Not all administrators encourage deviating from the focus on upping standardized test performance. Parents may not readily see the advantages of emphasizing talent development beyond the traditional three R's.

Multiple Intelligences in Teaching

Intelligence	Enjoy	Teaching Strategies
Logical-mathematical	Calculating, analyzing, questioning	Calculation, experiments, problem solving, computer games, library research
Linguistic	Writing, reading, telling stories	Books, discussion, reports, compositions, debates
Spatial	Drawing, visualizing	Art, puzzles, maps, visual images, mind mapping
Musical	Singing, playing instruments	Sing-alongs, musical instruments, background music, song writing
Bodily-kinesthetic	Dancing, running, touching	Gymnastics, hands-on activities, constructing things, physical games, drama, handicrafts, model building, skits, manipulatives
Intrapersonal	Reflecting, meditating	Independent study, introspection, self-paced learning, journaling
Interpersonal	Listening, helping, talking, leading, socializing, empathizing	Peer tutoring, games, surveys, cooperative learning
Naturalist	Sorting, categorizing, collecting specimens	Animals, ecology, plants, experimenting

Research suggests that instruction organized around multiple intelligences can yield increased responsibility in students, enhanced academic achievement, and more cooperative classroom behavior. To learn more about multiple intelligences, see Howard Gardner's Web site at pzweb.harvard.edu/PIs/HG.htm; check out the books listed in the resources; or take a course or workshop.

Emotional Intelligence

Daniel Goleman, author of the best-seller *Emotional Intelligence,* popularized the concept of emotional intelligence, which roughly corresponds to Gardner's interpersonal and intrapersonal intelligences. Goleman's five dimensions of emotional intelligence include self-awareness, self-regulation, empathy, motivation, and social skills.

Research indicates that conventional intelligence tests can account for only about 5 to 10 percent of the variability in real-life success and life adjustment. In one investigation, Dulewicz and Higgs (2000) found that emotional intelligence accounted for 36 percent of the variance in predicting successful managers, while traditional IQ accounted for only 27 percent.

Traits of People with High Levels of Emotional Intelligence

Emotional self-awareness	• Distinguishes and labels one's emotions
	• Comprehends the causes of emotions
	• Discerns the difference between emotions and behaviors
Managing emotions	• Exhibits frustration tolerance and anger control
	• Avoids verbal put-downs, fights, and classroom misbehavior
	• Expresses anger appropriately, without fighting
	• Exhibits less self-destructive or aggressive behavior
	• Has positive feelings about self, school, and family
	• Handles stress well
	• Experiences less loneliness and social anxiety
Motivation: harnessing emotions productively	• Behaves responsibly
	• Focuses on the task at hand; pays attention
	• Is seldom impulsive; shows self-control
Empathy: reading emotions	• Takes another person's perspective
	• Displays sensitivity and empathy to others' feelings
	• Listens well
	• Conveys warmth and understanding to others
Handling relationships	• Comprehends relationships
	• Resolves conflicts and negotiates disagreements
	• Works at solving problems in relationships
	• Behaves assertively
	• Tends to be popular and outgoing
	• Is friendly and invests in relationships with peers
	• Shows kindness
	• Cooperates in groups
	• Is helpful

Source: Goleman, D. (1995). *Emotional intelligence*. New York: Bantam.

Thirty-eight Strategies for Nurturing Emotional Intelligence

1. Encourage students to strive for excellence, not perfection.
2. Teach reframing to help students see events from a more positive perspective.
3. Incorporate goal-setting activities in your lessons.
4. Let students construct collages called Goal Posters, representing personal goals they hope to achieve.
5. Have students draw a picture of the hurdles they must clear to accomplish one of their goals.

6. Have students pick cards listing various feelings to mime or charade emotions for their classmates to identify.

7. Have students rate their feelings on a scale of one to ten as a way to encourage them to think about the intensity of their emotions. They can draw a feeling thermometer to indicate the intensity of their feelings.

8. Frequently use reflection-of-feeling statements to develop empathy with your students. (For example: "You feel disappointed because you didn't make the quiz-bowl team.") Encourage students to develop a rich vocabulary for feelings, beyond *mad, glad,* and *sad.*

9. Teach students to confront their own "stinkin' thinkin'"—to identify their own negative self-talk.

10. Invite students to suggest what different characters in a story might be feeling at different points in the story.

11. Obtain pictures of people expressing a variety of emotions. Devise learning activities or displays in which students try to detect what emotion the person in the picture is expressing.

12. Help students differentiate wants from needs.

13. Encourage students to think in terms of preference rather than musts. (For example, "I would prefer to be chosen first" rather than "I must be picked first!")

14. Use puppets, stuffed animals, or other props to gain insights into students' thought patterns. These can prove especially valuable for encouraging introverted children to express themselves.

15. Encourage students to get involved in community service projects or help individuals in need.

16. Teach students to use I-statements to express emotions more responsibly and without aggressiveness.

17. Help students see that people can have different opinions on how to accomplish the same goal, without either necessarily being wrong. Debates can be a constructive way to help students analyze contrasting viewpoints.

Helping people better manage their upsetting feelings—anger, anxiety, depression, pessimism, and loneliness—is a form of disease prevention.

—Daniel Goleman,
Emotional Intelligence

18. Have students draw a line down the middle of a page and list the pros and cons or advantages and disadvantages of a specific issue (for example, year-round school or a requirement that students wear school uniforms).

19. Infuse the development of listening skills into your class content. For example, have students paraphrase others' comments before adding their own.

20. Structure cooperative learning activities, which provide opportunities to develop a variety of social competencies.

21. Expose students to other cultures as a part of your regular lessons. Field trips, guest speakers, films, stories, projects, and ethnic celebrations present opportunities to experience diversity.

22. Teach basic conversation skills. Teach students interviewing skills such as clarifying questions or paraphrases. Encourage students to interview adults as a part of class assignments.

23. Use brainstorming activities to encourage students to generate alternative ways of handling daily problems.

24. Have students brainstorm a variety of ways to express a particular emotion.

25. Continually remind students that "To have a failure is not to be a failure." Emphasize the value of failures and mistakes as part of the learning process. The key is to learn from our mistakes. Selectively share your own mistakes and failures with students to let them know that these are part of being human.

26. Get a peer mediation program started if your school does not already have one.

27. Encourage students to come up with several different solutions to problems discussed in class. Anticipate the consequences.

28. Teach problem-solving skills as a part of your regular content.

29. Encourage students to develop self-contracts for small goals.

30. Help students see the difference between having a feeling and acting on the feeling. Help them see they have choices and can exercise control over their actions.

31. Teach some basic stress management techniques, such as deep breathing or progressive relaxation.

32. Help students think of large projects or goals as a series of little tasks. This makes the project seem less overwhelming.

33. Include anger management strategies in your lesson. Devise an option for students who become too upset to cool off.

34. Strive to develop flow in your lessons.

35. Invest in a psychological bank account with your students. Build up goodwill but treat them with compassion and respect. It will pay dividends.

36. Never emphasize that there is one right emotion for any specific situation.

37. Work closely with your school counselor to develop classroom guidance activities reinforcing the components of emotional intelligence.

38. Most importantly, model high emotional intelligence. Actions speak louder than words.

Preferred Learning Modalities

Research suggests that people learn through their senses and perceptions. Not only does perception supply much of what we remember, but it also anchors events in our memory to a particular place and time. While virtually everyone applies all the senses in learning, most individuals learn best through a particular sensory or perceptual channel—kinesthetic, tactile, auditory, or visual. That is, most people prefer to learn through their sense of touch and feeling, their sense of hearing, or their sense of sight. Their learning style, or modality, is the channel through which they best receive and retain information.

Every classroom likely contains a mixture of preferences—students who are kinesthetic or tactile learners, auditory learners, and visual learners. Research indicates that visual learners make up 65 percent of the population. Approximately 30 percent are auditory learners, leaving about 5 percent as kinesthetic or tactile learners. Research suggests that most teachers rely almost totally on print and aural modes of presentation.

Sensory preferences are developmental, with younger children being more kinesthetic and tactile. Typically, during the sixth grade, girls become more perceptually mature in the auditory channel, with boys following shortly. At about the eighth grade, girls usually develop greater visual-perceptual acuity, with boys catching up a year or two later.

Visual learners tend to process information through what they see, to think in pictures, and to have fertile imaginations. Auditory learners deal with information through what they hear. They tend to enjoy listening and like to talk things through. Kinesthetic learners manage information by doing, touching, and experiencing. Hyperactive students, 95 percent of whom are male, may have an extremely high kinesthetic preference.

Research suggests that matching teaching style with students' learning styles may increase student motivation and improve performance. The research also indicates that teachers almost always teach in their own preferred learning style. Visual teachers generally rely on visual techniques; auditory teachers depend on oral and listening techniques; and kinesthetic or tactile teachers tend to prefer Montessori methods.

Learning-style researcher Rita Dunn suggests that not every student need be assessed for learning style, only those who are having difficulty learning. Teachers accommodate different sensory modality needs by designing multisensory instruction. Because most children are able to learn through all sensory channels, teaching them through all modalities will help them attain optimal learning; what they don't learn from their preferred modality, they may attain from another. Teaching with varied multisensory techniques helps increase achievement of slow learners who had not progressed with conventional strategies.

Helpful Resources

Armstrong, T. (2000). *The multiple intelligences in the classroom.* Alexandria, VA: Association for Supervision and Curriculum Development.

Armstrong, T. (2003). *The multiple intelligences of reading and writing: Making the words come alive.* Alexandria, VA: Association for Supervision and Curriculum Development.

Attributes Signifying Modality Preferences

Auditory	Visual	Kinesthetic or Tactile
Likes music	Doodles	Likes handling objects
Enjoys talking	Notices details	Gestures while talking
Long, repetitive descriptions	Verbal directions often difficult	Often in motion
Distracted by noise	Enjoys drawing	Tapping feet or hands
Sings	Vivid imagination	May be fidgety
Talks to self	Solves problems deliberately	Likes to try things out
	Tends to be quiet	Jumping, pushing
	Distracted by movement	Often seems impulsive
	Remembers faces but forgets names	May be a poor speller
	Intense concentration when reading	Good motor memory

Helpful Instructional Strategies for Learning Modalities

Auditory	Visual	Kinesthetic or Tactile
Discussions	Drawing	Manipulatives
Debates	Note taking	Building models
Oral presentations	Watching videos	Hands-on activities
Listening to lectures	Guided imagery	Field trips
Listening to music	Demonstrations	Drama, role-playing
Reciting content aloud	Computer instruction	Allow to stretch or stand
Studying with peers	Color coding	Making flash cards
Reading aloud	Mind maps	Labs
Talk problems through	Time lines, flow charts	Walk-and-talk activities
Verbal mnemonics	Visual mnemonics	Stories with lots of action
Verbal analogies, metaphors	Use written directions	Interviewing
Reading dialogue and plays	Use pictures, diagrams, maps, and charts	Puppetry
Musical concerts	Flash cards	Writing at the board
Brainstorming	Highlight text with colors	Sculpture
Verbal directions	Independent learning	Action games
	Visual displays	Workbooks
	Transparencies	

Beachner, L., & Pickett, A. (2001). *Multiple intelligences and positive life habits: 174 activities for applying them in your classrooms.* Thousand Oaks, CA: Corwin.

Dulewicz, V., & Higgs, M. (2000). Emotional intelligence: A review and evaluation study. *Journal of Managerial Psychology, 15*(4), 341–372.

Forsten, C., Grant, J., & Hollas, B. (2002). *Differentiated instruction: Different strategies for different learners.* Peterborough, NH: Crystal Springs. Mahwah, NJ: Erlbaum.

Gardner, H. (1983). *Frames of mind: The theory of multiple intelligences.* New York: Basic Books.

Gardner, H. (1991). *The unschooled mind.* New York: Basic Books.

Gardner, H. (1993). *Multiple intelligences: The theory in practice.* New York: Basic Books.

Gardner, H. (1999). *Intelligence reframed: Multiple intelligences for the twenty-first century.* New York: Basic Books.

Goleman, D. (1994). *Emotional intelligence: Why it can matter more than IQ.* New York: Bantam Books.

Goleman, D. (1998). *Working with emotional intelligence.* New York: Bantam Books.

Stefanakis, E. H. (2002). *Multiple intelligences and portfolios: A window into the learner's mind.* Portsmouth, NH: Heinemann.

Assessing Student Performance

Some forms of assessment and grading of students' progress are inescapable parts of every teacher's job. *Assessment* means gathering information about individual students' level of performance or achievement. *Evaluation* is the process of making judgments about that information.

Evaluation involves comparing a student's achievement with a peer group (norm referencing) or with a set standard (criterion referencing). (*Norm-referenced grades* are calculated by comparing an individual student's performance relative to the rest of the class. *Criterion-referenced grades* are determined by assessing how well a student has met a specific set of standards, independent of how well anyone else did.) *Grading* is the subsequent assigning and reporting of a symbol (letter, number, or category) to the evaluation.

Formative vs. Summative Assessment

Two forms of assessment exist. Formative assessment is diagnostic in that it provides relatively immediate feedback to aid teachers and students during the learning process. Using this feedback, teachers can alter instruction to help students learn more effectively. Indeed, research has suggested that good formative assessment is one of the most powerful instructional devices in a teacher's toolbox.

Summative assessment is the assessment designed to determine what students know at a specific point of time, usually at the end of a term or year. Examples would be high school exit exams and final semester exams. Most standardized tests are summative. Summative evaluation is inescapable. Parents, students, administrators, and colleges expect end-of-course grades. States mandate exit and proficiency exams.

Done well, formative assessment is an extremely valuable means for improving student learning. It helps identify areas in which students are struggling in time for teachers to take corrective action. It assists teachers in making instructional decisions.

Ideally, student assessments provide teachers feedback on how well they are succeeding and diagnose areas needing additional attention. Assessment of students' progress is essential in determining whether instruction successfully met the lesson's objectives.

Good formative assessment deemphasizes marking and grading and depends less on rote memorization than most standardized tests do. Feedback on specific errors and gaps in learning are more valuable than are overall grades in enhancing learning. Receiving a B– on an essay is not of great value in helping students comprehend what they need to do to improve. Specific comments and grading rubrics provide useful data, particularly when paired with remediation and practice.

Formative assessments tend to be embedded within the learning process. Helpful formative assessment options include the following:

✓ Some tests

✓ Homework

✓ Quizzes

✓ Research reports

✓ Oral questions with adequate time for students to answer

✓ Feedback on seatwork

✓ Thoughtful, reflective class dialogues

✓ Grading rubrics

✓ Comments

✓ Checklists

✓ Self-evaluations

✓ Teacher conferences

✓ In-class writing assignments

✓ Lab worksheets

✓ Student journals

Self-assessment is an essential ingredient in the formative assessment process. In a 1998 *Phi Delta Kappan* article, Paul Black and Dylan Wiliam wrote (p. 143), "self-assessment by pupils, far from being a luxury, is in fact *an essential component of formative assessment.* When anyone is trying to learn, feedback about the effort has three elements: recognition of the *desired goal,* evidence about *present position,* and some understanding of a *way to close the gap* between the two. All three must be understood to some degree by anyone before he or she can take action to improve learning." Ideally, formative assessment encourages students to assume responsibility for their own learning.

Feedback on performance is crucial for improvement. Hence, good formative assessment is a prerequisite to effective teaching.

Grading Student Performance

Grading students' work meets a different set of educational and social purposes. For some students (mostly those already doing well), grades motivate and control behavior. Grades make categorization of students easier—for promotion, selection, and grouping. Parents also expect feedback from the school on how well their children are performing in school. Traditional grading schemes (A, B, C, D, and F; satisfactory or unsatisfactory) still prevail. But teachers, subjects, and schools vary so much that deciphering the meaning of one student's B provides little information about that student's level of achievement.

There are risks in assigning grades to student performance. Traditional norm-referenced grades, approximating the normal curve, probably work very well for the top one-third. They can develop positive academic self-esteem and generally reap the bulk of rewards that schools dole out. The lowest one-third, however, suffer from overtly competitive grading systems. They enter an environment each day that communicates "You are a loser. You are valued less than others." Howard Gardner suggests that these students may possess important intelligences (musical, spatial, interpersonal, intrapersonal, or bodily-kinesthetic). Unfortunately, our schools tend to value and reward only the logical-mathematical and linguistic intelligences. We should not be surprised that research reveals that students who drop out of school experience an immediate increase in self-esteem.

Student evaluations must be based on a variety of measures: assignments, projects, exhibits, tests, quizzes, observations, journals, presentations, products, performances, self-evaluations, and peer evaluations.

Though assessment and evaluation play important roles in the learning process, research provides little evidence that grades themselves have much educational value. Yet the practice persists, and most every teacher is mandated to submit a grade (usually a letter) for each student at the end of periodic grading terms. Here are some suggestions to make that process as painless and as fair as possible.

Variability in Assessment

Remember that different teachers grading the same materials show a variability of grades, especially for essays and other subjectively rated products. Different teachers employ different criteria in assigning grades. Even when using the same criteria, teachers may judge differently how well students have met those criteria.

Teachers' grades reflect many factors besides students' academic achievement: students' efforts, persistence, classroom deportment, and a host of subtle biases that can creep into subject assessments. Research studies have found each of the following biases to influence teachers' judgments of essays:

✓ Students with neat handwriting get higher marks on essay tests, especially from teachers with neat handwriting.

✓ A halo effect exists in the assignment of grades: students who performed well on previous essays tend to receive higher ratings on subsequent ones, even if the quality diminishes.

✓ Longer essays get rated higher than shorter essays, even when the shorter essays are better in argument, organization, and grammar.

✓ Students with common names (Sally, Mike, Jane) get rated higher than students with unusual names (Elmo, Zeke, Evangeline).

✓ Students deemed attractive tend to get rated higher than students rated as homely or unattractive, even when the essays are identical.

An objective view of the research reveals that grades do somewhat predict one thing: future grades. However, the higher up the educational ladder, the less accurately do grades predict grades at the next level. However, grades have proven of little value in predicting individuals' success in any field after they finish school.

Twenty Tips for Making Grading as Painless as Possible

1. Involve students in the grading process to minimize disagreements over grades. Make sure they fully understand how grades are assigned.

2. Have students grade some in-class assignments for immediate feedback. Sometimes it is valuable to allow them time to improve their effort after the self-assessment.

3. An elementary school teacher may use recess time for grading the previous period's papers. The teacher goes around to each pupil's desk and grades all the papers at once. On returning from recess, the students receive immediate reinforcement of their work. This saves time at night and also saves the time needed for passing out and collecting papers.

4. It is not essential for the teacher to correct every student assignment. As much as possible, allow students to swap and grade papers. Spot-check to prevent cheating.

5. For seatwork or some homework, provide keys that the students use to score their own work and add up their point totals for the week. Spot-check a few papers.

6. For checking students' homework, assign a set number of points to an assignment if it is complete and on time. Let the students check their own answers in class as a whole group. This allows homework to be a learning experience and saves time grading papers.

7. Require students to keep a page in their notebook on which they record each test or quiz grade when they receive it. That way they always have a tally of their scores and need not continually check with you.

8. Some teachers find it more efficient to keep the cumulative total of each student's test and quiz points. When entering a score, add it to the previous total. You might mark this new sum on the student's test paper. You'll save time at the end of the semester by not having to refigure each student's grade. This is an especially easy task if you use a computer grade-keeping system.

9. Stagger the due dates for major projects, papers, and examinations. Receiving a barrage of paper can be overwhelming. You'll manage your time more efficiently if you space the assignments out. Students who have you for more than one class will also appreciate it and probably do better work.

10. It is also a good idea to insist that students keep all graded papers until the end of the term. If there is a discrepancy in what you have recorded in your grade book and what they believe they have earned, they have the final proof.

11. Some teachers have each student turn in a cassette tape with their name on it along with their writing activities. The teacher records comments about the written work as they read it. Students may take the tape home to listen to it or do so on a recorder in class during free time.

12. Some teachers assign each student a number, which may correspond to the one appearing beside their name in the grade book. Each assignment or test must include that number. It is much quicker to find that number when entering scores than to hunt the student's name.

13. One advantage of seating students alphabetically is that papers you collect are already in alphabetical order, making grades easier to record in your grade book.

14. To keep clear records in the small spaces in most teachers' grade books, code many events that influence the grade. For example:

    Writing A in a corner of the box means "absent."
    Outlining the box means the work was handed in late.
    D means the assignment was done over.
    S indicates a parent signature on the paper.
    (*Source:* Contributed by Betsy Redd)

15. Generally, it is better to record test and quiz grades as numbers, not letters. Numbers are easier and quicker to convert into grades at the end of the term.

16. When grading multiple-choice examinations, use a computer scoring system if one is available. If not, develop answer sheets and a master key that you hold over the answer sheet to facilitate scoring.

17. Require students to double-space all essays or other written assignments. That provides more room for comments than just using the margin.

18. Develop checklist forms for evaluating essays and other products. List the specific criteria you are assessing and provide a separate rating for each criterion. Some criteria might be weighted higher than others. If you are only concerned with whether the feature is included in the assignment, a simple checkmark beside that item will suffice. Structure the form to minimize the amount of writing required of you.

19. Teach students to edit and revise their papers before turning them in to save you the time of repeatedly reading rough drafts. Let them work in cooperative groups to help edit each other's papers.

20. Some elementary teachers send home a weekly work folder with each student. The parents read the week's projects and then sign and return the folder with the student. This is a valuable way to maintain effective home-school communication.

Tests and Quizzes

The most effective teachers assess student learning often. This discourages student procrastination and cramming and provides a more accurate assessment of student learning. Here are some tips for making evaluation of student work easier and more effective:

✓ Strive for higher-order levels of thinking in your questions. The biggest disadvantage of multiple-choice questions is the overreliance on rote memorization. One research study found that students forget 80 percent of what they learn within one year. Most of what students forget are facts they memorized for one quiz or test.

✓ Develop a file for your old tests and worksheets. A large three-ring binder or manila file folder will work. After using a test, jot notes on the top as to which questions need replacing because they are too hard or too easy.

✓ If you give diagnostic tests at the beginning of the year, code the test items related to each skill area. Students then receive a checklist indicating their deficiencies. The checklist can also reference pages in the textbook. On the final exam, students only have to complete those areas in which they did not show mastery on the pretest. (*Source:* Contributed by Barb Wagner)

✓ Some teachers choose to make the first test relatively easy to build students' confidence.

✓ Run two-page tests on both sides of a sheet of paper and grade one side at a time. When done with the whole stack, just turn it over and begin grading the other side. This way you don't waste time turning all the pages over before you can start grading the second page. Also, you don't have to flip the pages back to page one to begin scoring. Just turn the stack over again. Tests run double-sided do not require collating and stapling. Answer sheets help with multiple-page objective tests. You may only have to grade one sheet instead of flipping through several pages. You can then save the test copies for future use without having to run them off again. (*Source:* Suggested by Barb Steinhauser)

✓ Use publishers' textbook tests when possible, but feel free to adapt them to your objectives.

✓ Use as few items as necessary to assess a skill or knowledge. Why use a fifty-item test if twenty items will give you the same information?

✓ Some teachers give makeup exams only for extended absences. By allowing each student to throw out his or her lowest grade, the teacher makes sure a single missed test does not penalize the student.

✓ Develop a computer test file. A variety of software is available to develop a test bank. Tests and quizzes are easily and quickly generated. Some software lets you save performance data, allowing you to eliminate ineffective questions.

✔ Do try to include questions of a higher cognitive level. Students tend to forget items they merely memorized as soon as the test is over.

✔ Provide adequate notice and help in preparing your students for examinations.

✔ Let students review in study teams before an exam.

✔ Set up a self-checking station for students to grade their own multiple-choice quizzes and homework assignments. Have a laminated answer key and colored marking pens available. Students are not allowed to bring their own pens or pencils to the checking station, and only one student at a time is allowed at the station. When done, the corrected work is left in a tray at the station. As you record grades, spot-check the work for accuracy and honesty. Research shows that students are generally quite accurate in their self-scoring.

✔ Fill out evaluation sheets on a computer or PDA as you assess the student's essay or product. Print or e-mail a copy to the student, keeping the data on file.

✔ Experiment with giving collaborative tests. Groups of three students get to work together on the test. You might randomly assign groups each time or carefully select a stratified sample to include one high- and one low-ability student in each group. Success requires that a cooperative climate is already established in your room.

✔ Give some attention to reducing test anxiety among your students. One tactic for reducing test anxiety and helping students prepare for an examination is to permit them to ask any question about the test that you can answer with "yes" or "no." (*Source:* Contributed by Barb Wagner)

✔ Immediately before an examination, lead the class in some relaxation exercises: focused breathing, positive affirmations, stretching, perhaps even shoulder rubs.

✔ Provide adequate feedback on students' test performance. Help them to understand where they erred and to correct mistakes and misunderstandings. Any assessment should help a student learn.

✔ Some teachers use cooperative learning groups to take weekly quizzes together and then individual final examinations. The cooperative group members may then meet after the examinations are scored to help each other understand questions missed.

✔ If any students are very upset about their exam scores, offer to meet with them the next day. Give them some time to cool off first. Make it a policy never to argue with a student about a grade in front of the class. Nobody wins, and the results usually will be unpleasant.

✔ If a large number of students do poorly on an exam, reconsider its worth. While it is tempting to blame large numbers of failures on incompetent, apathetic students, sometimes it is the instruction or assessment that was defective. Try to remain objective.

Grade Contracts

The grade contract is an option that many teachers use, especially in middle and high school. A contract is an agreement between two parties stipulating that when a specified event has occurred, a particular positive consequence will follow. Because completion of the grade contract is dependent on attaining a preset standard of performance rather than relative position within a group, it is a criterion-referenced form of evaluation rather than a norm-referenced one.

In the most common form of a grade contract, the teacher specifies a relatively small number of assignments that are required of all students, with each higher-level grade requiring one or more additional tasks. Generally, the student signs a contract at the start of the course for an A, B, or C. Students who contract for an A but fulfill only the required tasks for a lower grade present a dilemma for the teacher. Should these students be penalized for failing to reach the contracted goal or rewarded for the performance level that they successfully attained? Another option is to specify the tasks required for each grade category but not to require students to identify their target grade ahead of time. At the end of the grading period, students receive the grade corresponding with the contract tasks they completed.

The contracted tasks reflect the course's expressed or hidden objectives. The teacher may wish to attain other goals, but students will tend to emphasize the ones being evaluated.

The Multiple-Option Grade Contract

An extension of the grade contract system, the multiple-option grade contract maximizes the advantages of a criterion-referenced contract system while eliminating some of the deficiencies of standard grade contracts. The model presented here is a flexible grade contract that teachers have used successfully with a variety of grade levels and subjects. The multiple-option grade contract is flexible to incorporate the teacher's teaching style, needs, and objectives while also incorporating differences in students' learning styles and individual talents.

At the first class meeting, students receive a handout describing the contract's terms and specifying the minimum number of points needed to qualify for each letter grade. A sample contract might list the following cutoff points: one hundred points equal an A; eighty points equal a B; sixty points equal a C.

Don't specify a target grade of D. Suggest instead that those shooting for a D should come see you later and you'll negotiate a number; this often gets a laugh. Rarely will anyone ever take you up on such an offer. Identify a grade of C as the minimum competency level for your class objectives.

Each week students receive a set of from two to ten activities and projects. These assignments are keyed to the course objectives. Successful completion of each task is accepted as mastery of a particular objective or skill. Some activities, reflecting vital skills or concepts, may be required of everyone. There may be alternate means available for demonstrating attainment of the same skill. Many learning tasks are optional; students choose those that best reflect their individual needs, interests, and learning styles. The fact that students have active choices, even among a limited set of alternatives, enhances motivation.

The total number of points available should exceed the sum required for an A, usually at least double. The contract is cumulative and positive. The student receives points for achievement and effort. Points are not subtracted for poor performance; rather, nothing is added to the student's total.

Students are encouraged to propose assignment options that will demonstrate their learning. Class presentations, reports, book reviews, and interviews are all valid learning experiences that should be encouraged. The student and teacher can negotiate a mutually acceptable point value for such assignments. It is essential that at least an approximate point value be negotiated as part of the contract.

Individual assignments may be evaluated as pass or fail, indicating that the student achieved minimal criteria or that a student's assignment may be prorated and thus receive partial credit. If a pass-fail assessment is used, you may give students the option of redoing assignments until they fulfill the minimum criteria for success. (These criteria can be set quite high as the students have the option of taking more time to attain the level of success.)

It is possible to grade tests and quizzes on a point basis. Give each a specified point value, such as five, ten, or twenty points. Reward students for high performance. Poor performance is not rewarded, but one bad test score does not doom students for the duration of the term. Because the points are cumulative, not an average, test anxiety is decreased.

The contract must clearly specify assignments in order for it to be successful. Students should not have to guess what you expect. What are the minimal criteria for success? It helps to have high-quality sample products or assignments received from previous classes. Students will not perceive the contract as fair if they have to constantly rewrite because they guessed wrong about what you wanted. To discourage procrastination, set specific deadlines for all the assignments.

The multiple-option grade contract places the responsibility for grades on the students. The relationship between performance and grades is apparent. Students always know how many points they have accumulated and how many they need to attain the grade they seek.

The multiple-option grade contract provides an opportunity to individualize instruction and assignments. A menu is presented to the students. Essential skills or experiences may be required of all students, but in many instances alternative routes to a goal exist. Students may be able to demonstrate mastery of a skill or concept in a variety of ways.

This method of grading forces the teacher to carefully reflect on the desired course goals. In what way will students be different when they leave from when they entered this class? How will the teacher know whether students have achieved skills or mastered concepts in the course objectives?

Students are competing against themselves, not their peers. No one's grade is dependent on how well others in the class perform. The student is striving toward a preset standard of performance.

It is fair. Students know where they stand and are in control of their destiny. The contract minimizes the subjective elements of psyching out the teacher, leaving the teacher in the role of a resources person. There are no last-minute surprises. This also minimizes disputes over grades earned.

The primary purpose of grades is to communicate a level of performance. The flexible contract represents a fair and consistent method of evaluating academic accomplishment without damaging students' self-esteem.

Authentic Assessments

In 1949 the distinguished educator Ralph Tyler proposed an enlarged concept of student evaluation, encompassing other approaches besides tests and quizzes. He urged teachers to sample learning by collecting products of students' efforts throughout the year. That practice has evolved into what we now call authentic assessment, which encompasses a range of approaches including portfolio assessment, journals and logs, products, videotapes of performances, and projects.

Authentic assessments have many potential benefits. Diane Hart, in her excellent introduction to *Authentic Assessment* (1994), suggested the following benefits:

✓ Students assume an active role in the assessment process. This shift in emphasis may result in reduced test anxiety and enhanced self-esteem.

✓ Authentic assessment can be successfully used with students of varying cultural backgrounds, learning styles, and academic ability.

✓ Tasks used in authentic assessment are more interesting and reflective of students' daily lives.

✓ Ultimately, a more positive attitude toward school and learning may evolve.

✓ Authentic assessment promotes a more student-centered approach to teaching.

✓ Teachers assume a larger role in the assessment process than in traditional testing programs. This involvement is more likely to assure that the evaluation process reflects course goals and objectives.

✓ Authentic assessment provides valuable information to the teacher on student progress as well as the success of instruction.

✓ Parents will more readily understand authentic assessments than the abstract percentiles, grade equivalents, and other measures of standardized tests.

Authentic assessments are new to most students. They may be suspicious at first; years of conditioning with paper-and-pencil tests, searching for the single right answer, are not easily undone. Authentic assessments require a new way of perceiving learning and evaluation. The role of the teacher also changes. Specific assignments or tasks to be evaluated and the assessment criteria need to be clearly identified at the start.

It may be best to begin on a small scale. Introduce authentic assessments in one area (for example, on homework assignments) and progress in small steps as students adapt.

Develop a record-keeping system that works for you. Try to keep it simple, allowing students to do as much of the work as feasible.

Portfolio Assessments

Portfolio assessment is a valuable form of authentic assessment being widely adapted in schools today. Hart (1994, p. 23) defines a *portfolio* as "a container that holds evidence of an individual's skills, ideas, interests, and accomplishments." The ultimate aim in using portfolios is to develop independent, self-directed learners. Long-term portfolios provide a more accurate picture of students' specific achievements and progress and the areas that need attention.

Portfolios make it easier to develop grading schemes that emphasize assessing individual student growth rather than competition with other students. Because self-evaluation is an integral part of portfolio assessment, a highly competitive climate will prove counterproductive. Students will be reluctant to focus on their deficiencies if they believe this will put them at a disadvantage in the competition for the top grades. Often portfolios are used to supplement, not replace, traditional assessment procedures.

Here are some useful tips from veteran teachers on how to effectively incorporate portfolio assessment into student assessment:

✓ Students should develop their own portfolios, not the teacher. Students should have freedom in selecting items to include in their portfolios. Making the whole portfolio process a collaborative teacher-student effort allows the teacher to become more of a consultant to the student. The teacher functions more as a coach than a director.

✓ Any item that provides evidence of a student's achievement and growth can be included in a portfolio. Commonly used items include the following:

- Examples of written work
- Journals and logs
- Standardized inventories
- Videotapes of student performances
- Audiotapes of presentations
- Mind maps and notes
- Web pages
- Group reports
- Tests and quizzes
- Charts and graphs
- Lists of books read
- Questionnaire results
- Peer reviews
- Self-evaluations

✓ Each item in the portfolio should be dated to facilitate the evaluation of progress through the year.

✓ Typically, teachers hold periodic individual conferences with their students to review their portfolios. During this interview it is important to listen to the student's assessments of the portfolio items. The focus of the discussion should be on the products included in the portfolio. The teacher and student work together to set a limited number of objectives for future work. Strive to achieve a dialogue, not a lecture.

✓ Much of the portfolios' value derives from the students' reflection on which items are worth including in their portfolios.

✓ The portfolios may be kept in folders, file boxes, assigned drawers, or other appropriate containers. Whatever the storage container, it must be readily accessible to the student.

✓ Portfolios are especially helpful at parent conferences. Help the parent examine the portfolio, pointing out evidence of progress and areas that need improvement.

✓ Be patient. Portfolios are a new concept to most students and parents. There is a learning curve involved in adapting to the process. Experiment to determine what works, and feel free to modify as needed.

✓ In some schools students' portfolios are made available to their teachers the following year to aid in diagnosis. A few schools are experimenting with developing a permanent portfolio that follows the students throughout their total school experience. (This would be separate from their cumulative record folder.) On graduation the students would keep their portfolios.

✓ Prepare your own teaching portfolio as a means of facilitating your professional development. It also can prove invaluable in tenure assessments and future job searches. Your professional portfolio might include videotapes of successful classes, curriculum materials you have developed, course syllabi, sample lesson plans, professional development goals and objectives, workshop classes attended, published writings, student evaluations, awards, certificates, professional affiliations, principal's and supervisor's evaluations, and your teaching philosophy.

✓ A large three-ring binder is a practical way to organize your portfolio. Use tabs to indicate the various categories. You might occasionally share your portfolio with students to model the processes you are urging them to follow.

✓ With the wide availability of computer technology, many teachers encourage students to develop electronic portfolios. These multimedia presentations may incorporate student-designed Web pages, pictures, sounds, video, and text. Electronic portfolios are stored digitally on computer hard drives or on removable media such as CDs or DVDs. Tammy Worcester, an instructional technology specialist in Hutchinson, Kansas, developed a rubric to guide students in creating electronic portfolios. The rubric, which helps both teachers and students in evaluating the portfolios, can be found online at www.essdack.org/port/rubric.html.

Performance Assessments

Performance assessments require students to demonstrate mastery of a skill or procedure by performing it. Performance assessment has long been a part of the curriculum in certain courses. Directly evaluating a student's sewing, welding, dancing, typing, piano playing, or woodworking is not a new idea.

Direct assessments have the advantage of greater validity because the objective being assessed is observed directly. Indirect measures, such as a paper-and-pencil test on cooking a soufflé, may not accurately predict how well a person would perform baking a real soufflé. Performance assessments are more useful in assessing complex skills and high-level understanding.

Though not new, the trend toward including live performances and products in educational assessment schemes has grown in recent years. The growing interest in performance or authentic assessments is largely a reaction to the limitations and disparities of paper-and-pencil tests. Here are some ideas:

✓ The events or activities to be assessed are content specific and emerge from the course objectives. The tasks may be very brief or long and complex. The performance tasks may be completed individually or in groups.

✓ Problem-solving tasks related to real-world problems are often used in performance assessments. They may be embedded in a simulated or case-study scenario.

✓ Some schools have adapted a rite of passage experience, often required for graduation. These might consist of mastery exhibits, oral presentations, a résumé, essays, products, artwork, and role-plays.

✓ Classmates may be able to evaluate any performance task. It is essential to provide a checklist with the evaluative criteria listed with some form of rating scale for each criterion.

Self-Assessments

The ultimate aim of education is to produce lifelong, independent learners. An essential component of autonomous learning is the ability to assess one's own progress and deficiencies. Student self-assessment should be incorporated into every evaluation process. Its specific form may vary with the student's developmental level, but the very youngest students can begin to examine and evaluate their own behavior and accomplishments. Here are some tips:

✓ Instead of grading all assignments, allow students to correct some themselves. You may choose to spot-check these for accuracy.

✓ Share the specific evaluation criteria (or rubric) that students should employ in assessing various tasks or assignments. Provide them with criteria checksheets (or have the class generate them) that specify exactly what constitutes a good product.

✓ Provide models of successful products, answers, or performances. These might be tacked to the bulletin board, set in a display case, or played on videotape. Share the model before students begin the project. For creative activities avoid encouraging students to simply copy someone else's product. Lead students through an evaluation of the outstanding model, using the evaluation criteria to demonstrate why the model is an exemplar. To minimize peer pressure or harassment, use a previous student's work for the model rather than a current student's.

Schedule individual sessions to discuss students' progress. Have each student evaluate his or her own performance, applying specific criteria.

Thirty Alternative Assessments

The two main purposes of student assessments are to determine what students have learned and to reveal their strengths and weaknesses. Besides tests and quizzes, teachers can tap an array of alternative assessment devices. Here are thirty alternative assessment techniques that other teachers have found helpful:

Develop a portfolio.	Design a game.
Teach a class.	Draw a map.
Maintain a journal.	Present an oral report.
Design a Web page.	Conduct a debate.
Demonstrate a skill.	Make a storyboard.

Conduct an experiment.

Write a report.

Implement a group project.

Create a chart or diagram.

Make a mind map.

Present a drama.

Build a model.

Produce a musical interpretation.

Solve a real-world problem.

Produce a video.

Compile a notebook.

Write a poem.

Draw a picture.

Take photographs.

Make a slide show.

Draw up behavioral checklists.

Create a poster or bulletin board.

Record an interview.

Prepare a self-evaluation.

Create an exhibition.

For More Information

Black, P., & Wiliam, D. (1998). Inside the black box. *Phi Delta Kappan, 80*(2), 139–149.

Cohen, J. H., & Wiener, R. B. (2003). *Literacy portfolios: Improving assessment, teaching, and learning* (2nd ed.). Upper Saddle River, NJ: Merrill/Prentice Hall.

Hart, D. (1994). *Authentic assessment: A handbook for educators.* Parsippany, NJ: Dale Seymour.

Luongo-Orlando, K. (2003). *Authentic assessment: Designing performance-based tasks.* Markham, Ontario: Pembroke.

Montgomery, K. (2001). *Authentic assessment: A guide for elementary teachers.* New York: Longman.

Payne, D. A. (2003). *Applied educational assessment* (2nd ed.). Belmont, CA: Wadsworth Thomson Learning.

Rudner, L. M., & Schafer, W. D. (2002). *What teachers need to know about assessment.* Washington, DC: National Education Association.

Spinelli, C. G. (2002). *Classroom assessment for students with special needs in inclusive settings.* Upper Saddle River, NJ: Merrill/Prentice Hall.

Tombari, M. L., & Borich, G. D. (1999). *Authentic assessment in the classroom: Applications and practice.* Upper Saddle River, NJ: Merrill/Prentice Hall.

Thurlow, M. L., & Ysseldyke, J. (2002). *Including students with disabilities in assessments.* Washington, DC: National Education Association.

Tyler, R. W. (1949). *Basic principles of curriculum and instruction.* Chicago: University of Chicago.

Wilson, L. W. (2002). *Better instruction through assessment: What your students are trying to tell you.* Larchmont, NY: Eye on Education.

Guidelines for Fair Use of Copyrighted Educational Materials

Federal statute guarantees copyright protection of one's creative products. A fair use policy was established to specify conditions under which teachers and others can legally use copyrighted materials without first seeking permission of the copyright holder.

The guidelines are somewhat complex and have evolved from both law and judicial rulings. The law providing for fair use is guided by four basic assumptions:

1. The purpose and character of the use: nonprofit, educational uses are given more leeway than commercial uses. The principle of fair use permits more protection when the purpose is for criticism, research, comment, teaching, or news reporting.

2. The nature of the copyrighted work: for example, the courts have been more accepting of fair use of nonfiction than fiction.

3. The amount and substantiality of the portion used in relation to the copyrighted work as a whole: this is a murky area, for it is not an absolute guarantee of protection. Copying only a small portion of a work may still be seen as a violation if that tiny portion captures the heart of the creative work.

4. The effect of the use on the potential market for or value of the copyrighted work: How much harm is the copying likely to do to the copyright holder?

The guidelines for fair use are not always clear and absolute. From copyright laws and court interpretations, the following guidelines are generally accepted as defining the boundaries of fair use of copyrighted material:

✓ Teachers may copy one chapter from a book, provided the material copied does not exceed one thousand words or 10 percent of the total book.

✓ A single copy of a story or article, not to exceed twenty-five hundred words, from an encyclopedia or anthology may be copied.

✓ A poem no longer than 250 words may be copied.

✓ A single article from a periodical may be copied.

✓ One cartoon, photograph, or chart may be copied from a book.

✓ Copying a copyrighted computer program without permission is illegal.

✓ Video recordings of television programs may be recorded and shown to students. Programs from noneducational television channels may be shown to students twice within ten days of the original broadcast. Teachers are permitted to keep such recordings for up to forty-five days for evaluation purposes. Video recordings from educational channels may be used for seven days only.

✓ Such copying must be done on the spur of the moment at the teacher's initiative. The intent of the fair use policy is to permit limited use of instructional items for which there is not time to request permission from the copyright holder.

✓ The same item may not be repeatedly copied year after year.

✓ Students may not be charged for the costs of copying the item(s).

✓ Only one item by the same author may be legitimately copied.

✓ Only nine individual items may be copied per semester or term.

✓ Consumable items, such as workbooks or standardized tests, may not be copied.

Seeking Permission to Use Copyrighted Material

In soliciting permission to copy items, it is essential to contact the actual copyright holder, which may not necessarily be the author. Most periodicals include information on how to request such permission. For book publishers or other sources, start with their Web site to identify the appropriate contact information. A reference librarian can be very helpful for locating names and addresses.

The safest practice is to get permission from the copyright owner before using copyrighted materials.

Public Domain

Items not protected by copyright are considered to be in the public domain. Anyone is free to use such items without permission. Works that were never copyrighted or for which the copyright has expired will generally fall under public domain. Facts, ideas, slogans, and titles cannot be copyrighted. Government documents generally are not copyrighted, unless an independent contractor authored the item and may still hold the copyright.

Generally, items published before 1923 are in the public domain. For a list of songs now in the public domain, check the Public Domain Info Web site at www.pdinfo.com/.

Protecting Your Creative Works

Add the following copyright notice on all items you create and want to protect:

Copyright © 2005 (your name)
All Rights Reserved

It is probably wise to insert this copyright notice on any Web pages you design, as well as your original worksheets, study guides, stories, poems, or other creative works. Technically, copyright protection is provided immediately and automatically when you add the copyright notice to your creative work. However, by registering your work with the U.S. Copyright Office, you gain the right to sue in case of copyright infringement. The current fee for registering a copyright is $30. You can download the necessary forms from the U.S. Copyright Office at www.copyright.gov/.

Sample Letter Requesting Permission to Copy

Rebecca Cabaniss
Chenoa High School
1330 Hazel Avenue
Bowling Green, OH 43402

October 22, 2004

Permissions Department
Popular Culture Magazine
60 Beaumont Drive
San Francisco, CA 94103

Greetings,

   I teach U.S. History at Chenoa High School. I am requesting permission to photocopy and distribute to my classes the article titled "Fads and Fancies of the 1920s" by Charley Rogers. The article appeared on pages 40–43 in the April 2004 issue of your magazine. I have approximately sixty students in my classes each year. This article would provide valuable supplemental information for my class and would likely prove valuable in capturing my students' interest.

   If permission is granted, please sign below and return this letter to me in the enclosed self-addressed stamped envelope.

Sincerely,

Rebecca Cabaniss

Permission is granted to Rebecca Cabaniss to copy and distribute the above article for use in her U.S. history class.

_____   _____
Date   Signature

Assignment Record

Name _____

Week _____

Subject	Monday	Tuesday	Wednesday	Thursday	Friday

Skill Assessment Form

Name _____ Date _____

Subject _____

Teacher _____

Skill	Yes	No	No Evidence	Comments

Test tomorrow

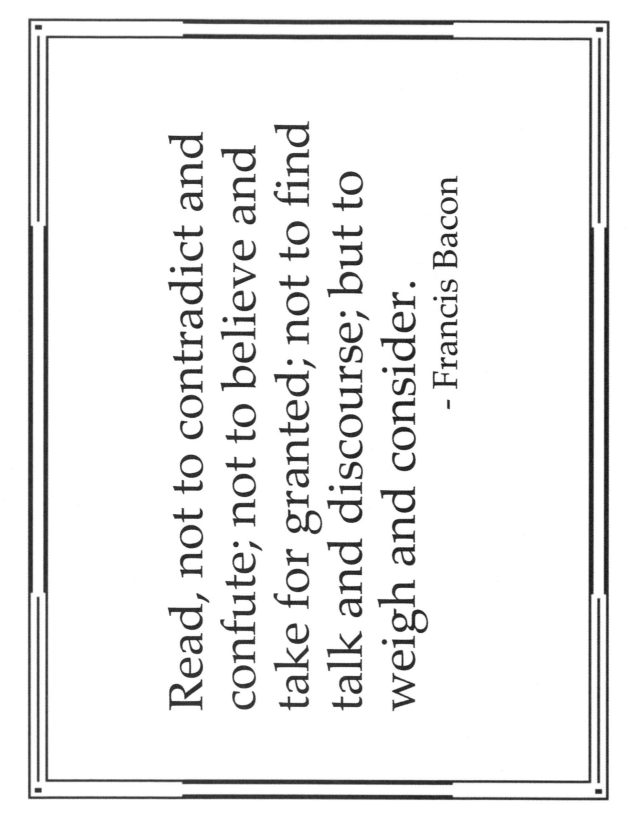

Read, not to contradict and confute; not to believe and take for granted; not to find talk and discourse; but to weigh and consider.

- Francis Bacon

knowledge is a treasure,

but practice is the key.

- English proverb

Homework Pass

Good for one
homework assignment.

_____
Student's signature

Homework Pass

Good for one
homework assignment.

_____
Student's signature

Homework Pass

Good for one
homework assignment.

_____
Student's signature

Performance Record

Class _____ Term/Year _____ Teacher _____

Name																						

Storyboarding Form

Chapter Three

Alternatives to Lecturing

Because most teachers were taught primarily by lecture, the natural response is for them to choose being the proverbial talking head in front of the class as the favored mode of instruction. Despite a growing body of research evidence demonstrating lecture's limitations as the primary instructional strategy, many persist in the practice. Head nods and whiplash are pervasive in these classrooms as students struggle to stay awake. While lecture can be useful in certain situations, many other more valuable teaching tools are available. The most outstanding teachers have a variety of instructional techniques in their repertoire.

Twenty-two Hot Tips for Asking Effective Questions

 A substantial body of research affirms that questions are still the most frequently used teaching tool. However, not all questions are created equally. Some are highly effective; others can be useless or even harmful. There is an art and a science to effective questioning. Here are twenty tips gleaned from outstanding teachers and research for improving teachers' use of questions:

1. As part of lesson planning, list the processing questions to ask. Effectively worded questions can make a good lesson superb. Develop a logical sequence and strive for clarity in your questions.

2. Challenge the whole class to mentally respond. When you ask a question, pause and then select the person to respond. Choosing the answerer randomly provides the opportunity for even the shyest child to become involved in the class discussion. The teacher's encouragement and support can reduce anxiety and make the lesson a successful learning experience. It is best for the teacher to build on small successes by asking open-ended questions rather than factual-recall questions. Unfortunately, researchers have observed that teachers ask low-ability students fewer questions and praise them less often when they respond correctly.

3. Wait at least five seconds after directing a question before saying anything else. Most teachers allow their students fewer than two seconds on the average to answer a question. Permitting the student a reasonable amount of thinking time is essential, especially if you are asking for more than recall of a single fact. The length and quality of students' responses increase when teachers allow increased wait time.

4. Use closed-ended questions when you are seeking information, facts, or a commitment. In attempting to assess student mastery of specific facts, the closed-ended question is most effective. Generally, avoid asking yes-or-no questions in your lessons.

5. Open-ended questions (beginning with *how, why,* or *what*) usually allow greater latitude in the student's response with a variety of possible answers (How can air pollution be decreased? Why do people change careers?). A single correct answer does not exist. Such open-ended

questions are most crucial in stimulating students' creative abilities and developing higher-level cognitive processes such as evaluation, hypothesis generation, analysis, and synthesis.

6. What the teacher does after a student responds to a question significantly influences the group discussion process. Students who are ridiculed or intimidated will become increasingly reluctant to participate in discussions. No constructive end can come from putdowns, whether the teacher or students initiate them. People, including students, have a right to make mistakes and a responsibility to learn from those mistakes. A positive class climate is attained when students feel accepted and sufficiently open to take risks—even at the price of sometimes being incorrect.

7. Encourage students to respond in some fashion, even if they aren't completely sure of the answer. Rephrase the question or provide cues, but don't just accept "I don't know."

8. Probe students' responses for clarification and to stimulate further reflection. "Why?" is an effective probing question to force the student to a deeper level of thought.

9. Avoid multiple questions. Barraging students with a series of questions often only confuses them and obscures the lesson's purpose. One question at a time posed clearly and concisely will more likely yield a clear and concise response.

10. Effective teachers keep a balance between calling on volunteers and nonvolunteers. Particularly when it is likely many nonvolunteers know the answer, calling on a nonvolunteer is better.

11. Occasionally have all students jot down an answer to your question before calling on one person to share the answer.

12. For variety have all students share their answer to your question in pairs or small groups. Call on a few groups to report their best answers to the whole class.

13. Difficult and challenging questions seem most effective for classes of high-ability students. A mixture of higher-order and lower-cognitive-level questions seems to work best with mixed-ability classes. Low-level cognitive questions seem to work best when teaching basic skills. Effective teachers ask a combination of both low- and high-level cognitive questions.

14. Strive to ask questions that yield a high level of correct responses; research suggests around 70 percent is the optimal success level. Some evidence suggests that the most successful strategy is to begin a lesson with lower-level questions and to use higher-level questions as the lesson progresses.

15. Learn to allow students to talk more. Typically, teacher-talk consumes 70 percent of class discussion time.

16. Acknowledge correct responses, but be specific in your praise. What exactly was appropriate or creative about the student's response? Avoid

the cliché "Very good" in response to every question. Save genuine praise for the response that is truly exceptional.

17. Occasionally ask the student to repeat the question before replying. This assures students are listening and understand the question.

18. Give students an equal opportunity to respond to your questions. Research shows that students down the middle and across the front of the classroom get called on more frequently. Also, higher-ability students tend to get called on more than lower-ability students when they raise their hands.

19. Research supports permitting call-out answers with students of a lower socioeconomic level, particularly at the elementary level. With classes at a higher socioeconomic level, students should be acknowledged before giving their answers. In the latter students are typically more assertive and eager to respond, creating more chaos. Without having to seek permission to speak, lower-ability students are more likely to contribute. A risk of permitting call-out responses is that a few students may dominate class discussions.

20. Don't accept an obviously incorrect answer. Gently yet clearly help identify a more appropriate response. Acknowledge if an answer is partially correct, but solicit a more complete response from the class before continuing. Have the student reflect a bit more on the question or your rephrasing of it. Don't immediately call on someone else.

21. Encourage students to ask questions, but don't just do it by saying, "Any questions?" Have each student write down one question, or have them pair up to make a list of questions related to the topic. Real learning is most likely when students are genuinely curious and enthusiastically generate their own questions. Encourage them to ask questions of each other as well as of you.

22. Be wary of asking *why* questions to confront misbehavior. When we ask *why* questions in reference to a person's behavior ("Why did you do that?"), we are generally seeking an argument, not an explanation. *Why* questions often put the student on the defensive, yielding a wisecracking defensive answer. A question such as "What are you doing?" is more effective in focusing the student's attention on his or her misbehavior.

Question and Answer

Questions are a most valuable instructional skill when used effectively. The question-and-answer method can be useful in a variety of ways in the classroom. Most commonly, teachers ask questions and students answer. The Socratic method of stimulating the creative or critical thinking in students through skillful questioning can be especially valuable. On a lower level, it may take the form of rote drill, with the teacher firing a barrage of questions around the room and soliciting answers. This form of question and answer is most effective when the content is fairly concrete. See the previous section on questions for tips on the effective use of teacher questions.

The question-and-answer method may also consist of students asking the teacher questions. The least effective method of doing this is to simply ask, "Are there any questions?" especially at the very end of the class period. Most students are hesitant to openly ask questions in front of the whole class, even if they have some in mind. One useful technique is to have each student jot down one question about the topic on a sheet of paper. Then you might collect them and respond to a few. Another possibility is to have small groups generate a list of two to five questions to submit. Rather than answering these questions, direct some of them back to the class, to consider either in a whole-group discussion or in small groups.

In facilitating question-and-answer sessions, try to stand across the room from the student speaking. This forces the student to speak in a louder voice, allowing everyone else to hear him or her. This will require you to keep moving during the discussion but will pay off in better interaction. As you call on students, you might nonchalantly pace toward the opposite side of the room. A secondary benefit of maximizing your distance from the student speaking is that it broadens your range of vision, allowing you to better monitor the rest of the class.

Brainstorming

Brainstorming, first introduced by Alex Osborne in the advertising industry, can be an effective technique for stimulating creative thinking in groups. It can be incorporated into almost any lesson. Brainstorms lasting one to four minutes are a quick and effective means of energizing a group when their interest wanes. Some advance training on the principles of effective brainstorming is essential. Consider displaying the four basic rules of brainstorming as a poster or transparency. When you first explain brainstorming, discuss the following rules:

1. Generate as many ideas as possible. The more ideas a group has, the greater the probability of discovering a good one. The emphasis for now is on quantity, not quality.

2. Delay evaluation. Later the group will evaluate its ideas, but to nurture free and open brainstorming, students must not be worried about whether others are going to criticize their ideas. Innovation only occurs when individuals are able to see with fresh eyes, stripping away the tunnel vision that usually limits creativity. Positive evaluation is also prohibited, as those not receiving positive comments from the group will assume their ideas are inferior. Record each idea without evaluation. Introduce the idea of creativity crunchers (see page 142) that we commonly use to squelch each other's creativity.

3. Encourage wild, zany, half-baked ideas. Even if it doesn't quite make sense now, a suggestion might be the stimulus for a great idea. Record it; later it may blossom into something worthwhile.

4. Build on others' ideas. Listen to their ideas and use them to stimulate additional ideas.

Creativity Crunchers

No way!

Don't be silly.

It's too risky.

We tried that before.

It would take too long.

The administration will never go along.

We don't have the money.

Let's form a committee.

You've got to be kidding!

It will never work.

Yes, but . . .

They'll never let us.

It'll never sell.

That's not our problem.

The time isn't right.

The main office won't let us.

It's too new.

Put it in writing.

We'll discuss it later.

Why do it now?

It will never be approved.

What for?

Nobody needs it.

It's against our rules.

The union won't go along.

It's too faddish.

What will the community think?

Let's table it for now.

Don't rush into things.

It's politically unwise.

Too radical.

We're too small.

It's too much work.

Let's wait and see.

Let me think about it.

What good will it do?

We already have enough problems.

It'll never happen.

You're dreaming.

It's a nice theory, but . . .

You don't understand.

We're too big for that to work here.

Why?

Maybe someday.

It'll never fly.

They'll laugh at us.

We have too many obstacles.

It's reactionary.

We don't have proof it will work.

It will offend someone.

It's too late.

It's not our policy.

Are you serious?

We need more data.

It didn't work the last time.

Costs too much.

Baloney!

Someone else should do it.

They aren't ready for it yet.

There's no use trying.

It's not our job.

Dud!

Nobody cares anyway.

We don't have enough details.

Don't you think there is a better way?

Too corny.

It's too soon.

That's not new.

It's illogical.

Get practical.

Here we go again.

That's fine, but . . .

Whose idea is that?

It's too simple.

It's too complicated.

That's just plain dumb.

Each group should have a scribe record on paper—ideally on a large sheet of newsprint for all to see—all ideas as the group generates them. After the initial brainstorming exercise, you might assign the group the task of discussing their ideas and selecting (and possibly ranking) their top five or ten solutions.

When you first introduce brainstorming, give your students an opportunity to practice applying it to unusual, interesting, and novel problems; for example, generating lists of unusual uses for common items. You might even hold up an object when assigning the brainstorming task. Here are some possibilities of objects for brainstorming unusual uses:

Chalkboard eraser	Cafeteria tray
Box of unmatched socks	Wallpaper sample book
Softball	Carpet scraps
Used auto tires	Empty paper towel tubes
Soda straws	Used CDs
Pie pan	Plastic milk jugs

Another fun activity for practicing brainstorming is to encourage students to project what would likely happen if some major change occurred. How would the world be different? Just suppose any of the following were true:

✓ All people looked the same.
✓ Everyone had the same voice.
✓ We no longer had trees.
✓ Televisions were banned.
✓ Men could not vote.
✓ Everyone was given a million dollars.
✓ There were no telephones.
✓ We had no thumbs.
✓ There were no traffic laws.

Curriculum expert and teacher trainer Cerylle Moffett suggests an interesting adaptation of the brainstorming technique that she calls carousel brainstorming. Several topics are listed on newsprint and posted on the wall around the room. The class is divided into an equal number of groups. Each group gathers at a different post. Give the groups three to five minutes to brainstorm and record their ideas on the topic written on the sheet in front of them. When you call time, everyone rotates clockwise around the room to the next post. Give them a set time limit to read the previous group's ideas and continue the brainstorming process, recording their ideas on the sheet. Repeat the cycle until each group has considered each of the ideas posted.

FIG. A
(25 WATTS)

FIG. B
(10,000 VOLTS)

BRIGHT IDEA VS. BRAINSTORM.

Another technique, sometimes called rapid brainstorming, involves posting a variety of topics on separate sheets of newsprint displayed around the room. A group is assigned to each topic and gathers in front of its sheet of newsprint. All groups brainstorm all the responses they can in two to three minutes. Each group then shares its ideas with the whole class. Another variation is to have each group rotate to the next topic and spend two minutes trying to add ideas to those already posted. Continue rotating until each group has brainstormed on each topic. Another variation is to have the groups remain seated in their groups and to pass the sheets of paper around the groups.

Another idea from Cerylle Moffett is the mail call. This technique works well in considering several related problems. Break the class into groups of four or five. Identify several problems for brainstorming. Each group needs a set of envelopes with each problem written on a different envelope. Place all the envelopes in the center of a table. Each person in the small group writes one idea on a note card and puts it in each envelope. Use newsprint or the chalkboard to record the various brainstormed solutions generated in each group.

One more option: instruct students to silently brainstorm their ideas for a minute. Each student then jots down his or her ideas on a sheet of paper. Then, in the small brainstorming groups, each shares two ideas. Afterward the group follows normal brainstorming procedures.

Brainwriting

Brainwriting is a variation on the brainstorming technique. It assures that everyone has an opportunity to participate and minimizes the effects of premature evaluation of each other's ideas. A topic or problem is assigned to a small group (four to seven members), and each student is given three note cards (or small sheets of paper). Each student writes a different idea about the problem on each card, then places the cards facedown on a table or desk. When all cards are facedown, the students take turns drawing one card and reading it aloud. It is then placed face up on the table for all to see. As similar ideas are read, they are grouped into clusters. After all the groups have read and grouped their ideas, they can be shared with the whole class and recorded on the board or newsprint. This is a useful technique for generating class rules at the beginning of the school year.

The card swap is an extension of brainwriting: each individual passes one of their cards to the person on their right. Each recipient reads the card they received. Next they can be instructed to do one of several things with the card:

✓ Allow the card to stimulate a new idea.

✓ Modify in some fashion the idea on the received card.

✓ Simply pass the card on around the circle.

List Making

List making can be combined with several other techniques, such as brainstorming or brainwriting. It may be done individually, in small groups, or as a whole class. Here are some ideas for possible lists:

✓ Causes (economic depressions, the Civil War, fights, fires, success, trust, decay of organic matter, substance abuse, the civil rights movement)

✓ Effects, real or projected (of chemical fertilizers, unemployment, alcohol abuse, global warming, soil erosion, television, decline of communism)

✓ Characteristics or traits (properties of organic matter, components of a healthy diet, parts of an airplane, forms of mental illness)

✓ Criteria for judgments (selecting a college; choosing a friend, a good novel, a successful employee)

✓ Members of sets (countries of Africa, religions of the world, elements of the periodic table, nineteenth-century American authors, species of birds, proverbs)

✓ Solutions (for decreasing crime, lengthening our life span)

Lists are easily incorporated into consensus-building activities. Students are assigned the task of first individually ranking the list in priority. Afterward small groups discuss their lists and attempt to arrive at a final group ranking. It is important to prohibit simple voting; students must present and negotiate the issues.

For examples of how lists can be used in various classes, see the following: Ron Partin, *Social Studies Teacher's Book of Lists* (Jossey-Bass, 2003); Helen D. Hume, *The Art Teacher's Book of Lists* (Jossey-Bass, 1998); *or* Marian D. Milliken, *The Physical Education Teacher's Book of Lists* (Parker Publishing, 2001).

Class Discussions

Class discussion is a useful strategy for stimulating critical thinking and encouraging students to reexamine their attitudes. For a discussion to be effective, students must possess some general information about the topic under consideration, unless you are using the discussion as an advance organizer to introduce a new topic.

The teacher's role in a class discussion is as a moderator. The teacher poses the initial question, facilitates thinking with follow-up questions, and assures that everyone has an opportunity to participate. He or she also introduces bits of information, but generally it is best if the teacher refrains from offering an opinion. If the teacher does choose to take a position, it is probably wise to wait until the end. It is essential that the teacher merely facilitate, not dominate, the discussion. Here's how:

✓ Whole-class discussion is best facilitated with the group seated in a large circle or a horseshoe. If they can see each other, students are more likely to respond to each other rather than engage in a series of successive dialogues with the teacher.

✓ Do give some forethought to the stimulating questions you will ask to promote the discussion. It is best to write them down. Overall, the less you have to participate to keep the discussion going, the better. It is also essential to establish the procedures for taking turns speaking. Does the student need to be acknowledged by the teacher before speaking?

✓ Begin the discussion by introducing the topic. Students need to be aware of the discussion's general theme and have a sense of its purpose. A couple of sentences and an opening question may suffice.

✓ Discussions can serve a variety of purposes. They may focus on examining a problem, analyzing its causes, effects, and potential solutions. A discussion may be used to debrief an activity such as a simulation, role-play, or experiment. Discussion may focus on predicting some future event or explaining some past phenomenon. To meet any of these aims, the discussion must progress beyond the knowledge level. Higher-level cognitive questions must be asked.

✓ The class may be broken into small groups to stimulate discussion. Each group might discuss the same topic or have separate topics to consider. It is helpful to provide the groups a written list of questions, either as a handout or displayed on the overhead projector or chalkboard. Without a clear purpose and a task for which students will be accountable, the discussion will quickly degenerate into a conversation. It is usually a good idea to appoint a group leader who is responsible for keeping everyone on task, recording the group's ideas, and reporting back to the whole class. (See the handouts section: Strategies for Selecting Group Leaders.)

✓ To facilitate only one person talking at a time, bring a sponge ball or other soft object to class. In order to speak, a student must be in possession of the ball. When a student wants to contribute to the discussion, he or she must raise a hand. The individual may speak only after he or she receives the ball from the previous student.

✓ Avoid overincluding high-ability students in an effort to keep the discussion going.

✓ A tactic teachers commonly use to prevent several persons from dominating the discussion is to allocate each student three or four poker chips or other tokens. Each time

a student makes a comment, he or she must turn in one token to the teacher. Once their chips are gone, they may add no more comments to the discussion. Another way to control the monopolizer is to first break students into small groups and designate a reporter from each group to share the group's conclusions. Another option is to appoint the monopolizer to a role that inhibits his or her participation; for example, as a silent observer or recorder.

✓ Don't allow the discussion to deteriorate into a shouting match. Emphasize the value of having a free and open discussion and supporting positions with facts. Emphasize that reasonable people may sometimes interpret those facts differently.

✓ End the discussion before it begins to stagnate. Do something different: have each student take one minute to write an answer to a question, introducing some relevant facts.

✓ Provide some structure to the discussion so that it is not too divergent. It must have focus to encourage serious reflection. An exchange of unexamined opinions is of minimal educational value.

✓ Provide closure to the discussion. One way is for the teacher or volunteers to summarize the main points emphasized. Another is to have students reflect and/or write about how the discussion may have changed their view of the topic.

✓ Thank students for their contributions. It generally works best to reinforce but not grade participation in discussions.

✓ Provide a transition to the lesson's next phase. Point out how the discussion fits into the overall lesson objectives.

✓ Occasionally, it is helpful to lead a postdiscussion review of the discussion's process and techniques. Encourage the class to analyze what went well and which areas might need improvement. Encourage reflection on the level of thinking that occurred during the discussion. Sometimes appointed observers can provide feedback on the group dynamics.

Fishbowls

A fishbowl consists of a small group that discusses an issue while seated in the center of the classroom, with the rest of the class seated in a larger circle around the fishbowl. This technique is most effective for topics in which students have a lot of interest and some disagreement exists. Often an empty chair is included in the fishbowl. Anyone in the outer circle who wishes to inject a comment may temporarily join the fishbowl. The student contributes a comment, then returns to his or her seat on the outside, leaving the chair vacant for the next volunteer.

It works best to prepare a list of questions in advance to structure the discussion and keep it on task. It is essential that those in the outer circle remain quiet during the discussion. They may talk only if they join the fishbowl in the empty chair. Observers should take notes during the discussion (for example, recording the topic's pros and cons). One option is to have the fishbowl participants and observers reverse roles and continue the discussion. Allow time for debriefing at the end of the discussion. The fishbowl technique can also be used as a lesson in effective group processes.

Another option is to break the class into several smaller discussion groups to examine a controversial topic. Each group then selects a representative to participate in the fishbowl and express his or her group's concerns on the issue. After fifteen or twenty minutes of discussion, the representatives might rejoin their groups for feedback and new "ammunition" to share once they rejoin the fishbowl.

Artwork

Most students still love to draw, especially if they are not being evaluated. For variety, experiment with art media in your regular classes. Crayons, colored markers, colored pencils, and chalk seem to immediately grab students' attention. Students who otherwise find self-expression difficult may be able to communicate deeper ideas and feelings through artistic media. Art has been used successfully to build students' self-esteem and self-confidence. The following art tips can tap all students' creativity and imagination.

✓ Experiment with inserting a five-minute art activity into a lesson. Rather than having students write out their responses to a discussion question, have them draw a depiction of their answer. It provides a reenergizing break from the left-brain focus of most lessons.

✓ Added motivation comes with the use of scented markers (Mr. Sketch is one brand) available at most office supply stores.

✓ Play music in the background while students are doing their artwork to further stimulate creativity.

✓ Encourage students to draw in their journals to represent some of their ideas. Have them take a sketchpad along on field trips to record their observations. Drawing helps students focus their attention and process their perceptions.

✓ Drawing murals cooperatively can enrich students' reflection about the academic content while developing social skills.

✓ Discourage competition among students in their artwork. Be cautious of effusive public praise for obviously talented students. It may discourage less artistically inclined students. Private praise is probably much more effective.

✓ Have students draw a vertical and a horizontal line to create four equal boxes. In each box the students draw a different item in response to four different questions about the topic being studied in class. (For example, it could be four causes of the Civil War, four kinds of clouds, four effects of inflation, or four career possibilities). Or each box might be used to address a different question. (For example, the first box might show a cause of some problem being studied. An effect and two possible solutions might be drawn in the other three boxes.)

✓ Keep the directions to any art assignments general. Let the students use their creativity and imaginations to construct their vision of reality. Give them as much freedom as possible to choose the form and media they believe best expresses their ideas.

✓ Encourage the use of color by having assorted markers, pens, crayons, or pencils available for students to use if they do not provide their own.

✓ Incorporate the construction of advertisements into your lessons. Ads may take the form of posters or magazine layouts. Their ads should express some relevant concept related to the topic being studied.

✓ Collages can be adapted to a great many purposes in classes other than art. Though most art collages consist of pictures and captions clipped from magazines, most any item that can be pasted to a piece of poster board can be included in a collage (for example, photographs, fabrics, drawings, leaves, buttons, ribbon).

✓ Individuals or groups can compose collages. Ask students to bring in a variety of old magazines as sources of pictures to cut out. Have students attach titles to their collages.

✓ Check out Betty Edwards's excellent book *Drawing on the Right Side of the Brain* (J.P. Tarcher Publishers, 1989) for many practical ideas for incorporating drawing into your lesson plans.

Music

Music has many uses in the classroom. It can be used in the background to set the mood for a lesson; to energize, relax, inspire, cue transitions, focus attention, reinforce a theme; or for fun. Music affects our physiological systems, our emotions, and our spirit. Music can influence your students' mood and behaviors.

> *When words leave off, music begins.*
>
> **—Heinrich Heine**

It is generally best to select instrumental music, although vocals might be used during breaks or if the lyrics pertain specifically to the lesson. Pay special attention to the musical selection's beat. A march is hardly going to soothe and calm a group of hyperactive, rowdy students. Baroque and soft New Age instrumentals work well as background music during individual seatwork. Here are some ideas:

✓ Special effects or emphasis can be achieved by using themes from famous movies or television programs. (The theme from *Jeopardy* during a spelling bee or oral quiz lightens the atmosphere.) Continually be aware of the purpose you want to achieve with each musical selection.

✓ Incorporate humorous novelty songs into your lessons. This is especially effective if the song's theme relates to the topic under study.

✓ Put a part of your lesson to music. If you are bold, try singing an announcement or assignment to a rap beat.

✓ Allow students to bring a favorite tape to play before class begins or during lab or project work. The privilege of selecting the tape for the day can be used as a reward for outstanding performance.

✓ If you play a musical instrument, bring it to class and feature a brief selection as part of the lesson or use it as a novelty reward. It reinforces the value of music.

✓ Some teachers play music before class. Stopping the music is a cue that it is time to begin class.

Be sure to cue your recordings at the appropriate spot and adjust the volume before class begins. You'll lose momentum and effect if you have to waste class time searching for the segment you want to use. Have them out of their boxes and clearly labeled and ready to use.

Guided Imagery

Guided imagery can be used effectively to stimulate students' problem solving, goal setting, and hypothesis building in studying complex issues. In affective education guided imagery is used to help students explore their feelings and attitudes. The guided imagery lesson aims to immerse the students in the subject. Guided imagery is the next best thing to being there. It is an active, not passive, instructional strategy.

Careful thought must be given to the topic chosen as the focus of a guided imagery. Some teachers employ guided imagery to help students focus on a reading assignment. For example, in teaching about the drafting of the Constitution, a teacher might lead the students through a visualization of the scene in Philadelphia, with vivid descriptions of the people present, the debates, the weather, and other details, setting the stage for the drama to unfold. The students' prior experience and knowledge about the topic must be considered in designing the lesson. It may be necessary to present some background information before introducing the imagery. The questions to be included must be given careful thought. Here are ideas to help you use guided imagery:

✓ It is best to allow students the option of not participating in fantasy trips or visualizations. Though this is rare, some students might not wish to participate for religious or emotional reasons. Don't make a big fuss, but avoid forcing student participation. Provide an alternate assignment, perhaps a written theme on the same topic.

✓ When you introduce the visualization, make clear that no one will be forced to share their thoughts or feelings afterward. In debriefing, call only on volunteers for responses.

✓ Introduce the visualization by encouraging students to make themselves comfortable, to take several deep breaths, and to relax. You may choose to turn the lights off. Some may prefer to close their eyes to eliminate distractions, but do not insist that they do so.

✓ Carefully script the visualization the first time. Pause after each line to allow time for students to create their fantasy response.

✓ Design visualizations that encourage students to use all their senses as they progress through the visualization. For example, "What sounds are outstanding?" Or "What do you see from the top of the hill?"

✓ In debriefing the visualization, invite students to share whatever observations they choose. This might be perceived as safer if done in pairs or small groups. A large-group discussion might then elicit any generalizations or conclusions.

To imagine is everything.

—**Anatole France**
(***The Crime of Sylvester Bonnard,*** **1881**)

Journal Keeping

A valuable instructional device for encouraging reflection, review, application, and creativity is the student journal. As most commonly used, each student periodically makes entries into a spiral-bound notebook, which is occasionally handed in to the teacher. The teacher scans the journals, making relevant comments in the margin or a separate column. Student journals can serve a variety of purposes: to improve writing skills, to remind the student of important things to remember, or to strengthen self-reflection skills. The following will help you get started:

✓ Learning logs or journals function as course diaries. Students enter summaries of the major content they have been studying. These might be major points from class lectures, formulas and other important pieces of information they need to memorize, or procedures and directions. It might be kept in the form of a mind map.

✓ Reflective journals serve as a medium to stimulate and record thinking about what students experience in the class. This form of response journal may be turned in to the teacher and returned with the teacher's comments, creating a teacher-student dialogue. Each can ask the other questions.

✓ Journals can also serve as logs, helping the students and the teacher track the books read, experiments completed, Web quests completed, or use learning activities done or objectives attained. Journals can also help students monitor their progress.

✓ Experiment with assigning specialized journals, such as a conflict journal. Students record instances in which they encounter conflict in their daily lives, their response to the conflict, the outcome of their reactions, and other options they might have taken. Other topics for specialized journals might include stress, use of time, successes, anger, joys, positive and negative consequences, nutrition, or exercise. Of course, the journal assignments should be relevant to the subject you are teaching.

✓ Journals can also function as field notebooks for recording observations of processes or phenomena you want students to examine over time. Students can keep journals on weather patterns, wildlife observed, progress of experiments, social or psychological observations (for example, violence on television, smiles), child development, political developments, books read, or field trips.

✓ Provide instructions as to the format of students' journals. What medium (spiral notebook, notebook paper, computer disk) may be used? How frequently will they be writing in it? What is the minimum amount they should write? When will the teacher read it?

✓ When you give a journal-keeping assignment, be sure to explicitly describe its purpose. Journals are frequently used as a learning log to record new knowledge gained each day. This is especially valuable with experiential learning.

✓ When emotions become aroused during heated discussions, it is often helpful to call a time-out for students to reflect on the issue at hand and enter their thoughts and feelings into their journals. This encourages them to summarize the main points on both sides of an issue.

✓ Another strategy for using journals is to have students list three important points or ideas from the day's class that they think will be most helpful to them. You might then encourage them to share these thoughts in pairs or seek volunteers from the class at large. This facilitates review of the day's lesson and encourages application.

✓ To stimulate students' journal writing, ask them to answer specific, open-ended questions in their journals.

✓ As part of introducing a new topic, particularly ones of natural interest to students, ask each student to enter in their journals two or three questions they hope the upcoming lesson will answer. Near the end of the lesson, you might ask students to check their list of questions for any that remain unanswered.

✓ Have students assume a role related to the topic being studied (for example, antebellum plantation owner, colonial merchant, entrepreneur, union organizer, Underground Railroad conductor, or explorer). Students make their journal entries as though they were the person in the role they are assuming. Or the student might be assigned to study a real person, such as George Washington, Clara Barton, Eleanor Roosevelt, Madame Curie, or Albert Schweitzer. Students are to make their journal observations as they believe their assigned persons would have responded.

✓ Some teachers have successfully employed the use of team journals. Teams of five students are each given a journal. Periodically the teacher assigns a topic for the class to consider and enter their reactions in their team journal. The team leader, a rotating position, writes the first entry in the journal. Other members are then responsible for adding their comments. Each student, except for the team leader, is supposed to comment on at least one previous entry. The teacher then reads each journal and adds an entry. It encourages students to write regularly and to assume a position and defend it.

✓ Consider having students keep their journals on computer files that they can exchange and forward to the teacher.

Field Trips

The entire world can be a learning resource if a knowledgeable guide shows the way. Well-planned, organized field trips can be one of the most valuable ways of helping students apply their textbook and classroom learning to the greater world. Here are twenty-three practical tips for making field trips into profitable learning experiences:

1. Any class trip should have a meaningful purpose that is explicitly communicated to the students. It is also essential to communicate that purpose to any off-site presenters and any parents or others serving as chaperones. Any field trip should have a legitimate aim, directly related to the subject being taught. A class trip cannot be justified if its sole purpose is to entertain or fill time. It should enrich and expand your regular curriculum.

2. Clarify your school's procedures and requirements before you begin planning a field trip. Will parental permission be required? If so, is there a special form you must use? (See the handouts at the end of this chapter: Field Trip Permission Form.) When and where must the permission forms be filed? Will chaperones be required? How many? Always notify your principal in writing.

3. How will transportation be provided? Going in buses is generally preferable to traveling in private automobiles. It is simpler, easier to control students' behavior, and less likely to create liability issues.

4. If chaperones will be accompanying you on the trip, be sure to communicate your expectations of the role they should take. It is best to send a note to each chaperone detailing when they should be at school and exactly what you expect of them. Are they only to monitor student behaviors? Which behaviors are unacceptable? How should they handle rowdy students? Will the chaperones have a role in the learning associated with the trip?

5. Send information to the parents about your field trip, describing its purpose and specifics of the travel arrangements. If you are seeking parents to accompany the class, be sure to give ample notice (ideally, at least two weeks). Are any costs involved? If so, how are they to be handled? Will lunch be provided?

6. Be sure the proposed visit is age-appropriate for your students. Is this site used to having visits from students? Will a guided tour be provided? If so, are the hosts used to talking to students of this age group? Will cameras be allowed? Is any special attire required?

7. Strive to make the field trip an active learning experience. The more hands-on the experience is, the better. If it is a guided tour (for example, a factory or battlefield), provide students (either individually or in cooperative groups) specific tasks to accomplish during the visit. The class should in some way be accountable for learning that occurs during the trip. This can be in the form of word puzzles, word scavenger hunts, or a study guide to help direct their attention and reflection. It is often useful to break the class into learning teams, each with a different task to accomplish. The next school day, they can exchange their insights and completed tasks.

8. As much as possible, the field trip should be integrated into a sequence of planned class activities. Before the trip prepare the students with background information about the field trip's topic. The day after the visit, allow class time for reflection and discussion of the experience. Plan a lesson that allows them to apply this new knowledge.

9. Be reasonable about what you can accomplish on a field trip. Often teachers try to accomplish too much, especially if it is a daylong trip. Once students become bored or tired, less learning and more misbehavior are likely.

10. Be sure to confirm the field trip a couple days ahead of time. Contact the site, chaperones, transportation providers, and your principal.

11. Try to arrange for parents to meet with you fifteen minutes before the group is to leave so that you can share any last-minute details and coordinate efforts. It's generally a good idea to have one more chaperone than you think you'll need. If parents will be driving, be sure to give each one a map of the route to take.

12. Adequately prepare your students before the day of the trip. Clarify your expectations for both appropriate behavior and any learning assignments associated with the trip. Are there special dress requirements? Will seats be assigned on the bus? What should students do if they get separated from the group?

13. If possible, give your planned trip a dry run. How long will it take to get there? Try to meet any guides or presenters who will be leading your group. Will eating arrangements need to be made en route or on-site? Make note of details, such as locations of bathrooms, parking, and so on. Is the site fully accessible for any students with disabilities? Determine precisely where and when you are to arrive with your group. How will any admission fees be handled?

14. Count noses before you leave the school and again when you meet to return home.

15. With older students identify a landmark where all should meet at a set time if they become separated.

16. Carry a notepad or cards with you on the field trip. During the excursion jot down ideas for process questions or points to emphasize back in the classroom.

17. It is probably wise to take along a first-aid kit, tape, safety pins, needle and thread, tissues, and coins or a cell phone for emergency phone calls. On a long bus ride, carry a couple of bags for students who experience motion sickness—and hope you don't need them.

18. Be sure to make a provision for a restroom stop during the field trip.

19. Take along a digital camera to take shots that can be made into a PowerPoint presentation, included on your class Web site, or used in bulletin board displays.

20. During a tour carry an easily identifiable object, such as a colorful umbrella, that you can hold up to help students find their group. With

small children some teachers use a rope, instructing the children to cling to it in a single file throughout the walking tour.

21. After the field trip, send a thank-you note to the organization or person that facilitated the visit. If appropriate, you might encourage your students to draft a letter to send.

22. Evaluate the field trip. Did it fulfill your educational purposes? Solicit feedback from the students. What would have improved the experience?

23. If you plan to use that field trip site in the future, jot down any reminders of changes that would make the trip more profitable next time. You might file these along with copies of your form letters and permission slips, student activities, and any promotional brochures.

Ideas for Potential Field Trips

Airport	Hospital
Amusement park	Laboratory
Aquarium	Law enforcement agency
Arboretum	Legislative session
Art exhibit	Library
Artist's studio	Military base
Assisted living facility	Museum
Bank	Neighborhood
Battlefield	Newspaper office
Book publishing company	Observatory
Botanical garden	Park (local, state, national)
Brokerage firm	Planetarium
Cemetery	Political rally
City council meeting	Power plant
College or university	Presidential library or home
Concert	Printing plant
Conservation area	Science museum
Conservatory	Seashore, river, or lake
Courthouse	Sewage treatment plant
Cultural fair or festival	Ship
Factory	Special exhibition
Farm	State capitol building
Fire department	Television or radio station
Forest	Theatrical performance
Geological site	Train ride
Historical museum	Weather station
Historical site or building	Zoo

Field Trip Supply List

_____ Binoculars

_____ Camcorder

_____ Cell phone or coins for pay phone

_____ Clipboards

_____ Digital camera

_____ Driving directions and map

_____ First-aid kit

_____ Flashlight

_____ Food

_____ Garbage bag

_____ Important phone numbers

_____ Insect repellent

_____ Money

_____ Name tags

_____ Field trip permission form

_____ Participant roster, two copies

_____ Pencils

_____ Resealable plastic bags for collections

_____ Sunscreen

_____ Student medications

_____ Trip schedule

_____ Water bottles

_____ Whistle

Field Trip Follow-up Activities

✓ Allow teams of students to create a CD or DVD of the trip using digital photos or video clips taken during the outing. Share the product at a parent-teacher open house.

✓ Encourage the class to send thank-you notes to the on-site field trip guides.

✓ Create a display depicting the material learned and featuring any specimens collected. Invite other classes to view the display.

✓ Solicit volunteer students to help create a bulletin board depicting the trip's content.

✓ Invite students to evaluate the field trip experience. What was their favorite part of the field trip? What would they suggest to make the trip more worthwhile? Did it meet the preannounced goals?

✓ Select a student to write a story about the field trip for use in the class newsletter to be sent to parents.

✓ Assign teams to make reports on various aspects of the trip. These might be presented in a variety of modes (PowerPoint presentation, a video, oral presentation, learning center).

Virtual Field Trips

The Internet offers easy access to a broad array of virtual field trips relating to almost every subject area. Many historical, art, and science museums now host splendid online educational tours.

Virtual field trips allow students to visit remote places that would normally be impossible to visit. Online tours avoid the hassle of arranging chaperones and transportation, and they can be completed during normal class hours.

Several excellent catalogs of online museums and field trips can be found on the Web. Try the following:

Best Virtual Field Trips Online
surfaquarium.com/virtual.htm

The "OOPS" Virtual Field Trip Page!
oops.bizland.com/vtours.htm

Virtual Schoolhouse
www.ibiblio.org/cisco/trips.html

✓ As with off-campus field trips, virtual trips require planning. Be sure to meticulously preview any virtual field trip before introducing it to your students. You want no surprises.

✓ Some teachers send home a permission form for virtual field trips, just as they would for off-campus field trips. Be sure to include the site's URL so that parents can check it out. It is always wise to forestall problems by keeping parents informed.

✓ Prepare goals and instructional activities for students to complete as they explore the site's offerings. For example, design a scavenger hunt with information that small

Sample Virtual Field Trips

American Museum of Natural History
ology.amnh.org/

At the Tomb of Tutankhamen
www.nationalgeographic.com/egypt/
index.html

Boston Museum of Science
www.mos.org/

Fisheye View Online Camera
www.fisheyeview.com/

Journey with CARE to Ghana
careusa.org/vft/ghana/care_ghana.asp

Library of Congress
www.loc.gov/exhibits/

Metropolitan Museum of Art
www.metmuseum.org/

Ontario Science Centre Online
www.ontariosciencecentre.ca/

Smithsonian American Art Museum
www.nmaa.si.edu/

groups of students work on together. Design a follow-up activity for students to complete to extend and crystallize the knowledge they gained.

✓   Teachers must monitor students to assure they are on task and not abusing Internet privileges.

Questions to guide evaluation of potential virtual tours include the following:

✓ Who is sponsoring the site?

✓ Are there any costs?

✓ Is the content nonpartisan and factual?

✓ Is the site easy to navigate?

✓ Is the site sufficiently interactive?

✓ How current is the information?

✓ Where do any external links lead?

Guest Speakers and Panels

The use of guest speakers, either individually or as a panel, can provide a valuable educational opportunity. Outside presenters can enrich a lesson, provide special expertise, stimulate interest, and help students connect classroom learning to real-world applications. Guest speakers provide variety: a different voice and a new face. A bonus benefit is the public relations value of inviting parents and community members to share their wisdom, skills, and views with young people.

However, as with any instructional approach, planning and preparation are crucial for success. A poor speaker is worse than none at all. Not only will precious educational time be lost, but also the speaker may leave with a lower opinion of schools and your students.

Here are some ideas for potential speakers:

✓ Anyone who has traveled to a foreign country

✓ People representing different careers

✓ Persons with unusual hobbies or interests

✓ College and university professors

✓ Elected officials

✓ Local citizens of other nationalities

✓ Area business owners or executives

✓ International students attending local schools or colleges

✓ Governmental agency employees

✓ Someone with an interesting collection

✓ Physicians, lawyers, and other professionals

✓ School alumni

✓ Representatives of trade associations, unions, or service organizations

✓ Local radio, television, or newspaper celebrities

✓ Federal government employees

✓ Local newsmakers

✓ Better Business Bureau, consumer agencies, and advocates

Guest speakers should be arranged well in advance. Here are some ideas for guiding your planning process:

✓ Determine why you are using the speaker (or panel). What benefit do you expect students to gain from being exposed to this speaker or panel? Without using jargon, communicate your objective to the speakers when you invite them.

✓ Give careful thought to whom you invite to participate in your class. What are their credentials? Parents, senior citizens, local celebrities, civic leaders, skilled artisans, artists, professors, and local businesspersons can potentially contribute much to your students.

✓ When you extend an invitation, be specific as to the date, topic, and time limits. What format are you suggesting: lecture, demonstration, question and answer, a panel discussion? Have they spoken before in front of groups this age? How will they relate to students? Some persons are more comfortable participating as a member of an informal panel discussion than as the sole presenter.

✓ Confirm the visit two or three days ahead of the scheduled presentation.

✓ Give your speakers as much support as possible. Tell them about the kinds of students you have. Alert them to potential behavioral problems they might encounter and your plans to deal with such disruptive students. See if the speakers need any special equipment or supplies. Encourage them to use props and to involve students as much as possible.

✓ Encourage the speaker to solicit questions from students. This makes the experience more interactive and responsive to students' interests.

✓ Short presentations are generally preferable, at least the first time you have a speaker present on a specific topic. If it is well received, more time can be allotted the next time.

✓ Prepare your students for the speaker(s). Before the speaker arrives, clarify who is coming and why. Clarify what behaviors you expect from your students. You might suggest they formulate some questions ahead of the presentation. Make it an active learning experience.

✓ Ask permission to videotape the speaker's presentation for use in the future or with students who were absent.

✓ Be sure to send thank-you notes to your panelists or presenters. If students express high interest in the subject, invite them to write thank-you notes, either individually or as a group.

✓ Invite persons who have some expertise in the subject under discussion to share their knowledge in a panel discussion. These might be parents, community members, or representatives of a particular organization, occupation, or interest group. Most people feel more comfortable participating as a panel member than giving a stand-up solo presentation. Generally, a panel consists of three to five participants. The panelists might discuss the topic among themselves as well as respond to questions from your students. Another option is to select a group of students who study a particular topic and present it to the rest of the class as a panel discussion.

✓ Before the panel takes place, it is often a good idea to give students a few minutes in class (or as homework) to write one or two questions they could submit to the panel. This might also be done as a small-group exercise. You serve as a moderator, posing questions when the discussion lags. Avoid dominating the discussion, however.

✓ Arrange chairs at the front of the room so that the panelists can see each other and be seen by all the class. Keep track of the time and try to allow for some closing thoughts by each panelist.

✓ Another useful variation is to allow fifteen to twenty minutes at the end for the panelists to meet with small clusters of students and permit individual questioning and discussion.

Debates

The debate can be a powerful motivational and instructional device. Though formal debate has perhaps become a lost art, seldom practiced outside of law schools, the debating process can successfully be adapted to any educational level. Informal debates can be used in almost any subject. Debates are an effective tool for honing students' thinking skills. The debate also reinforces data gathering, persuasion, public speaking, and listening skills. The ability to analyze a position and persuasively present a case for or against that position will benefit students throughout their lives. One of the most valuable gains from debates is the appreciation for more than one way of viewing issues.

Informal classroom debates need not follow all the procedures of a formal debate, though you will need to teach some basic rules to structure the debate. Each side should have the same amount of time to present its case. Students take turns presenting their arguments with time to rebut the opponent's points.

Any topic on which people might disagree can be selected for a debate assignment. This might include local or school-related issues, or national or international events. Most any proposal for change meets resistance, with advocates for both sides. Though some students may initially be reluctant, most really do find classroom debates exciting; and even the academically less-talented students can become involved. Debates frequently are quite lively and elicit postdebate discussion on the issue. Here are some tips:

✓ The first time you use the debate in class, keep it fairly simple. With experience your students can successfully take on more complicated issues. The more complex the issue, the more time needed for preparation. Adjust your expectations to your students' intellectual level.

✓ Present some of the basic principles of effective argumentation, such as distinguishing opinions and emotions from facts. If you aren't familiar with these skills, find a book from the library (see the suggestions that follow). Invite a lawyer or a debate coach to speak to your class about effective debating.

✓ Debates generally work best as a cooperative learning activity. Students will feel much more comfortable as a member of a panel than as a sole debater. Emphasize the collaboration within each team more than the competition against other teams.

✓ Another adaptation of the debate is to assign a variety of debatable topics to pairs of students. Each pair works collaboratively to identify the best arguments for and against their assigned proposition. The teacher then randomly assigns one student to present the pro and another student to present the con position in a five-minute presentation. Allow them two minutes to review their notes before presenting to the whole class. Everyone in the class gets to speak, but the time is brief enough not to arouse undue anxiety in most students.

✓ For variety debate with yourself in front of the class. Choose a stimulating issue and argue one point of view, perhaps in a relevant hat or shirt. Then quickly don the other costume and argue the other position. Switch back and forth for rebuttal. With a bit of practice, you can present a most entertaining as well as enlightening debate. The hat serves as a cue that the roles are shifting back and forth.

✓ Provide the option for your students to demonstrate their debating skills by presenting their argument to an outside audience, perhaps the board of education, city council, the school administration, or viewers of the local cable television channel. This would require students to carefully research the issue, analyze the supporting data, and rehearse their presentations.

For More Information

Daley, P., & Dahlie, M. S. (2001). *Fifty debate prompts for kids.* New York: Scholastic Professional Books.

Driscoll, W., & Zompetti, J. P. (2003). *Discovering the world through debate: A practical guide to educational debate for debaters, coaches, and judges.* New York: International Debate Education Association.

Ericson, J. M., Murphy, J. J., & Zeuschner, R. B. (2003). *The debater's guide* (3rd ed.). Carbondale: Southern Illinois University Press.

Fine, G. A. (2001). *Gifted tongues: High school debate and adolescent culture.* Princeton, NJ: Princeton University Press.

Snider, A., & Schnurer, M. (2002). *Many sides: Debate across the curriculum.* New York: International Debate Education Association.

Films, Videotapes, and DVDs

Films, videotapes, and DVDs can be tremendous instructional assets. The challenge facing teachers using video presentations in class is that their students have been overexposed to the medium at home. Many students spend more time facing a television or movie screen each year than they do in class. And much of what they have seen is action-packed, lusty, and very professional. Educational films, which are usually low budget and often of low technical quality, can be weak competition for students' attention.

Yet when used effectively, films and videos can be a powerful learning aid. The visual media can take students places they could never visit, help them see things they might never experience, and make the things they have read about come alive. Good films and videotapes can be very effective in arousing interest and motivating students. Many excellent documentary videos are available via commercial or educational broadcasting stations. *The Civil War* series produced by Ken Burns demonstrated the power and appeal of well-done video broadcasting. (See Chapter Two for copyright laws and fair educational use of videotaped programs.)

Selecting the right film or video is crucial. It must clearly fit into the lesson, not simply be an add-on or time killer. It is only a tool for helping you attain your instructional objective. A good film or videotape does not replace good teaching; it complements it. The following suggestions will help you:

✓ Check with your local library or television station about the availability of these programs. Many commercial organizations lend free films and videos. Colleges and governmental organizations are also sources of free or inexpensive films or videos.

✓ Whatever the source, the cardinal rule in using any audiovisual material is to preview it first to determine its appropriateness. You don't want any surprises in class! Evaluate the film or video for accuracy, age-appropriateness, cultural or gender bias, relevance to your class, and production quality. A bad program is worse than none at all.

✓ As you preview a film or videotape, jot down potential processing questions and main points you want to stress in the debriefing. If only portions of the film or video are worth showing, observe the timer to determine when the desired segment begins and ends.

✔ The biggest risk of audiovisual media is that it can become a passive learning experience for students, little more than a recorded lecture. Successful learning from films and video hinges on the teacher's ability to actively engage students in the experience. One way is to assign students a task to accomplish while viewing the presentation. This may take the form of two or three questions to answer, behaviors to count, words to define, or examples to observe.

✔ Another way to keep students actively involved in visual media is to stop the film or video occasionally and ask them questions about what they've seen or ask them to predict what they think will happen next. To affect learning the subsequent processing of the film or video is as important as what students see and hear. Ask questions that stimulate reflection about the experience. Help students connect what they have learned in this presentation with prior knowledge and skills.

✔ Do not put on a film or video and then leave the room while students watch it, even if you have seen it fifty times. Apart from the liability issues of leaving a classroom unmonitored, your absence suggests to students the film is just being used to fill time and really isn't very important.

✔ Don't feel compelled to rewind the film immediately. Proceed directly to your debriefing activity and rewind the film later.

✔ Experiment with just using small clips from films and videos to augment lectures. A brief two- or three-minute segment illustrating an important point adds variety to any lesson and can enhance attention and retention. It is crucial that you cue up the desired segment and focus and set volume levels before the lesson begins. It is also imperative to adjust the lighting for optimal viewing of the screen.

✔ After the film or video, solicit candid feedback from your students as to how helpful it really was. If it gets low marks, don't use it again. You might even have them complete a brief rating form. Don't just ask if they liked the film; ask what they learned from it.

✔ If you have not learned how to work the VCR or thread the film projector, find someone in the school to teach you. It is much better to know how to do this than to always depend on finding someone else to do it.

✔ Be sure you know where to quickly locate a projector replacement bulb and how to change it if help is not immediately available.

Digital video equipment and editing software are now available in most schools. All video-editing software comes with self-paced tutorials. However, it is best to learn under the tutelage of an experienced user. This may be a techie student!

With user-friendly software, teachers and students can add high-end special effects and export their project to the Web, DVD, or videotape. Macintosh users may find Apple's iMovie and Final Cut Pro 3 reasonably easy to learn. Adobe Premiere or Avid Xpress are two of the more popular software packages for video editing on PCs.

Videotaping

Camcorders and VCRs are widely available in schools and homes. Used wisely, video recording can be a versatile, powerful instructional tool. It can also motivate reluctant students. Current models of camcorders are simple to use, requiring little experience to operate. As with any other instructional technique, the key to success is careful preparation and planning. Keep the following tips in mind:

✓ Before you attempt to use a camcorder in class, be sure you have practiced using it. Double-check that the battery is fully charged.

✓ If you use the same videotape repeatedly, mark on the label the length of time the tape consumes. That will make planning the class time to allot easier the next time. Also file processing questions and any related student activities with the tape for easy access.

✓ One teacher can videotape parts of the opening day discussion of rules, routines, expectations, and grade policies. If the principal has an opening presentation, that might also be included on the tape. Students joining the class after the first day sign out the video to view it in the library or at home in the evening. This can also be a useful option for assisting hearing-impaired students or others for whom English is not the primary language. Any student who wants to review the first day might choose to check out the tape overnight. Some parents might even be interested in viewing it to learn more about your class.

✓ Take the camcorder along to tape field trips, special speakers (with their permission), or other interesting lessons.

✓ Videotape class activities to send to students who are absent with extended illnesses.

✓ Record various interesting class experiences throughout the year to show at the parents' open house or when making a presentation at a parent-teacher association meeting.

✓ Use a camcorder to record various activities and events throughout the school year. On the last day of the year, show the videotape in your class. Students will love seeing themselves and recalling some of the highlights of their year.

✓ As more schools turn to portfolio assessments, videotaping will be incorporated as part of the student evaluation process. Each student might have his or her own videotape to periodically update.

✓ Some high-quality class-produced videotapes might be shown on the local cable channel. While providing a valuable educational service, you are also creating good public relations for your school.

✓ Videotape students involved in successful lessons. Send these clips home with students to show their parents or play them when parents come to an open house. Most parents will love the opportunity to see their kids involved in schoolwork.

✓ Don't overlook the value of reviewing videotapes of your own teaching as a means of self-improvement and professional development. The videotape creates a truthful memory of the lesson. Use the videotape to stimulate reflection on your teaching. Retain videotapes of successful teaching experiences to include in your professional portfolio.

For More Information

Print Publications

Appleman, R. (1996). *Videoediting: The pictorial sequence, Vol 2.* Greenwich, CT: Association for Educational Communications & Technology.

Chambers, M. (2002). *CD & DVD Recording For Dummies.* New York: Hungry Minds.

Herrell, A. L., & Fowler, J. P. (1998). *Camcorder in the classroom: Using the video-camera to enliven curriculum.* Upper Saddle River, NJ: Prentice Hall.

Rubin, M. (2002). *The little digital video book.* Berkeley, CA: Peachpit.

Wright, S. (2002). *Digital compositing for film and video.* Boston: Focal Press.

Online Resources

DVD Help
www.dvdrhelp.com/

FOCUS Enhancements
www.focusinfo.com/educators/

Project-based Learning with Multimedia
pblmm.k12.ca.us/

Videomaker Magazine
www.videomaker.com/

Free online tutorials

Atomic Learning
atomiclearning.com/freesamples

Butte College radio-TV/film program
RTVF 40 Camcorder Video Production course textbook
www.bctv.net/telcom/te140text/toc.h

How-to information and books for videographers
videoexpert.home.att.net

Slides

Although newer technologies are rapidly making slides obsolete, they are a relatively inexpensive way to add visuals to your class presentations. You can take slides either as you travel to places related to your subject or by using a copy stand to take slides of photos in books. Take slides of outstanding student projects for use in future classes. Take slides of students working in class on different activities. Use these to prepare a slide presentation for use at open houses or to show your students at the end of the school year. Of course, many commercially prepared slides are available for almost any topic. Discarded filmstrips can be cut into individual frames and placed in cardboard or plastic slide mounts. Here are suggestions to help you:

✓ With a copy stand, you can easily take pictures from books and magazines. Construct inexpensive title slides on a computer and photograph the layout directly from the monitor. You will need to mount your camera on a tripod and tilt the camera to assure that the lens is parallel with the monitor. Another option is to print (preferably with a laser printer) your title slides on colored papers and photograph these on a copy stand. Either way use large fonts (at least thirty-six point).

✓ Be sure you know how to take a carousel off a projector if a slide jams. By placing a coin in the slot in the center of the slide tray and twisting, you can release the carousel from the projector.

✓ Carousel trays that hold eighty slides are less prone to jamming than the ones for 140.

✓ Students in the farthest corners of the room must be able to clearly read your slides. Using too small a font is perhaps the biggest mistake in using slides.

✓ A horizontal format is best because it fits the screen better. It is visually distracting to alternate back and forth between horizontal and vertical formats. Fill up the screen with the largest image possible.

✓ The lower quarter of the screen is difficult to see from the back of the room. For that reason it is best to project only onto the upper three-quarters of the screen.

✓ Insert black slides at the beginning and end of your slide program. Avoid blinding your students with a white, light-filled screen.

✓ The biggest disadvantage of slides is that the room must be sufficiently darkened that they project sharply on the screen. Turning out or dimming some of the room lights will usually suffice. Avoid totally dark rooms, as they are conducive to sleeping and mischief.

✓ Preview your slides to make sure you have placed them in the correct position and sequence.

✓ Have a spare bulb available and know how to change it.

✓ When showing slides, stand off to the side so that you do not block any student's view.

✓ Use a remote control with an extension cord to allow you freedom to move away from the projector.

Dyadic Encounters

A dyadic encounter is a structured dialogue between two (or occasionally three) students. It works best to prepare a sheet or a small booklet of directions and questions. A booklet of ten to twenty pages works better than a single sheet as the students are more likely to fully focus on one question at a time and not race ahead. (*Hint:* make minibooklets by cutting an 8½-by-11-inch sheet of paper into four smaller sheets.) On the first page, include a brief paragraph giving directions on how to proceed through the stimulus questions.

A dyadic encounter can work with any topic in which you want students to reflect on their experiences, opinions, or attitudes. The booklet may contain questions (for example, "What qualities do you most value in a friend?" or "What do you think are the most pressing problems facing our country today?") or sentence stems (for example, "One thing I would like to be better at is . . . "; "The character in *Moby-Dick* most like me is . . . "; or "If I could have dinner alone with one historical character it would be . . . "). Both students respond to each question or stem and take turns going first. Encourage students to ask each other's questions and to help clarify each other's responses. The intent of the dyadic encounter is to stimulate thought about a specific topic.

A variation on the dyadic encounter is the talk-walk exercise. Students conduct their dyadic encounter while walking around. This can work well on a nice day when you can take the class outside. Establish restrictions on where they may roam. As they walk together, they discuss the assigned topic. At a whistle or other cue, they all return to the classroom.

Demonstrations

Demonstration is an essential step when you are teaching a skill, providing an opportunity for students to see the task modeled. Adequate preparation is the key to effective demonstrations. Have any needed equipment or materials readily available. Pay attention to the details in your preparation. Assure that all students can clearly see the demonstration. If necessary, allow those in the back to stand to gain an unobstructed view. One option is to have someone who has mastered the skill demonstrate it while you narrate the process.

As you introduce the demonstration, be sure to explain its purpose. Focus students' attention on each step as you proceed. You might choose to demonstrate a task or skill at regular speed and then repeat the demonstration in slow speed, stopping to discuss each step in more detail. Explain why you are doing each step as you proceed. You might occasionally ask students questions at crucial points in the demonstration. In most instances it is best to keep your demonstration short, probably no longer than five minutes. Attention will begin to wane if it drags on much longer.

Ideally, your demonstration should be followed by an opportunity for the students to practice the skill you have just demonstrated. Supervise their practice and permit opportunities to receive feedback from the teacher or from peers.

Board Work

Math teachers have traditionally had students work through problems at the chalkboard (and now the whiteboard). While this can be an effective means of giving students practice at problem solving and assessing progress, with some creativity it can be even more instructive and fun. Some teachers have problems already written on the board before the class begins. As students enter the room, they might be assigned to work on these problems at the board in pairs. The teacher can offer hints to pairs that are having difficulty. Students who are not working at the board are called on to analyze the completed problems. Here are a few tips for effectively using chalkboards or whiteboards:

✓ Use legible handwriting. Make sure it is large enough to be read from the back of the room.

✓ Erase items from the board (or ask a student volunteer to help) at the end of the lesson so that a clean board will be available when needed.

✓ Put a cloth towel into a plastic sandwich or freezer bag along with a few drops of lemon oil. The oil will soak into the towel, creating a superb chalkboard cleaner. Add oil as needed to keep the cloth damp.

✓ Use a variety of colored markers on whiteboards for emphasis and increased interest.

✓ Old white socks work well for cleaning whiteboards.

✓ Check the view of the whiteboard at various times of the day to detect reflection from sunlight.

✓ Clean the whiteboard periodically; markings left for a long time leave a faint stain.

✓ Avoid using light colored pens on the whiteboard. Red often doesn't show well from the back of the room.

✓ Use a digital camera to capture whiteboard graphics or writing that you want to save. Download images to a computer for manipulation.

The interactive whiteboard, connected to a computer, offers tremendous instructional potential. Software can capture images and video from any electronic source—multimedia CDs or DVDs, the Internet, or any software program—and project it onto the whiteboard. A multitude of creative applications can be done on the projected images. Anything written on the interactive whiteboard (such as a mind map) can be saved to a computer for later retrieval. Teachers can write notes and drawings with a stylus on an electronic tablet and project their writings onto the whiteboard.

Originally developed for use in business meetings, this new technology has begun to find its way into a few classrooms. Unfortunately, the price sets this technology beyond the reach of most K–12 classrooms. As with most technology, declining prices will likely spread its use in the next decade. The technology will be particularly valuable to teachers involved in distance education courses.

Action Research

Action research is an effective learning device for teaching the process of scientific investigation and systematic problem solving. Involving students in gathering data and systematically studying real-world problems enhances the relevance and authenticity of classroom instruction. This may take the form of a case study, an experiment, a survey, or interviews.

Students learn how to ask the right questions, gather data, tabulate results, draw conclusions, and present findings. Action research can be conducted in cooperative teams or as a whole-class project with various delegated tasks. Guest speakers may be invited to provide the class with some background information on the problem under investigation. The final report might be presented orally or in written form to a group or organization, such as the city council or board of education.

Interviews

Many lessons can be enriched with the use of interviews, which are best used as a homework assignment. Potential targets of interviews might include parents, grandparents, local government leaders, peers, civic leaders, neighbors, or businesspersons. Besides enriching students' knowledge and motivation through active learning, interviews are also a good public relations tool. People in the community, especially parents, generally enjoy being asked about their experiences and opinions. Interviewing invites parents and others to have discussions with young people that might never otherwise occur.

It is best to have students develop in class a set of questions that they will use to structure their interviews. Give them sufficient time and specific instructions on whom to interview and a deadline for reporting their results. The interview results can be submitted as a written assignment or discussed in class as a large group or in small groups.

One variation of the interview is a mock press conference, in which one or more class members assume the role of a person or group being studied in the class (astronaut, president, explorer, author, scientist, and so on). They should be given time to research their role and instructed to answer all questions from the assigned character's point of view. The rest of the class assumes the role of television or newspaper reporters who then interview the celebrity. A moderator or panel can also be appointed, and a *Meet the Press* format can be used.

Construction

Building or making things is an integral part of many courses. Examples include baking cakes, building models, sewing a tie, constructing a house, making a stained-glass window, reconditioning a piece of furniture, taking and developing photographs, reproducing a chair, making a clay pot, composing a song, making a quilt, or constructing a poster.

Such hands-on projects are among the most valuable learning experiences. They closely approximate reality or rehearse activities actually used in the world outside schools. Students tend to become highly motivated when involved in real-life tasks.

It is important to clarify the assignment's boundaries, including any evaluation criteria. Deadlines must be specified. For very large projects, it is often desirable to have several checkpoint deadlines prior to the final due date.

Tell students what help they may receive from others. There are many advantages to using group projects where feasible.

See that particularly outstanding products are publicized, with the student's permission. Some might be exhibited in government buildings, malls, fairs, festivals; on local cable television; or at school open houses. Consider inviting the local newspaper or television to do a feature story on your students' noteworthy accomplishments.

Almost daily, local and national newspapers, television, and professional journals highlight outstanding learning activities. Keep an idea notebook of ones you might adapt to your class.

Card Sorts

Card sorts are useful devices for helping students narrow a range of options, clarify criteria, or set priorities. Potential topics for a card sort might include career options, life goals, interests, criteria for selecting a career or college, or funding priorities. Any choice in which more than a dozen alternatives are available can be adapted to a card sort.

The first step is to generate a list of alternatives. This can be done as a large-group brainstorm, listing the alternatives on the chalkboard or newsprint. After the list is constructed, each student prints each option on a separate card or slip of paper. (It works well to precut or have students cut 8½-by-11-inch sheets of paper into eight equal slips, 4¼-by-2¾ inches each.) After each student has a complete deck of cards, give directions for the card sort. Instruct the students to sort their cards into three piles: yes, maybe, and no. After the initial sort, have them count the number of cards in the yes pile. If they have more than ten or twelve, ask them to sort through one more time, sorting that stack into two more piles: those they feel red hot about and those they feel lukewarm about. The goal is to get the options down to fewer than ten.

Once the cards in the yes pile are down to ten, instruct the students to spread out all the cards in their yes pile so that they can see them all at once. Direct the class to study their cards carefully. After a pause instruct them that they may have only one card. "Which one will it be? Pick it up and hold it in your hand." After everyone has made their selection, tell them they may have one more card, which they are to pick up and place behind their first choice. After everyone has made their second choice, instruct them to continue picking up their cards one at a time until the entire stack of yes cards is in their hand. They should then record the list in order on paper.

Once the card sort is completed, you may process the activity in a large-group discussion or in small groups. Another option is to construct a large grid on the board revealing the group's top priorities. Experiment with variations on the card sort. It can be used successfully in almost any subject.

Surveys and Questionnaires

Instruments such as questionnaires and surveys can serve a number of valuable purposes: to enhance interest and motivation in a topic; to introduce a new lesson; or to assess prior knowledge, attitudes, and experiences. Tell students whether they will keep their answers private or be asked to share them. Experiment with using soft music in the background while students are completing the instrument.

Teachers can construct their own surveys or questionnaires; or they can easily adapt them from newspaper and magazine articles, especially those reporting survey results pertaining to topics the class is studying. Many teacher guides also include brief surveys or questionnaires.

A variety of follow-up activities can be used with the survey or questionnaire. A large-group discussion might be held to process the students' answers. Students can talk about and compare their answers in pairs or small groups. Tabulate the answers on a chart or graph to synthesize the group data. A small fishbowl discussion in the middle of the class can be used to facilitate examination of the content. If comparison data are available from other groups, you might share them with the class.

As an introduction to a new topic, construct your own questionnaire to include significant facts related to the subject. Be clear that it is not a quiz and will not be graded. As each question is scored, you are reinforcing the information included in the questionnaire.

Oral Presentations

Oral presentations have long been used as an instructional strategy in American schools. At their worst, they are frightening to give, boring to watch, and a waste of time. Used effectively, oral presentations can be stimulating and motivating learning aids. For an oral presentation to be of maximum benefit, the teacher must appropriately structure it. Most students do not know how to give a brief, focused presentation. When making the assignment, it is important to provide adequate coaching on the project's *why, what,* and *how.* The following suggestions might be adapted to improve your students' presentations:

✓ To reduce the anxiety of talking in front of the group, begin with safe topics the students know well. Themes such as "my dream vacation" or "my favorite game" tap a student's experiences. Permit students to teach a skill they know or talk about a favorite possession; these are topics students can present with little extra study.

✓ Letting two students do a presentation together provokes less anxiety for the speakers.

✓ Assign students to read magazine articles related to an assigned subject area. The students should take notes summarizing the key points of the article and prepare a four- to five-minute talk. Specify the main parts of their presentation. The talk could be split between two students, dividing the content between them.

✓ In most instances individual oral presentations should be limited to ten minutes. Few students possess the skills and enthusiasm to hold their listeners' attention longer. Little is gained and much precious time is lost if your class must endure a succession of long, boring reports. They probably won't be too exciting for you either.

✓ It is helpful to demonstrate the oral presentation you are assigning. Model the parts of the demonstration and process the presentation afterward, providing a written outline of its parts. Another option is to videotape your five-minute presentation

and replay it, pointing out the different parts of the talk. Encourage the class to critique the presentation. It is best if it is not perfect. If you can point out your own errors or deficiencies, they will realize they don't have to be perfect.

✓ If students have some experience in giving oral presentations, allow two to three minutes at the end of the talk for the rest of the class to ask questions of the presenter. This develops the ability to think on their feet and to speak extemporaneously.

✓ Sometimes teachers provide an opportunity for the class to offer feedback to the presenter, perhaps in writing: "List one thing the speaker did well," or "Describe one part of the presentation that needs improvement."

✓ Another tactic for developing oral presentation skills is to develop a persuasive speech. This assignment requires students to take a stand on an issue, research it, and develop a brief persuasive presentation.

✓ It is best to set a time limit for student presentations. The time should be appropriate to your students' age and developmental level. Seldom should a solo presentation exceed ten minutes, even for high school students. For elementary students three to four minutes are generally sufficient, especially if everyone in the class is assigned to do one.

✓ The debate format is also a most useful alternative for developing the skills of oral persuasion.

✓ Require students to speak from note cards. Don't let them write out a verbatim script, and discourage them from trying to memorize the whole speech. Encourage them to use a visual aid or prop. This serves as a cue, creates added interest, and gives them something to do with their hands.

✓ Oral presentations can also be incorporated into cooperative learning activities, with each team member presenting a different part of the program. It is easier to stand in front of the class as a member of a supportive group than alone.

✓ Having students interview a student can be a valuable learning experience. Establish the focus of the interview ahead of time. Again, it is easier if the topic is one the student already knows. Another option is to assign students to various historical or fictional roles. The students then study the lives and times of the characters they are playing. The class interviews them as reporters with the role-player answering in character.

✓ It is sometimes helpful to videotape the presentations and allow students to review them later either alone, in teams, or with the teacher. Students might be allowed to check the videos out overnight to show their parents. Some of the better ones might be saved for use at the parent open house.

Role-Playing

Role-playing is a valuable technique for simulating real-life situations. Role-plays provide a safe environment for students to experiment with new behaviors and skills. The role-play can arouse interest in a topic, as well as encourage students to empathize with differing viewpoints. Because students become totally involved in their roles, the learning is holistic, involving their emotional and psychomotor domains as well as the cognitive. The role-play is one activity in which students don't have to be anxious about coming up with the single right answer. Giving them permission to make mistakes encourages even more risk taking and experimentation. Even low-ability students can experience success. The creativity of all students can be unleashed through role-playing activities.

Role-plays are typically very short, seldom more than fifteen minutes. In a role-play two or more students improvise a specific, assigned scenario. These roles may be ones that are familiar (for example, introducing a new student to a friend) or beyond their realm of experiences (for example, a World War II resistance fighter, a nuclear scientist, or a U.S. president). The actors receive only a sketchy outline of the scenario. Role-plays may be set in the past, present, or future. The directive may be no more than a sentence or two. For example, two students in a French class may role-play a job interview or order a meal from a menu.

Here are some suggestions for using role-plays effectively:

✓ Plan role-plays to support your instructional objectives. Depending on their function, role-plays can be used in the beginning of a lesson to introduce a new topic, in the middle to help teach a skill or concept, or at the conclusion to tie together and reinforce the whole lesson. Whenever used, role-plays should have a sound educational purpose.

✓ Generally, you should clearly explain the purpose of the role-play ahead of time. In some role-plays, where the purpose is to sensitize students to their attitudes, it would be detrimental to fully explain the intent beforehand. In such instances seek their cooperation by explaining that you'd like their help in an experiment. It is important to avoid forcing students into roles that may prove embarrassing.

✓ To overcome some of the initial resistance to role-playing, it may be best not to use the word *role-play* the first time you use the activity. Many students have preconceived notions about role-plays. Describe it as an experiment or simply say, "Assume for a moment you are . . . " or "Respond as though you really were . . ."

✓ It's usually best to seek volunteers for the role-play unless everyone is going to be participating. You will likely encounter less resistance to role-plays if everyone participates in small groups. (Groups of three seem to work well.) When people assume roles, they must talk: there is no place to hide as in group discussions.

✓ You must provide a safe climate for students, or they will not get into the roles. After students have gained some experience in small-group role-plays, some (but not

all) will feel more comfortable role-playing in front of the class. Do invite and encourage participation by the introverts as well, but it's probably best not to force very shy children to role-play in front of the whole class.

✓ Explain the roles or give brief written descriptions to each role-player. Keep the scenarios and role descriptions brief. A sentence or two are usually sufficient. Assign non-participants to make structured observations of the role-play. An observer's worksheet is helpful in focusing their attention. Rearrange the room to enable everyone to see. If several simultaneous role-plays are occurring, spread out the groups so that they do not interfere with each other.

✓ Students are more receptive to role-plays if they have some freedom in choosing how to play them.

✓ Keep the introduction to the role-play simple. The more you build up the role-play, the more anxiety you are likely to create. Succinctly convey the essentials. One tactic that some teachers use is to wave a wand and say, "You're a [role to be played]!"

✓ Giving the role-players props, a costume, or a hat sometimes adds a touch of realism and increases their motivation to assume the role. Having something in their hands seems also to reduce anxiety.

✓ At least the first time you use role-plays, assign roles they can easily play. You may have to provide some prompts for initial dialogue.

✓ Have students use fictitious names rather than their own. It makes getting into the role a bit easier. It adds a touch of humor to make up funny nicknames for them to use.

✓ One tactic often used is to interrupt the role-play and have two people reverse roles. Or have another student step into a role and continue the role-play.

✓ Immediately after one group completes a role-play, have a second group repeat the same role-play with a different twist.

✓ Another option is to have the audience participate by giving the role-players directions. For example, in a foreign language class, the audience might suggest a scenario or responses to help structure the role-play.

✓ Adapt the empty chair technique that Gestalt therapists use in exploring conflicting situations. It is a good way to look at two sides of an issue. Only use this technique with content that is safe and doesn't evoke strong feelings in the student. A student volunteer sits in a chair facing an empty chair. The student begins by arguing for a particular issue or course of action (for example, compulsory education, banning cigarettes, curfews). After fifteen to twenty seconds, say "Switch." The student then moves to the other chair and argues the opposite point of view. After another fifteen to twenty seconds, again call "Switch." Repeat three to four times or until the student runs out of things to say. A safe way to introduce this is to have everyone in class do it simultaneously, or break the class into groups of three with one volunteer in each group who engages in the empty chair.

> ## Debriefing Role-Plays
>
> Morry van Ments, author of the revised *The Effective Use of Role-Play* (Nichols, 1989), suggests the following steps in debriefing a role-play:
>
> 1. Bring players out of the role.
> 2. Clarify what happened (get the facts).
> 3. Correct any mistakes or misunderstandings.
> 4. Dissipate any anxiety or tension.
> 5. Discuss the assumptions, feelings, and changes that occurred during the role-play.
> 6. Give the players an opportunity to develop self-observations.
> 7. Develop observation skills.
> 8. Relate the outcome of the role-play to the original objectives.
> 9. Analyze why things turned out as they did.
> 10. Draw conclusions about the behaviors observed.
> 11. Reinforce or correct concepts learned.
> 12. Draw out new points for consideration.
> 13. If appropriate, deduce ways of improving behaviors.
> 14. Generalize to other situations.
> 15. Link with prior learning.
> 16. Provide a plan for future learning.

✓ A commonly used role-play is the press conference. One or more students assume roles, such as famous historical characters, scientists, explorers, or authors. The rest of the class act as reporters and interview the celebrity. As a variation, use a *Meet the Press* format, with a panel of two to four journalists who conduct the interview with a moderator.

✓ Videotape the role-play. As it plays back, occasionally stop it to process significant points. This is especially valuable in introducing new skills. Students might even take the video home to study their own progress.

✓ Don't allow the role-play to run on too long. Try to cut it off at a high point. If the scenario has run its course, cut off the role-play and debrief. If it isn't working, cut it off but don't belittle the actors for their efforts.

✓ Thank students for participating in the role-play. If they have been asked to take a special risk, such as performing in front of the class, praise or a small reward is sometimes appropriate.

✓ Don't criticize students' role-playing performances (unless it's a theater class). The threat of evaluation will surely stifle students' willingness to engage in role-plays. Keep the focus on the actions, not the acting.

✓ Be sure to always allow time afterward for processing the role-play. This is the most important part of the role-play; don't rush it. Debriefing is absolutely essential if the role-play has evoked conflict or negative emotions. Ideally, it should immediately follow the role-play. Solicit feedback from the observers as well as the role-play participants. Ask questions that explore content as well as feelings. It is important to help students make connections between the role-play situation and real-world events.

✓ Be patient. Role-playing may be a new experience for some students. As a more trusting class climate emerges, students will feel more comfortable taking risks and less inhibited.

✓ If the role-play went well and you would like to use it again with future classes, make notes on any refinements you might want to make the next time.

Dramatization

In dramatization students act out a skill or situation before the class, with or without scripts. A dramatization is a miniplay. The roles are much more defined than in a simple role-play. Students receive instructions as to the role they are to demonstrate and suggestions as to the behaviors and techniques to include. Students will usually rehearse the dramatization before presenting it to the whole class.

Strive to minimize participants' potential embarrassment by matching the roles to the students' personality as much as possible. Creating a safe atmosphere for the dramatization is important so that all participants feel at ease. Generally, it is best to explain what you will be asking the students to do before soliciting volunteers. Don't force anyone to participate.

Some dramatizations will require advance preparation. Rather than using verbatim scripts, assign roles and provide guidelines for the students' roles. Occasionally, you may employ improvisation to encourage students to develop their creativity.

Experiment with using puppets to create your dramatization. Most students find it much easier to become involved in a role by using a puppet. Costumes, props, hats, or masks can also arouse students' enthusiasm for the skit.

Group processing of the experience is an integral part of the learning process. Give careful thought to developing good open-ended processing questions. Help the class clearly understand the purpose and different aspects of the dramatization.

Here are some examples of dramatization that teachers have used in various subject areas:

✓ Some foreign language teachers have students enact soap operas in their new language.

✓ Conduct a mock constitutional convention.

✓ Present past or current U.S. presidential debates.

✓ Conduct a press conference of famous scientists, artists, explorers, or inventors about their accomplishments.

✓ Present a public hearing of an agency on some social or environmental issue. Each side has to prepare testimony and present it to the panel, which must ask the witnesses questions.

✓ Conduct a mock trial of either a character from literature or a historical figure.

✓ Allow the class to write their own drama and then present it to the rest of the school. Be sure to videotape it for parents.

Games and Simulations

Games and simulations can be powerful learning strategies. However, only use them when they have sound educational purposes related to the topics you are teaching. Academic games should require some use of intellectual skills, rather than chance, to succeed. The skills students use in this game should have application to the real world. Academic games may be very brief, requiring only a few minutes of class time; or they may continue over a number of days, perhaps stretched out over several weeks or longer. Some tips:

✓ Besides using games to build skills, use them as rewards for good performance.

✓ It is best to avoid games that end with only one winner. While the winner feels good, the negative emotions that the losers experience make it an unpleasant experience for most students. They will have plenty of opportunities outside the classroom to confront defeat and know how losing feels. Team competition is preferable to individual competition.

✓ As with all learning activities, explain the purpose of the game or simulation. There may be some emotional insights you expect to explore and may not want to describe overtly ahead of time.

✓ Some form of scoring system should be included in the game's structure. To score well one must be required to use the academic skills rather than luck.

✓ Ask the following questions in considering a game for use in your class:

- Is it fun?
- Is it challenging for your students?
- What is the purpose of the game?
- How will this game further my learning objectives?

- What skills does this game develop?
- Is this game age-appropriate?
- Are skills, rather than luck, required to win?
- Are the rules relatively simple? Do they need modification?
- Does the game require team rather than individual competition?
- Will the game reward inappropriate behavior?
- How are scores determined and recorded?

✓ Consider redesigning an existing game to fit your classroom needs.

✓ Educator Robert Slavin promotes the use of teams-games-tournament as a cooperative learning activity. Students are broken into heterogeneous teams allowing students within each team to collaborate in mastering new content. The teams then compete against each other in academic contests. For the tournament phase, students compete against students of similar ability, and their success contributes to their teams' score.

✓ To keep track of small game pieces, store them in plastic sandwich or freezer bags.

✓ Laminate any paper game items that will be used repeatedly.

✓ One kind of game students love is the television quiz show. Adapt the format of *Jeopardy, Who Wants to Be a Millionaire, Hollywood Squares,* or other popular television programs to entice students into review, reinforcement, and assessment of your classroom content. Such activities add variety, energy, and enthusiasm to your curriculum. Although some element of competition is involved, try to structure the game so that everyone wins; downplay the competitive aspect.

✓ Read the group energy level. When the enthusiasm for the game begins to wane, end the game and proceed to the debriefing phase.

In simulations students assume roles and make choices as though they were the person in that role. A simulation is more complex and evolving than a role-play that focuses on a single incident. As a structured activity, the simulation provides consequences for the choices the players make. For a simulation to succeed, students must be convinced to realistically act out their roles. They must try to think and act like a real-world person in that role.

Margaret Gredler, author of *Designing and Evaluating Games and Simulations* (Gulf Publishing, 1994), categorizes simulations according to the types of tasks and nature of interactions between participants. Tactical-decision simulations require students to interact in resolving a complex problem or crisis and to arrive at a logical, safe resolution. The participants must interpret data, develop options, and implement strategies. Simulations that require management of economic resources fall under this category. In contrast, social-process simulations encourage students to interact to address social challenges or to attain a political or social goal. Participants must interact and react to each other in a social milieu. Such simulations often involve interviewing, negotiating, cooperating, questioning, or persuading. Communication or empathy-building simulations are of this variety.

The most important learning occurs after the simulation, when the participants reflect on what happened during the game. This debriefing should encourage them to examine the thoughts, feelings, and actions that the simulation elicited. Generalizations of these insights for future real-world application should also be examined. Teachers must facilitate this reflection, not leaving it to chance.

Processing done in small groups may assure that more people actively participate. A good way to facilitate small-group thinking about the game is to provide several written questions for each group to discuss. Each group should have a recorder. Later the whole class discusses the group answers.

The latest development in the world of academic games and simulations is the wide availability of the computer and thousands of computer games and simulations. Much of it is commercial, although many good free or shareware programs are also available and easily accessible through the Internet or computer user clubs. There are indeed some pearls in this sea of computer simulations and games, but there is also a lot of garbage. While the potential of computer applications with multigraphics, sounds, and instantaneous feedback is attractive and possesses a great deal of potential, the teacher must use sound criteria in selecting those games and simulations to use in class. A risk is that the eye-catching graphics can distract the player from the game's real purpose. Don't just use a game because you have it. Use as rigorous criteria in selecting a computer game as you would a board game. Is it worth class time? A major disadvantage of most computer games is that only one or two persons at a time can usually participate.

For suggestions in designing original effective simulations see one of the following resources.

Helpful Resources

Books and Games

Ellington, H., Gordon, M., & Fowlie, J. (1998). *Using games and simulations in the classroom.* London: Kogan Page.

Fischer, M. W. (1995). *Geography simulations.* Westminster, CA: Teacher Created Materials.

Fischer, M. W. (2001). *Mysteries of antiquity: Lessons to engage middle school students in ancient/medieval history.* Boulder, CO: Social Science Education Consortium.

Gredler, M. E. (1994). *Designing and evaluating games and simulations.* Houston: Gulf Publishing.

Hall, K. P. (1997). *Math simulations: Intermediate.* Westminster, CA: Teacher Created Materials.

Hess, F. M. (1999). *Bringing the social sciences alive: Ten simulations for history, economics, government, and geography.* Boston: Allyn & Bacon.

Lasher, D., Graham, P. W., & Heyde, A. T. (2000). *Underground railroad* [game]: *A simulated journey from slavery to freedom.* Carlsbad, CA: Interaction Publishers.

Stix, A., & Hrbek, F. (2001). *Using literature and simulations in your social studies classroom.* Westminster, CA: Teacher Created Materials.

Online Resources
Educational Simulations, Inc.
www.simulations.com/

Interact Simulations
www.interact-simulations.com

North American Simulation and Gaming Association
www.nasaga.org

River Deep
www.riverdeep.net

Ten "Mistakes" Commonly Made by Persons
Designing Educational Simulations and Games
www.stsintl.com/articles/ten_mistakes.html

United States Institute for Peace
www.usip.org/class/simulations/instructions.html

Cooperative Learning

The traditional argument for adhering to the bell-shaped normal curve in distributing class grades was that students needed to be prepared for the competitive, dog-eat-dog world of work. However, the dramatic changes in the global economy have forced a revolution in the workplace. The emphasis is on teaching employees to work cooperatively. Quality circles and work teams are now in use almost universally. Employers realize that to be competitive in the world economy, their employees must be skilled in working collaboratively.

Cooperative learning consists of a variety of techniques that requires students to collaborate in mixed-ability groups, helping each other learn the material. Students are taught to take greater responsibility for their own learning. The ultimate goal of cooperative learning is to enable each student to become more successful in school.

The essential focus of cooperative learning is that students are not competing with other students for success. They are seeking to top their own level of achievement. By helping each other, all students can improve. How many people a student defeats in the race for grades would no longer define success. Cooperative learning succeeds when students become convinced that their success is determined by how well they help each other. They must become interdependent in their use of the available learning resources.

Numerous research studies have found cooperative learning does work. Indeed, it may be the most validated instructional strategy in practice today. It results at achievement gains in every grade level, for both high- and low-ability students.

Research has found cooperative learning to enhance student self-esteem, mutual helping, and more positive attitudes toward teachers and learning. Contrary to what some people fear, high-ability students do not suffer when they work cooperatively with middle- and lower-ability students.

Direct teaching of the interpersonal skills necessary to collaborate is an essential component of cooperative learning.

Cooperative learning is widely used across all grade levels and subjects; probably every school in the United States has some teachers using cooperative learning. The major spokespersons for it have been Roger and David Johnson and Robert Slavin. These educators are among those offering outstanding training programs on using cooperative learning. A thorough presentation of cooperative learning is beyond the scope of this book, but do consider taking a course or workshop to learn more about implementing the various cooperative learning strategies available. See Performance Learning Systems (www.plsweb.com/) for an example of one such course, or contact a college of education near you.

> The reason cooperative learning is so successful is that the context of a work group is more important than the content of the group. If you have a group of people who care for and are committed to one another, they are going to achieve the goal of the activity much more quickly than if each were to attempt the task alone.
>
> —**Harry Wong, *The First Days of School***

The following tips may prove helpful in implementing cooperative learning activities in your classes:

✓ Merely participating in a group activity will not assure success. Several conditions must exist. The students must be working toward a common goal, and their success in attaining that goal must depend on their interdependence. Ideally, students must also have to depend on each other to share resources. There is evidence that the use of group rewards enhances students' cooperative learning efforts but only if the rewards are contingent on all group members' individual learning.

✓ Cooperative learning activities can succeed only if a supportive class climate is established. Students must feel free to take risks and make mistakes.

✓ Be creative in how you form groups. For most temporary groups, randomly dividing the class into the desired number of groups will assure a sufficient degree of mixed abilities in each group. Simply counting off and grouping the ones, twos, threes, and so on is the most common tactic. Inject some humor and interest by using unconventional ways of forming equal-sized groups. For example, have students line up against the wall in order of their birthdays, without talking. Then break them into the desired number of groups.

✓ Group size can vary with the activity's objective. Generally, a maximum of five seems to be advisable. Heterogeneity in gender, ability, and ethnicity are desirable. The research shows that students involved in cooperative learning become much more accepting of other students, including those different from themselves.

✓ Clear directions are essential for cooperative learning groups' success. Provide written instructions in assigning any complicated tasks. Give careful thought to your directions' completeness and clarity. Encourage students to ask questions if they do not understand what to do.

✓ Each person in a group has a job. The number of jobs required to complete the assignment determines the size of the cooperative learning group. Sometimes the teacher may assign each member specific jobs; other times the group may decide how to break up the functions.

✓ Cooperative learning develops the social skills necessary to work with others: seeking and giving help, listening to others' points of view, and resolving conflicts. Provide students special training to develop the skills they need for collaborative work. Assessment of each student's social skills is an essential component of successful cooperative learning. Training in the constructive management of conflict is vital for success. For many students cooperation may be a new mode of classroom learning. Patience and guidance will be necessary.

✓ Cooperative groups can be especially valuable in editing group members' written compositions. Students should be provided with a checklist of criteria to use to evaluate each other's compositions. The peer editor places his or her signature on the criteria checklist. At each step of the writing process—from conceptualization through polished product—the cooperative team members aid each other. Ideally, everyone submits a high-quality written product while saving the teacher much time reading and rereading rough drafts.

✓ Some teachers have their students explain and grade their homework assignments in cooperative learning groups. An efficient routine must be established for the procedures to follow, with several roles assigned (accuracy checker, grade recorder, coach, explainer). An advantage of this group approach is that students have the opportunity to help each other understand why they made the errors they did and to obtain corrective feedback.

✓ Cooperative learning groups are sometimes permitted to take examinations or tests together. The day prior to the test, groups may help each other review. It is essential that the groups be heterogeneous in ability. On the test day, students may take individual examinations. After turning in the answer sheet, students meet with their cooperative learning group and collaborate on the examination. They turn in the second answer sheet, with the teacher recording each student's performance on both exams.

> *Cooperative learning methods are creating a classroom revolution. No longer is a quiet class thought to be a learning class; we know now that learning is often best achieved in conversation among students. Teachers all over the world are breaking up the rows in which students have sat for so long, and are creating classroom environments in which students routinely help each other master academic material.*
>
> —**Robert Slavin,** *A Practical Guide to Cooperative Learning*

For More Information

Books

Aronson, E., & Patnoe, S. (1997). *The jigsaw classroom*. New York: Longman.

Blanchard, K., Bowles, S., Carew, D., & Parisi-Carew, E. (2001). *High five! The magic of working together*. New York: William Morrow.

Cuseo, J. (2002). *Igniting student involvement, peer interaction, and teamwork: A taxonomy of specific cooperative learning structures and collaborative learning strategies*. Stillwater, OK: New Forums Press.

Forest, L. (2001). *Crafting creative community: Combining cooperative learning, multiple intelligences, and nature's wisdom*. San Clemente, CA: Kagan Publishing.

Gut, D. M., & Safran, S. P. (2002). Cooperative learning and social stories: Effective social skills strategies for reading teachers. *Reading and Writing Quarterly: Overcoming Learning Difficulties, 18*(1), 87–91.

Jacobs, G. M., Power, M. A., & Inn, L. W. (2002). *The teacher's sourcebook for cooperative learning: Practical techniques, basic principles, and frequently asked questions*. Thousand Oaks, CA: Corwin.

Johnson, D. W., & Johnson, R. (2002). *Meaningful assessment: A manageable and cooperative process*. Boston: Allyn & Bacon.

McConnell, D. (2000). *Implementing computer supported cooperative learning*. Sterling, VA: Kogan Page.

Thousand, J. S., Villa, R. A., & Nevin, A. I. (Eds.) (2002). *Creativity and collaborative learning: A practical guide to empowering students and teachers*. Baltimore: P. H. Brookes.

Special-Interest Groups

Computers and Cooperative Learning
Contact: Howard Budin
Teachers College
Box 8
525 West 120th Street
New York, NY 10027
(212) 678–3773

Cooperative Learning in Higher Education
Contact: Jim Cooper
California State University, Dominguez Hills
1000 E Victoria Street
Carson, CA 90747
(213) 516-3524

Cooperative Learning Network
Contact: Harlan Rimmerman
North Kansas City Public Schools
2000 NE 46th Street
Kansas City, MO 64116
(913) 621-3073
www.sheridanc.on.ca/coop_learn/cooplrn.htm

Cooperative Learning: Theory, Research, and Practice
Contact: Kary Smith, chair
Cooperative Learning Center
University of Minnesota
202 Pattee Hall
150 Pillsbury Drive SE
Minneapolis, MN 55455
(612) 624–7031

Human Relations Skills Network for Outdoor Leaders
Contact: Kathy Henchey, manager of professional development
American Camping Association
State Road 67 N
Martinsville, IN 46151
(765) 342-8456
www.acacamps.org/education/ols.htm

International Association for the Study of Cooperation in Education
P.O. Box 1582
Santa Cruz, CA 95061-1582
(408) 462-7926
www.iasce.net/

Mid-Atlantic Association for Cooperative Learning
www.geocities.com/~maacie/

National Learning Communities Project
Contact: Washington Center for Undergraduate Education
L 2211
The Evergreen State College
Olympia, WA 98505
(360) 867-6910
www.learningcommons.evergreen.edu

Online Collaborative Learning in Higher Education
Central Queensland University
Australia

Faculty of Informatics and Communication
Central Queensland University
Bundaberg
Queensland 4670
Australia
clp.cqu.edu.au

Periodicals
Cooperative Learning: The Magazine for Cooperation in Education
www.iasce.net/Newsletters

Published by the International Association for the Study of Cooperation in Education,
P.O. Box 1582, Santa Cruz, CA 95061-1582.

Cooperative Learning and College Teaching
www.csudh.edu/SOE/cl_network/

Published by the Network for Cooperative Learning in Higher Education.

Online Cooperative Learning Resources
Ted's Cooperative Learning e-book (Ted Panitz)
home.capecod.net/~tpanitz/ebook/contents.html

Collaborative Learning Discussion Forum
mathforum.org/discussions/co-learn/

Cooperative Learning Center, University of Minnesota
www.cooplearn.org/

Cooperative Learning Elementary Activities
Springfield (Missouri) Public Schools
204.184.214.251/coop/ecoopmain.html

DeLiberations on Cooperative Learning
www.lgu.ac.uk/deliberations/collab.learning/

Jigsaw Classroom (Elliot Aronson)
www.jigsaw.org/

Software Evaluation Guide

Software title _____

Company _____ Cost _____

Multiple-user and site licenses available? _____ No _____ Yes

Platforms supported: _____ Macintosh _____ Windows _____ Palm

System requirements _____

_____

Age or skill level _____

Objectives of software _____

_____

Target audience: _____ Individual _____ Collaborative groups

Assess each criterion with a score from 1 (poor) to 5 (excellent).

Criteria	Poor				Excellent
	1	2	3	4	5
Ease of Installation					
Alignment with standards and curriculum					
Accuracy of content					
Technical quality					
Interest and motivation					
Degree of interaction					
Multicultural and gender sensitivity					
Effectiveness					
Clarity of directions					
Documentation					
Ease of use					
Internal record management					
Total points					

Recommend software? _____ No _____ Yes _____ Undecided

Sample Letter to Parents at Beginning of School Year

(Date)

Greetings:

Do you have a special talent? Do you enjoy an interesting hobby or activity? What skills do you use in your work? Have you traveled to an interesting or exciting place? Have you had a significant life experience from which young people might learn something? Please consider sharing any of these special abilities or events with my class sometime during the school year.

If you will complete and return the section below, I will contact you to arrange a mutually convenient time when you might visit my class. This is a valuable opportunity to become a part of the school community and to show your child you are interested in his/her education.

Sincerely,

(Your name)

Name _____

Phone _____

E-mail address _____

Address _____

_____

What talent, experiences, or hobby would you be willing to share with my students?

_____

_____

_____

_____

_____

_____

_____

_____

_____

Few people think more than two or three times a year. I have made an international reputation for myself thinking once or twice a week.

— George Bernard Shaw

Strategies for Selecting Group Leaders

First person to stand up

Whoever got up earliest this morning

Tap the person on your right and congratulate him or her.

Drives the oldest car

Lowest last two digits in their phone number

Draw cards.

Youngest or oldest person in the group

Born farthest from or closest to school

Stayed up the latest last night

Most or fewest brothers and sisters

Traveled the farthest to get here

Has the most pets

Been to the movies most recently

Nearest birthday

Shortest pinky

Last name comes first in alphabet

Moved most recently

Most recent vacation

Born earliest in the year or month

Went swimming most recently

Person to left of the last group leader

Came into the room last

Has the most eyelets in their shoes

Ate peanut butter most recently

Wearing the largest shoe

Has moved the most times

Mowed the grass most recently

Rented a video most recently

Most years in their current home

Appointed by the last leader

Shortest or tallest

The most letters in name

Bought a _____ most recently

Lives closest to where they were born

Most recent airplane ride

Longest or shortest hair

Sitting closest to the door

Sitting nearest the instructor

Everyone points to the next leader on the count of three.

Ask for a volunteer who then appoints the next leader.

Field Trip Checklist

Site _____   Date of trip _____

Contact person _____   Phone _____

Departure time _____   Return time _____

Chaperones _____

Before the Visit

_____ Identify the purpose of the trip.

_____ Contact site to arrange date and time.

_____ Obtain administrative approval if necessary.

_____ Distribute permission forms.

_____ Send a letter to parents describing details of the visit.

_____ Solicit chaperones.

_____ Arrange transportation.

_____ Make any necessary lunch arrangements.

_____ Develop active learning worksheets.

_____ Collect and turn in permission forms.

_____ Construct map and directions to the site.

_____ Discuss behavioral and academic expectations with students.

_____ Remind chaperones and students the day before the trip.

Day of the Visit

_____ Meet chaperones a few minutes early.

_____ Give drivers maps and directions.

_____ Distribute any worksheets.

_____ Remind students of when and where to meet after the visit.

After the Visit

_____ Debrief students and help them connect the visit with prior learning.

_____ Write thank-you notes to chaperones and the site coordinator.

_____ Note any changes to make for the next field trip.

_____ File forms, brochures, and lesson plans to use next time.

Field Trip Permission Form

Student's name _____

We are planning a class field trip on _____

to _____. We are seeking your approval for your

child to participate. We will be leaving at approximately _____ and

will return to the school at _____. We will be traveling by

_____. The trip will be appropriately supervised. I believe

this visit is of sound educational value. Please call me if you have any questions. I need this

form returned to the school by _____.

The above student has my permission to participate in the above field trip.

_____

(Parent or guardian)

- -

Field Trip Permission Form

Student's name _____

We are planning a class field trip on _____

to _____. We are seeking your approval for your

child to participate. We will be leaving at approximately _____ and

will return to the school at _____. We will be traveling by

_____. The trip will be appropriately supervised. I believe

this visit is of sound educational value. Please call me if you have any questions. I need this

form returned to the school by _____.

The above student has my permission to participate in the above field trip.

_____

(Parent or guardian)

Audiovisual Request Form

To _____   Today's date _____

From _____   Room no. _____

Equipment	Date Needed	Time	
		From	Until

Team Record

Team name _____ Class _____

Team Members	1	2	3	4	5	6	7	Totals
Team Score								
Average Score								

Tasks:

1. _____

2. _____

3. _____

4. _____

5. _____

6. _____

7. _____

Chapter Four

Building a Learning Community

Twenty-four Hot Tips for Working with Other Teachers

Most experienced teachers have learned to avoid the potential isolation of the classroom. In many schools a teacher can go through an entire day with little more than superficial contact with other adults. What happens behind the closed classroom door is still guarded as private in some schools. Beginning teachers used to enter the profession with full responsibility from the first day, learning to teach largely on their own by trial and error or the sink-or-swim method. Fortunately, there are signs that the school culture is opening up. Increasingly, teachers are collaborating, working in teams, and engaging in peer coaching. Attention to developing collegial relationships and nurturing positive school climates is growing. Here's what to do:

1. Talk about teaching with your colleagues. This should involve more than complaining about insufficient supplies or how terrible kids are these days. Nor should conversations be limited to trading war stories. Encourage a positive focus on sharing strategies for improving classroom teaching, solving school problems, or seeking innovative ways of doing old tasks.

2. Experiment with peer coaching. Invite teachers you respect to observe your teaching and provide suggestions for improvement. Let the observer know which areas you are seeking to improve. Of course, if you solicit their feedback, listen to it objectively. Don't discount their views and become defensive.

3. Ask for help from colleagues. Share your concerns about what you would like to do better. In every building there are successful teachers. Seek them out and learn from their experience.

4. Acknowledge your fellow teachers' successes. Relay positive comments you hear from students about other teachers.

5. Send special notes and cards to your colleagues recognizing their successes or offering words of comfort during difficult times. Eschew jealousy over other teachers' success. Your value as a teacher or person is not diminished by others' accomplishments. To be appreciated is one of the most fundamental human needs.

6. Share curriculum resources or creative ideas you bring back from professional workshops or read in journals.

7. After attending school in-service programs, discuss the content with other teachers. Try to remain open-minded in examining new ideas, always seeking new ways to improve your teaching. Convey to your colleagues that you value improvement and appreciate their ideas.

8. Avoid joining the staff saboteurs whose main function is to prevent any efforts at improvement. Their primary activities are complaining, gossiping, nit-picking, whining, and ridiculing. Rarely do they offer positive solutions or acknowledge their own deficiencies. They blame all their problems on others. Often they will be found sitting in the back at faculty meetings or clustered in faculty lounges before and during school. Treat them cordially, but resist their venomous game. They are an emotional and economic drain on their schools, taking far more than they contribute. It is unlikely they find much joy in teaching.

9. Avoid gossiping about other teachers, students, or the administration. Gossip serves no constructive purpose and poisons the school climate. It is unprofessional as well as destructive. If you hear gossip, don't spread it. Be especially careful in what you say about students or faculty outside of school.

10. Organize or join a study group or peer support group. Peer coaching is gaining acceptance in many schools. Do whatever you can to nurture mutual support and the development of collegial, professional relationships.

11. Participate in professional improvement activities with your colleagues. Attend workshops, classes, or conferences together. Watch videotapes or discuss education-related books. Nurture each other's professional development.

12. Strive to develop connections with teachers beyond your area or grade level. Much can be learned from all good teachers, regardless of the subject or grade they teach.

13. Observe outstanding teachers in their classrooms. The truly effective ones will welcome your presence. They are not threatened by having visitors in their classrooms.

14. Never criticize fellow teachers in front of students. Such unprofessional conduct serves no constructive purpose. Always assume that whatever you say about a colleague will eventually get back to that person. Communicate directly with the other teacher if you believe his or her behavior creates a problem for you or the students. If the grievance is serious, pursue it through your principal. Remember, you will probably be working with that teacher for some time.

15. Be willing to do your share of the work. Volunteer for some committee assignments: chaperoning dances, organizing events, or supervising students.

16. A friendly "hello" or "good morning" plants the seeds of an inviting relationship with your colleagues, even those you don't know very well or who treat you coolly.

17. Help create goodwill. Celebrate special occasions by bringing cookies, fruit, or other treats to a faculty meeting or to the lounge in the morning.

18. Avoid associating only with a favorite clique. Try to develop cordial relationships with all teachers, even the ones with whom you disagree. Try to get to know them as people. Discover their interests, family news, and achievements.

19. Respect your colleagues' rights. Avoid causing students to be late to their classes. Don't undermine colleagues' authority and credibility with their students. Remain considerate of your fellow professionals' needs.

20. Don't borrow materials, books, supplies, or equipment without asking. If you do use someone else's things, be sure to return them promptly.

21. Be extremely cautious of reprimanding other teachers' students, especially while the students are under their supervision.

22. Try to resolve conflicts in a mature, assertive fashion. Any school will have occasional disagreements over policies, perceptions, solutions, or actions. Feelings can get hurt, intentions misperceived. Seldom is one person right and the other absolutely wrong. Colleagues are rarely evil, though occasionally they may be thoughtless or inconsiderate. Don't overreact. The first step is to let the person know in an assertive, not hostile, way that you perceive a problem to exist. Seek collaborative problem solving. Really listen to their point of view. Avoid petty squabbling.

23. Be patient with your colleagues. Like you, your fellow teachers are humans. They will have bad days and will make mistakes. Don't expect them to hold the same values and perspectives as you.

24. Treat all colleagues as professionals, even if you don't believe they are treating you with full respect. Work at being tolerant of those who have views different from yours. Treat all others decently. Your initial perceptions of people can be wrong; you don't know all that is happening in their lives beyond school.

Working with a Mentor

Teaching is challenging work, even for the most experienced teachers. The most enthusiastic beginning teachers can find entering their very first class to be a frightening experience. Approximately a third of all new teachers leave the profession within three years. Clearly, new teachers need support.

Ask veteran teachers for their advice. It makes them feel valued if you are genuinely interested. You don't have to reinvent the wheel. Others have faced the same challenges and taught the same content. Learn what works for them.

Many schools have established formal mentoring programs to make the transition smoother for beginning teachers. Indeed, some states have mandated such programs. An abundance of research supports the wisdom of well-implemented mentoring programs.

Seek out the best teachers in the school and ask their permission to observe their classes. It doesn't matter what subject they are teaching. There is no substitute for seeing outstanding teachers in action.

A Hampton, Virginia, program matches beginning teachers with retired teachers. The program is a collaboration among the Virginia Education Association, the NEA-Retired Association, the local school district, and area universities.

A number of excellent publications outline the procedures for setting up effective mentoring programs. Hopefully, your school has followed those guidelines. A well-matched mentoring relationship benefits both the mentor and the protégé. And in the end, students greatly benefit.

Having an effective role model to provide a friendly ear, objective feedback, support, and encouragement has tremendous potential for enriching one's professional development. Effective coaches and mentors help novice teachers gain confidence, improve their skills, and achieve their full potential. Mentored teachers are more likely to stay in the profession and enjoy teaching more.

While the tendency is to focus largely on classroom management issues early on in the mentoring process, it should move on to include lesson planning, curriculum goals, collegiality, and instructional improvement.

Here are some concrete tips on how to reap the most from a mentoring relationship:

✓ If your school doesn't have a formal mentoring program, ask your principal about creating one. Suggest one or two teachers you admire as potential mentors.

✓ If you are a beginning teacher or having difficulty, find a mentor. Identify a teacher whom you respect and whose style and personality is simpatico with yours. Seek someone who is genuinely enthusiastic about teaching and is an exemplary instructor. Share your difficult problems with them and listen openly to their advice.

✓ Get to know your mentor. If possible, meet him or her before the school year begins.

✓ Enter the mentoring relationship with an open mind. Your mentor is not there to judge or evaluate you. Even if you don't agree with something your mentor says, treat him or her with respect.

✓ Take responsibility for initiating contacts with your mentor when you need help. Your mentor cannot anticipate all your needs and concerns. Try to set up regular meetings with your mentor.

✓ Being an effective mentor takes a serious commitment of time and effort. Respect your mentor's time. Don't monopolize his or her time or become overly dependent.

✓ Accept suggestions and constructive criticism. Avoid taking criticism personally. Try to avoid becoming defensive. You will make mistakes and aren't going to be perfect.

✓ If possible, visit your mentor's classroom to observe him or her in action. Take notes about what you see and initiate a discussion later about what you observed. Focus your observations on specific aspects, such as the way this teacher asks questions, the teacher's nonverbal behavior, the use of praise and encouragement, the teacher's way of handling transitions, or the pace of the lesson.

✓ Clarify what you think the mentor is communicating. Ask follow-up questions or paraphrase what you think you have heard. Clarify your assumptions.

✓ Periodically express your appreciation for your mentor's help. If your mentor is especially helpful, be sure to convey that message to the principal or superintendent. Doing so multiplies the effect of your gratitude.

✓ Share your successes with your mentor. Give your mentor credit for helping you improve. Develop a warm-fuzzy file of compliments, positive notes from parents or students, and mementos of any other successes you cherish. Paste these in a scrapbook and reread them anytime you begin to feel a bit discouraged.

✓ Keep a daily journal, noting concerns, challenges, questions, successes, and insights. Reflect on insights you gain. These notes may serve to structure meetings with your mentor. This writing is not a formal paper, so write whatever comes to mind in whatever style flows naturally. Reread your journal later in the year. Save it. Who knows? It might become a book someday!

✓ Give the mentoring relationship a fair chance to succeed. If after a couple months, you find that your mentor is not very helpful, develop an informal mentor relationship with a teacher you admire. If you have a trusting relationship with your principal, candidly discuss your concern.

✓ At the end of the year, do something nice for your mentor. A letter of appreciation, an invitation to lunch, or a small gift would likely be most appreciated. For many the mentoring relationship blossoms into a lifelong friendship.

Telementoring

In a creative application of developing computer technology, many teachers have linked up in telementoring projects (also known as e-mentoring or telecoaching). Some telementoring projects are formally set up by schools or universities, some by for-profit organizations, and others by informal arrangements between two teachers. Most of the communication occurs through e-mail exchanges. The mentor can be thousands of miles away yet still develop a helpful relationship with the protégé.

The North Carolina Science Leadership Association sponsors an e-mentoring program that matches new teachers with online partners who provide support and teaching ideas. The mentor and mentee communicate by e-mail through- out the school year. More information about this program may be found online at www.ncsla.net/leadership/ementor.html.

Teachers may also request an e-pal mentor through the Teacher.net Web site, at www.teachers.net/, or Mentor Net, at stone.web.brevard.k12.fl.us/mentornet/mentor.html.

For more about telementoring see the following Web sites:

CCCCD: Telementoring
iws.ccccd.edu/telementoring/

The Mentor Center
www.teachermentors.com/

Telementoring Web
www.tnellen.com/cybereng/mentor/

Guidelines for Collaborative Teams

The ability to arrive at group decisions has become a vital skill for today's teachers, as schools increasingly incorporate site-based management (directly involving local staff in decision making), collaborative teams, and shared decision making. The opportunity to participate more broadly in the school decision-making process has several potential benefits. Giving teachers a greater voice in the school decision-making process, like the quality circles that businesses are adapting, assures that those having the best available information will make decisions and be responsible for implementing them. Participatory decision making also gives the participants a greater sense of control and is more likely to yield a commitment to the resulting decisions.

The ability to effectively arrive at good group decisions requires a set of learned skills that teacher education courses of study have only rarely included. It is risky to assume that all members of a team possess the skills of group problem solving. Unfortunately, most persons assume that everyone knows how to arrive at group decisions. A substantial body of research suggests this is a most erroneous supposition. To be effective, specific training in collaborative decision making should be available to any staff moving toward greater use of teams. The preponderance of evidence also shows training in group problem-solving skills leads to more creative ideas, both in quantity and quality.

Whenever two or more persons must jointly arrive at decisions, expect two things: (1) the process will take more time, and (2) the process will bring friction. While any group can arrive at a decision, the barometer of success is whether the group considered the best available information in making its choice. When groups effectively tap all their members' resources, they are capable of achieving synergy, meaning the group product is superior to anything any one individual could have achieved alone. Here are some tips:

✓ Be sure that everyone in the group clearly understands the issue to be decided. Occasionally, group members discover they have been arguing over different issues. Early in the group process, the group should attain some agreement on the mutual mission and define the problem and goals.

✓ Ask open-ended questions to elicit all points of view. Some participants are going to be more reluctant to share their views openly without encouragement.

Paraphrasing for understanding and clarity is another valuable communication tool for group decision makers.

✓ Occasionally ask others to clarify with examples and specifics. Don't necessarily assume that you know what another person means.

✓ In the early stages of searching for possible solutions, employ the strategy of group brainstorming. To succeed brainstorming must adhere to four rules:

- Elicit as many ideas as possible. The focus in this stage is on quantity, not quality. The more ideas you have, the greater the possibility of discovering a good one.
- Delay evaluation. Later you will apply criteria of judgment to your ideas, but premature criticism nips creativity in the bud.
- Encourage wild, far-out, half-baked ideas. One may be the diamond in the rough.
- Listen to others' ideas and use them as springboards. Let their ideas stimulate your search. For this reason it helps to record the group ideas on newsprint for all to see.

✓ Elicit different points of view. View such disagreements as a healthy part of the group search for the optimal decision. Avoiding conflict is not productive in arriving at good group decisions. Research shows that the most effective decision-making groups encourage minority opinions to be aired. It is important to discuss sources of resistance openly rather than to let them fester and later sabotage the implementation of the decision.

✓ The goal should be to arrive at a win-win consensus rather than a compromise about which no one is particularly enthusiastic. For that reason avoid such conflict-reducing techniques as voting or averaging. While they may save time, they often yield inferior decisions that lack all members' commitment.

✓ It is also important for groups to arrive at their own definition of consensus. It could mean that everyone must enthusiastically endorse any group decision, that everyone agrees the solution might work and should be tried and later reevaluated, or simply that everyone can live with the recommendation.

✓ Consensus building is most likely when all group members seek to identify areas of disagreement and the common ground. The group should fairly analyze the advantages and disadvantages of all possible solutions.

✓ Don't change your mind merely to avoid conflict. Disagreement among persons with different needs and assumptions is a legitimate part of the group process. Conversely, it is important to challenge others' ideas, especially when they offer little support for the position.

✓ When conflicting views emerge, strive to identify the needs and interests rather than merely the positions of the opposing group members.

✓ Show your respect for others by listening to their ideas. When you share your opinions, try to be nonconfrontational. Present your point of view without putting down those who disagree. Focus on issues, not personalities.

✓ If necessary, leave the decision for a later time. This permits some incubation time. New, more creative solutions may emerge from this reflection. Such a delay is especially warranted if the discussion has become excessively volatile or if the group lacks information necessary to make a sound decision.

✓ Groups have very limited attention spans and tend to digress from the issue at hand. Gently refocus the group's attention with such open-ended questions as "What additional information do we need?" or "Are there any other options we have not considered?"

✓ Be sure to have a team recorder keep a written record of your team's decisions and create the group memory. This helps the team keep focused on its task and assures a future record of what the group has decided.

✓ Create opportunities to celebrate your team's successes: a gag gift, a funny ritual, a special meal, or a party.

✓ A team must assume responsibility for decisions that don't succeed. Part of the price of the freedom to make decisions is accepting their consequences.

✓ Capitalize on each team member's strengths and talents. Match the tasks required with your team members' skills.

✓ Training should be available on group roles, group problem solving, planning, and stages of group development. The group might read and discuss some of the resources that follow.

> ## Suggestions for Effective Action Planning Teams
>
> Select a group leader. Things seem to go more smoothly if one person serves as the facilitator.
>
> Do not prematurely seek the ultimate solution. Spend time clarifying the issues related to the problem. Examine the problem's causes and effects.
>
> Discuss what additional information is needed to make an intelligent decision. Where can you get that information? Divide up the information-gathering tasks. Ask for help if you need it.
>
> After gathering relevant information, spend adequate time fully brainstorming options without prematurely evaluating. Remember the four rules of effective brainstorming:
>
> - Strive for as many ideas as possible.
> - Delay evaluation.
> - Encourage novel, creative ideas.
> - Build on others' ideas.
>
> Elicit ideas from each other without dominating the discussion. Remember to differentiate facts from opinions.
>
> Components of an effective action plan should include the following:
>
> - Specific steps to be taken
> - Who will be responsible for each component of the plan
> - A reasonable time line for implementing each component
> - Estimates of any costs for implementation and suggestions as to the source of these funds
> - A target deadline for reevaluating progress toward implementation of your plan
>
> Set a time and place to meet again if needed.

✓ The group should be conscious of and occasionally examine its group process to see if it is working effectively. By enhancing its group process, the team can arrive at better choices. Some teams find it helpful to take five minutes at the end of each meeting to complete a Team Process Assessment form such as the one at the end of this chapter.

Helpful Resources

Basham, A., Appleton, V. E., & Dykeman, C. (2000). *Team building in education: A how-to guidebook*. Denver, CO: Love Publishing.

Friend, M. P., & Cook, L. (2003). *Interactions: Collaboration skills for school professionals*. Boston: Allyn & Bacon.

Smialek, M. A. (2001). *Team strategies for success: Doing what counts in education*. Lanham, MD: Scarecrow Education.

Smialek, M. A. (2002). *Inside teams in education*. Bloomington, IN: Phi Delta Kappa Educational Foundation.

Working with Your Principal

A principal who truly serves as an instructional leader is of immense value to any school. The role of the principal and the nature of school leadership are being redefined as increasing numbers of schools turn to site-based management, total quality schools, teaming, restructuring, peer coaching, decentralization, and other paradigm shifts.

Whatever the exact configuration of leadership functions in a specific school, teachers and their principals are locked in an interdependent relationship. They need each other to succeed. The less friction and stress between principal and teacher, the more enjoyable both will find their jobs. Evidence also suggests that the quality of the teacher-principal relationship greatly influences the overall school climate, which in turn affects the students' success in the classroom.

Investing in a positive, professional teacher-principal relationship should be a top priority for any beginning teacher. While some principals are more talented leaders than others, students are ultimately the winners when principals and teachers can work in harmony. No one gains and ultimately students lose when a poisonous, adversarial relationship exists between principal and teachers. Successful teachers strive to develop partnerships with their principals. Here's what to do:

✓ Keep your principal informed of both budding problems and your triumphs. Don't wait to surprise him or her with major problems. It is best for the principal to have ample information directly from you before he or she hears about a problem from others. No decision can be better than the information on which it is based. Take time to communicate your interests and needs.

✓ Avoid visiting your principal only when you have problems. Share some good news or ask his or her advice. Invest time in nurturing a positive relationship. If you are experimenting with a new instructional technique or a novel assignment, alert your principal and seek his or her support. Only through frequent interactions does mutual trust evolve.

✓ When your principal has done something considerate or particularly helpful, drop him or her a note. Let the principal know that you appreciate his or her efforts. Like department store managers, principals often hear only the complaints.

✓ For special achievements send an unsolicited letter of recognition or support for your principal to the superintendent. Anytime you want to give someone major recognition, don't just tell them; tell their superior.

✓ Avoid dumping your problems on your principal. Especially avoid sending kids to the office for misbehavior unless it involves persistent or serious infractions, such as fighting. Relying on the principal to solve your student behavior problems on a daily basis creates the impression that you cannot control your own classroom.

✓ Avoid backbiting or ridiculing your principal, even if he or she falls short of your expectations. It simply isn't professional, and it really doesn't accomplish anything positive. Don't join in the game even if others are playing.

✓ If you have a complaint or disagree with the principal on an issue, communicate your case clearly and rationally. This never calls for yelling, name-calling, or sarcasm. Stick to the facts. If you have difficulty controlling your emotions in direct conversation, articulate your position in a letter. Remember, you still have to work with him or her tomorrow. Your aim is to influence the principal's decision, not to alienate him or her. In all contacts act maturely and professionally.

✓ Choose your battles carefully. In any relationship you have only a limited amount of credit available in the other's emotional bank account. Don't squander your assets on minor skirmishes; save them for the truly important issues. If you rarely complain, you are more likely to be heard when you do.

✓ When you take a problem to your principal, prepare at least one or two possible solutions. Anticipate the consequences of each, the risks, and the resources needed. Be succinct in your presentation. Be rational in what you expect the principal to do to solve your problems.

✓ Find opportunities to make your principal look good. One way is to publicize in the community the students' outstanding achievements. Any noteworthy school accomplishment reflects positively on the principal.

✓ Don't make the principal's job more difficult than it needs to be. Submit grades, attendance records, and reports on time. Some amount of paperwork has to be done to make a school work smoothly. It may sometimes be inconvenient, but it must be done. Avoid using the principal's time for petty problems.

✓ Try to see things from the principal's point of view. Being principal is not an easy job. Principals have many interests to please: teachers, noncertified staff, boards of education, central office, students, parents, and taxpayers. Most every decision they make irritates someone, especially with the limited resources available to most schools. They are also sometimes obliged to enforce school policies they may not like. Be a bit empathetic. That doesn't mean you have to sacrifice your principles, that you shouldn't advocate for those issues to which you are passionately committed. However, recognize you won't always get what you want when you want it.

✓ Take the initiative in inviting your principal to visit your classroom. If you have a particularly interesting or successful lesson coming up, try to schedule an observation. Strive to view the principal as an instructional ally, even if you do disagree on your teaching effectiveness.

✓ Avoid interpreting criticisms of your teaching effectiveness as personal attacks. No teacher is perfect. Avoid becoming defensive. Reality-test any criticisms by asking other administrators or teachers to observe your teaching. Invite the principal to observe you again to reassess your teaching. A goal you both should share is to provide the best instruction possible to all your students. Build on that common purpose.

✓ Avoid asking for special privileges. It unfairly puts the administrator on the spot. If you have a request for special resources or exemption to school policies, consider how your fellow teachers will accept that request if it is granted.

✓ Share articles you read on school improvement practices with your principal. Occasionally, ask his or her opinion on an educational trend or innovation.

✓ A good time to get to know your principal better is during the summer. Most are on an extended schedule. Stop by to see the principal during the summer. She or he will have more time than during the school year, when daily crises consume the principal's time.

✓ Show your principal you are thinking of him or her. Small considerations such as a birthday card, a holiday card, homemade cookies, or a vacation postcard are fruitful investments in a positive relationship.

Improving Parent-Teacher Relations

You have much to gain from developing a constructive working relationship with your students' parents and guardians. If invited, parents can play a valuable role in your teaching success. They can offer support and reinforcement for your academic and behavioral goals. They can provide assistance in a variety of ways, both in your classroom and from their homes. Many possess talents, interests, and ideas that can augment what you offer. Many parents (and other community members) don't become more fully involved in their schools simply because they haven't been invited. Here are suggestions:

✓ Before the school year begins, send notes home to your students' parents or guardians introducing yourself and inviting them to become a part of the school community. Some teachers include a checklist of hobbies, talents, and interests that the parents might be willing to share with the class at some time during the year. Emphasize that you believe they play an important role in their child's education.

✓ Send periodic notes to parents, recognizing their children's positive achievements or behavior in your class. Typically, parents hear from the school only when their children are in trouble. Set aside ten minutes each week to send two or three notes to different parents. Don't just acknowledge the students who are getting A's. Recognize the student who has been reluctant to participate but is now contributing in class, the student who did an outstanding job on one project, or the student who had been getting C's and is now getting B's. It will pay dividends!

✓ Occasionally call parents to communicate some good news about their child's accomplishments. It will catch them off guard, but they will likely be most appreciative.

✓ Develop home-school contracts with the parents of students who are having difficulty completing homework or behaving appropriately in class. If the student fulfills the contract, the parents offer a special privilege or reward. You might have a checksheet that both you and the parent must sign each day or week. This forestalls students from reporting "I didn't have any homework" and other similar "inaccurate" communications they sometimes relate to parents.

✓ Invite parents to become involved in your classroom. Tap their talents as special volunteers not only for field trip supervision and class parties but also as teacher's aides and speakers. You might send a survey home to obtain information about their skills, interests, and willingness to help.

✓ If feasible, make home visits to meet your students' parents. Not only will you learn much more about your students through these visits, but you will also be communicating to the student's family that you genuinely are interested in their child.

✓ Be sensitive in making assumptions about the constellation of your students' families. It is likely that some of your students reside with only one parent (not necessarily the mother) or with grandparents, older siblings, aunts, uncles, unrelated guardians, or foster parents. It is also possible that some of your students have parents who are deceased, incarcerated, or hospitalized. Tactfully determine the child's living arrangements before contacting the home. You can avoid potentially embarrassing situations.

✓ Let parents know early if their child is having difficulty in your class. Don't wait until grades are sent home.

✓ Consider sending parents a class newsletter several times a year to let them know what is happening in your class. You might even give your students responsibility for writing, editing, and printing it. News of field trips, special class projects, guest speakers, birthdays, and features recognizing individual students' achievements are all good content to include.

Parental Involvement Pays

Research shows that students are more likely to earn mostly A's when their fathers are highly involved in school. This connection holds for fathers in two-biological parent families, for stepfathers, and for fathers heading single-parent families. Mothers' involvement is similarly related to high grades. When mothers are involved in school, students in sixth through twelfth grades have a lower rate of suspension and expulsion.

High parental involvement was defined by participation in at least three of four school activities: attending a general school meeting, attending a regularly scheduled parent-teacher conference, attending a school or class event, and volunteering at school.

Source: National Center for Education Statistics. (2001, May). *Fathers' and mothers' involvement in their children's schools by family type and resident status.* Available online at http://nces.ed.gov/surveys/. Reprinted from *The Heart of Teaching* newsletter, Performance Learning Systems.

✓ Sponsor a family fun night in which parents and their children come to school to participate in some fun, interesting activities together. These might be related to your subject area or simply a chance to interact and have fun together. Some schools very successfully offer workshops in topics of interest to parents, anything from flower arranging to parenting skills. If your faculty cannot teach the workshop, find someone in the community who can.

> *If you promise not to believe everything your child says happens at this school, I'll promise not to believe everything he says happens at home.*
>
> —**English schoolmaster,** *Wall Street Journal,* **January 4, 1985**

✓ Designate one evening a month as an informal open session to which all parents are invited to visit your room to discuss any concerns or ask more about what their children are learning. Provide coffee, tea, or cookies. If no one shows, you can get some extra work done.

✓ Some schools sponsor a grandparents' day. Students are invited to bring their grandparents to school for a visit. You might even encourage grandparents to participate in the lesson of the day (for example, a discussion of the 1950s or how technology has changed). Grandparents are also a valuable though underused source of school volunteers.

✓ Send special cards or notes to parents for special family celebrations: birth of a new child, a new home, special award received, and so on. Clip newspaper articles featuring any family members and send them to the parents with a note of congratulations.

Do whatever it takes to get parents or guardians involved in school. This is no small challenge. Not all adults have pleasant memories of school. They avoid schools, even in adulthood. Not all parents are responsible caring adults. Nonetheless, we must do all that we can to break down the barriers between the school and the home. We must make schools inviting and persuade the adults in our students' lives to get involved in their education.

There are many examples, even in the most depressed schools, of programs that have experienced success in involving parents. Parental involvement is no panacea, but the odds of success are greater when schools and families make a team effort to help children get the most they can out of their educational opportunity.

Parent or Guardian Conferences

The prospect of a parent-teacher conference can arouse intense emotions in both the teacher and the parent. Beginning teachers can be especially anxious about meeting parents for the first time. For adults whose memories of school are less than pleasant, the parent-teacher conference can be intimidating and dreaded. However, the reality is that most parents really do want their children to have a positive school experience and prefer to develop a cooperative home-school relationship. Professionally conducted parent-teacher conferences can prove a most valuable strategy for improving student classroom behavior as well as enhancing learning. Here are some ideas that successful teachers have used to reap the maximum benefit from parent-teacher conferences:

✓ Before the conference date, plan what you hope to accomplish. What information do you want to share with the parent or guardian? What problems need solving? Do not overwhelm the parent. Settle on no more than two or three concerns to address. A laundry list of complaints will only discourage or alienate them.

✓ If you are requesting the conference in response to a specific problem with the child, allow some time to cool off before meeting with the parent. You'll be less emotionally charged and more objective after a couple of days. Remember, you are a professional educator.

✓ When a student begins to misbehave in class, record specific disturbances on an index card. Include the name, date, description of the problem behavior, and the action taken. Make your notes as soon after an incident as possible. This will help you to identify patterns and give more credibility to your complaint when talking with the child's parent.

✓ If possible, clarify ahead of time who will be attending the conference and their relationship to the child. Is this person the child's mother, father, guardian? Also verify from the school records the person's name. Do not assume their surname will be the same as the student's. Don't make a big point of it in front of the parent, but a bit of advance checking can help avoid potentially embarrassing gaffes during the conference. Some teachers have mistakenly assumed that an older parent was the student's grandparent.

✓ Within reason try to accommodate the parent's schedule. Many parents cannot readily take off work to attend school conferences. If parents have more than one child, attempt to coordinate their appointments so that they have to come to school only once. Such small considerations can reap significant cooperation.

✓ Consider sending a reminder of the time, date, and place to the parent a couple of days before the scheduled conference. If special directions are needed for parking or for finding your room, include those as well. If you are seeing several parents back-to-back, inform them how much time is allotted for their appointment.

✓ Put your name on the door to make it easier for parents to locate your room.

✓ Create an inviting room atmosphere. Displays of students' work, projects in progress, bulletin boards, posters, learning centers, and "Welcome Parents" signs can all help create a warm atmosphere.

✓ Arrange the room setting to minimize potential distractions or interruptions during the conference. Close the door if necessary.

✓ Assemble samples of the student's work and a list of his or her grades before the conference. It will save you the time of having to look them up during the appointment. Some teachers have their students assemble a work portfolio. This might include a greeting from their child. You might also include a page where the parent can return a positive note to their child about the schoolwork.

✓ Many teachers keep a note card for each student, recording points to discuss at the parent-teacher conference. Try to anticipate any questions a parent might ask and note your thoughts related to that issue.

✓ Greet parents cordially when they arrive, again being sure to verify their names immediately. Ideally, try to greet them at the door. Thank them for coming to see you.

✓ Be the gracious host. Some teachers set up coffee, juice, or snacks for parents, especially if they might have to wait in the hallway while you finish a prior conference.

If they must wait in the hall, provide some chairs and perhaps copies of your textbooks or other materials to scan while waiting.

✓ Practice the very best of manners, treating each parent with full respect and dignity. Whatever their occupation or socioeconomic status, treat all parents as you would the president of a corporation or a physician. Strive to make them feel as welcome and comfortable as possible.

✓ Address all parents by their last names preceded by the appropriate *Mr., Mrs.,* or *Ms.* until they invite you to use their first names.

✓ Don't hide behind your desk. It can be a barrier to developing a working relationship. If possible, sit beside the parent at a table. Also avoid seating parents in small children's chairs.

✓ Begin the conference on a positive note. Think of two or three positive descriptors for each student (for example, "Michelle is so eager to help" or "Braedon seems well liked by his classmates"). You might jot these down on each student's card or file to stimulate your memory. It is important to find something to praise with each student.

✓ Establish rapport with the parent. This need not take long, but try to establish a personal connection and create an inviting atmosphere. If you know about the parent's job, hobby, or special interest, make a brief inquiry (for example, "Matt tells me you've been working on your family genealogy"). Help put the parent at ease.

✓ Do question the parent about the student's special talents, interests, or accomplishments. Express a genuine interest to better understand their child's successes and strengths as well as challenges.

> *The only reason I always try to meet and know the parents better is because it helps me to forgive their children.*
>
> **—Louis Johannot, headmaster, Institut Le Rosey, Switzerland, *Life* magazine, May 7, 1965**

✓ Be specific when discussing difficulties the student is experiencing. It is generally better to be candid but not place blame. It is unwise to mislead the parent into thinking all is well if there is a problem with their child. Stick to the facts, giving concrete examples rather than broad generalities.

✓ Don't dwell on any student's attributes that are unlikely to change or over which the parents have little control.

✓ It is best to avoid getting emotional in discussing problems you may be having with the student. Remember, your goal is to enlist the parent's cooperation in resolving any difficulties the student may be experiencing in your class.

✓ Actively listen to the parent. Practice the reflection of feeling skills discussed in Chapter One. Respond empathically to feelings the parent expresses (for example, "You are disappointed Laurie isn't getting more individual attention in class"). This communicates that you really are trying to understand the parents' perspective; it does not imply that you necessarily agree with their view. Such active listening is an especially effective way to handle the angry parent.

✓ Encourage parents to ask questions, and respond fully yet tactfully. Avoid jargon, "educationese," or psychological labels. Allow parents time to talk.

✓ Inquire about home routines (responsibilities, homework habits, play, and so on). Seek information that might help you gain a better understanding of the student's talents, interests, and challenges.

✓ Try to offer two or three specific suggestions that the parent might implement at home to help the student. Offer them not as commands but as ideas that have worked with other students.

✓ Invite the parents to contact you with any future concerns about their child's classroom progress.

Facilitative Conferences: Alliances for Success

Betty Jo Simmons, professor of education at Longwood College, urges teachers to engage in facilitative conferences to nurture productive parent-teacher relationships. Simmons proposes five keys to successful problem solving in facilitative conferences:

- Be honest. Provide parents with specific and accurate information in a calm, nonaccusatory manner.
- Assure parents that their child is liked. Convey that you care about their child and that he or she is important.
- Describe the responsibilities to be shared. Clarify the roles of parent, teacher, and student in achieving success.
- Involve the student. Include the child in discussion of academic progress or behavior concerns.
- Provide encouragement. Reassure parents that whatever difficulties the student faces can be resolved with collaboration.

Source: Simmons, B. J. (2002). Facilitative conferences: Parents and teachers working together. *The Clearing House, 76*(2), 88–93.

✓ Some traps to avoid: discussing family problems, discussing other teachers' classroom treatment of the student, comparing the student with siblings, arguing with the parent, attempting to psychoanalyze the student, or blaming the parent for the student's misbehavior.

✓ End the conference in a hopeful tone. Summarize the main points discussed and any steps to be taken to resolve identified problems. Using the Parent Conference Record from the end of this chapter emphasizes the importance of following through on any actions. Again commend parents for coming to the conference.

✓ If other parents are waiting, be sure to end the meeting at the scheduled time. Ideally, allow yourself a few minutes between sessions to permit time to note any major points discussed during the conference. If necessary, offer to schedule another conference with the parent.

✓ Do follow up with a note or a phone call, especially if the conference has identified a particular problem for attention.

The Successful Open House

Many schools sponsor open houses for parents and guardians. The open house can be a valuable opportunity to get parents more involved in their children's education.

✓ Videotape several interesting learning activities in your class. Have these playing on the VCR as parents enter the room. You might play selected segments to give them a flavor of what your class is like. It is best to edit your tape first to avoid having to fast-forward. Five or ten minutes of videotape are sufficient.

✓ Avoid getting into prolonged discussions with individual parents about their child's progress. Do offer to arrange appointments with any parents who would like to discuss their children's work in more detail.

✓ Create an especially inviting atmosphere. Remember, some parents do not have fond memories of school and may be a bit anxious about being in a classroom.

✓ Greet parents at the door. If you do not already know them, introduce yourself to each as they enter.

✓ Some teachers have each student create a folder of exemplary work throughout the term. Have these available for parents to examine as they first enter.

✓ Create a "Welcome" sign with your name and subject clearly posted on the door so that parents are sure they are in the appropriate room.

✓ Attractive bulletin board displays featuring student work is a plus. If students create or build projects, have these on display.

✓ If parents are visiting several rooms, do not keep them past the time they should be moving to the next class.

Tips for Helping Substitute Teachers

Substitute teaching can be a challenging experience, but you can help assure that it will be constructive for both the substitute and your students. It is essential that learning continue even in your absence. Advance preparation can make a substitute's visit run more smoothly and assure that useful learning occurs. Here's how:

✓ Early in the year, inform the students of your expectations of acceptable behavior when a substitute is present.

✓ Agree with a nearby teacher to help the other's substitute when one of you is absent. The teacher can help the substitute get settled and become familiar with your procedures.

✓ Develop a substitute's notebook that includes all information he or she will need to make the experience successful. Be sure your notebook is clear and precise, avoiding special codes or abbreviations the substitute may not understand. Here are items many teachers include:

- Lesson plans.
- Daily schedule of activities.
- Class roster(s). The substitute can make notes on these (for example, checking off homework completed).
- Attendance forms and procedures.
- Hall passes and procedures for going to the rest room, library, guidance office, and so on.
- The names of teachers, administrators, clerical staff, or students they can turn to for help with special problems or questions.
- Seating charts for each class.

- Classroom rules. It is helpful if the students already have a copy and they are posted for everyone to see.
- If you have established any special classroom routines or behavior management programs, be sure to leave details about these. Also inform the substitute of any students with special needs who will require attention.
- Jot down any special nonteaching duties you must perform (for example, playground or lunchroom supervision).
- Bus information. Note times and procedures for dismissal and getting students to and from their buses.
- A map of the school building.
- Student handbook.
- Instructions on where all textbook manuals and supplies are kept.
- Teacher handbook.

✓ Don't forget to inform the substitute of any special scheduled interruptions (assemblies, class pictures, field trips, homerooms, and so on).

✓ If you know ahead of time you will be absent, leave a lesson plan to cover the material you want taught. It may not be the same lesson you would have taught, but it should be something of instructional value. It is a good idea to have a couple of special learning activities that can be plugged into the schedule at any point in the year. Keep these in a special place with all the necessary materials and directions. Try to help the substitute by including something you know your students will enjoy. Don't just use tests and seatwork on the days that substitutes are covering your class.

✓ If you know ahead of time that you will be absent, make a videotape for the substitute to show at the beginning of class. In this presentation you can give the students instructions on what you expect them to do that day. You might also videotape and save demonstrations or some lectures from previous years for the substitute to use.

✓ Expect the day to be used constructively. Most substitutes are qualified professionals with the training and motivation to do a good job. Treat them as professionals and with due respect.

✓ If you know you will be absent several days, invite your substitute to visit your class beforehand to meet your class and to discuss your lesson plans and classroom procedures with you.

✓ Ask your substitute to leave a note describing how the day went. It helps to remind your students ahead of time that you will be soliciting feedback from the substitute. You might express your appreciation to your students (through praise or special privileges) if the report is favorable.

✓ If you have a substitute who does perform particularly well, drop him or her a note to express your appreciation. Let your principal know as well. Specify that individual to take your place when you are absent. That will permit that substitute teacher to become more familiar with your routines and your students. If you will have frequent absences, it also alleviates the stress of getting the students accustomed to another person. Trust the substitute to provide a meaningful learning experience for your students (with your help).

Working with Support Staff

Successful teaching is a team effort. Teachers will be much more successful with the support of other competent professionals: counselors, secretaries, nurses, custodians, aides, cafeteria workers, and librarians. Each has a valuable function to play in creating a smooth-running and effective school. Special efforts should be made to make them feel included and valued as part of the school community.

✓ Learn the names of the support staff. Ask them how they would prefer to be addressed. Don't assume they want to be called by their first names.

✓ Attempt to discover what is important to them. Their jobs and needs are different from yours. Wherever possible, help them get their needs met.

✓ Acknowledge their contributions. An occasional thank-you note for any special assistance or a particularly outstanding contribution will be most appreciated. Offer verbal comments that convey you do value their efforts. Seek genuine opportunities to offer sincere compliments.

✓ Let others know what is happening. If you are planning a special activity that is going to affect someone else's job, check it out with them first. Try to minimize any disruption of their work. Seek their advice on how to proceed. Even if they don't have any suggestions, they will appreciate being asked.

✓ Always treat support staff (and all other persons) with courtesy. Accompanying requests with a *please* or *thank you* will plant the seeds of a cooperative, mutually respectful relationship. Always greet them with a smile and pleasant acknowledgment in the morning.

✓ Whenever someone puts forth an extra special effort to help you, acknowledge it with a note, small gift (cookies, bread, flowers from your garden), or even a note to his or her supervisor.

✓ If you see a positive news article about any staff members or their family, clip it out and send it to them with a note of congratulations.

✓ Treat all, including those with less education, as equals. Never assume that more education makes you a superior human being. Chances are that persons with less education than you have experiences, talents, or knowledge you do not.

✓ Sooner or later you are going to need a favor from a support staff member. You are much more likely to gain his or her compliance with your request if you have invested in a collegial relationship.

Working with Volunteers and Aides

Time is the teacher's most precious resource. There is always too much to do in too little time. Someone other than a teacher could complete many essential tasks, if such help were available. Using aides, either paid or volunteer, is one valuable way to get more help in the classroom, freeing you to spend more time on the most important teaching tasks. One estimate is that over five million persons volunteer to help in schools each year, and probably many more would help if they were invited. Many adults in your community have valuable talents that could be tapped to enrich your instructional program.

One benefit of using aides, whether paid or volunteer, is that they share the challenges and achievements of your school with the greater community. They can become valuable public relations spokespersons simply by sharing their experiences with friends and neighbors. These paraprofessionals from the community are more likely to become advocates for their schools. There is also evidence that student achievement improves in schools that use volunteers extensively. Teachers who are freed from many of their noninstructional tasks have more time and energy to focus on their teaching responsibilities. Additionally, individual students gain more of the teacher's attention, as well as the added contact and reinforcement from the paraprofessional helper.

The paraprofessionals working in their community schools also gain. Many feel a greater sense of social responsibility and personal enrichment from using their time to aid children's development. Many feel more positively about themselves, knowing that their talents and knowledge are valued and needed. For others, especially college students, working in the classroom provides an opportunity to develop skills and knowledge that may enhance their employment prospects. All classroom assistants gain a greater appreciation and insight into the inner workings of their local school.

Volunteers can help in a variety of ways, depending on the students' age group, the volunteer or aide's skills and knowledge, and the teacher's willingness to delegate tasks and train the paraprofessional to assume these duties.

If your school does not regularly provide aides, discuss the idea of using volunteers with your principal. You will need to consider concerns such as legal limits and liabilities and delegated responsibilities. You might want to start small at first to determine how best to use classroom assistants.

Send out a call for all potential volunteers, not just to your students' parents. An announcement in the local newspaper or through the parent-teacher association newsletter may encourage others to volunteer. Senior citizen groups and your students' grandparents are also potential sources of volunteer aides. College students, especially teacher trainees, may value the opportunity to work in a classroom. Elementary teachers sometimes use high school students. You might also survey local businesspersons to determine if they might be willing to help occasionally. Some companies provide release time for their employees to help in schools. The regular school open house is an excellent recruiting opportunity. Create and prominently display a recruiting poster describing the specific ways parents can help. Follow up the open house with a letter inviting parents to volunteer. Make a special effort to recruit parents who speak languages other than English.

Parents and others are generally reluctant to volunteer because they are unsure they have anything to contribute. Be sure to list specific tasks parents are capable of handling. Where possible, provide options, allowing parents to choose those activities they find most attractive. While some parents may be able to work every week, let parents know that you value their help even if only for a onetime visit to share some talent or their jobs with your class or help with one activity. Some parents might be able to help even if they cannot come to school. Many tasks can be done in their homes: typing, sewing, baking, or entering computer data.

Many volunteer aides or paraprofessionals lose interest because they feel underused or taken for granted. Here are some tips for effectively using the aides' services:

✓ Interview each volunteer, preferably in person. Assess whether you think you can work comfortably with each individual. You likely will need more than one volunteer to cover the week. Determine how much time each day you want an aide or volunteer in your room. You'll also need to decide whether to schedule volunteers for specific tasks as needed or for the same block of time each week. Some persons might wish to help weekly; others will be able to assist only occasionally. Be sure to call everyone who volunteers.

✓ Appropriate training is essential for effective use of paraprofessional help. Allow time for them to observe you interacting with students and doing tasks you will expect them to fulfill. They will also note the routines you have established. If you are using several volunteers, you might schedule an orientation session where you can provide training for all at once. Also provide ample time for them to ask questions. It is helpful to let them just observe for a day before you have them work directly with students.

✓ Develop a handbook for your assistants. It should describe tasks to be done (with samples when possible), disciplinary procedures, rules, and responsibilities. It is also important to emphasize confidentiality so that volunteers don't gossip about the individual children's problems.

✓ Do try to get to know your classroom helpers. Ask about their families and interests. When appropriate, seek their suggestions on how to make improvements in the classroom.

✓ Develop a file, tray, or box in which you place work for your aide or volunteer to do when time is available. This prevents them from having to interrupt you to get instructions on what to do. A desk or table designated as their workstation would be helpful. Be sure to provide an adult chair if you teach young children. Also designate where they can store personal items and clothing.

✓ Construct and post a chart depicting the schedule for your assistants. Ask them to call when they are not able to come. It is helpful to send reminders to volunteers who are coming for a special project. If you are scheduling a parent to help with one class, remember it is easiest for most parents to come first thing in the morning or late afternoon. Be considerate of their schedules.

✓ Make sure you always have something useful for them to do. They will get bored or discouraged if they arrive to find they really aren't needed. Keep a running list of things for your helpers to do. Try to give them meaningful, interesting tasks at least part of the time.

✓ Design a system so that you need to spend only minimal class time supervising your assistant.

Common Tasks for Volunteers and Aides

Take attendance or lunch count.

Help students get on the bus.

Tutor individual students.

Supervise field trips.

Escort students through the hall.

Demonstrate an experiment.

Listen to students read.

Grade objective tests and quizzes.

Collect and distribute materials.

Find materials in the library.

Make phone calls.

Monitor students.

Converse with individual students.

Facilitate small-group activities.

Supervise recess.

Complete certificates for students.

Praise students.

File papers.

Set up displays.

Record grades.

Type.

Operate instructional equipment.

Administer quizzes and tests.

Photocopy.

Help with computer software.

Laminate materials.

Supervise learning centers.

Compute grades.

Do desktop publishing on the computer.

Order free materials.

Help organize games.

Requisition supplies.

Administer routine first aid.

Take students to the nurse.

Help returning students make up
missed work.

Assist with club meetings.

Paint murals.

Help with seatwork.

Prepare instructional resources.

Record observations about students
and classroom activities.

Proofread.

Do housekeeping chores: water plants,
arrange desks, clean, and so on.

Put up bulletin boards.

Direct a play.

Provide enrichment activities.

Make costumes.

Restock supplies.

Share a hobby.

Monitor computer use.

Prepare visual aids.

Mediate student disputes.

Conduct storytelling.

Coordinate volunteers.

Share career guidance information.

✓ In front of students, always address your aide or volunteer as you would any other professional in the building, generally by title (Mr., Mrs., Ms.). Insist that students also address them as they would a teacher and that they treat any paraprofessionals with courtesy and respect.

✓ In the beginning delegate tasks you are quite sure the paraprofessional can handle, assuring initial success. As they gain confidence and your trust, assign more challenging duties. Provide an opportunity for your assistants to learn and grow. Encourage them to ask questions if they are not sure how to complete a task.

✓ Remain tactful yet clear in providing suggestions and feedback to your assistants. Always treat them with respect. Show them that you have confidence in their ability to fulfill their duties. When appropriate, seek their opinion on items related to classroom success.

✓ Allow your classroom assistants an opportunity to work with all students, not just the ones having difficulties. Discourage parent volunteers from working only with their child.

✓ Give ample recognition and appreciation to your aides. Never take them for granted; strive to always make your assistants feel needed. Here are ideas some teachers have used to show their appreciation to their paraprofessional helpers:

- Give them certificates.
- Award them plaques.
- Praise them.
- Send them special thank-you notes.
- Write newspaper features on volunteers.
- Invite them to lunch.
- Honor them at recognition ceremonies.
- Give them small gifts.
- Invite them to a staff development program.
- Buy them a soft drink, coffee, or tea.
- Send them a birthday or holiday card.
- Delegate additional responsibility.
- Seek their opinion.
- Take them to the faculty lounge.
- Introduce them to other school personnel.
- Offer to write them letters of recommendation.
- Celebrate their achievements.
- Nominate them for volunteer awards.
- Smile.
- Send a letter of appreciation to their boss.
- Treat them as professionals.
- Bring a cake for their birthday.
- Praise them in front of your principal.
- Greet them by name.
- Take time to listen to their ideas.
- Give them a space of their own.

While volunteers do save the teacher time and having parents in the classroom may enhance parent-teacher relationships, the bottom line is that extra help in the classroom benefits students.

Invitation to Open House: Sample Letter to Parents

(Date)

Greetings,

Kalida Elementary School will be holding its annual open house on Monday, October 15. We ask all parents and guardians to first meet in the school auditorium at 7:00 P.M. After a brief introductory program, you are invited to join me in room 68.

I will have several samples of your child's work available for you to examine. While we will not have time to discuss your child's performance in detail, I would be willing to schedule a private conference if you desire. I do hope to briefly explain some of the activities we will be doing this year and to respond to any questions you might have about our classes.

I very much value the help and support my students receive at home. Together, we can assure that your child has a successful year. I hope to see you at our open house.

Sincerely,

Mrs. Ritter

Parent Survey

I believe the parents in our school community possess a great many talents and skills that would be of benefit to our students. I would like to invite you to become involved in our class activities during this year. To help me identify the special interests or skills you might possess that would be most helpful, please complete this survey and return to me at school. If you are willing to help in any fashion, I will contact you later to determine when you would be available to help.

Name _____   Child's name _____

Address _____

Phone _____   Occupation _____

E-mail _____

What special hobbies or interests do you have that you might be willing to share with my class?

With which of the following activities would you be willing to help?

_____   Supervise field trips

_____   Teach a hobby or skill (Describe: _____)

_____   Create a bulletin board

_____   Tutor individual students (Subject: _____)

_____   Assist in the classroom (filing, tutoring, monitoring, grading, and so on)

_____   Help with computer hardware and software

_____   Other (Specify: _____)

Team Process Assessment

At the end of the team meeting, each member should indicate his or her assessment of how that meeting went. Circle the number that represents your rating of each dimension. The group should then spend a few minutes discussing the group's responses.

Participation

1	2	3	4	5	6	7

Some did not participate at all.   There was significant participation by all.

Group Focus

1	2	3	4	5	6	7

The group tended to digress from   The group stayed on task
the session agenda or objective.   throughout the meeting.

Listening Process

1	2	3	4	5	6	7

Participants did not seem to   Participants made outstanding
be fully listening to one another.   efforts to fully hear each other.

Commitment Check

1	2	3	4	5	6	7

I am not supportive of the   I am very supportive of
meeting outcome.   the group decision.

Quality of the Group Effort

1	2	3	4	5	6	7

The session did not produce   The final outcome was excellent.
an effective outcome.

Team Meeting Form

Team _____   Date _____

Agenda Topics

_____

_____

_____

_____

_____

_____

Decisions

_____

_____

_____

_____

_____

_____

Assignments and Deadlines

_____

_____

_____

_____

_____

_____

Creativity Crunchers

No way!

Don't be silly.

It's too risky.

We tried that before.

It would take too long.

The administration will never go along.

We don't have the money.

Let's form a committee.

You've got to be kidding!

It will never work.

Yes, but . . .

They'll never let us.

It'll never sell.

That's not our problem.

The time isn't right.

The main office won't let us.

It's too new.

Put it in writing.

We'll discuss it later.

Why do it now?

It will never be approved.

What for?

Nobody needs it.

It's against our rules.

The union won't go along.

It's too faddish.

What will the community think?

Let's table it for now.

Don't rush into things.

It's politically unwise.

Too radical.

We're too small.

It's too much work.

Let's wait and see.

Let me think about it.

What good will it do?

We already have enough problems.

It'll never happen.

You're dreaming.

It's a nice theory, but . . .

You don't understand.

We're too big for that to work here.

Why?

Maybe someday.

It'll never fly.

They'll laugh at us.

We have too many obstacles.

It's reactionary.

We don't have proof it will work.

It will offend someone.

It's too late.

It's not our policy.

Are you serious?

We need more data.

It didn't work the last time.

Costs too much.

Baloney!

Someone else should do it.

They aren't ready for it yet.

There's no use trying.

It's not our job.

Dud!

Nobody cares anyway.

We don't have enough details.

Don't you think there is a better way?

Too corny.

It's too soon.

That's not new.

It's illogical.

Get practical.

Here we go again.

That's fine, but . . .

Whose idea is that?

It's too simple.

It's too complicated.

That's just plain dumb.

Parent Conference Record

Teacher _____ Date _____

Student _____ Parent(s) _____

Objective: _____

_____

_____

_____

_____

Suggestions for improvement: _____

_____

_____

_____

_____

_____

_____

_____

_____

_____

_____

Signed: _____   _____
                                                                        Teacher

_____   _____
Parent(s)/Guardian(s)   Student

Chapter Five

In Search of Educational Excellence

Twenty-two Tips for Becoming an Effective Teacher

While teaching is a complex and challenging profession, some teachers are more successful than others. Their students perform better on achievement tests, are more likely to succeed in future grades, and remember their teachers more fondly. Many outstanding teachers are creative and successful in facilitating their students' academic as well as personal growth. We need not search only for those gaining national recognition, such as Jaime Escalante, featured in the real-life drama *Stand and Deliver,* or Kay Tolliver, the East Harlem teacher touted in the PBS production *Good Morning, Ms. Tolliver.* In every school exciting, creative, and effective teaching is happening. A growing body of educational research has focused on what these exemplars are doing that makes them successful. Use every opportunity to observe outstanding teachers in action; you can learn much from them. What follows is a compilation of the characteristics of these effective teachers that researchers have identified:

1. The A+ teachers tend to have realistic yet high expectations for their students. They require students to use higher-level mental processes, such as critical thinking, deeper understanding, creativity, and problem solving. They present the appropriate level of challenge in their lessons.

2. They incorporate student questions and comments into their lessons. Their classes tend to involve significant amounts of class discussion and group exploration. This is especially important in teaching high school students.

3. The best teachers actively involve their students in the learning process. Their students spend less time doing seatwork, passively watching, or waiting. When these teachers do employ seatwork, it is more interesting and varied.

4. Much thought and planning go into their instruction, yet they remain flexible in their teaching to allow for spontaneous discovery as opportunities present themselves. They are especially sensitive to cues that their lessons are not working, and they adapt them on the spot. They continually seek ways to improve their teaching. They produce lessons that enhance student mastery.

5. The best teachers tend to conduct their lessons in a businesslike, task-oriented style. They maintain a strong academic focus in their classrooms. They are effective in designing lessons that enhance student mastery.

6. Effective teachers match their instructional activities to their students' developmental level and then gradually lead them to higher levels of mastery. This involves recognizing and correcting deficiencies in students' skill level.

Great teachers rely not on charisma. Instead, they rely on the inner qualities of love, integrity and commitment.

—Eric Jensen,
Teaching with the Brain in Mind

7. They employ structuring comments or advance organizers at the beginning of their lessons. They are also careful to use language appropriate to their students.

8. Teachers whom students rated highest tend to use more humor in their classrooms. This humor does not typically come from telling jokes but rather from the good-natured banter they carry on with their students. This contributes to developing good rapport with their students.

Effective teachers let students know they are somebody, not some body.

—William Purkey

9. They genuinely believe in the value of their subject matter. Almost without exception, they exude enthusiasm for what they are teaching; and they teach in a manner that exhibits that passion. You can sense the energy and animation in their teaching. The research suggests this is especially important at the junior high and high school levels.

10. The best teachers possess a can-do attitude, sometimes referred to as efficacy. Although they face the same problems as less effective teachers, they have confidence in their ability to cope with the challenges they face. They feel their efforts can make a difference in their students' lives.

11. The memorable teachers exhibit empathy toward their students, striving to see the world from their point of view. Such caring and desire to genuinely understand their students is sometimes characterized as teacher warmth. This includes a sensitivity to the students' cultural background as well. One opportunity to do that is by arriving at class early to chat with students as they enter. These teachers' classes are more student-centered than subject-centered.

12. Top-performing teachers seek help from others. They discuss teaching ideas with colleagues and seek input from parents, students, administrators, and educational specialists. They also read more educational magazines and books and are more likely to attend professional development programs.

13. They provide opportunities for students to seek extra help if they fall behind. They are approachable. They are also observant of cues that individual students are not learning or are uninvolved. They more frequently check students' progress and proceed only when students have shown mastery of the content being taught.

14. The A+ teachers avoid embarrassing students and do not resort to intimidation to gain their cooperation. They avoid showing favoritism toward selected students. Not surprisingly, the better

The Whistling Dog

A man reported to his friends that he had taught his dog to whistle. His friends coaxed the dog to whistle. Despite their fervent pleas, nothing happened.

In exasperation one finally retorted, "I thought you taught him to whistle."

The man replied, "I did. But he just didn't learn."

Successful teachers are vital and full of passion. They love to teach as a writer loves to write, as a singer loves to sing. They are people who have a motive, a passion for their subject, a spontaneity of character, and enormous fun doing what they do.

—Thomas Cronin, 1991

teachers tend to have more positive opinions of students, as well as of fellow teachers and administrators. Research shows that ineffective teachers are more prone to use sarcasm, shame, ridicule, shouting, and scolding. High-achieving classrooms are cooperative, warm, and convivial.

15. The top teachers give clear instructions in assignments and demonstrate clarity in their presentations. They also attend to the nonverbal cues that suggest that students do not understand, and they adjust lessons in midstream as needed.

16. Excellent teachers are more likely to incorporate a variety of instructional strategies into their lessons. They tend not to do the same thing in the same way for too long. They possess a broad repertoire of teaching skills.

17. They encourage more than they criticize. Indeed, criticism is negatively related to student achievement. However, outstanding teachers do provide corrective feedback whenever necessary to help students rectify mistakes.

18. The most effective teachers are in control of their classrooms but are not obsessed with the idea of control. They invest time and effort into preventing discipline problems by developing positive student relationships and planning well-organized, interesting lessons. To the outside observer, these teachers seem to exert relatively little effort to maintain an orderly environment. They are more apt to intervene to nip problems in the bud before they escalate into major disruptions. They are also less likely to send students to the principal, punish their students, or call parents to complain about students' misbehavior.

19. Successful teachers continually monitor their classrooms; they are aware of what is happening at all times. They often do this by moving about the room and maintaining frequent eye contact with all students.

20. Good teachers teach their students classroom routines, such as what to do when they finish an assignment early or how to obtain extra help.

21. Not surprisingly, effective teachers actually spend more time teaching. They use class time to maximize student learning and try to minimize distractions, chaos, and interruptions. Indeed, teachers who are less able to manage their time well tend to leave the teaching profession.

22. The truly outstanding teachers are not necessarily charismatic and dynamic individuals; but they enjoy and believe in what they are teaching, work hard at it, and spend time planning well-organized lessons.

Suggested Reading on Effective Teaching

Burden, P. R., & Byrd, D. M. (2003). *Methods for effective teaching* (3rd ed.). Boston: Allyn & Bacon.

Kauchak, D. P., & Eggen, P. D. (2003). *Learning and teaching: Research-based methods* (4th ed.). Boston: Allyn & Bacon.

Stephenson, Jr., F. J. (Ed.). (2001). *Extraordinary teachers: The essence of excellent teaching*. Kansas City, MO: Andrews McMeel Publishing.

Stronge, J. H. (2002). *Qualities of effective teachers*. Alexandria, VA: Association for Supervision and Curriculum Development.

Wilen, W., Kindsvatter, R., Ishler, M., Hutchison, J., & Ishler Bosse, M. (2004). *Dynamics of effective secondary teaching* (5th ed.). Boston: Allyn & Bacon.

Wiseman, D., & Hunt, G. H. (2001). *Best practice in motivation and management in the classroom*. Springfield, IL: Charles C Thomas.

> ## Characteristics of Successful New Teachers
>
> - Able to motivate students
> - Child-centered
> - Consistent
> - Empathetic
> - Team-oriented
> - Willing to serve
> - Cooperative
> - Flexible
> - Good interpersonal skills
>
> *Source:* Breeding, M., & Whitworth, J. (1999). *Increasing the success of first year teachers: A synthesis of three studies.* Paper presented at the annual meeting of the American Association of Colleges for Teacher Education (ERIC Document No. ED428056).

Teacher Expectations Revisited

Since Rosenthal and Jacobson first proposed the idea of the self-fulfilling prophecy in their much-publicized 1968 study, *Pygmalion in the Classroom,* research has verified that teacher expectations are a complex, not yet totally understood, variable. Many researchers have found that, under certain conditions, teacher expectations can affect student behavior and achievement. Scholars are still debating the magnitude and predictability of these effects. However, UC Berkeley psychology professor Rhonda Weinstein found that teacher expectations appear to affect the amount of effort that students are willing to put into their schoolwork.

Weinstein's research has also revealed that children as young as age six can sense where they fit in the academic pecking order. This is especially so in schools that strongly emphasize differences in academic achievement. While many teachers believe students cannot detect favoritism toward "pet" students, empirical research suggests that students are indeed accurate in reading such favoritism through teachers' nonverbal behaviors (Babad, 1992). Teachers express their expectations differentially through their nonverbal cues (body

Effective Teacher Checklist

Do you . . .

_____ Listen to your students?

_____ Know your students' names by the end of the first two weeks of school?

_____ Try to see things from your students' point of view?

_____ Smile in class?

_____ Believe all your students are capable of learning your subject?

_____ Convey your enthusiasm for what you are teaching?

_____ Continue to improve your teaching effectiveness?

_____ Believe in the value of what you are teaching?

_____ Have clear objectives for each lesson?

_____ Clearly communicate your expectations to your students?

_____ Strive to create an inviting room environment?

_____ Establish routines the first week of school?

_____ Try to get to know all your students as individuals?

_____ Encourage cooperation more than competition in your classroom?

_____ Demonstrate a sense of humor in working with your students?

_____ Praise your students for specific accomplishments?

_____ Fairly and consistently enforce your rules?

_____ Use more positive statements than negative statements in your classes?

_____ Vary your seating arrangement according to your teaching needs?

_____ Communicate students' positive achievements to their parents?

_____ Make positive comments on students' papers?

_____ Permit your students to make mistakes as they learn new content and skills?

_____ Avoid overreacting to minor misbehaviors?

_____ Create interesting lessons that actively involve students?

_____ Encourage students to ask questions when they don't understand some part of your lesson?

_____ Capitalize on spontaneous learning opportunities when they occur?

_____ Attend workshops or classes to continue improving your teaching skills?

_____ Maintain at least an 80 percent on-task rate in your classes?

_____ Compliment students individually and as a group?

_____ Create a sense of family among your students?

_____ Make effective use of class time?

_____ Strive to link current lessons to students' prior knowledge?

_____ Provide reflection time for all students?

_____ Give students guided practice?

_____ Provide appropriate pacing for your lessons (neither too slow nor too fast)?

_____ Employ a variety of instructional techniques besides lecture?

_____ Regularly communicate with the parents of students having difficulties?

_____ Consider the variety of learning styles of your students in planning your lessons?

_____ Incorporate students' questions and comments into your lessons?

_____ Adapt your lessons on the spot when they aren't working?

_____ Provide opportunities for students to seek extra help if they fall behind?

_____ Feel confident in your ability to handle the challenges you face in the classroom?

_____ Greet your students as they enter the classroom?

_____ Avoid the use of sarcasm or ridicule in interacting with students?

_____ Have everything ready for the day when you enter the building in the morning?

_____ Control your classroom without being obsessed with the idea of control?

_____ Effectively nip behavior problems in the bud before they escalate?

_____ Constantly keep aware of what is happening in your classroom through continual monitoring?

_____ Strive to minimize distractions, chaos, and interruptions?

_____ Love teaching?

Scoring Directions: Count the number of items you checked and find your score in the categories below.

41–50	Outstanding	A master teacher. Others can learn much from you.
31–40	Good	You're on the way to success. A few areas need attention.
21–30	Challenged	It's not too late to seek help in improving your classroom effectiveness.
0–20	Struggling	Teaching is probably not very enjoyable. Considering a career change might be wise.

language and facial cues) when interacting with low- and high-expectation students (Babad & Taylor, 1992). These differential cues are quite fine and subtle yet detectable (Babad, 1992).

In her book *Reaching Higher,* Weinstein (2002) argues that the current focus on extensive standardized testing fails to incorporate the substantial body of research on developing positive prophecies for students. She argues that the school culture should stress developing students' talents instead of testing and sorting. She concludes that current massive testing programs will inevitably yield large numbers of student failures, resulting in increased special education placements, tracking, retention, and mandatory summer school—all approaches that research has shown to be counterproductive and damaging to children's opinions of themselves, destructive to their self-expectations, and generally counterproductive.

For More Information

Babad, E. (1992). Teacher expectancies and nonverbal behavior. In R. S. Feldman (Ed.), *Applications of nonverbal behavioral theories and research* (pp. 167–190). Hillsdale, NJ: Erlbaum.

Babad, E., & Taylor, P. J. (1992).Transparency of teacher expectancies across language, cultural boundaries. *Journal of Educational Research, 86,* 120–125.

Rosenthal, R., & Jacobson, L. (1968). *Pygmalion in the classroom.* New York: Holt, Rinehart & Winston.

Weinstein, R. S. (2002). *Reaching higher: The power of expectations in schooling.* Cambridge, MA: Harvard University Press.

Why Teachers Fail

Teachers sometimes fail. In a survey that asked school administrators about reasons for teacher failure (dismissal, reprimand, reassignment), Professor Jack Riegle found teachers are more likely to get fired because of poor human relations skills than lack of knowledge about their subject matter. Respondents most frequently mentioned the following reasons:

✓ Inability to organize and control a classroom of students

✓ Lack of knowledge concerning how children grow and develop as pertaining to pupil-teacher interactions

✓ Inability to work effectively with other educators

✓ Inability to work effectively with parents

✓ Subject matter inadequacies

✓ Other: immorality, insubordination, absenteeism, child abuse, senility, or drugs and alcohol

Source: Riegle, J. D. (1985). What administrators say about why teachers fail. *The Teacher Educator, 21*(1), 15–18.

Twenty-seven Mistakes Teachers Commonly Make

1. Consistently talking in a monotone
2. Using sarcasm
3. Embarrassing students in front of their peers
4. Talking down to students
5. Not knowing students' names
6. Being inconsistent or unfair in classroom discipline
7. Using sexist or culturally insensitive language
8. Not being adequately prepared
9. Overrelying on lecture
10. Being disorganized
11. Using inappropriate humor
12. Allowing too many interruptions
13. Expecting perfection rather than excellence
14. Ignoring the bottom half of the class
15. Not clarifying expectations, rules, and routines
16. Screaming at students
17. Not knowing the subject
18. Talking to the chalkboard or whiteboard
19. Trying to impress the students
20. Not using variety in instruction
21. Trying to fake it
22. Not having clear objectives in designing lessons
23. Setting expectations too low
24. Poor grooming or personal hygiene
25. Rewarding inappropriate behavior
26. Isolating themselves from colleagues
27. Not learning from their mistakes

Thirty-two Strategies for Nurturing Peak Performance in Others

Charles Garfield has made a career of studying high performers in an array of professions. His research has revealed that some work environments are more likely to elicit high levels of performance. Teachers can help their colleagues (from custodians to principals) do their jobs better. Here are thirty-two suggestions for helping your colleagues attain peak performance:

1. Minimize criticism. Most people need role models more than they need critics. Use questions to encourage reflection and creative thinking. Criticize sparingly and in private. Praise often and in public.

2. Help others get what they want. In the end it is the surest way to get what you want.

3. Communicate clearly and concisely. Provide consistent but constructive feedback.

4. Use I-language in conveying your complaints. For example, "I would prefer we begin our meetings on time." Learn to be responsibly assertive rather than aggressive or nonassertive.

5. Clarify expectations and goals. Don't just assume others know what you need or expect. Check it out.

6. Assure that colleagues have access to the information and resources they need in order to do their jobs effectively.

7. Clarify priorities. Don't expect others to read your mind.

8. Do not promise what you cannot deliver, and keep the promises you do make. That is the root of trust.

9. Don't let the urgent things crowd out the important. Don't overwhelm colleagues and subordinates with so many urgent tasks that they don't have time to deal with more important ones.

10. Be more concerned with effectiveness than efficiency. One can be very efficient without being very effective.

11. Invite feedback from others. Listen with an open mind.

12. Always strive to be empathetic. Try to see things from the other person's point of view.

13. Nurture relationships. Develop a psychological bank account with every colleague. Try to make at least a small deposit each day.

14. Master the art of saying thank-you. Seek every opportunity to provide genuine appreciation and recognition for others' successes and achievements.

15. Strive for excellence, not perfection.

16. Demonstrate respect for colleagues' time. Avoid creating unnecessary interruptions.

17. Follow the cardinal rules for effective meetings: always publicize the agenda; begin and end on time; keep them on task; record and circulate decisions made. Don't dominate the meeting.

18. Describe the traits of the worst boss or colleague you've ever had. Would your colleagues find any of these characteristics in you?

19. Support others when they are down. Learn to be a compassionate listener.

20. Share credit with as many people as possible.

21. The details are important. Be prepared.

22. Strive to view the challenges you face at work as problems in need of solutions. Seldom are they great moral choices with only one correct answer. Open-mindedly examine the advantages and disadvantages of each option. Relinquish the need to convince others you are right.

23. Be skeptical of simplistic solutions for complex problems.

24. Nothing conveys respect more than learning your colleagues' names.

25. View mistakes as an opportunity to learn. They are essential to effective learning. Fear of failure hinders taking risks and tackling challenging tasks. Encourage calculated risk taking and experimentation.

26. Don't punish desired behaviors or reward undesired behaviors. Do not ignore persons when they do the job right.

27. Avoid participating in gossip. You have nothing to gain and much to lose. Others will assume you are talking the same way about them behind their backs.

28. Assign reasonable workloads. Students are most productive when challenged with meaningful tasks and least productive when they are overwhelmed.

29. Strive to reduce the stress level in your building. Increased illness, job burnout, and higher turnover are all related to high levels of stress.

30. Don't dump your problems on other people. Always treat colleagues with dignity and respect.

31. Share journal articles of value with your colleagues.

32. Encourage all to participate in quality professional development activities.

Effective Schools

In the past two decades, scholars have given substantial attention to studying effective schools (see the work of David Berliner, Michael Fullan, and John Goodlad). While no universal blueprint exists, we can draw some generalizations from the myriad of research studies available. The exact causal nature of these characteristics is difficult to determine. However, the most outstanding schools possess a number of specific traits. Research has identified the following characteristics as exemplifying the most effective schools:

✓ The professional staff is committed to the belief that all students can learn. The time required to learn the same content may vary greatly, however.

✓ Teachers hold high expectations for their students. Teachers also believe their efforts make a difference in students' lives.

✓ Students believe their success in school is related to how hard they work rather than just innate ability.

✓ The principal functions as an instructional leader, setting high goals for the school and inspiring staff to move toward those goals.

✓ A safe and orderly school environment is provided.

✓ Continued professional development is encouraged and facilitated.

✓ Firm, consistent, and fair enforcement of appropriate student behavior is emphasized. Disruptive and dangerous behaviors are not tolerated. Rules and expectations are clearly communicated to all.

✓ A climate of cooperation exists among the staff. The faculty works as a team. Collaboration becomes part of the school culture. Mutually supportive relationships exist between the principal and the staff.

✓ Students exhibit a high level of school spirit. They identify with their school and feel good about attending their school.

✓ Academic learning time is safeguarded. Frivolous interruptions of class activities are minimized.

Faced with the choice between changing one's mind and proving there is no need to do so, almost everyone gets busy on the proof.

—John Kenneth Galbraith

✓ Parents feel welcome in the school. The community is supportive of its schools.

✓ Student progress is systematically monitored.

✓ Staff input into instructional decisions is invited.

✓ Students' level of on-task behavior is relatively high.

✓ The emphasis is on developing basic academic skills in students.

✓ Continuity of instruction from one grade level to the next is emphasized.

For More Information

Berliner, D. (2001). Teacher expertise. In F. Banks & A. S. Mayes, *Early professional development for teachers* (pp. 20–26). London: David Fulton.

Corbett, H. D., Wilson, B., & Williams, B. (2002). *Effort and excellence in urban classrooms: Expecting, and getting, success with all students*. New York: Teachers College Press.

Fielder, D. J. (2003). *Achievement now! How to assure no child is left behind*. Larchmont, NY: Eye on Education.

Fullan, M. (2003). *Change forces with a vengeance*. New York: RoutledgeFalmer.

Ginsberg, M. B., & Wlodkowski, R. J. (2000). *Creating highly motivating classrooms for all students: A schoolwide approach to powerful teaching with diverse learners*. San Francisco: Jossey-Bass.

Hawley, W. D., & Rollie, D. L. (Eds.). (2002). *The keys to effective schools: Educational reform as continuous improvement*. Thousand Oaks, CA: Corwin Press.

Goodlad, J. I. (2004). *A place called school*. (20th anniversary edition). New York: McGraw-Hill.

Kaplan, L. S., & Owings, W. A. (2001). *Enhancing teaching quality*. Bloomington, IN: Phi Delta Kappa Educational Foundation.

Marzano, R. J., Pickering, D. J., & Pollock, J. E. (2001). *Classroom instruction that works: Research-based strategies for increasing student achievement*. Alexandria, VA: Association for Supervision and Curriculum Development.

Mastropieri, M. A., & Scruggs, T. E. (2002). *Effective instruction for special education*. Austin, TX: Pro-Ed.

Shellard, E. (2000). *Effective teaching: How do we know it when we see it?* Arlington, VA: Educational Research Service.

Taylor, B. M., & Pearson, P. D. (Eds.). (2002). *Teaching reading: Effective schools, accomplished teachers*. Hillsdale, NJ: Erlbaum.

Tileston, D. W. (2000). *Ten best teaching practices: How brain research, learning styles, and standards define teaching competencies*. Thousand Oaks, CA: Corwin Press.

Indicators of Quality

The following indicators of quality summarize the findings of numerous research studies examining the most successful schools:

1. *Enriched environment*

    The physical environment is uncluttered and inviting.
    Flexibility in the room arrangement is possible.
    Students are actively involved in hands-on experiences.
    A variety of multimedia resources are used.
    Learning resources augment peripheral learning.

2. *Safe, supportive learning environment*

   Appropriate humor is used.
   Rules are fairly and consistently enforced.
   Opportunities for extra help are provided.
   Teacher treats students courteously.
   Teacher uses students' names.
   Teacher monitors the classroom with eyes and movement through class.

3. *Choice*

   Students are involved in classroom decisions.
   Options are provided in learning activities.
   A variety of instructional techniques are employed.
   Teacher is sensitive to learning-style differences.
   Opportunities are provided for learning through different sensory modalities.

4. *Meaningful content*

   Relevant, real-life learning experiences are provided.
   New content is anchored to prior knowledge.
   Subject matter is age-appropriate.
   Teacher conveys enthusiasm for the content.
   Learning situations appropriately challenge students.
   Lessons support interdisciplinary and real-world connections.
   Critical thinking is emphasized more than seeking the right answer.
   Curiosity, novelty, and interest are embedded in learning experiences.

5. *Collaboration*

   Instruction is student-centered rather than teacher-centered.
   Time is provided for interaction with other students.
   A sense of community is evident among the students.
   School-home collaboration is nurtured.
   Students are provided with opportunities to learn interpersonally.

6. *Time usage*

   Teacher employs efficient routines for handling daily tasks.
   Students are appropriately engaged.
   Interruptions and distractions are minimized.
   Students are allotted adequate time to totally process learning tasks.
   Teacher adapts lesson to student energy level.

7. *Ongoing feedback*

   Mistakes are treated as learning opportunities.
   Teacher listens to the students.
   Teacher uses more positive than negative comments.
   Constructive peer feedback is encouraged.
   Students are encouraged to ask questions.
   Emphasis is on moving from extrinsic to intrinsic motivation.
   Students' responses modify teacher approach.

8. *Assessment*

> Teacher clearly communicates expectations to students.
> Learning is assessed in a variety of ways.
> Assessment of progress is provided.
> Mastery is valued more than memorization.
> Assessment emphasizes application of lesson content.
> Students demonstrate how-to knowledge.
> Students are encouraged to assess their own performance.
> Students have options in choosing the assessment techniques by which they are evaluated.

High Schools That Work

What would the top 1 percent of high schools look like? Portland's newspaper *The Oregonian* assigned two of its reporters to gather data on the crème de la crème of West Coast high schools.

The investigators sought out high schools that ensured success for virtually every student. Selection criteria included high student achievement, a low dropout rate, a high rate of college attendance, and subsequent success in college. These outstanding schools also received no more funding than comparable area schools and had a mix of students, including significant numbers of minority, special education, and low-income students.

The paper concluded: "High schools must invigorate ties between adults and students, so teens aren't left to find their own way. And they must demand more challenging and meaningful work from students."

The Oregonian reported ten qualities that highly successful high schools possess. The high-performing schools they studied demonstrated nearly every one of these ten practices:

1. Expect high performance from all students and discontinue dumbed-down tracks. For example, one school required every student to take algebra. It did not offer general math or pre-algebra classes.

2. Assure that no teacher has more than 150 students. By adapting with block schedules or a trimester format, teachers had the same class size but spent longer time with fewer students.

3. Nurture teachers talking with their colleagues. The top schools made in-depth conversations about school effectiveness a top priority.

4. Assign schoolwork "worthy of being showcased." Many of the best high schools use student portfolios featuring authentic, high-quality projects. For example, students from San Diego's High Tech High School made documentaries on World War I, built a working submarine, and sponsored a public debate on evolution.

5. Form student advisories. Many of the top schools see that every student has a faculty adviser. The authors concluded, "Making every educator an adviser helps ensure that no teen drifts through high school unnoticed."

6. Make every minute matter. The best schools are obsessed with eliminating absences and tardiness. Interruptions are discouraged, and classes begin on time.

7. Assist students in selecting courses. Some schools require students to obtain the permission of their most recent teachers in a subject before students can enroll in an advanced class. Students are encouraged to talk with teachers they respect about the most appropriate courses to take.

8. Turn seniors into mentors. Older students are encouraged to provide positive guidance to younger ones, creating a more inviting and friendlier school environment.

9. Give parents, students, and teachers more say. Site-based management with heavy involvement from teachers and parents is a hallmark of the most successful schools. Students have an active role in the running of the school.

10. Challenge students with authentic lessons. Connecting the academic curriculum to real-world problems and job-related skills captures students' interest and boost enthusiasm.

Source: Hammond, B., & Graves, B. (2004, January 13). Road map to success. *The Oregonian.* Online at www.oregonlive.com.

National Teaching Standards

Standards, testing, and *accountability* have become buzzwords in the educational arena since the 1990s. A significant portion of the nation's educational resources (money, time, and energy) has been devoted to accountability. Along with the offshoot buzzwords *curriculum alignment* and *high-stakes testing,* these phenomena dominate contemporary educational journals and professional educational conferences.

Some suggest that the origin of the movement for national standards dates to the successful Soviet launch of the Sputnik spacecraft in 1957. This event sparked an enormous response, focusing on what was being taught in our schools. Attention to national standards regained momentum in 1983 when the U.S. Department of Education's National Commission on Excellence in Education published the report *A Nation at Risk.* This much ballyhooed document strongly recommended that graduation requirements be strengthened and that higher standards be implemented for teacher preparation and professional growth.

In 1989 the National Council of Teachers of Mathematics published *Curriculum and Evaluation Standards for School Mathematics,* and the American Association for the Advancement of Science published *Science for all Americans.* Other subject areas soon had their own sets of standards.

Passage of the federal No Child Left Behind (NCLB) Act in 2001 greatly influenced the development of state standards, timetables of state exit exams, and local school districts' priorities.

Writing in a 2001 issue of *Educational Leadership* (59[1], 14–18), Marge Scherer made the following observations about national standards: "High and rigorous academic standards are

✓ A way to establish what all students need to know and be able to do

✓ A result of a public and political outcry for increased accountability in schools

✓ Not yet well implemented in most schools, although not for want of trying

✓ Fraught with challenges and difficulties, but still an opportunity to raise achievement of all students, including minorities

✓ A bipartisan reform that offers a common ground on which advocates of good education can unite"

Proponents argue that standards will boost achievement by clearly defining what is to be taught and what kind of performance is expected. The underlying theory is that higher expectations produce better performance. The intent behind the national standards movement is to set clear standards for what students must learn, evaluate student improvement, and hold students and teachers responsible for the results.

Curriculum alignment is the idea that test content should be congruent with subject area content specified in state or national academic standards. Teachers and schools are continually urged to align their curriculum and assessments with state standards.

The standards movement is not without opposition. The overwhelming number of standards is the biggest impediment to successfully implementing standards, according to Robert Marzano, senior fellow at the McREL Institute. He argues that the number of standards should be cut at least by two-thirds. Marzano suggested we would have to switch from K–12 to K–22 to have time to cover all the standards. The McREL Web site (www.mcrel.org/standards-benchmarks) lists over forty-one hundred benchmarks distributed among 256 standards.

In the McREL database, mathematics contains nine standards and 223 benchmarks. For example, one standard, "Understands and applies basic and advanced concepts of probability" encompasses eighteen benchmarks, such as "Determines probability using simulations or experiments " (grades 6–8) and "Understands the concepts of independent and dependent events and how they are related to compound events and conditional probability" (grades 9–12).

High-Stakes Testing

All states, except Iowa, have established statewide testing programs and curriculum standards. With increasing pressure from the federal government, by 2003 nineteen states had implemented standards-based external exit examinations, often called proficiency tests or competency tests. This national trend is often labeled high-stakes testing. Another five states plan to have exit exams in place by 2008.

Tests in and of themselves do not improve the quality of education; teachers do. Unless testing programs are coupled with comprehensive strategies for disaggregating and interpreting data and implementing curricular and instructional approaches to school improvement, it is unlikely anything will change.

—**Harold C. Doran of New American Schools**

"New American Schools Helps Schools Make the Grade," interview in *Education World* (**www.education-world.com/ q_issues/issues324.shtml**)

California's High School Exit Exam is fairly representative. Beginning with the class of 2006, students must pass the test to receive a diploma. Students take the exam, consisting of English language arts and mathematics sections, in the tenth grade and may retake each section of the pass-fail exam up to five times. Also fairly typical is the mandate that schools must offer assistance to students who do not demonstrate progress toward passing the exam. However, the state does not provide districts with additional funds for this purpose.

Arguing for making tests a cornerstone of educational improvement practices, the Educational Testing Service, which produces many of the standardized tests used in the effort, states: "Tests provide answers. They help teachers make better instructional choices for their students. They help students—and their parents—understand how well they are learning what they are supposed to know and how they compare to other students. Good tests identify strengths as well as weaknesses" (ETS Web site at www.ets.org/letstalk/formula.html).

The NCLB policy requires states to meet established adequate yearly progress goals. Schools that do not are sanctioned. This legislation has its share of vocal critics. In his book *Making the Grade* (2002), Harvard's Tony Wagner argued that the theory underlying the high-stakes testing effort is inherently flawed. He concluded that the high-stakes testing approach seems to increase school failure and dropout rates, broadening the gap between high and low achievers.

Richard Emore (2003, p. 6), senior research fellow at Harvard, warns that the NCLB policy was flawed by overrelying on testing and underinvesting in "capacity building," by which he means boosting teachers' and schools' ability to deliver high-quality instruction. The estimated $1.9 billion to $5.3 billion price tag for the testing components of the NCLB legislation have challenged state budgets.

Recent national polls by the Kettering Foundation revealed a strong sentiment among the public that while tests are necessary, accountability should be founded on more than test results. A 2003 poll by Johnson and Duffet found that 89 percent of teachers and 75 percent of parents agreed with the statement "It's wrong to use the results of just one test as a basis for promotion."

The American Psychological Association (APA) cautions that public officials and educational administrators using tests to make high-stakes decisions must be alert to "the instances when tests have unintended and potentially negative consequences for individual students, groups of students, or the educational system more broadly." Its Code of Fair Testing Practices in Education policy (APA, 2004) further states, "It is only fair to use test results in high-stakes decisions when students have had a real opportunity to master the materials upon which the test is based."

Educators and public critics have become increasingly vocal in urging that schools use multiple indicators (including grades, performance assessments, attendance, and advanced placement coursework) in making decisions about promotion, graduation, retention, or rewards.

Most states have initiated incentives (and sometimes punishments) for schools and teachers when their students' test performance falls short of set standards. When California implemented incentive bonuses for teachers whose students showed gains in their SAT-9 scores, over one thousand teachers earned bonuses of $25,000 when their students attained 10 percent gains in their test scores.

In a survey of teachers from states with high-stakes testing, Pedulla (2003, p. 44) found that 80 percent indicated they "feel pressure from the building principal to raise scores on the test." Only 30 percent of teachers agreed with the statement "Overall, the benefits of the state-mandated testing program are worth the investment of time and money" (p. 46).

Arguments For High-Stakes Testing

- ✓ Tests help schools focus instructional programs.
- ✓ Tests can provide teachers with valuable information about instructional programs' quality and individual students' achievement.
- ✓ The same high expectations and the same evaluation criteria hold for all students.

> We need to acknowledge that tests, although useful, are also fallible indicators of achievement. We also need to recognize that when test scores are linked to high-stakes consequences, they can weaken the learning experiences of students, transform teaching into test preparation, and taint the test itself so that it no longer measures what it was intended to measure.
>
> —**Lisa Abrams and George Madus**
> *Educational Leadership,*
> **November 2003**

> Decisions that affect individual students' life chances or educational opportunities should not be made on the basis of test scores alone.
>
> —**American Educational Research Association, "Position Statement Concerning High-Stakes Testing in PreK–12 Education"**

School officials using such tests must ensure that students are tested on a curriculum they have had a fair opportunity to learn, so that certain subgroups of students, such as racial and ethnic minority students or students with a disability or limited English proficiency, are not systematically excluded or disadvantaged by the test or the test-taking conditions. Furthermore, high-stakes decisions should not be made on the basis of a single test score, because a single test can only provide a "snapshot" of student achievement and may not accurately reflect an entire year's worth of student progress and achievement.

—**American Psychological Association,**
Appropriate Use of High-Stakes Testing
in Our Nation's Schools

✓ Tests help identify children's strengths and weaknesses.

✓ Tests allow policymakers to reward high-performing schools and teachers.

✓ The exams force schools to better align curriculum with state standards.

✓ It is easier to make school-to-school comparisons.

Arguments Against High-Stakes Testing

✓ Teachers feel they must use instructional strategies they don't believe are good educational practices.

✓ State tests seldom take into account errors in measurement.

✓ School graduation rates decline.

✓ Teachers only teach to the test.

✓ Rote memorization tends to be rewarded more than critical-thinking skills.

✓ Standardized test scores correlate highly with parents' income and level of education.

✓ Too much time is spent preparing students to take tests.

✓ Content not tested tends to become neglected.

✓ As the curriculum narrows, students will become less well rounded.

✓ Less time is spent on noncore areas, such as the fine arts and foreign languages.

✓ Tests encourage teachers to become lockstep and uncreative.

✓ Making such important decisions based on performance on one test is unfair.

✓ The tests have little correlation with success outside of school.

✓ Testing programs are extremely expensive.

For More Information

Books and Articles

American Psychological Association (APA). (2001). *Appropriate use of high-stakes testing in our nation's schools.* Washington, DC: APA.

APA. (2004). Code of fair testing practices in education. http://www.apa.org/science/fairtestcode.html.

Carnoy, M., Elmore, R., & Siskin, L. S. (2003). *The new accountability: High schools and high-stakes testing.* New York: RoutledgeFalmer.

Elmore, R. F. (2003). A plea for strong practice. *Educational Leadership, 61*(3), 6–10.

Jones, M. G., Jones, B. D., & Hargroves, T. Y. (2003). *The unintended consequences of high-stakes testing.* Lanham, MD: Rowman & Littlefield.

Pedulla, J. J. (2003). State-mandated testing: What do teachers think? *Educational Leadership, 61*(3), 42–46.

Peterson, P. E., & West, M. R. (Eds.). (2003). *No child left behind? The politics and practice of school accountability.* Washington, DC: Brookings Institution Press.

Scherer, M. (2002) Perspectives: Making standards work. *Educational Leadership, 59(1),* 5.

Wagner, T. (2002). *Making the grade: Reinventing America's schools.* New York: RoutledgeFalmer.

Online Resources

Mid-continent Regional Educational Laboratory
www.mcrel.org

Search national standards database for all subjects.

StateStandards.com
www.statestandards.com/

State educational standards are linked to lesson plans and resources.

Professional Development

Teaching should be more than just a job. It is a profession and a career. It is a long-term commitment to doing your best to help young people blossom intellectually, emotionally, and behaviorally. It is a position of incredible importance; teachers with passion and compassion can profoundly influence their students' lives. At the worst, teachers also have the power to discourage, humiliate, and crush their students' spirit. Either way the lives we teachers touch become part of our heritage, our immortality.

Outstanding teachers are not born but develop. True, some personality types are probably more attracted to education, but the art and craft of teaching is gradually honed through years of study, experimentation, reality testing, and reflection. Development of the effective teacher does not end with the receipt of an undergraduate or even master's degree. A diploma is but a license to learn. The more true professionals learn, the more they realize there is to learn.

Any teacher can become a better teacher; and with enough determination and hard work, probably any teacher could become a successful teacher. However, teaching is hard work. Knowing your content is a necessary, though wholly insufficient, prerequisite to becoming an outstanding teacher. Many in the teaching profession are brilliant, possessing great knowledge and understanding of their chosen field of study, yet they will never be successful teachers. The skills of effective teaching are complex. It is not enough to be a scholar; a good teacher is also part salesperson, entertainer, psychologist, counselor, leader, mediator, conductor, guide, evaluator, advocate, and cheerleader. Different teachers develop different combinations of these talents, but all are helpful.

> *Insanity is doing the same thing over and over again, but expecting different results.*
>
> **—Rita Mae Brown,**
> ***Sudden Death***

Believe it or not, many teachers rarely read anything related to their teaching area. Their teaching repertoire is limited to what they knew when they walked into the classroom the first day. Imagine going to a physician, auto mechanic, or any other professional who had not remained current with the latest techniques, research, and technology related to their profession. Indeed, an argument can be made that the person who fails to learn and use the most effective practices available to his or her profession is being both negligent and unethical.

Create a purposeful plan of professional development. It is too important to be left to chance. Here are some ideas that successful teachers have used to enhance their professional skills:

✓ Continued learning keeps you fresh. Experiment with new ways of doing old tasks. Include new content and skills in your courses or volunteer to develop new courses. It is impossible to maintain enthusiasm and peak performance while teaching the same things the same ways year after year. "Rust out" or burnout are inevitable if we do not incorporate professional rejuvenation.

✓ Allow time, ideally each day, for reflection. Examine what works and what doesn't and how you might improve each lesson. Write it down in a journal or in the margins of your lesson plans. Keep an idea notebook to incubate and brainstorm teaching ideas.

✓ Peer-coaching groups are now an integral part of many staff development programs. This is an effective, proven approach to improving instructional and classroom management skills. If your school does not yet have a peer-coaching group, suggest it to your colleagues. Many will be threatened by the thought of another teacher observing them. The truly professional teacher will welcome the opportunity.

✓ Develop or join a support group among fellow teachers. It may take the form of a study group where you read and discuss relevant educational materials, or it might be a more unstructured gathering to offer mutual support and problem solving.

✔ Draw up a professional development plan each year, even if your school does not require it. It should target two or three areas for improvement. It might be in classroom management skills, developing specific teaching strategies, or in expanding your knowledge of some content area. Share your plan with your principal and seek suggestions. You are also more likely to later receive support (in either release time or money) if it is obvious your request is a part of a professional development plan and not a whim.

✔ Create your own independent study. Each year identify a new topic you intend to study in depth. Attend workshops or classes, read books and journal articles, interview experts, or develop your own field trips. Within a year of concentrated effort, you can develop a reasonable degree of expertise in most any subject.

✔ Don't overlook the benefits of acquiring a mentor, even if you are a veteran teacher. It may be a more experienced teacher, a supervisor or administrator, a professor, or perhaps an individual working in your subject area outside of a school setting. Working with a mentor should be a mutually rewarding experience. Show your appreciation of your mentor through verbal acknowledgment, token gifts, and time spent helping him or her in special projects.

✔ Learn by observing good role models. Every building contains creative, successful teachers. Find them and study their style, techniques, and ideas. Seek their advice.

✔ If you have an opportunity to participate in a sabbatical, take it—even if it entails some financial sacrifice. The trade-off in mental health and renewed vigor are well worth the price.

✔ Each year try to attend at least one state or national conference related to your teaching field. Ask fellow teachers or local professors which ones are most worthwhile. These programs can provide refreshing

Personal Independent Study

For twenty-five years, I have satisfied my thirst for learning by annually setting up a personal independent study project. Each year I select a topic that piques my curiosity and embark on a quest to learn all I can about it in roughly a year. My research involves reading relevant articles and books, attending workshops and seminars, and interviewing any available experts. The Internet has facilitated access to a treasury of hard-to-find resources.

In my independent study, I am accountable to no one but myself. No grades or reports are required. No one is going to evaluate my progress. There is nothing magical about the length of time a project takes. Some topics run their course in less than a year. I sense it is time to move on when what I am reading or hearing becomes redundant or when the topic becomes less interesting.

While I was teaching college, the content of my inquiries tended to be academic; for example, the use of time in schools, stress management, creative problem solving, perfectionism, and classroom management. More recent topics have included learning to design Web pages, building stained glass windows, and calligraphy.

You can develop a fair amount of expertise on any topic if you focus on it for a year. Interestingly, the next topic often emerges from the previous year's study, appearing almost subconsciously as an itch that needs scratching. I anticipate that my independent study practice will continue as a lifelong habit.

and energizing experiences. Bring back samples and ideas to share with interested colleagues. If you are a regular at a conference, consider sharing your classroom experiences as a presenter. If you can't attend, most conferences provide tapes of many sessions. Borrow or buy these to listen to while commuting.

✔ Subscribe to at least one useful publication related to your teaching area. You need not feel obligated to read every issue cover to cover, but do scan it looking for new teaching ideas.

✔ Recognize that teaching as a profession cannot be limited to forty hours per week for nine months per year. If education is really a passion, you will eagerly devote the time necessary to improve your lessons, develop new skills, and reflect on the daily challenges of the classroom.

✔ Attend in-service programs and workshops with an open mind. It is easy to develop a red-pencil mentality and stubbornly refuse to rationally listen to new ideas. Of course, they have to be reality tested back in your classroom the next day, but give them a chance. Like developing any new skill—riding a bike, mastering a computer, or learning a new hobby—innovative teaching techniques will require a start-up learning curve. It may seem unnatural or awkward at first. Experiment. After a fair trial, discard those things that clearly don't work for you; and adapt those things that do. That is how we improve in any endeavor—whether golf, knitting, or painting; we keep the behaviors and ideas that work and eliminate those that do not. It is embedded in the concept of continuous improvement, constantly fine-tuning our performance.

✔ Develop options. If you have only one way to teach a concept or handle misbehavior, what will you do when your tactic does not work? If you have a smorgasbord of alternatives available, you can pragmatically experiment until you find one that succeeds.

✔ Use a student evaluation form appropriate to your students' age level. Carefully and objectively read the results to see how your students rate your teaching effectiveness. While there are some limitations of student evaluations, they do provide one valuable source of information that should not be ignored.

✔ Examine your students' scores on standardized achievement tests related to your subject area. Are there any areas in which they seem to consistently score low? Is it important for your students to master these skills or concepts? How can you better teach these concepts in your class?

✔ Resist the temptation to rationalize poor student performance or behavior in your classes. Claims such as "I'd be a better teacher if I had better students" may be true, but they don't excuse poor teaching. Imagine a physician lamenting that only sick people come to her office. Yes, kids are not the same today as when you went to school, and they probably never will be. Yet the fact remains that school represents the best hope that many kids have. A true professional is committed to doing the very best possible with the skills, resources, and students available.

✓ Don't automatically discount critical feedback you receive from others about your teaching performance. Supervisors' or principals' observations can be one, though not the only, valuable source of information. Listen objectively, not defensively. If you disagree with some aspect of an observer's conclusions, rationally present whatever documentation or evidence you might have to rebut the point. However, avoid arguing or quibbling to protect your ego.

✓ Develop relationships outside the field of education. One way of recharging your batteries is to cultivate interests beyond school. Interacting only with other teachers invites too much shop talk and commiserating. While some colleagues are likely to be included in your circle of friends, seek a balance with others from diverse careers and experiences.

✓ Become a risk taker. Don't repeat the same half-baked lessons year after year from habit. Experiment. Try new things. Don't be afraid to make mistakes. Free yourself from the shackles of perfectionism. Strive for excellence, not perfection.

✓ Become an actor, not a reactor, on the stage of life. You possess a free will to choose how you will conduct your life, both in and out of the classroom. When we become reactors, we surrender control of our thoughts, actions, and feelings to those around us. When we worry about possible disapproval from our colleagues or about not living up to others' expectations, we yield control of our lives. When we defensively respond with revenge, gossiping, backbiting, sulking, and withdrawal, we have surrendered our autonomy. When we become creative problem solvers, we affirm our competence and efficacy. When we become tolerant of the foibles of others while admitting and occasionally laughing at our own, we reap dignity and the respect of our colleagues and students. True power arises from acceptance of ourselves and of those around us.

National Board Certification

The pinnacle of professional development today is attainment of National Board certification. This is a voluntary national credential that complements state licensure. Administered by the National Board for Professional Teaching Standards, the rigorous certification process guides teachers through self-reflection and examination of their teaching practices. Over thirty-two thousand of the nation's 2.5 million teachers have been designated as National Board Certified Teachers (NBCTs).

As of November 2003, all but one state had enacted special incentives and recognition for teachers achieving National Board certification. Most states subsidize all or part of the $2,300 certification fee. The state of Washington provides a $3,500 salary enhancement for NBCTs. New Mexico certification earners gain a onetime $4,000 bonus. Oklahoma offers $5,000 annually to certificate recipients. Iowa does the same for the first ten years, dropping the amount to $2,500 after the renewal. Many local school districts offer additional annual payments (typically, $500–$2,500) for successful attainment of this certification.

Over twelve hundred colleges and universities will grant graduate credits for completing the board certification process. A complete list of these cooperating institutions can be found at www.acenet.edu/calec/corporate/coop-colleges.cfm. The American Council on Education may award three semester hours of graduate credit to teachers who complete the application process and an additional three credit hours to those receiving National Board certification.

The National Board's mission, according to its Web site (www.nbpts.org), is to maintain "high and rigorous standards for what accomplished teachers should know and be able to do." The National Board certification process is based on five basic assumptions underlying the practices of excellence in teaching:

✓ Teachers are committed to students and their learning.

✓ Teachers know the subjects they teach and how to teach those subjects to students.

✓ Teachers are responsible for managing and monitoring student learning.

✓ Teachers think systematically about their practice and learn from experience.

✓ Teachers are members of learning communities.

The National Board assessment involves two components, a professional portfolio and a series of assessment-center exercises. The portfolios include videotapes of the applicant's teaching, samples of students' learning products, and additional teaching artifacts, as well as a detailed analysis of the teacher's instructional practices. Trained assessors examine how teachers put knowledge and theory into practice.

The assessment-center component requires teachers to write answers to questions pertinent to their specific content areas. The intent of these exercises is to verify that the knowledge and competencies demonstrated in the portfolio truly reflect the applicants' performances and to allow applicants a chance to exhibit proficiencies not included in their portfolios. Candidates may complete the computer-administered assessments at any of more than three hundred testing centers located in every state in the nation.

Teachers report spending an average of two hundred hours working on their certification process. National Board certification is valid for ten years, at which time a teacher must undergo a renewal requirement. A growing body of research relates National Board certification with improved student achievement.

To learn more about receiving this certification, check the National Board's Web site at www.nbpts.org.

Educational Research

Every professional educator must be a savvy consumer of educational research. The obligation to follow the best practices that have been supported by sound, empirical research is a hallmark of any profession. It is every professional's duty to continuously improve his or her skills and knowledge. A doctor who is practicing outdated procedures that have been scientifically shown to be inferior is in violation of that profession's ethical code.

A vast body of sound educational research is available. Some of it is pure muck—poorly designed, inaccurate, and misleading. The fact that it is in print offers no assurance that a research study is valid. Being able to sort the wheat from the chaff is an essential skill for professional teachers. That is why virtually all master's degree programs in education include research and statistics courses. To remain ignorant of the principles of sound research and basic statistics is to put oneself at the mercy of charlatans and zealots plying political and personal agendas.

While a full tutorial in educational research and statistics is beyond the scope of this book, a general set of guidelines for assessing the quality of good educational research follows.

The Scientific Method

The scientific method is the foundation of sound research, enabling investigators to objectively gather data to solve problems. It consists of four parts.

1. *State the problem.* Einstein suggested that a well-defined problem is half solved.

2. *Form a hypothesis.* A potential solution is tentatively created after gathering information about the problem. This step involves examining the current body of knowledge related to the problem at hand, including observations, theories, and prior research efforts.

3. *Test the hypothesis.* An experiment is planned and conducted to determine whether the hypothesis solves the problem or not.

4. *Draw conclusions.* A conclusion is reached as to whether the hypothesis was correct or not. The results are often stated in research articles in terms of the statistical probability that the observed results could have occurred by chance.

Types of Research

Different disciplines may rely on somewhat different modes of research, depending on the types of problems being studied and the feasibility of collecting necessary data. Research designs fall into two broad categories: qualitative or quantitative.

Qualitative research designs involve compiling narrative data to learn about variables of interest. Data analysis includes coding data and synthesizing the information to draw conclusions about the phenomena under study.

Quantitative research designs rely on collecting numerical data to understand, predict, and explain phenomena. The analysis is essentially deductive, involving primarily statistical analysis.

Research designs tend to fall under one of the following seven categories:

✓ Ethnographic research strives to describe group behavior and social interactions. It employs qualitative techniques, particularly structured interviews, careful observation, and meticulous documentation of actions and social interactions.

✓ Descriptive research tries to depict and explain present phenomena. It uses both qualitative and quantitative data assembled from interviews, observations, surveys, written documents, and test results.

✓ Historical research seeks to describe and explain past events. It usually depends on qualitative data, such as oral histories or written documents.

✓ Correlational research explores relationships among variables or tries to make predictions. It analyzes the correlation between two or more measures, such as test scores and attitudinal instruments.

✓ Action and evaluation research assesses the value of a procedure, program, or product. It often takes place on-site (such as in the classroom or school building). Its goal is usually to improve the organization. Action or evaluation research does not attempt to generalize results to a broader population.

✓ Causal comparative research attempts to explore cause-and-effect relationships. It relies on both qualitative and quantitative data such as written documents, interviews, test scores, and so on. Pretest and posttest control group projects in which the subjects are randomly assigned to the control group or experimental group provide an ideal research structure for making valid claims of causality. The difficulty in controlling relevant variables (such as students' home environment) makes pure control group experiments difficult in some areas of educational and social research.

✓ Experimental research examines cause-and-effect relationships. Experiments are designed to manipulate specific variables to create different kinds of effects. It uses primarily quantitative data such as test results and performance measurements. The independent variables are the factors the experimenter controls.

Common Flaws in Research Articles

Causation vs. Correlation

The fact that the rooster crows every morning does not mean that its crowing causes the sun to rise. The mere fact of two events occurring together does not mean that one causes the other. It reveals a relationship (what researchers call a correlation) between the two events but does not imply causation.

A common error in the public press is to misinterpret correlation between two variables as causation. Statistically, a clear correlation can be shown between the price of cigarettes and the salaries of ministers in this country. Would anyone be so naive as to suggest that somehow ministers are profiting from the sale of tobacco? Of course not, they are obviously both caused by a third variable, economic inflation. But equally invalid assumptions commonly find their way into the popular media and are spread as gospel.

Sound research designs can provide evidence of a causal relationship between variables. Some are too complex to cover here, but most involve some form of control group, which does not receive the procedure under study. It serves as a comparison group for the variable under investigation. Data from the experimental group, which does receive the procedure under study, is then statistically compared to that of the control group.

Sampling Errors

Seldom is it feasible to include every individual or event in a research project. A legitimate research practice is to study a representative sample of a particular population. The safest way to assure that the individuals included are truly representative of the total population is to randomly select a sufficiently large group. Random selection means that every individual in the total population had an equal chance of being selected.

A research investigation may lead to erroneous conclusions if a poor sample of the population under study is selected. Erroneous conclusions are likely if the sample is drawn in a biased manner or from a group not representative of the population being studied. It would be risky to use data from ten teachers to generalize that all teachers would possess the same characteristics.

Measurement Error

Ineffective or inappropriately used instruments will usually lead to erroneous conclusions. Tests, questionnaires, and other assessment devices must be designed using fair and unbiased procedures. Two essential qualities, reliability and validity, must be evident and should be reported in any legitimate research article.

Reliability is a statistical indicator of the instrument's ability to obtain consistent results. Imagine trying to measure the length of something using an elastic ruler.

A test (or other instrument) possesses validity if it measures what it says it is measuring. One form of validity is predictive validity. For example, the SAT claims to be a valid predictor of student success in college. Note that reliability is a necessary but not sufficient condition for validity.

Biased test instruments can put some students at a great disadvantage. Much of the debate on intelligence testing and today's high-stakes competency tests centers on potential cultural biases. Fairness of testing may be questioned if the test penalizes students with disabilities or those with limited English proficiency.

Poorly worded questions on a survey can distort the results, intentionally or unintentionally yielding inaccurate interpretations. Unclear or incomplete directions can adversely affect test or questionnaire results.

Lack of Standardization

The instruments and procedures used in any research endeavor must be standardized, such that all subjects or cases in a comparison group receive the same treatment under precisely the same conditions. For example, the Trends in International Mathematics and Science Study (TIMSS, nces.ed.gov/timss/) report, which annually compares U.S. students with other students worldwide, seldom reports that the United States is one of the very few countries to prohibit the use of calculators on the TIMSS tests. Furthermore, the TIMSS tests use only the metric system in problems involving measurements. All other participating countries use the metric system almost exclusively in their instruction. This is an example of comparing apples and oranges. Too often a researcher may make inferential leaps in analyzing data and make side-by-side comparisons that are inappropriate.

Additionally, researchers' inattention to detail or carelessness can produce errors. "Fuzzy" operational variables must be clearly and concretely defined.

Lack of Objectivity

In reading a piece of research, it is wise to ask some questions. Who sponsored the study? What are the researcher's credentials? Who has a vested interest in the results? Are hidden political or social agendas being plied? Does the research project have inherent biases?

Lack of Peer Review

Be extremely skeptical of research that is distributed solely by mass media (news releases, television sound bites, and popular magazines). Legitimate research is published in peer-reviewed publications. These professional research journals employ a rigorous and objective process to evaluate the appropriateness of the research design, data analysis, and interpretations. A list of the major education-related research journals is included later in this chapter.

The Importance of Statistics

In applying the scientific method, a researcher generates a hypothesis about some observed phenomenon and proceeds to objectively collect data to test that hypothesis. The researcher then analyzes the data to either confirm or refute the hypothesis. This may take the form of an experiment specifically designed to test the hypothesis.

Frequently, the researcher measures the data. Anytime one collects a series of measurements, some variation will occur. Statistical analysis helps a researcher determine whether differences between two (or more) sets of measurements occur purely by chance or if some other variable caused the differences.

Basic Research and Statistics Glossary

correlation The most commonly used measure of association. It indicates the strength of a linear relationship between two variables. Remember that correlations do not support causality.

correlation coefficient A measure of the relationship between variables. It is expressed numerically with a value between –1.0 and +1.0. A zero represents no relationship at all. A negative sign before the coefficient indicates an inverse relationship between the variables: as one variable increases, the other decreases. A positive number indicates a positive relationship: as one variable increases, so does the other.

hypothesis A tentative statement predicting the relationship between variables.

mean, median, and *mode* The three mathematical calculations are used to provide a picture of a group of measurements. These three calculations are measures of central tendency. They represent different concepts.

The *mean* is the statistical average of a group of numbers. It is calculated by adding all numbers in a set of numbers and then dividing by the number of observations in the set. Examples would include grade point average, the Dow Jones, or average daily temperature. The mean is the most commonly used measure of central tendency. One disadvantage is that extreme numbers can distort the mean or average. Imagine the effect of including Bill Gates in a calculation of the average annual salary of a group of people.

The *median* is the middle value in an ordered selection of measurements. It is the midpoint: half the cases would be above, and half would be below the median. If a set contains an odd number of figures, the median is the middle number. Typically, the median is a better indicator of central tendency than the mean when there are some extremely small or large measurements.

The *mode* is the most frequent value in a set of observations. The mode is a particularly useful measure when the data are not numbers but categories (for example, shoe sizes, cities). For example, in the set of values 1, 3, 5, 5, 5, 7, the mode would be 5 because this value occurs most frequently in the set. A distribution can have two modes (hence, bimodal).

normal distribution A bell-shaped graph of data. It is highest in the middle and lowest on the sides, and the right and left halves are symmetrical. Many biological, physical, and social phenomena are normally distributed.

null hypothesis Generally a hypothesis that no difference or relationship exists between two or more variables. The researcher applies a statistical procedure to either accept or reject the null hypothesis. When the null hypothesis is rejected, the researcher describes the results as statistically significant.

probability The chance of a particular event occurring. A statistical probability is expressed as a number between one and ten. The closer the number is to one, the greater the probability of occurrence. Flipping a coin for heads or tails would carry a .5 probability of either result.

random sample A sample in which each member of the population has the same probability of inclusion.

range The statistical range is the difference between the lowest and highest numbers in an array of numbers. For example, the range of heights of boys on a high school basketball team was from five feet eight inches to six feet seven inches.

replication An independent verification of a research study's results.

sample A subset of the total population or universe.

standard deviation A statistic that describes how tightly all the data are clustered around the mean in an array of data. When the instances are closely bunched together and the bell-shaped curve is steep, the standard deviation is small. When the data are wider apart and the bell curve is flatter, the standard deviation will be large.

validity The extent to which an instrument measures what it's supposed to be measuring.

variable A trait or characteristic of a person or an item that can have different values within the population of interest.

For More Information

Carroll, S. R., & Carroll, D. J. (2002). *Statistics made simple for school leaders: Data-driven decision making.* Lanham, MD: Scarecrow Press.

Fraenkel, J. R., & Wallen, N. E. (2002). *How to design and evaluate research in education* (5th ed.). Boston: McGraw-Hill.

Gay, L. R., & Airasian, P. (2003). *Educational research: competencies for analysis and applications* (7th ed.). Upper Saddle River, NJ: Merrill/Prentice Hall.

Gravetter, F. J., & Wallnau, L. B. (2004). *Statistics for the behavioral sciences* (6th ed.). Belmont, CA: Thomson/Wadsworth.

McMillan, J., & Wergin, J. (2002). *Understanding and evaluating educational research* (2nd ed.). Upper Saddle River, NJ: Merrill/Prentice Hall.

Checklist to Use in Evaluating Whether an Intervention Is Backed by Rigorous Evidence

Step 1. Is the strategy supported by "strong" evidence of effectiveness?

   A. The quality of evidence needed to establish "strong" evidence: randomized controlled trials that are well-designed and implemented. The following are key items to look for in assessing whether a trial is well-designed and implemented.

Key items to look for in the study's description of the intervention and the random assignment process

- ☐ The study should clearly describe the strategy or intervention, including: (i) who administered it, who received it, and what it cost; (ii) how the intervention differed from what the control group received; and (iii) the logic of how the intervention is supposed to affect outcomes.
- ☐ Be alert to any indication that the random assignment process may have been compromised.
- ☐ The study should provide data showing that there are no systematic differences between the intervention and control groups prior to the intervention.

Key items to look for in the study's collection of outcome data

- ☐ The study should use outcome measures that are "valid"—i.e., that accurately measure the true outcomes that the intervention is designed to affect.
- ☐ The percent of study participants that the study has lost track of when collecting outcome data should be small, and should not differ between the intervention and control groups.
- ☐ The study should collect and report outcome data even for those members of the intervention group who do not participate in or complete the intervention.
- ☐ The study should preferably obtain data on long-term outcomes of the intervention, so that you can judge whether the intervention's effects were sustained over time.

Key items to look for in the study's reporting of results

- ☐ If the study makes a claim that the intervention is effective, it should report (i) the size of the effect and (ii) statistical tests showing the effect is unlikely to be the result of chance.
- ☐ A study's claim that the intervention's effect on a subgroup (for example, Hispanic students) is different [from] its effect on the overall population in the study should be treated with caution.

☐ The study should report the intervention's effects on all the outcomes that the study measured, not just those for which there is a positive effect.

B. Quantity of evidence needed to establish "strong" evidence of effectiveness.

☐ The intervention should be demonstrated effective, through well-designed randomized controlled trials, in more than one site of implementation;

☐ These sites should be typical school or community settings, such as public school classrooms taught by regular teachers; and

☐ The trials should demonstrate the intervention's effectiveness in school settings similar to yours, before you can be confident it will work in your schools/classrooms.

Step 2. If the intervention is not supported by "strong" evidence, is it nevertheless supported by "possible" evidence of effectiveness?

This is a judgment call that depends, for example, on the extent of the flaws in the randomized trials of the intervention and the quality of any nonrandomized studies that have been done. The following are a few factors to consider in making these judgments.

A. Circumstances in which a comparison-group study can constitute "possible" evidence:

☐ The study's intervention and comparison groups should be very closely matched in academic achievement levels, demographics, and other characteristics prior to the intervention.

☐ The comparison group should not be comprised of individuals who had the option to participate in the intervention but declined.

☐ The study should preferably choose the intervention/comparison groups and outcome measures "prospectively"—i.e., before the intervention is administered.

☐ The study should meet the checklist items listed [here] for a well-designed randomized controlled trial (other than the item concerning the random assignment process). That is, the study should use valid outcome measures, report tests for statistical significance, and so on.

B. Studies that do not meet the threshold for "possible" evidence of effectiveness include: (i) pre-post studies . . .; (ii) comparison-group studies in which the intervention and comparison groups are not well-matched; and (iii) "meta-analyses" that combine the results of individual studies which do not themselves meet the threshold for "possible" evidence.

Step 3. If the intervention is backed by neither "strong" nor "possible" evidence, one may conclude that it is not supported by meaningful evidence of effectiveness.

Source: Institute of Education Sciences. (2003). *Identifying and implementing educational practices supported by rigorous evidence: A user friendly guide.* Washington, DC: U.S. Department of Education.

Learning What Works: Action Research

Action or evaluation research is concerned with assessing the effectiveness of a particular treatment or procedure. In the classroom it usually involves teachers gathering and analyzing data about their own practice to improve it. The focus is on resolving practical problems and systematically testing new ideas.

Action research can serve several purposes simultaneously: professional development, curriculum development, school improvement, and self-reflection. It can also give teachers greater confidence in the quality of their classroom decisions.

Because the data analysis is generally qualitative rather than quantitative, an in-depth knowledge of statistics is not required. Often teachers collaborate with colleagues on action research projects. Action research can be an integral part of teachers' mentoring or peer-coaching process. Some teachers work together with university professors on an action research project.

Projects may take from a few weeks to several months. Here are the steps involved:

1. *Identify a research question or classroom problem.* The first step is to select an issue or methodology you would like to research. Usually it is a technique or activity that has potential for improving some aspect of instruction or academic life. It should be something important that is of genuine interest to you.

   Sample Research Questions

   - How does self-efficacy affect the achievement of students?
   - What impact does including the student in parent conferences have?
   - How can I get my students to take better notes?
   - Has block scheduling improved student learning?
   - Does cooperative learning improve students' attitudes toward school?
   - What effect does participation in a service project have on classroom civility?
   - What strategies will decrease classroom teasing?

2. *Review the research literature.* Do some background reading of previous research related to the issue under study. Why reinvent the wheel? Build on what others have already done. An Internet search can provide useful information, though its credibility must be carefully assessed.

3. *Implement a potential solution.* If feasible, use two comparable groups to test the potential solution. The experimental group receives the proposed treatment; the control group does not.

4. *Collect data.* A wise person once quipped, "Gathering data is like gathering garbage. You'd better know what you are going to do with it before you collect it." Don't accumulate more than you need. Focus precisely on the specific issue under examination. To adequately assess the impact of an innovation, collect data from a variety of sources and from alternative points of view. Collecting pre- and posttreatment data is helpful in detecting treatment effects.

Potential Data Sources

Anecdotal records	Parent-teacher conference notes
Attendance	Photographs
Audiotapes and videotapes	Portfolios
Case studies	Questionnaires
Cumulative records	Student journals
Grades	Student work samples
Interviews	Surveys
Observations	Test scores

5. *Analyze the data.* Does the project make a difference? Do you see clear patterns in the data?

6. *Take action.* Implement successful solutions. Revise partially successful ones or seek alternative solutions.

7. *Share what you have learned.* Communicate the results to colleagues or parents. This might be done through journal articles, online discussion groups, conferences, or workshops. Include copies of action research projects in your professional portfolio.

For More Information

Books

Arhar, J., Holly, M. L., & Kasten, W. C. (2000). *Action research for teachers: Traveling the yellow brick road.* Upper Saddle River, NJ: Prentice Hall.

Johnson, A. P. (2002). *A short guide to action research* (rev.). Boston: Allyn & Bacon.

Meyers, E., & Rust, F. (Eds.). (2003). *Taking action with teacher research.* Portsmouth, NH: Heinemann.

Mills, G. (2000). *Action research: A guide for the teacher researcher.* Upper Saddle River, NJ: Prentice Hall.

Schmuck, R. A. (1997). *Practical action research for change.* Glenview, IL: Skylight.

Stringer, E. T. (1999). *Action research: A handbook for practitioners.* Newbury Park, CA: Sage.

Online Resources
Action Research at Queen's University
educ.queensu.ca/projects/action_research/

Action Research/Teacher as Researcher
Mid-continent Research for Education and Learning
www.mcrel.org/lesson-plans/action.asp

Educational Action Research
www.triangle.co.uk/ear/

Networks: An On-line Journal for Teacher Research
education.ucsc.edu/faculty/gwells/networks/

Professional Organizations

American Alliance for Health, Physical
Education, Recreation and Dance
1900 Association Drive
Reston, VA 22091
(800) 213-7193
www.aahperd.org/

American Association of Physics
Teachers
One Physics Ellipse
College Park, MD 20740-3845
(301) 209-3311
www.aapt.org/

American Council of the Teaching of
Foreign Languages
6 Executive Plaza
Yonkers, NY 10701-6801
(914) 963-8830
www.actfl.org/

American Federation of Teachers
555 New Jersey Avenue, NW
Washington, DC 20001
(202) 879-4400
www.aft.org/

American Library Association
50 E. Huron Street
Chicago, IL 60611
(800) 545-2433
www.ala.org/

American School Counselor Association
801 N. Fairfax Street, Suite 310
Alexandria, VA 22314
(703) 683-2722
www.schoolcounselor.org

American Speech-Language-Hearing
Association
10801 Rockville Pike
Rockville, MD 20852
(800) 638-8255
www.asha.org

Association for Career and Technical
Education
1410 King Street
Alexandria, VA 22314
(800) 826-9972
www.acteonline.org/

Association for Childhood Education
International
17904 Georgia Avenue, Suite 215
Olney, MD 20832
(301) 942-2443
www.udel.edu/bateman/acei/

Association for Educational Communications and Technology
1800 N. Stonelake Drive, Suite 2
Bloomington, IN 47408
(877) 677-2328
www.aect.org/

Association for Experiential Education
2305 Canyon Boulevard, Suite 100
Boulder, CO 80302-5651
(303) 440-8844
www.aee.org/

Association for Supervision and
Curriculum Development
1703 N. Beauregard Street
Alexandria, VA 22311
(800) 933-2723
www.ascd.org

Council for Exceptional Children
1110 North Glebe Road, Suite 300
Arlington, VA 22201
(703) 620-3660
www.cec.sped.org

Council for Learning Disabilities
P.O. Box 4014
Leesburg, VA 20177
(571) 258-1010
www.cldinternational.org/

International Reading Association
800 Barksdale Road
P.O. Box 8139
Newark, DE 19714-8139
(302) 731-1600
www.reading.org/

International Society for Technology
in Education
480 Charnelton Street
Eugene, OR 97401-2626
(800) 336-5191
www.iste.org

Kappa Delta Pi
3707 Woodview Trace
Indianapolis, IN 46268-1158
(800) 284-3167
www.kdp.org/

Learning Disabilities Association of
America
4156 Library Road
Pittsburgh, PA 15234-1349
(412) 341-1515
www.ldanatl.org/

Modern Language Association
26 Broadway, Third Floor
New York, NY 10004-1789
(646) 576-5000
www.mla.org/

Music Teachers National Association
The Carew Tower
441 Vine Street, Suite 505
Cincinnati, OH 45202-2814
(888) 512-5278
www.mtna.org/

National Alliance of Black School
Educators
310 Pennsylvania
Washington, DC 20003
(800) 221-2654
www.nabse.org/

National Art Educators Association
1916 Association Drive
Reston, VA 22091
(703) 860-8000
www.naea-reston.org/

National Association for Bilingual
Education
Union Center Plaza
1220 L Street, NW, Suite 605
Washington, DC 20005
(202) 898-1829
www.nabe.org/

National Association for Gifted
Children
1707 L Street, NW, Suite 550
Washington, DC 20036
(202) 785-4268
www.nagc.org/

National Association for the Education
of Young Children
1509 16th Street, NW
Washington, DC 20036-1426
(800) 424-2460
www.naeyc.org/

National Association of Biology Teachers
12030 Sunrise Valley Drive, Suite 110
Reston, VA 20191
(800) 406-0775
www.nabt.org/

National Association of Elementary
School Principals
1615 Duke Street
Alexandria, VA 22314
(800) 386-2377
www.naesp.org/

National Association of School
Psychologists
4340 East West Hwy., Suite 402
Bethesda, MD 20814
(301) 657-0270
www.nasponline.org/

National Association of Secondary
School Principals
1904 Association Drive
Reston, VA 22091-1596
(703) 860-0200
nassp.org/

National Business Education
Association
1914 Association Drive
Reston, VA 22091-1596
(703) 860-8300
www.nbea.org/

National Catholic Education
Association
1077 30th Street, NW, Suite 100
Washington, DC 20007
(202) 337-6232
www.ncea.org/

National Council for the Social
Studies
8555 Sixteenth Street, Suite 500
Silver Spring, MD 20910
(301) 588-1800
www.ncss.org/

National Council of Teachers
of English
1111 W. Kenyon Road
Urbana, IL 61801-1096
(217) 328-0977
www.ncte.org/

National Council of Teachers of
Mathematics
1906 Association Drive
Reston, VA 22091-1596
(703) 620-9840
www.nctm.org/

National Education Association
1201 16th Street
Washington, DC 20036
(202) 833-4000
www.nca.org/

National Middle School Association
4151 Executive Parkway, Suite 300
Westerville, OH 43081
(800) 528-6672
www.nmsa.org/

National Rural Education Association
820 Van Vleet Oval, Room 227
University of Oklahoma
Norman, OK 73019
(405) 325-7959
www.nrea.net/

National Science Teachers Association
1840 Wilson Boulevard
Arlington, VA 22201-3000
(703) 243-7100
www.nsta.org

Phi Delta Kappa
P.O. Box 789
Bloomington, IN 47402-0789
(800) 766-1156
www.pdkintl.org/

Teachers of English to Speakers of
Other Languages
700 South Washington Street, Suite 200
Alexandria, VA 22314
(888) 547-3369
www.tesol.edu/

Education Journals

General Education Periodicals

American Education
American Educator
American Journal of Education
American School Board Journal
American Secondary Education
American Teacher
Changing Schools
Clearing House
Computers and Education
Computers in the Schools
Contemporary Education
Curriculum Inquiry
Curriculum Review
Education
Education, U.S.A.
Education and Urban Society
Education Digest
Educational Forum
Educational Horizons
Educational Leadership
*Elementary School Guidance and
   Counseling*
Elementary School Journal
Harvard Educational Review
High School Journal
History of Education
Instructional Science
Instructor
Interchange
International Education

Issues in Education
Journal of Classroom Interaction
Journal of Computer-Based Instruction
Journal of Curriculum and Supervision
Journal of Developmental Education
Journal of Education
Journal of Education and Psychology
Journal of Educational Thought
*Journal of Humanistic Education and
   Development*
Journal of Indian Education
Journal of Instructional Development
Journal of Modern Education
Journal of Moral Education
Journal of Negro Education
Journal of Philosophy of Education
Journal of Special Education
Kappa Delta Pi Record
Learning
Lifelong Learning
McGill Journal of Education
Merrill-Palmer Quarterly
Middle School Journal
NASSP Bulletin
NEA Today
*New Directions for Teaching and
   Learning*
New Education
Notre Dame Journal of Education

Open Learning: Teaching and Training at a Distance
Peabody Journal of Education
Phi Delta Kappan
Pointer
Progressive Education

Scholastic Education
School Review
Teacher
Theory into Practice
Today's Education

Research Journals

American Educational Research Journal
Educational Record
Educational Research
Elementary School Journal
Human Development
International Journal of Educational Development
International Journal of Educational Research
Journal of Counseling and Development
Journal of Educational Psychology
Journal of Educational Research
Journal of Experimental Education
Journal of Instructional Psychology
Journal of Nonverbal Behavior
Journal of Research and Development in Education
Journal of Research in Science Teaching

Journal of School Psychology
Journal of Teacher Education
Journal of Verbal Learning and Verbal Behavior
Journal of Vocational Education Research
Journal of Youth and Adolescence
Learning and Motivation
Learning Disability Quarterly
National Forum of Applied Educational Research Journal
Oxford Review of Education
Research in Mathematics Education
Research in Science Education
Research in the Schools
Review of Educational Research
Review of Research in Education

Subject Specialty Journals

American Biology Teacher
Arithmetic Teacher
Art Education
Business Education World
Childhood Education
Education and Training of the Mentally Retarded
Educational Theatre Journal
Electronic Learning
Elementary English
Elementary Teachers' Guide to Free Materials
English Education
English Journal
Exceptional Child
Exceptional Children

Focus on Exceptional Children
History and Social Science Teacher
History Teacher
Gifted Child Quarterly
Gifted Child Today
Journal of Business Education
Journal of Chemical Education
Journal of Drug Education
Journal of Economic Education
Journal of Environmental Education
Journal of Industrial Teacher Education
Journal of Nutrition Education
Journal of Physical Education, Recreation and Dance
Journal of Reading

Journal of Reading Behavior
Journal of School Health
Journal of Sex Education and Therapy
Journalism Educator
Language
Language Learning
Language Teaching
Mathematics in School
Mathematics Teacher
Mathematics Teaching
Modern Language Journal
Physical Educator
Physics Education
Psychology in the Schools
Reading
Reading Improvement
Reading Teacher

Scholastic Coach
School Arts Magazine
School Counselor
School Health Review
School Science and Mathematics
Science and Children
Science Education
Science Teacher
Social Education
Social Studies Professional
Social Studies Review
Speech Communication Teacher
Studies in Science Education
Teaching English
Teaching Exceptional Children
Technology Teacher
TESOL Quarterly

Online Education Journals

The number of free, full-text online journals is rapidly increasing, encompassing virtually every academic discipline. Check portals such as Magportal (www. magportal.com/) or BestEzines.com for updated lists of online journals related to your interests.

American School Board Journal
National School Boards Association
www.asbj.com/

American Teacher
American Federation of teachers
www.aft.org/publications/
american_teacher/

Bilingual Research Journal
National Association for Bilingual
Education
brj.asu.edu

Converge
Center for Digital Education
www.centerdigitaled.com/converge/

*Current Issues in Comparative
Education*
Columbia University, Teachers College
www.tc.columbia.edu/cice

Current Issues in Education
Arizona State University
College of Education
cie.asu.edu

Education Next
www.educationnext.org

Education Review
Arizona State University
www.ed.asu.edu/edrev/

Education Week on the Web
www.edweek.org

Education World
www.education-world.com

*Electronic Journal of Literacy through
Science*
sweeneyhall.sjsu.edu

Electronic Journal of Science Education
unr.edu/homepage/jcannon/ejse/ejse.html

Electronic Magazine of Multicultural Education
Eastern University
www.eastern.edu/publications/emme

Electronic School
www.electronic-school.com/

From Now On: The Education Technology Journal
www.fno.org/

Journal of Career and Technical Education
scholar.lib.vt.edu/ejournals/JCTE/

Journal of Industrial Teacher Education
National Association of Industrial and Technical Teacher Educators
scholar.lib.vt.edu/ejournals/JITE/

Learners Online
www.learnersonline.com

Meridian
North Carolina State University
www.ncsu.edu/meridian

Perspectives on Urban Education
Graduate School of Education
University of Pennsylvania
www.urbanedjournal.org

Practical Assessment, Research and Evaluation
University of Maryland
edresearch.org/pare/

Reading Online
International Reading Association
www.readingonline.org

Research and Issues in Music Education
www.stthomas.edu/rimeonline

Special Education News
www.specialednews.com

Teacher Magazine
www.teachermagazine.org

Technology and Society
International Forum of Educational Technology and Society
ifets.ieee.org/periodical/

THE Journal
http://www.thejournal.com/

For a more comprehensive list of online journals, check the following Web sites:

Library of Congress
News and Periodical Resources on the Web
lcweb.loc.gov/rr/news/lists.html

NewJour Electronic Journal and Newsletter Archive
gort.ucsd.edu/newjour/

Serials in Cyberspace
University of Vermont
www.uvm.edu/~bmaclenn/

Stress and Burnout in the Classroom

Stress is an inescapable part of any teacher's job. Indeed, Hans Selye, pioneer stress researcher, suggested that the absence of stress is death. Stress is part of the price of living. The greater risk occurs when persons spend long periods of time under conditions of constant stress or tension. Researchers have identified some professions, including teaching, as particularly prone to stress. Over a period of time, teachers can begin to experience a condition commonly referred to as burnout. Psychologist Christina Maslach has identified three phases of burnout. The first consists of emotional exhaustion, a loss of energy and enthusiasm, of being used up with nothing left to give. The second stage is characterized by insensitivity, cynicism, and callousness. The language of this stage is depersonalized, with teachers referring to students as "the animals" or "the beasts." Distrust and even dislike of one's students is evident. Of course, this creates the spiral effect of making students behave in even more distrustful and unacceptable ways. The final phase embodies a feeling of despair that all one's efforts have been fruitless and the teacher is a failure. In short, burned-out teachers have lost their initial idealism, compassion, zeal, and energy. There is a discrepancy between one's efforts and the perceived rewards one gains from that effort, accompanied by a sense of sadness, hopelessness, helplessness, and lower self-esteem.

Of course, most teachers don't burn out in the classroom. Researchers suggest that approximately 3 to 4 percent of the teachers still in the classroom exhibit chronic symptoms of burnout. Many others leave the profession at the onset of burnout. Some struggle, feeling trapped. Surveys have suggested that about 30 percent of American teachers would prefer to be doing something else. Various researchers have identified the following symptoms of burnout: physical exhaustion, absenteeism, abuse of alcohol or drugs (some areas have "teacher bars," where teachers congregate after work), chronic fatigue, boredom, depression, cynicism, moodiness, impatience, ulcers, headaches, excessive eating, blaming the students for their own problems, stubbornness, and resistance to change.

A first step in preventing burnout is to recognize its potential sources. It is the cumulative combination of many events over a period of time, not merely one event, that ultimately leads to burnout. Teacher burnout and stress have received a great deal of attention from educational researchers, who have identified the following items as particularly stressful for teachers:

✓ Management of disruptive students

✓ Involuntary transfers

✓ Overcrowded classrooms

✓ Unrealistic expectations or standards

✓ Lack of planning time

✓ Competency testing

✓ Class interruptions

✓ Curriculum changes

✓ Faculty strikes

✓ Being threatened

✓ Lack of adequate supplies, materials, and books

✓ Incompetent administrators

✓ The first week of school

✓ Receiving low evaluations

✓ Angry parents

✓ Verbal abuse from students

✓ School reorganization

✓ Vandalism and destruction of personal property

Stress Management in the Classroom

Teaching will always entail some potentially stressful events. However, teachers can develop strategies to inoculate themselves against the tensions of school life. Here are suggestions for reducing stress and preventing the onset of burnout:

✓ Avoid the loneliness of teaching. Adult contact can become very rare for some teachers. It is tempting for beginning teachers to isolate themselves, avoiding contact with the more experienced teachers. You can gain much from interacting with your colleagues.

✓ One of the single best predictors of who will avoid burnout is interaction with a supportive group of colleagues—at least one or two people who understand your frustrations and can listen with empathy. Find one or two people you can eat lunch with each day. Many schools develop support groups that meet periodically to share problems and search for creative solutions.

✓ At the first sign of burnout, do something different. Change grade levels, plan a new unit, or try teaching a different subject. Experiment with different curricular approaches: cooperative learning, independent study, learning centers, field trips, peer tutoring, teaming, or learning contracts. Continue to seek new challenges and break up old routines. Bring as much variety into your teaching as possible.

✓ Explore professional rejuvenation through continued education. Take a graduate course, subscribe to professional journals, attend professional workshops, or commit yourself to learning everything you can about a new topic. Learn something novel that you can incorporate into your teaching: some magic tricks, storytelling, drama, graphic design, or public speaking.

✔ Remember, you can't be all things to all people all the time. You are but a fallible human. The greatest baseball players in the world don't bat one thousand, and you don't have to be perfect either. You won't win them all no matter how hard you try. What counts is that you strive to do your best, to continually improve, and to learn from your mistakes.

✔ Set priorities. One source of stress for many teachers is overcommitting themselves. Feeling overwhelmed by all the demands on one's time is a cue that it's time to set priorities. Establishing which things are truly both urgent and important helps allocate one's energies and time. The more thought you give to what you value and your professional and personal goals, the easier it is to set priorities.

The only difference between a rut and a grave is the depth.

—Anonymous

✔ Learning to say no to unimportant, distracting activities is an essential stress-prevention technique. Learn to judiciously use the phrase "I have a previous commitment" when asked to commit yourself to unimportant activities. You need not elaborate on the exact nature of that commitment (well, you might want to give your spouse more detail!). You must save some reserve of private time to recharge your batteries and renew your enthusiasm. You do no one a favor if you say yes to so many requests that you have little energy left to fulfill those commitments. Learn what your limits are.

✔ Don't try to do everything yourself. Delegate some tasks to students, aides, volunteers, or colleagues.

✔ Take care of your body. Substantial research concludes that we are more susceptible to stress and burnout when our bodies are fatigued, out of shape, and deprived of proper nutrition. Make exercise and play a top priority. Get sufficient sleep and eat a healthy balanced diet. Remember, if you take care of your body, your body will take care of you!

✔ Many schools have incorporated sabbaticals as an option for their teachers. If available, take advantage of one to renew your professional commitment.

✔ Learn how and when to ask for help. Most people around you really do want you to succeed. Learn from others' successes and failures. If symptoms of burnout persist for several weeks, consider getting professional help from a qualified counselor.

✓ Get away. Take advantage of your summers to travel. Take short weekend excursions.

✓ It is essential to find some time to be alone every week, even if only for a few minutes. Some do it through quietly walking, playing a musical instrument, meditating, praying, or simply resting.

✓ Monitor your stress level. When you notice yourself becoming more tense, do something about it. Become proactive rather than reactive. Remember, the time to relax is when you can least afford to. Take time for yourself.

✓ Seek a balance in your life. Develop interests beyond teaching. Save time for social activities, hobbies, and community service. Avoid talking only about school when you are with friends.

Laughter makes good blood.

—Italian proverb

✓ Above all, strive to maintain a healthy sense of humor. It helps keep things in perspective. Remember Henry Ward Beecher's warning that people without humor are like wagons without springs: they are jolted by every pebble in the road.

✓ Most important, always remember the adage that it is not events in our lives that cause stress but rather what we say to ourselves about those events. Self-defeating, irrational assumptions about the things that happen to us invite feelings of despair, depression, and anger. Challenge that illogical thought pattern. Strive to change "I must . . . " to "I would prefer . . ."

For More Information

Brock, B. L., & Grady, M. L. (2000). *Rekindling the flame: Principals combating teacher burnout.* Thousand Oaks, CA: Corwin.

Burmark, L., & Fournier, L. (2003). *Enlighten up! An educator's guide to stress-free living.* Alexandria, VA: Association for Supervision and Curriculum Development.

Carlyle, D., & Woods, P. (2002). *The emotions of teacher stress.* Stoke-on-Trent, England: Trentham.

Glanz, J. (2000). *Relax for success: An educator's guide to stress management.* Norwood, MA: Christopher-Gordon.

Greenberg, J. S. (2002). *Comprehensive stress management.* Boston: McGraw-Hill.

Joseph, R. (2000). *Stress free teaching: A practical guide to tackling stress in teaching, lecturing and tutoring.* Sterling, VA: Kogan Page.

Skovholt, T. M. (2001). *The resilient practitioner: Burnout prevention and self-care strategies for counselors, therapists, teachers, and health professionals.* Boston: Allyn & Bacon.

Stress Busters and Sanity Savers

Take a walk.

Meditate.

Take three slow, deep breaths.

Learn a new skill.

Talk to a friend.

Participate in an aerobic activity.

Read a book.

Avoid unnecessary arguments.

Take a vacation.

Get a massage.

Cultivate new relationships.

Find some time to be alone.

Stretch.

Ask someone for help.

Get organized.

Challenge your irrational self-talk.

Listen to your favorite music.

Set long-term goals.

Take a nap.

Clean.

Apologize.

Dance.

Pursue a hobby.

Meet new people.

Write a letter.

Have a plan.

Eat a healthy diet.

Just listen.

Decorate your environment.

Try biofeedback training.

Never make important decisions
 after midnight.

Avoid perfectionism.

Volunteer for a worthy cause.

Problem solve.

Eliminate a self-defeating behavior.

Smile.

Be prepared.

List your strengths and successes.

Take a warm bath.

Keep a journal.

Shop during off-hours.

Take a break.

Maintain a sense of humor.

Visualize a calming scene.

Learn responsible assertiveness.

Distinguish between needs and wants.

Have a good belly laugh.

Relax your jaw.

Monitor your bodily reactions.

Reexamine conflicting goals.

Avoid getting too wrapped up in yourself.

Keep a balance in your activities.

Know and accept yourself.

Learn to say no.

Treat others with kindness.

Stop to smell the roses.

Strive for an open mind.

Be an actor, not a reactor.

Unclutter your life.

Make effective planning a habit.

Eliminate needless worry.

Reexamine your shoulds and musts.

Take time for a good lunch away from work.

Allow open time in your schedule.

Clarify your expectations.

Invite someone to lunch.

Live in the present.

Clarify others' expectations.

Avoid catastrophizing.

Get adequate rest.

Seek a different perspective.

Associate with people from other professions.

Try to remain flexible.

Try acupressure.

Hug someone.

Be thankful.

Develop self-affirming habits.

Recall a pleasant experience.

Forgive.

Challenge your assumptions.

Help someone.

Set priorities.

Join a self-help group.

Do one thing at a time.

Play a musical instrument.

Get professional help.

Try progressive muscle relaxation.

Develop a contract for change.

Look for a new job.

Make a list.

Keep things in perspective.

Remember that tomorrow is a new day.

Choose to be happy.

Avoid putting yourself down.

Remember to play.

Cry.

Have a pet.

Get up ten minutes earlier.

Sing.

Develop a support network.

Professional Development Record

Activity	Goals	Date/Time Spent

Stress Management Contract

Goal: Select one stressor that you would like to eliminate or reduce. It should be one you can reasonably hope to decrease in the next four to six weeks. Write this as a goal.

My stress reduction goal is to _____

_____

_____

Action Plan: Develop a strategy for accomplishing your stress reduction goal.

My strategy for achieving my stress reduction goal is _____

_____

_____

Obstacles to my success might be _____

_____

_____

I will need support from _____

_____

_____

My reward for achieving my goal will be _____

_____

_____

Each day I will _____

_____

_____

How committed are you to achieving your stress reduction goal?

1	2	3	4	5	6	7
Not at all committed						Extremely committed

Stress Symptoms

Directions: Check off the symptoms that affect you. Although this is not a scientific instrument, it can serve as a warning of the cumulative effects of stress. Sudden increases in the number of symptoms may signal that remedial or other professional care is needed.

Physical Symptoms (Body)

_____ Increased heart rate
_____ Increased perspiration
_____ Rapid breathing
_____ Headaches
_____ Tense muscles
_____ Dry mouth
_____ Frequent colds
_____ Stomach ache
_____ Muscle aches
_____ Back pain
_____ Lightheadedness
_____ Sleep difficulties
_____ Trembling or shakiness
_____ Frequent fatigue

Emotional Symptoms (Feelings)

_____ Crying
_____ Resentment
_____ Feeling overwhelmed
_____ Irritability
_____ Nightmares
_____ Feeling out of control
_____ Hopelessness
_____ Easily discouraged
_____ Loneliness
_____ Mood swings
_____ Anxiety, panic, nervousness
_____ Tenseness, edginess
_____ Unexplained sadness
_____ Anger
_____ Boredom
_____ Self-pity

Cognitive Symptoms (Thoughts)

_____ Frequent worrying
_____ Confusion, inability to concentrate
_____ Difficulty making decisions
_____ Loss of creativity
_____ Lethargy
_____ Inability to laugh
_____ Forgetfulness
_____ Apathy
_____ Distrust
_____ Negative self-talk

Behavioral Symptoms (Actions)

_____ Talking rapidly
_____ Abusing alcohol or drugs
_____ Neglecting responsibilities
_____ Grinding teeth
_____ Laughing nervously
_____ Increasing tobacco use
_____ Losing sex drive
_____ Becoming unable to get things done
_____ Overeating
_____ Being accident prone

Famous Americans Who Also Taught School

John Adams, U.S. president
Madeleine Albright, secretary of state
Louisa May Alcott, author
Chester A. Arthur, U.S. president
Clara Barton, founder of American Red Cross
Alexander Graham Bell, inventor
Dan Blocker, actor who played Hoss on *Bonanza*
James Carville, political adviser and author
Clarence Darrow, attorney
Amelia Earhart, aviator
Geraldine Ferraro, vice presidential candidate
Abigail Fillmore, first lady
Roberta Flack, singer
Margaret Fuller, transcendentalist author, social reformer
Art Garfunkel, singer
John Wesley Hardin, outlaw
Janis Joplin, rock star
Lyndon B. Johnson, U.S. president
William McKinley, U.S. president
Anne Murray, singer
Carry Nation, temperance leader
Pat Nixon, first lady
Thomas Paine, colonial patriot
General John Pershing, World War I leader
William Quantrill, Confederate guerilla leader
Dixie Lee Ray, governor of Washington
Eleanor Roosevelt, first lady, author, lecturer
Gene Simmons, member of rock group KISS
Margaret Chase Smith, U.S. senator from Maine
Mary Church Terrell, social reformer

Source: Partin, R. L. (2003). *The social studies teachers' book of lists.* San Francisco: Jossey-Bass. Used with permission.

Chapter Six

Effective Use of School Time

The Erosion of School Time

In the past century, schools have been charged with greater and greater responsibilities. Each time society faces a new problem, schools are expected to become part of the solution, creating a perpetual add-on curriculum. We have added consumer education, drug education, sex education, moral education, character education, driver education, and career education. Schools are expected to turn out students who are good citizens, have positive self-esteem, have mastered the basics, have employable skills, and can act as mature and responsible adults. In short, we expect a lot of our schools.

Reports such as *A Nation at Risk* (National Commission on Excellence in Education, 1983), *Educating Americans for the 21st Century* (National Science Board Commission on Precollege Education in Mathematics, Science, and Technology, 1983), and *Prisoners of Time* (National Education Commission on Time and Learning, 1994) suggest that even more must be demanded of our schools, urging a longer school day and extended school year. Proponents of the standards-based and high-stakes testing trend have focused attention on the most precious of resources in the education of youth: time.

With the spectrum of goals competing for time in the curriculum, the necessity of using it wisely is paramount. Because time is a finite resource, each wasted minute decreases the amount of time available for higher-priority goals.

To increase learning time, we are faced with two alternatives or some combination of the two. We can increase the number of hours of schooling by lengthening the school day, at a considerable expense—estimated in the billions. Beyond the financial restraints are the social and psychological impacts on children and their families. Such a move is a policy decision that legislators and educators are debating. That debate is likely to continue for some time.

A more immediate alternative is to use the presently scheduled school day more effectively. Research has found that as little as 50 percent of the scheduled school minutes are actually used for academic instruction.

Teachers vary greatly in their ability to manage classroom time. The ability to use time wisely in pursuing curricular goals is the most valuable teaching skill. Time-management skills are essential for survival in the classroom. Where else in modern society do we place thirty people in one room with a single leader for six hours a day and expect constant, productive activity?

A School Day

There is no such thing as a typical school day. Although on paper a teacher's daily schedule may look fairly routine, the fact is that the unexpected will occur, as witnessed in the workday of a hypothetical teacher, Mr. Tom Dudley.

Tom has taught three years at Rollover Junior High. This year he has taken on the job of assistant track coach of the junior high team. With fewer younger teachers on the staff, he has been under increasing pressure to accept additional extracurricular activities. He can use the extra money, but it really doesn't pay that much considering all the extra time it consumes.

He meant to be at school early this Thursday to call the athletic director about ordering more tape and gauze. He mentally reminds himself that he must call during his free period.

Tom can hear the bell ring as he wheels into the parking lot. Of course, it's not his fault he is late. He left in plenty of time today. In fact, he was almost at school when he remembered he'd forgotten to bring the tests he was giving second period. He had taken them home to staple together last night. After returning home, he was caught ten minutes by a train.

Rushing into his classroom, Tom finds most of the students lined along the windows watching two dogs fighting. As he begins to get them moving toward their desks, the school counselor pops in to remind Tom of the career interest inventory scheduled during his fourth-period class. They briefly exchange comments about last night's board of education meeting and make arrangements to play racquetball Saturday. It is now six minutes into the period.

Tom takes attendance, reads the morning announcements, and reminds the students that class dues will be collected the next morning. He collects today's homework and returns assignments handed in Monday.

A girl asks permission to go to her locker to get her book; permission granted. Another girl wants to go to the restroom; permission denied. She had plenty of time before class!

The lesson begins. The bell rang nine minutes ago.

His lecture begins smoothly except for the momentary distraction of an ambulance roaring down the street. He reminds Steve to quit tilting his desk and threatens to send Alice to the office if she doesn't stop chatting. Two girls are passing notes at the back of the room, but Tom doesn't notice.

Ten minutes before the end of the period, he gives directions for tomorrow's homework and instructs the class to use the remaining time to begin working on it. After working for a couple of minutes, two students approach his desk for clarification of the instructions. Realizing that others may have the same problem, Tom again explains the assignment to the whole class. As they return to their work, Tom walks to the office to check on the film he needs to use right after lunch. Luckily, the film arrived this morning. Between classes he must remember to request the projector from the teacher in charge of the audiovisual equipment.

By the time Tom leaves school at the end of practice, he is exhausted. He laments to himself that he didn't get everything done he had hoped to do. He carries his loaded briefcase home, promising to get caught up by Monday—just too much to do in too little time.

Tom's day isn't all that unusual. Interruptions, distractions, unanticipated problems, and decisions plague all teachers. Some may handle them more efficiently, but the challenges are there. Handling time demands is essential for classroom success!

The School Calendar

The upper limits of academic learning are set by the time school is in session. The average U.S. school year is 180 days or almost one-half of the days in a year (Goodlad, 1985). This compares with 243 days in Germany and 240 days in Japan. However, in Sweden, whose students have done fairly well on the Trends in International Mathematics and Science Study (TIMSS) tests, the academic year is only 170 days.

In the United States, the average school day is approximately six hours long, yielding an annual scheduled school calendar of 1,080 hours. However, no school is ever in session the total hours scheduled. Schools close for snowstorms, fog, windstorms, ice, floods, and water shortages. Some buildings have been closed for fuel shortages, broken water lines, bomb threats, vandalism, funerals, or flu epidemics. Work stoppages by faculty or other school employees have caused some schools to close. A few school systems have a history of periodic strikes interrupting the school year. Schools have canceled sessions because their basketball team was competing in the state championship. In recent years many have shut the doors for weeks because they ran out of money.

On days that schools are closed, teachers cannot teach and students do not receive supervised instruction. Most school closings are unavoidable, but they yield vastly different amounts of exposure to instruction among schools.

More time is lost for delays of one or two hours because of inclement weather. In some areas frequent fog may force schools to delay opening more than ten or fifteen mornings per year. Impending storms occasionally force early dismissals. Some systems excuse students early for faculty meetings or parent conferences. Others have shortened the school day by moving to double shifts to alleviate overcrowding.

Even when school is in session, students are not always there. Absenteeism may severely limit some students' academic exposure. Certainly, legitimate illnesses keep some students at home. Religious holidays or deaths in the family are also viewed as excused absences. Some parents keep their children home to baby-sit, go on early vacations, or help with work. Parents still schedule doctors' and dentists' appointments during school hours. In many rural schools, it is not unusual for boys to miss school the first day of hunting season. Some students still play hooky. Indeed for many schools, especially in the inner city, it is not unusual for as many as one-half of the students to be absent. This represents a serious loss of learning time.

Schemes for rearranging the way time is distributed (most notably, block scheduling and year-round schools) have gained in popularity. These innovations, however, do not necessarily increase the total number of hours spent in the classroom.

Instructional Time

Even when school is in session and the student attends, not all time is available for classroom instruction. Transitions, recesses, and assorted scheduled activities erode available instructional time.

The time allocated to academic classes varies widely from school to school and even within the same building. The power to allocate school time among the various content areas is a most significant tool in determining school effectiveness—one that unfortunately has been abused in some instances. Differences as large as sevenfold have been observed in the amount of time spent on content areas such as math or reading, even within the same school system. In a large national study, John Goodlad (1985) reported that the hours of time allotted to instruction ranged from nineteen to over twenty-seven hours per week, with an average of 22.5 hours per week. Wide discrepancies were also found at the secondary level.

The obvious explanation for such wide variation in time allocated to instructional areas is that the needs of students vary, demanding individualization. But little evidence suggests that this is the reason. The data to date suggest that students are exposed to large differences in content coverage merely because of the school they happen to attend or the teacher they are assigned. For example, one teacher reported that she spent very little time teaching fractions because she didn't like them. Her students will pay for such preferences later. Indeed, in the Beginning Teacher Evaluation Study, the amount of time allocated to reading and mathematics instruction and achievement test scores were significantly correlated.

Scheduled events such as standardized testing, school pictures, assemblies, fire or tornado drills, or pep rallies cut into the time scheduled for instruction. Individual students are often absent from the room for school-sanctioned activities, such as visits to the counselor's office, special pull-out programs, in-school suspensions, or athletic events. In the spring high schools may excuse a third of the students early to travel to athletic contests. Teachers may be reluctant to introduce any new material to the remaining students, virtually eliminating the last period of the school day.

Teacher Time-on-Task

Not all regularly scheduled class time is devoted to academic instruction. Most teachers lose time for clerical tasks such as collecting milk money, taking attendance, collecting and distributing papers and materials, counting books, reading announcements, or writing passes—all tasks that do not require a college degree.

Classroom research studies have recorded that as much as 18 percent of class time may be consumed by discipline matters. The simplest reprimand may further consume time by creating a break in the lesson's momentum, causing the whole class to go off task. The inertia of the lesson must be regained. Most time is used in managing student behavior; for example, giving students permission to go to the restroom or sharpen pencils eats away at class time.

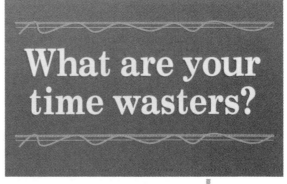

What are your time wasters?

Beginning the class a few minutes after the scheduled starting time or stopping the lesson a few minutes before dismissal robs more learning time, as much as ten minutes of the class period. By poor preparation and planning, a teacher can consume more time on non-instructional activities, such as hunting for misplaced papers and materials, clarifying directions, or setting up audiovisual equipment.

Additional class time is absorbed by a variety of interruptions: students arriving late, drop-in visitors, telephone calls, outside noises and distractions, equipment breakdowns, or ill students.

Transitions from one activity to another consume many minutes over the course of a year. Some teachers have been guilty of using class time poorly by reviewing the previous week's big game, making the class wait while one student is helped, or excessively chatting about personal stories that are irrelevant to the lesson.

While the individual time robbers may vary from room to room, all schools lose a large proportion of time to noninstructional activities. Indeed, several research studies have found that less than 50 percent of the school day is actually spent in academic instruction! That is 540 hours of the 1,080 allotted to teach the basics, develop minimal competencies, and meet all the other assorted objectives that society imposes on schools.

The Pace of Instruction

The pace of instruction represents how fast a teacher covers the content during the time allotted to a content area. In the same span of time, two teachers may cover different amounts of content.

Student achievement test results have been found to be higher for teachers who push their students through the material at a faster rate. In one study math teachers producing the greatest achievement gains covered 40 to 50 percent more pages during a time span than did teachers of lower-scoring students. This should not be interpreted as a maxim that faster is always better. Such research only reflects average gains for comparison groups. The faster pace may benefit middle- and upper-ability students, but harm the lower portion of the class.

The guiding principle in pacing instruction is to aim for appropriateness. Too fast a pace and the student is left behind. The teacher is moving on to new material for which the student has not yet mastered prerequisite skills. Instruction paced too slowly becomes inefficient, producing boredom, repetition, and lack of interest.

The reality of understanding students' individual differences is that not all require the same amount of time to master a concept. Research from mastery learning suggests that most concepts and skills taught in schools can be mastered by 80 to 95 percent of all students if they are given an appropriate amount of time. The lockstep pacing of the traditional classroom moves everyone at the same pace, some before they are ready, others long after. Observational studies have found that teachers typically move on when approximately 80 percent of the class has grasped the concept or skill. Of course, conscientious teachers have always made attempts to provide remedial instruction to the lagging 20 percent through individual tutoring, small-group instruction, or homework assignments. Indeed, totally individualizing pacing of instruction remains a challenge to the most dedicated of teachers. With varying degrees of success, teachers have sought to individualize pacing through programmed instruction, peer tutoring, computer-assisted instruction, contract learning, enrichment activities, learning centers, and ability grouping. Matching the time provided with the time required for learning is the key to improving learning gains for all students but especially low achievers. We must continue to experiment with new techniques that provide the appropriate level of pacing. Part of the key is freeing teachers from routine clerical and noninstructional tasks to provide the optimal instructional time for each student.

Student Time-on-Task

Just because teachers are teaching doesn't mean that students are learning. Educational efficiency is eroded further by student inattention and ineffective instruction. Two teachers may allocate the same amount of time to instruction, but their students may be engaged in that instruction at vastly different rates. The percentage of time-on-task or engagement rate has come under increasing scrutiny as a contributor to learning effectiveness. The percentage of time-on-task has been reported to range from 50 to 90 percent, with an average engagement rate of 70 percent of the available instructional time. But remember that 50 percent of the day may already be lost to noninstructional activity; therefore, the student time-on-task may be less than 70 percent of 50 percent, or 350 hours out of the original 1,080 hours per year!

Wide variations in student engagement rates have been observed. Higher on-task rates are observed for girls, high-ability students, and good readers. The highest engagement rates are typically found in music, social studies, and foreign languages. The lowest on-task rates occur in mathematics, language arts, and reading (ironically, the subjects generally allocated the largest block of time). Students are also more attentive to those classes in which they are actively involved in activities, such as music and social studies.

The teaching format also influences time-on-task. Teacher-led discussions tend to elicit greater student involvement than do lectures, audiovisual presentations, or seatwork. Croll and Moses (1988) found that the more time the teacher spends working with the whole class, the greater the percentage of time students spend on a task, even when they are working independently. Small-group activities and seatwork tend to provide the lowest levels of on-task behavior. This does not mean that instructional activities with lower engagement rates should not be used. The benefits gained from a seatwork assignment or small-group project may justify its use.

Student attention to lessons is also influenced by the weather, season, and time of the day. Students experience the highest involvement at the beginning of the morning, but involvement decreases as the day passes. Days right before or after a major holiday or special event usually suffer lower attentiveness.

Not all engaged time is productive learning time. If students are attending to instruction that is ineffective, too easy, or too difficult, they are gaining little. The goal must be to seek high engagement in appropriate learning tasks.

Research shows that increasing the amount of time spent in learning benefits low-ability students more than it does the more capable students. Increased time-on-task shows the greatest benefit in highly structured courses; for example, math and foreign languages.

Out-of-school-time strategies, such as after-school or weekend programs, have been found to be effective in enhancing some students' academic achievement. Students in the early elementary grades seemed to profit most from out-of-school work in reading, while high school students gained the most from extra work in math. One-on-one tutoring in reading was found to be particularly helpful in improving reading skills.

While proposals to lengthen the school day or add days to the school calendar have an intuitive appeal, careful data analyses indicate that to have a significant impact, the number of instructional hours would have to be extensive. After reviewing related research, Cotton and Wikelund (2002) have concluded that the costs of extending the school day or year are not justifiable. Others caution that increasing time spent in school does little good if the instruction offered is ineffective.

Conclusion

Before the school year is lengthened or the school day is extended, it is imperative to make every effort to assure that the current available time is being used as effectively as possible. Teachers must create an environment that demonstrates that school time is to be safeguarded. Setting the expectations and standards on the effective use of time must be done the first week of school. Well-prepared, organized lessons are more likely to maximize student time-on-task. Beginning class on time and teaching until the end of the class period are two ways of gaining additional class time.

The educational community must work to assure that learning time is protected. Every effort must be made to free teachers from noninstructional clerical tasks and to minimize interruptions and other time robbers. A humane and fun yet businesslike learning climate should be sought.

References

Bloom, B. S. (1976). *Human characteristics and school learning.* New York: McGraw-Hill.

Cotton, K., & Wikelund, K. R. (2002). *Educational time factors.* School Improvement Research Series. Portland, OR: Northwest Regional Educational Laboratory.

Croll, P., & Moses, D. (1988). Teaching methods and time on task in junior classrooms. *Educational Research, 30,* 90–97.

Davidson, J. L., & Holley, F. M. (1979). Your students might be spending only half of the school day receiving instruction. *American School Board Journal, 161*(3), 40–41.

Ebmeir, H. H., & Zoimek, R. L. (1982, March). *Engagement rates as a function of subject area, grade level and time of day.* Paper presented at the American Educational Research Association, New York.

Fisher, C. W., Berliner, D. C., Filby, N. N., Marliave, R., Cahlen, L. S., & Dishaw, M. M. (1980). Teaching behaviors, academic learning time, and student achievement: An overview. In C. Denham & A. Lieberman (Eds.), *Time to Learn* (pp. 7–32). Washington, DC: National Institute of Education.

Goodlad, J. I. (1985). *A place called school.* New York: McGraw-Hill.

Harnischfeger, A. (1984, April). *School time and changing curricular goals.* Paper delivered at the American Educational Research Association, New Orleans.

Hiatt, D. B. (1979). Time allocation in the classroom: Is instruction being shortchanged? *Phi Delta Kappan, 61,* 289–290.

Karweit, N. L. (1973). *Time on task: A research review.* Baltimore: Johns Hopkins University, Center for Social Organization of Schools.

Karweit, N. L., & Slavin, R. E. (1981). Measurement and modeling choices in studies of time and learning. *American Educational Research Journal, 18,* 157–171.

Lauer, P. A., Akiba, M., Wilkerson, S. B., Apthorp, H. S., Snow, D., & Martin-Glenn, M. (2003). *The effectiveness of out-of-school-time strategies in assisting low-achieving students in reading and mathematics: A research synthesis.* Aurora, CO: Mid-Continent Research for Education and Learning.

Lowe, R., & Gervais, R. (1988). Increasing instructional time in today's classroom. *NASSP Bulletin, 72,* 19–22.

Murphy, J. (1992). Instructional leadership: Focus on time to learn. *NASSP Bulletin, 76*(542), 19–26.

National Commission on Excellence in Education. (1983). *A nation at risk: The imperative for educational reform.* Washington, DC: U.S. Government Printing Office.

National Education Commission on Time and Learning. (1994). *Prisoners of Time.* Washington, DC: U.S. Government Printing Office.

National Science Board Commission on Precollege Education in Mathematics, Science, and Technology. (1983). *Educating Americans for the 21st century: A plan of action for improving mathematics, science and technology education.* Washington, DC: Education for All.

Note: An earlier version of this section appeared in *American Secondary Education, 17*(4), 1989, 6–11. Reprinted with permission from *American Secondary Education.*

Prisoners of Time

In April of 1994 the National Education Commission on Time and Learning issued its report, *Prisoners of Time,* which examined the relationship between time and learning in the nation's schools. The commission concluded that schools were very much controlled by the clock and that true school reform must reexamine the allocation and use of time in the schools. Its report labeled school time as the rudder of school reform. The commission issued eight recommendations:

1. Reinvent schools around learning, not time.
2. Fix the design flaw: use time in new and better ways.
3. Establish an academic day.
4. Keep schools open longer to meet the needs of children and communities.
5. Give teachers the time they need.
6. Invest in technology.
7. Develop local action plans to transform schools.
8. Share the responsibility: finger-pointing and evasion must end.

Block Scheduling

The trend toward block scheduling in middle and high schools mushroomed during the 1990s. Block scheduling roughly doubles class periods. For example, instead of teaching six classes of forty-five minutes each day, a teacher might have three eighty- or ninety-minute classes per day. An estimated 40 to 50 percent of all high schools use some form of block scheduling, which has gained more support in some states than in others. A 2003 *Christian Science Monitor* article reported that 90 percent of North Carolina high schools are using block schedules.

Many schools have adopted a 4-by-4 block schedule. Under this plan students take four rather than six classes each quarter. What previously were yearlong classes now meet for only two quarters. Courses that met for a semester under the traditional calendar now meet for only one quarter. Many schools have adopted schedules that are variations or combinations of block schedules and traditional schedules.

To address some of the major criticisms of the 4-by-4 schedule, a variation known as the A-B-A-B or alternating system has emerged. Students attend four extended class periods the first day. The next day they attend four different classes. Students alternate daily between the two daily schedules through the entire year.

A major advantage of the block schedule is that longer periods allow more opportunity for more active learning activities. However, there is no guarantee of the outcome. Many teachers continue to lecture as they have before, perhaps tacking on a study period the last half-hour.

Alternative Day Block Schedule for Six Courses

Days	Monday A Day 1	Tuesday B Day 2	Wednesday A Day 1	Thursday B Day 2	Friday A Day 1	Monday B Day 2
Period	1	2	1	2	1	2
	1	2	1	2	1	2
	3	4	3	4	3	4
	3	4	3	4	3	4
	5	6	5	6	5	6
	5	6	5	6	5	6

4-by-4 Semester Block Schedule

Period		First Semester	Second Semester
	1	Class 1	Class 5
	2		
	3	Class 2	Class 6
	4		
	5	Class 3	Class 7
	6		
	7	Class 4	Class 8
	8		

Advantages of Block Scheduling

✓ Extra time supports more project-based learning.

✓ Teachers see fewer students each day.

✓ Time permits more cooperative and small-group learning.

✓ Greater depth and breadth of content is possible.

✓ Teacher has the opportunity to change role to facilitator.

✓ Less time spent in between-class transitions.

✓ Opportunity to vary instructional approaches.

✓ Blocks allow time for more one-on-one teaching and evaluation.

✓ Interdisciplinary teaching is easier to accomplish.

✓ Common teacher planning time is more feasible.

✓ Blocks allow opportunity for more hands-on learning.

✓ Students have less homework each weekday.

✓ Blocks allow time for integrating technology into instruction.

✓ Teachers may have longer planning periods.

✓ Instruction is less hurried.

Disadvantages of Block Scheduling

✓ Teachers face the challenge of holding students' attention.

✓ Subjects don't meet every day.

✓ Teachers must have a variety of instructional skills.

✓ Teachers have to spend more time with exasperating classes.

✓ Students lack daily reinforcement of content.

✓ Students find it harder to catch up after absences.

✓ Impact on achievement is still questionable.

✓ Substitutes have more difficulty making good use of time.

✓ Teachers may end up teaching more courses in a year.

✓ Student transfers between schools are more difficult to handle.

✓ Blocks may decrease participation in music programs (largely due to schedule conflicts with academic courses).

The wisdom of moving to the "block" is still being debated. Some teachers love it; others hate it. Block scheduling presents special challenges for teachers of special subjects, like music and gym. The semester format and longer class periods do not allow the daily reinforcement of skills.

Research on the effect of block scheduling is mixed and so far inconclusive. Much depends on the quality of the instruction offered. Research tends to find that students like the block-schedule format, particularly with teachers who are able to do more than lecture for the entire period. At least one study reported increased stress for teachers, at least initially, when moving to the block schedule. Other studies have found less use of lecture by teachers in block-schedule schools.

Research suggests that the longer teachers teach under block scheduling, the more they like it. Some evidence suggests that teachers' acceptance is related to how the decision to move to block scheduling was made, with earlier and active involvement correlating with more positive attitudes. Several studies have reported that after two to four years under block scheduling, 65 to 90 percent of teachers, students, and parents felt block schedules were effective and worth continuing.

Studies seem to consistently report decreased behavior problems and increased attendance rates for schools moving to block schedules. The benefits of block scheduling appear to be most pronounced for at-risk students. The main exception is mathematics achievement, which seems to suffer across the board under block scheduling.

For More Information

Gainey, D. D., & Brucato, J. M. (1999). *Questions and answers about block scheduling: An implementation guide.* Larchmont, NY: Eye on Education.

McCullough, L. L., & Tanner, B. M. (2001). *Assessment in the block: The link to instruction.* Larchmont, NY: Eye on Education.

Pettus, A. M., & Blosser, M. E. (2001). *Teaching science in the block.* Larchmont, NY: Eye on Education.

Porter, C. J. (2002). *"What do I teach for 90 minutes?": Creating a successful block-scheduled English classroom.* Urbana, IL: National Council of Teachers of English.

Queen, J. A. (2003) *The block scheduling handbook.* Thousand Oaks, CA: Corwin.

Queen, J. A., & Isenhour, K. G. (1998). *The 4x4 block schedule.* Larchmont, NY: Eye on Education.

Robbins, P., Gregory, G., & Herndon, L. (2000). *Thinking inside the block schedule: Strategies for teaching in extended periods of time.* Thousand Oaks, CA: Corwin.

Williams, R. B., & Dunn, S. E. (2000). *Brain-compatible learning for the block.* Arlington Heights, IL: Skylight Professional Development.

Eleven Tips on Minimizing Classroom Interruptions

Interruptions are the bane of every classroom teacher. Not only is precious class time lost but something even more essential: momentum. A class that is 100 percent on task suddenly becomes 100 percent off task as the interruption disrupts everyone's attention. The teacher must then refocus everyone's attention back onto the topic at hand. While many interruptions are beyond teachers' direct control (for example, fire drills, P.A. announcements, or drop-in visitors), some interruptions are created by the teachers (stopping a lesson to hunt for materials or to reprimand a student). Here are some suggestions for minimizing interruptions' impact:

1. To assess the amount of time that interruptions consume, carry a stopwatch for a day or week. Each time you are interrupted, start the watch. When the interruption ends, stop the watch. At the end of the day, record how much time has elapsed. An alternative is to ask a student to do the timekeeping for you.

2. Let the world know that intrusions are not welcome. Many interruptions occur simply because the offender is not aware that his or her behavior is disruptive. Open doors invite interruptions.

3. Outside their doors, many teachers hang a sign such as "Important Learning in Progress" (or use the "Please Do Not Disturb: Learning in Progress" sign included in this chapter). Tape a note pad and hang a pencil beside the door for messages.

4. Negotiate with the principal for custodians to schedule distracting work, such as mowing beside windows, before or after school. It may not always be possible, but let it be known that such activity detracts from learning.

5. If doors or windows provide too many visual distractions to students, rearrange the furniture to face away from the distraction.

6. Let other teachers know that sending students to borrow supplies during class is not welcome. Be tactful but assertive. Conversely, you have a responsibility to respect your fellow teachers' time. Do not send student messengers to their rooms during classes except in emergencies.

7. The best prevention of interruptions is a well-planned, organized lesson. Have the necessary materials and equipment ready before class begins. Stopping a lesson to thread a movie projector or hunt for a book is usually an avoidable distraction. Not only does it use precious class time, but it invites student misbehavior.

8. When an interruption does occur, your aims are to keep it as brief as possible, minimize the impact on the learning activity, and assure that the same interruption will not occur again. If you are interrupted by a telephone call, get to the point immediately. Be brief and assertive. If the call is going to take too long, give the caller a more convenient time to talk or volunteer to call back.

9. Most principals have discovered the potential abuses of the P.A., restricting announcements to the first and last five minutes of the day. If your school has not implemented such a policy, suggest that it does so. Some have stopped using the P.A. system for routine morning announcements; instead, teachers read them to their classes.

10. People who walk in unannounced cause many classroom interruptions. If someone comes to your door, stand in the doorway so that you can talk with the visitor yet face the class. Try to avoid leaving the room unattended. As much as possible, discourage drop-in visitors.

11. At the beginning of the year, when it is best to establish classroom routines, tell your students what they should do during such interruptions.

Teacher Time Robbers

The following list contains the activities that teachers most frequently cite as keeping them from doing their job better:

✓ Filling out forms, paperwork

✓ Repeating directions

✓ Dealing with unplanned interruptions

✓ Doing clerical tasks, photocopying

✓ Handling classroom behavior

✓ Grading student work

✓ Attending meetings, in-service programs

✓ Cleaning the classroom

✓ Supervising the playground, the lunchroom

✓ Keeping track of money

✓ Doing bus duty

✓ Taking attendance

Full-Time Teachers' Workweek

	Average Hours per Week Required to Be at School	Average Hours per Week Spent Outside of Regular School Hours in School-Related Activities Involving Students[a]	Average Hours per Week Spent Outside of Regular School Hours in School-Related Activities Not Involving Students[b]
Public	37.8	3.2	8.7
Elementary	37.6	2.1	8.9
Secondary	38.1	5.2	8.4
Private	38.2	3.1	8.6

Source: National Center for Educational Statistics. (2002). *Schools and staffing survey, 1999–2000: Overview of the data for public, private, public charter, and Bureau of Indian Affairs elementary and secondary schools.* Available online at nces.ed.gov/pubsearch.

Note: Data did not include public charter schools.

[a] School-related activities involving student interaction include coaching, field trips, tutoring, or transporting students.

[b] School-related activities not involving students include preparation, grading papers, parent conferences, or attending meetings.

Classroom Routines

Effective teachers have learned the importance of establishing classroom routines the first week of school. Many daily classroom events and tasks must be accomplished with a minimum of direction and must flow smoothly using the least amount of time possible. Don't assume students know what you want; train them the first week of school. As each task arises the first time, explain carefully exactly how you would like it to be done. It helps to carefully explain why the routine is helpful in getting things done. Invite questions from students to clarify the procedure. For some you might want to put the directions in writing. Review these routines occasionally if students begin to deviate from them. Research suggests it generally takes about a month to establish a new habit. Possible tasks for which you might wish to establish routines include the following:

✓ Beginning the day

✓ Taking attendance

✓ What to do when the student arrives late

✓ Making up missed assignments when returning from an absence

✓ Making up missed tests

✓ Taking lunch count

✓ Seeking help

✓ Signaling when to stop talking

✓ Turning in homework papers

✓ Information to be included on student papers (where they should write their name, period, date, and so on)

✓ What to do when they finish a test or seatwork early

✓ Leaving the room (restroom privileges, library, office, and so on)

✓ What to do when a visitor comes to the door

✓ Distributing and collecting materials, assignments, and so on

✓ What to do if they don't bring pencils, paper, and other supplies

✓ Appropriate responses to emergencies (fire, tornado, earthquake)

✓ Beginning class

✓ Leaving and returning from recess

✓ Signing out materials, tools, books, equipment, and so on

✓ Seating arrangement

✓ Using learning centers

✓ Procedures for moving about the building as a group

✓ Attending assemblies

✓ Cleanup

✓ Obtaining permission for field trips

✓ Leaving the room at the end of the day

✓ Transitions from one activity to another

Merely establishing a routine or procedure will not make it happen. You must clearly explain it to your students. If possible, demonstrate it or have a model for them to study. Then provide opportunities for your students to practice the routine. Walk them through it step by step if necessary. Reinforce them for complying with your routines. Show students you appreciate their cooperation.

Once the routines are explained, consider posting them on the wall. When a new student enrolls in your class, it is often helpful to appoint a partner who is responsible for teaching the new student the various routines. Here are some specific routines many teachers find helpful in running their classrooms' daily activities.

Taking Attendance or Lunch Count

Taking attendance is one of the necessary tasks of any teacher. There is no one way to take the class roll. Your school policy, the number of students, their grade level and maturity all influence the form of your attendance-taking routine. The important thing is to adopt a procedure that is least disruptive. Here are some tips:

✓ Many teachers prefer to get their students to work immediately and then to unobtrusively take the roll. Generally, after the first week of school, few teachers waste class time calling the roll aloud. Some have been ingenious in subtle ways to take attendance with little disruption and minimal time.

✓ Attach a library-book pocket for each student to poster board that hangs on the wall near the door. Put the students' names on these pockets. Attach a separate one in which you insert brightly colored cards. As students enter the room, they pull out a blank card and insert it in the pocket with their name.

✓ To make an attendance or lunch-count board, you need a board approximately fourteen-by-eighteen inches, spring-type clothespins (one for each student), a box or can to store the clothespins, a calendar, and attendance slips.

Decorate the board and box if desired. Print each student's first and last name on the clothespins. Store the clothespins in the box or can on a small table or desk. Have the calendar and attendance slips handy. After students hang up their coats, they go to the table, get their clothespins, and place them on the board in the appropriate slot to indicate that they are present or that they will be buying lunch. When school actually starts, a volunteer student goes to the desk and fills out the date, teacher's name, counts those buying lunch, and records the number on the slip. Any clothespins left in the box or can are students who are absent. The volunteer records these on the slip and takes the list to the teacher for approval. The volunteer then takes the slip to the office or clips it to the door, whichever is your school policy. When the student returns to the room, he or she is responsible for removing the clothespins from the board and putting them back in the box, ready for tomorrow. An alternative is to hang the pins around the rim of a bucket and have the students drop their clothespins into the bucket as they enter.

✓ If not required, don't begin every class by taking attendance or reading the roll. Jump right into the subject matter. Students most remember the first and last things you do in the class. You can quietly take attendance while they are busy with independent work later in the period. Other teachers have an assignment written on the board. As soon as students enter the room, they are to go directly to their seats and begin work on the day's assignment. Once everyone has begun work, the teacher can quietly take attendance using the seating chart.

✓ Have each student record his or her name on a three-by-five-inch index card. Different colors can be used for each class or grade level. Keep the cards in one small file box. When students are absent without being excused, their cards are turned sideways in the box and left there until the teacher receives a call or note. It is very easy to check who has not returned an approved absence slip.

✓ Keep a stack of brightly colored cards in a pocket attached to the wall near the door. Instead of having to take a lunch count, have the children be responsible for their own. Clip two folders (labeled "buy" and "pack") on the bulletin board, next to the folder containing the colored cards. Each day as students enter the room, they get a card and drop it in the "buy" pocket or "pack" pocket. A student volunteer can quickly count the number of cards in each folder, place the cards back in the original holding folder, and turn in the lunch count.

✓ For elementary school record each student's name on a paper animal cutout. Hang these with a short string to a poster. As the students enter the classroom, they turn their tags over. Those students whose names still show are absent. At the end of the day, a student helper can turn them all back over to reveal the names again. (*Source:* Contributed by Janet Smith)

✓ On the left side of an 8½-by-11-inch paper sheet of paper, type your class roster in a column, listing your name, room number, and the period at the top of the column. Copy or type the same information onto the right-hand side of the paper, giving you two identical lists of the class roster. Duplicate, cut, and staple these into pads of attendance rosters for each class. At the beginning of the class, all you need do is circle the names of the absent students on the top sheet and tear it off. The pads can also be used for field trips, lunch counts, and so on. The office staff will be most appreciative, especially if your hurried handwriting is illegible.

✓ Some teachers use a loose-leaf notebook to maintain attendance records. Create a section for each class, separating them by tabs. Within each section arrange sheets alphabetically by students' last names. At the top of each student's sheet, have them enter basic information, such as locker number, home address, phone number, parents' names, student identification number, and book number. Note each day when a student is absent, tardy, or fails to bring homework. If disruptive behavior occurs, note it on that student's sheet. You will be able to handle later problems much more smoothly with such documentation.

✓ Have students who are buying lunch stand up and count off. You have a quick head count. This also reinforces number skills for younger children.

Distributing and Collecting Materials

Getting tools, books, papers, and other materials distributed to students can be a time-absorbing, chaotic, stressful event if a smooth routine is not developed. Here's what you can do:

✓ Don't distribute too many things at once, and distribute things in the order in which students will need them.

✓ Assign a weekly monitor whose job is to assist you in distributing any materials.

✓ Don't count papers when distributing them in class. Instruct the person at the end of the row to pass them to one corner where a student puts extras in a neat pile for you.

✓ If students are working in groups, you can unobtrusively place papers or supplies they will need beneath one person's seat in each group. At the appropriate time, you can direct them to gather from beneath their seats the materials for their group.

✓ Delegate one student from each group to come pick up the materials the group needs.

✓ When collecting papers, have students pass them across the rows to one side of the room rather than down the front. There is less poking people in the back, and it is easier to monitor student behavior.

Regaining Students' Attention

Quieting a class to gain its attention is a challenge to many teachers. It is perhaps the first routine that should be taught the first day of school. Most successful teachers develop some form of signal or cue that tells students to stop what they are doing, be quiet, and focus their attention on the teacher. Here are some strategies that many teachers use:

✓ Use a bell, chord on the piano, or chime to signal it is time to stop talking and give the teacher attention. Some teachers have collected an assortment of bells, whistles, and other novelty sound instruments that they use for this purpose.

✓ Use hand signals to cue students to stop talking. Raise your hand palm up or hold up two or three fingers. Don't say anything until you have everyone's attention. Some teachers have their students join the teacher in raising their hands.

✓ Another commonly used cue to quiet a group is to hold your index finger vertically across your lips.

✓ Others signal it is time to give the teacher attention by standing in a designated spot in the room.

✓ Slowly clap your hands together three times. When students hear the first clap, they are to join in on the second clap. This grabs the attention of everyone who didn't hear the first one. Typically, the whole class offers the third clap simultaneously. Now the room is silent, and attention is focused on the teacher.

✓ Another strategy is to write a cue word (for example, STOP or QUIET) on the chalkboard. On seeing the teacher writing that word on the board, all students are to comply immediately.

✓ A different signal can be used to cue the class that group activities are becoming too noisy and should be brought down to a lower level. It might be helpful to have all students pause for fifteen to thirty seconds before resuming their activities. Some teachers flick the light switch. This tends to work if used sparingly.

✓ Some teachers have constructed a flashing red light that they switch on when it is time for students to stop talking.

✓ A useful way of indicating the time remaining without interrupting small-group discussion activities is to construct a picture of a traffic light, either on a poster or as an overhead transparency. When the discussion begins, show the light with a green light. When one minute is left, reveal the yellow light. That is the cue for students to wind up their discussion. When time is up, reveal the red light. This serves as a signal for everyone to stop talking.

Seeking Permission to Leave the Room

The first week of school, clarify whatever system you wish to use to handle restroom visits. Here are several suggestions:

✓ *Restroom pass:* Rather than have students raise their hands to ask to use the restroom, hang a sign from a string that has GO printed on one side and STOP printed on the other. If everyone is in the room, the sign is on GO. If someone needs to use the restroom, he or she turns the sign to STOP (meaning that no one else can leave the room because someone is out). When the person comes back, he or she must turn the sign back to GO, and someone else may go out. Of course, if this privilege is abused, it is restricted.

✓ *Nonverbal signals:* At the beginning of the school year, teach your students the following signals: raise an index finger to indicate a need to use the restroom; raise a pencil if it needs sharpening. Make eye contact with the student, and simply nod your head or raise your hand to indicate that the activity may be done. Using these signals avoids needless interruptions. Other nonverbal cues for signaling that students should be quiet and give you their attention might include holding up an interesting object; pointing toward the clock; flipping the light switch once; gesturing across the throat with your index finger; using chimes, slide whistles, or other noisemakers; holding your finger up to your lips; going to a specified spot in the room; or turning on a colored light.

✓ Laminate two pictures on cards—one for boys, one for girls. Add a string to hang the cards on a hook or nail beside the teacher's desk. When a student needs to use the restroom, he or she takes the card from the nail and shows the teacher without talking. The teacher sees the student and nods to give permission. The student places the picture on a hook by the door. When he returns, he puts the picture back on the hook beside the teacher's desk. Since neither student nor teacher talks aloud, there is no interruption of class.

✓ Save time when using written hall passes (such as those included at the end of this chapter). Have the student fill out all the information except your signature.

✓ Instead of using written passes, many teachers have one made of wood. It is best to make it large enough not to fit into the students' pockets. Paint your name and room number on it. You might choose to decorate it in an interesting way (or delegate the task to a student). By having only one pass, you assure that only one student at a time is out of the room.

Seeking Help

During seatwork students will occasionally need help from the teacher. It is important to let students know the procedure you expect them to follow to get help. If the teacher is not busy with other students, the simplest procedure is for the student to raise his or her hand until acknowledged by the teacher. (Teaching students to raise two fingers would help differentiate seeking help from wanting to use the restroom, which students might signal with just the index finger.) The teacher either comes to the student's desk or nods permission for the student to approach the teacher. With reasonably well-behaved students, some teachers permit students needing help to come to the teacher's desk without first having to gain the teacher's consent. A greater problem occurs when the teacher is busy working with another student or group. A signal or cue needs to be established to let the teacher know that help is needed whenever the teacher has a chance to assist the student. Here's how:

✔ Some teachers have a colored card taped to the front of each student's desk. When students need help, they flip the card down over the front of the desk. Another option is to have each student construct a stand-up placard by folding an 8½-by-11-inch sheet of card stock in half. They should print "I Need Help" on the face of the card. To signal the teacher, the student turns his or her card up so that it is visible to the teacher.

✔ Teacher educator Harry Wong suggests using a toilet paper tube with one end covered with red construction paper and the other with green. A student needing help turns the tube with the red end up and continues to work until the teacher comes to help.

✔ To avoid being disturbed while working with a group, use a see-me chair. If a student working independently has a question about his or her work that a classmate cannot answer, the student must sit in the see-me chair to ask for help. Check with the student when you have time.

✔ A signal that many teachers use is for students to turn their textbook up on edge when they need the teacher's help.

Students' Tools

For smooth operation of day-to-day instruction, students should know which supplies and tools they must provide, when they need them, and where to store them. The first week you should clearly specify all the materials they are required to provide. A written list works best.

It is important early in the year to clarify which items in the room are for student use and which are only for teacher use. Also clarify which items students can use with and without permission. Here are some tips:

✔ Keep a store of pencils that students can buy with cash or class points earned. Some teachers lend out pencils, but students must leave collateral (such as a dime or a shoe), which they redeem when they return the pencils.

✓ If they come without a pen or pencil, lend students a crayon. Some teachers scrounge vacated lockers the last day of school to collect all the leftover pencils. These become loaners the following year. Some break them in half, sharpen both stubs, and lend these. Students are less willing to depend on the teacher for writing instruments if they are not too attractive.

✓ Let students know when they may use the pencil sharpener. Some teachers let students sharpen pencils only before class and warn them to always bring two. Some teachers do not require students to seek permission to use the pencil sharpener as long as students do not abuse the privilege. Other teachers have students signal when they need to use the sharpener, usually by holding their pencil in the air. In either case it is wise to only allow one student at a time at the pencil sharpener.

✓ Must assignments be completed in pencil or pen? Let students know your expectations. At first it might even be a good idea to note on the top of the assignment sheet "Complete in pen only." That minimizes debate later about whether a student knew he or she was to use a pen.

Assignments and Homework

Procedures for completing assignments, turning them in, and returning them need to be established the first week of school. Here are some procedures that must be clarified:

✓ How will students be given each day's assignment? Will it be posted on the board each day when they enter the room? Will it be given at the beginning or end of class? Are they required to carry an assignment notepad? Will deadlines be announced?

✓ How do you want them to complete it? Where does the student's name go on the assignment?

✓ How and when should it be turned in? As students enter the class? Do they pass assignments in or place them in a basket or box at a designated time? Should the assignment be folded in any specific way?

✓ How should a student make up work after an absence? How do students find out the assignments? How long do they have to get caught up?

Storage Solutions

It is easier to maintain an organized classroom if sufficient storage facilities are provided. This includes cabinets, shelves, and furniture, as well as ample, accessible storage containers. Use an assortment of resealable, plastic sandwich and freezer storage bags to store game parts, bulletin board letters, crayons, art supplies, and any other small items that need to be kept together. Check out the following:

✓ Small hardware storage bins are ideal for storing many small items and supplies. Shoeboxes, especially the clear, plastic ones, are great storage containers for many items. Dishpans, wire or plastic baskets, and coffee cans also are handy and inexpensive containers. Though harder to find today, cigar boxes are still some of the finest storage bins available. Parents or garage sales are inexpensive sources for many storage containers.

✓ Obtaining and organizing adequate storage solutions is only the first step. You must train your students to put materials back in their designated places. It is much easier to teach everyone to put things back where they belong than for you to spend time sorting and shelving misplaced items.

✓ As much as possible, color code items and storage compartments to facilitate putting things back where they belong.

✓ Clearly label all storage containers and cupboards. This task could be delegated to a student volunteer or aide.

✓ Assign a student to be the postal clerk, librarian, or stock supervisor. The student's job is to see that everything is put back where it belongs that day. You might develop a checklist to facilitate the task. This can be especially helpful in laboratory or shop classes.

The Challenge of Paperwork

Two and a half trillion pages of paper are generated in the United States each year. According to a study by Partners for Environmental Progress, paper consumes 45 percent of the available landfill space. Another researcher found that 95 percent of all the pieces of paper that go into filing cabinets in America today will never come out again. To estimate how long a person has been in education, count the number of filing cabinets in his or her room and multiply by five. We seldom purge our cabinets. They simply fill up, and about every five years we requisition another one! Author Tom Parker estimated that each day Americans buy 426 bushels of paper clips—approximately thirty-five million!

Teachers consistently rate paperwork as their biggest time management problem. While some paperwork is inevitable in any profession, most teachers probably accumulate much more paper than they really need. Imagine how many pieces of paper you handle on a typical school day: magazines, quizzes, tests, attendance forms, grade records, requisitions, books, letters, forms, memos, mail, and meeting notices and minutes. Then multiply that figure by 180 school days. These reams and reams of paper we swap, hoard, file, and stack consume vast amounts of storage space; they also devour a significant proportion of our lives.

Causes of the Paper Deluge

Paper abounds for many reasons. Governmental, technological, and cultural forces interact to inundate us with paper. Psychological weaknesses often make it difficult for us to rid ourselves of paper once we have it. Here are some of the more pervasive causes of the paper deluge:

✓ Knowledge grows exponentially. The number of publications has exploded. In 1800 there were approximately one hundred scientific journals; today there are close to one hundred thousand. The number of nonscientific publications has increased as dramatically.

✓ In this age of litigation, many people are concerned with documenting anything that might possibly be the subject of dispute in the future. Certain disciplinary decisions, personnel dismissals or sanctions, and financial transactions should be carefully recorded. Keep only what is absolutely necessary, and file it so that you can find it when you need it. Purge these files after a reasonable time; if you haven't used a paper in the past two years, toss it in the recycling bin. This environment feeds insecurity, prompting some—especially administrators—to hoard paper to protect their backsides.

✓ Governmental red tape has proliferated. Additional state and federal mandates and standards require massive documentation, consuming not only the mounds of paper this generates but the valuable time of the school employees charged with tabulating, assembling, and submitting these documents. Every new educational program funded also creates a paper trail of accountability.

✓ The copy machine has abetted the paper explosion. Making ten copies is just as easy as making one, so we end up with nine more copies of everything just in case. And the photocopier makes it easy for others to send us copies of their paper collection.

✓ The computer, while having the potential of saving time and paper, has thus far failed to create the paperless society. Indeed, many argue that it actually makes generating more paperwork easier. With computers accessible to virtually everyone, the mass of form letters, targeted mailing lists, and databases abounds. Additionally, those of us who grew up before computers don't trust hard drives and CDs to hold our valuable information. We want papers we can touch, file, and carry.

Thirty-four Tips for Handling Paperwork

1. When in doubt, throw it out (or better yet, recycle it). Ask yourself, "What's the worst thing that would happen if I didn't have this piece of paper?" Few papers are totally impossible to replace if necessary.

2. Never save papers simply because you might need them someday. Rather ask yourself, "If I need this at some time in the future, where will I be able to find it?" Chances are that nine other copies are filed around the school system.

3. Set aside one day a year (perhaps during the summer) to purge all your files of any piece of paper you don't need. If you haven't used it in the last two years, you probably don't need it.

4. Time management experts advise that we strive to handle each piece of paper only once. While this is not always possible, the less we shuffle papers back and forth from our briefcase to our desk and back, the more effective we are likely to be in controlling the paper plague.

5. Label a basket or folder "To be filed." Set aside a few minutes every week to file papers. Don't let them accumulate longer.

6. Label twelve file folders with the names of the months. Keep this in a convenient file drawer near your desk. As you receive pieces of paper that you will need at some time later during the year, file them under the month they will be needed. At the first of each new month, pull out the corresponding file.

7. Tape or glue to your desk blotter important or frequently used lists, numbers, rosters, or schedules.

8. Save only one copy of papers you need in the future. Be sure to save one clean master (or a computer file) of handouts and letters you use each year.

9. In your desk or at the front of your file drawer, keep three folders; label the first Correspondence, the second Schedules, and the third Forms. Place master copies in these so you won't have to redo them the next time.

10. Keep a colored manila folder in your briefcase or book bag labeled To Do. Keep your to-do list in that folder as well as any memos, letters, forms, or other items you'll need in order to accomplish the tasks on your list. Keep it in your briefcase so that it is always with you.

11. Use colored folders or labels when you file papers. Use a different color for each subject you teach or for each period of the day. (If possible, match the color of your textbook. This minimizes the possibility of misfiling the folder in the wrong drawer.)

12. When file folders get too fat, split them into smaller categories or move all the papers to a large three-ring binder. The same principle holds for accumulating files on your computer hard drive.

13. Develop a test-question bank on note cards or on the computer. Several excellent test-generation programs are available from computer software suppliers (see the list in Chapter Seven). This makes construction of tests and quizzes much easier.

14. For each class you teach, keep a three-ring binder in which you file all lesson plans, handouts, assignments, samples, problems, and other items you want to have available when you teach the class again. It is helpful to have a different colored notebook for each class.

15. Plan to make photocopies at times when there is no line. Right before school in the morning is probably the busiest time.

16. Set aside a specific spot on your desk at school where you place items to go to the office. As you think of such items, always place them in that spot. Whenever you have to make a trip to the office, take those items

Never stack paper,
to stack is to stay!

—Don Ashlett,
Not for Packrats Only

with you. You should do the same thing with items you plan to take home each night. Strive to make every trip count.

17. Organize your work area at home with all the necessary supplies at hand (pens, paper, envelopes, stamps, paper clips, stapler, scissors, and so on).

18. Probably the hardest things for teachers to discard are books, no matter how outdated, unused, or duplicative. This is doubly difficult for hardcover books. If it is not a much-used reference book, ask yourself, "Will I ever read this book?" If the answer is not a definite yes, then donate it to a book sale or library or give it to a student. Put a bunch of discarded books in a box labeled Free for your students to pick the ones they want.

19. If you have forms you must complete for many students, complete one form with all the basic information that is the same for all students (for example, your name, date, school building, signature). Photocopy the necessary number of forms and complete by hand only the necessary individual information.

20. If professional journals accumulate unread for more than three months, give them away or cut out and file the most promising articles for future reference. Do not feel guilty if you do not read every publication cover to cover. They might contain only one or two articles really of interest to you.

21. If it is your magazine, cut out the articles you want to read later. Save these in a file folder to read in your free time. Some keep this file in their briefcase or take it with them when they are likely to be waiting, such as at the doctor's office or the airport.

22. You might put a blank label on the front cover of a magazine. As you read it, jot down the page numbers you would like to copy. Another way is to keep small strips of scrap paper handy and mark the page numbers on these slips, then insert them as page markers.

23. Cancel subscriptions to publications you don't have time to read or that really don't meet your needs. Avoid renewing simply out of habit. Set yourself a goal to reduce the volume of paper crossing your path.

24. Set limits on how long you will save various types of papers (for example, two years for professional magazines, six months for memos to parents, three years for grade books, two weeks for meeting minutes). Whenever you run across a piece of paper whose time line has expired, discard it.

25. Use three-ring notebooks to preserve masters of tests and handouts for copying. Keep your masters sequential and easy to find. Use a separate notebook for each subject area. Be sure to back up to floppy disks or CDs all computer files that contain your lessons and handouts.

> *Half of our life is spent trying to find something to do with the time we have rushed through life trying to save.*
>
> **—Will Rogers,**
> **The Autobiography of Will Rogers**

Junk mail in the U.S. alone consumes one hundred million trees each year.

—Native Forest Network

26. Keep a file box or drawer beside your desk for all the worksheets and homework sheets you will use in all your classes that week. In the box place manila file folders labeled by subject and day (for example, Science—Mon.; Science—Tues.; and so on). Duplicate all materials you're going to use on Friday and fill up your box. (Obviously, not every subject has a ditto or handout for every day.) This makes it very easy for the rest of the week. If handouts are used for that day, they are easily found. If you are absent, you don't have to worry about a substitute finding the handouts to use.

27. Always carry three-by-five-inch note cards in your purse or pocket to record ideas and facts as you think of them to use in class and on tests. Also list home needs and class needs on these cards. An ideal time to use them is when you are waiting for an appointment or meeting to begin.

28. Whenever possible, develop individualized form letters you can use for repeated correspondence. Also keep a file of letters you must send out every year so that you do not have to redraft them each time. This is even easier if you maintain these as a computer file.

29. Quickly sort your mail into four stacks: NEVER, which you throw out unread; NOW, which receives top attention because some degree of urgency or importance is attached to it; LATER, which deserves attention but is not urgent; MAYBE, which may get a cursory glance sometime but probably isn't important or urgent (for example, catalogs, general notices, and newsletters).

30. For routine interoffice mail and school memos, jot your response on the same piece of paper and return to the sender immediately. Of course, don't do that with important pieces of correspondence, like job offers.

31. As you read a piece of correspondence that will require a response, jot down a few notes in the margin to remind yourself of what you want to say. It is quicker to use postcards or e-mail rather than letters whenever possible.

32. If you spend lots of time commuting to and from school, keep a micro-cassette tape recorder in your car. You can dictate into it as you drive. It is a great way to create letters, to-do lists, quiz questions, teaching ideas, and so on.

33. Eliminate junk mail by contacting the Direct Mail Marketing Association online at www.the-dma.org. For $5 you can complete their Mail Preference Service Form to be placed on their suppression list. Another option for help in stopping junk mail is to contact the Stop Junk Mail Association, 3020 Bridgeway #150, Sausalito, CA 94965; (800) 827–5549.

34. A computer has the potential to help with all kinds of paperwork chores. You can get software to handle addresses, phone numbers, grades, to-do lists, and calendars. However, don't rush to put everything on a computer just because you can. Keeping your calendar on the computer may become an extra chore if you also have to carry a pocket calendar with you, duplicating the effort.

Communications

A teacher's job entails hundreds of communications each day. In addition to traditional oral and paper exchanges, technology innovations like voice mail and e-mail greatly expand the opportunity to give and receive messages. These additional communication channels can be a mixed blessing. Used effectively, they can make us more productive. Poorly used, they can become time robbers. Here are some helpful tips gleaned from other teachers:

✓ Leave notes for teachers, administrators, or students—rather than taking the time to wait for someone. The recipient can write a short response and leave it in your mailbox or on your desk. Both of you save time as there is little opportunity for idle conversation.

✓ Buy a Rolodex file that holds three-by-five-inch cards. Record not only names and postal addresses but also phone and fax numbers and e-mail addresses if available. File any numbers you have to look up more than twice. You can also note in the file special information about the individuals, such as birthdates, spouses' and children's names, or interests. The file is also a useful place to record membership or subscription numbers, lock combinations, directions to places, and other miscellaneous bits of information that are easy to misplace.

✓ If you hate to write, try writing postcards. Or better yet, make your own postcard by cutting 8½-by-11-inch card stock in half, yielding two 5½-by-8½-inch cards. Fold these in half to make inexpensive note cards.

✓ Use a carbon-backed form for parent conferences. It gives a record of what was discussed, comments, and so on. You can give the parent a copy and keep one for your class file. If necessary, you can send a copy to the guidance office or principal.

✓ Develop form letters to handle routine and repetitive correspondence. Storing your form letters as template computer files saves much time in written communications.

✓ Where available, transmit electronic text messages to colleagues and others with access to e-mail.

✓ Create mailboxes to organize your outgoing and incoming e-mail messages. Once you have read a message, move it into a mailbox folder based on subject areas (for example, parents, students, professional development, and courses).

✓ Use an e-mail filter to block spam and other unwanted messages.

✓ Use signatures. Rather than retyping your name and contact information at the end of each message, use a signature file with the relevant information. Your e-mail program will automatically append your signature file to the end of every outgoing message. Most e-mail software allows the user to have several different signatures to use with different groups (for example, friends, colleagues, parents, and students).

✓ Delete outdated e-mail messages and other unnecessary files from your computer.

Teacher Time Log

Keep a daily time log for three or four school days to get a more accurate picture of how your time is consumed. (A form is given at the end of this chaper.) Enter the data on the time log form from the time you get up until the time you go to bed. It is important to accurately record what you are really doing during these small segments to get a good reflection of where your time really goes. It does no good to enter what you *could* have done, *should* have done, or *would* have done. You must be honest for the time log to have any meaning.

Record the specific activity for each fifteen-minute block of time. You need not actually stop what you are doing every fifteen minutes to enter your information. A useful procedure is to carry a three-by-five-inch card with you and take fifteen to twenty seconds each hour to briefly note what you were doing in each of the previous fifteen-minute segments. At the end of the day, enter the information onto your time log form. At that time also enter comments reflecting on specific activities. What were your most frequent interruptions? Were there any patterns? Which activities would you like to increase? Which would you like to decrease? In the priority column, assign a value to each activity: A is for important activities that contribute to your essential life goals; B for activities that are urgent but not particularly important to fulfilling your life goals; C for maintenance activities, routine chores, not especially important.

Analyze the log at the end of the week. The following questions may be helpful in analyzing your record:

✓ What percent of your total time did you spend on A, B, and C items?

✓ What were your major interruptions? Was there a pattern (time of day, in person, activity)? How can you decrease them in the future?

✓ What activities would you like to eliminate or decrease?

✓ Which would you like to increase?

✓ What strategies will help you spend more time doing higher-priority items?

To-Do List

As the cartoon character Ziggy claimed, "I made a mental note of it, but I lost it." That's exactly what happens to many of our mental notes—we lose them. A simple written reminder or to-do list can effectively help teachers complete the many little tasks that make up the profession of teaching. Here are suggestions:

✔ The trouble with keeping to-do lists is that crossing things off is too much fun. At the end of the day, we take delight in crossing off twelve of the fourteen tasks. Unfortunately, the ones we cross off are too often the routine and petty tasks; we transfer the unpleasant or difficult ones to tomorrow's list. However, these are often the most important items on our list. If you are going to keep a daily to-do list, it is essential to indicate in some form the priorities of the list items. One way is to put an asterisk in front of the most important two or three items. Try to do the top-priority items first.

✔ Whenever you find yourself with a few minutes of free time, look at your list to see whether you can chip away any items. Many of the jobs, like returning a phone call or sending a note, may take as little time as a minute.

✔ Some find it more convenient to keep their to-do list on their calendar. This works well if you use a daily calendar that gives you one full page for each day. An alternative is to keep your list on sticky notes that you apply to the calendar each day. Rather than rewriting the list at the end of the day, scratch out those items accomplished, pull the list from today's page in your calendar, and stick it on tomorrow's page.

✔ Instead of keeping a daily to-do list, some people keep only a master list. The projects and tasks on this list do not have to be done today but do require attention within the next week or month. They need to be done but are not urgent—yet. Of course, if put off long enough, they could become urgent.

> *Everything I didn't do yesterday, added to everything I haven't done today, plus everything I won't do tomorrow completely exhausts me.*
>
> **—Anonymous**

✔ Examine your list to see which ones someone else can do. Which are really not important to you? Ask yourself, "What is the worst thing that would happen if I didn't do that?" Scratch out items that really don't have to be done. Some wise persons believe success is derived not so much from what we choose to do but rather from what we choose not to do. Effective time management is largely the ability to eliminate those activities that distract from the truly important ones.

✔ Duplicate and use copies of the to-do form included at the end of this chapter. Printing them on brightly colored paper makes it harder to misplace them.

Assessing Student Time-on-Task

For at least a century, educators have touted the importance of attention and time spent on learning activities, but the idea has gained renewed attention during the past decade. A growing body of evidence shows that student time-on-task is a modest predictor of learning but not a panacea. Research also emphasizes that increasing time-on-task is likely to have a greater effect for below-average students.

High engagement rates on ineffective or irrelevant instructional activities are of doubtful benefit. To result in learning gains, the instruction must be at the appropriate level for that individual student: too high and the student does not comprehend and is lost; too low and needless overlearning and perhaps boredom occur. Some educators have been guilty of focusing solely on time-on-task without attending to the other variables that contribute to instructional effectiveness. Time-on-task is best viewed as a necessary but insufficient condition for academic success.

Past research has generally found time-on-task rates around 70 to 75 percent. However, it is important to remember that this is an average. Researchers have reported rates as low as 30 percent for individual classrooms. If you experience engagement rates at the lower end of the range, it may be time to develop a plan of action. While striving for higher time-on-task, do not ignore the half of the teaching day that is lost to nonacademic activities. It accounts for a greater proportion of time lost than does student off-task behavior. A complete school time management plan must focus on decreasing noninstructional activity, as well as increasing student engagement rates. If the teacher isn't on task, the students can't be.

How effectively do your students spend their in-class time? Are they engaged more or less than the 70 percent norm? What are they doing when they are off task? These questions can best be answered by direct, systematic observation.

Your gut-level assessment may be a valid clue as to your students' on-task rate, but it may be biased and inaccurate. It is difficult to observe the rest of the class when you are preoccupied with one student or with a small group.

Trade observations with a fellow teacher, giving each other feedback and support. Select someone who is reasonably objective and candid. A single observation may not be representative of your teaching. Try to have at least three separate observations on different days. Avoid special days, such as right before or after holidays, since the results are likely to differ from typical days. Devise an observation form that fits your classroom situation and provides the information you want. (You might use the form included in this book.)

At five-minute intervals the observer should scan the entire class in the same sequence. For each student a tally is placed on the chart. If the observer cannot tell, after a few seconds of watching a student, whether the behavior is on task or off task, record it as being on task. Students should be recorded as out of class if they leave for the restroom, go to the principal's office, arrive late to class, or are told to leave.

Once the observations are complete, divide the number of students scored as on task by the total number of students included in each observation segment to arrive at your engagement rate.

Here are some things the observer can look for:

✓ How long does it take to get a class started?

✓ How much time is spent in clerical tasks, such as taking attendance and reading announcements?

✓ Which part of the class period suffers the most off-task behavior?

✓ How smooth are the transitions from one task to the next?

✔ What proportion of class time is allocated to seatwork?

✔ How much class time is spent on discipline?

✔ How many interruptions are there? How much time do they consume?

✔ How much time do students spend waiting for help?

The answers to these questions may assist in setting goals for improvement. Later observations can help assess whether progress is being made in increasing time-on-task.

Conquer Procrastination Now!

Are you eligible for membership in the Procrastinator's Club but haven't gotten around to sending your application? Some teachers have accepted the group's motto, "We're behind you all the way." Are you one? Test your eligibility right now! Don't put it off another minute.

Procrastination Payoffs

Psychologists and motivational researchers have studied procrastination for decades in an attempt to uncover its causes and cures. People procrastinate because they expect to gain or avoid something.

Procrastination likely develops over a period of years, beginning in childhood. Research suggests that many procrastinators tend to be perfectionists, immobilized by deadlines until they feel a masterpiece is achieved. They may feel that their work is of value only if it is perfect, and their self-worth is a reflection of their performance.

By doing jobs at the last minute, procrastinators may protect their egos, since their true ability is not judged, only their skill in doing jobs at the last minute under pressure. "Of course, I could have done a much better job if I had had more time!" may even elicit sympathy from some listeners. Another secondary gain is that if a person puts off a job long enough, someone else may do the job. Many adolescents are aware of this game. Their parents become impatient waiting for the garbage to be taken out or for their children to clean their bedrooms, so they do the chores for them. What motivation do these children have to change? None, they have a good thing going. Unfortunately, that pattern may continue into adulthood.

Procrastination may also serve as a defense to avoid difficult or unpleasant tasks, although the habitual procrastinator may begin to delay even minor and enjoyable activities. Seldom is the procrastinated task totally avoided; it is only delayed.

Sometimes procrastination is the result of poor skills or insufficient knowledge. Being poorly organized, setting goals without deadlines, attempting to make decisions with insufficient information, and being unable to say no may all contribute to procrastination.

Educators' Procrastination Society Eligibility Form

Answer each of the following now.

	Yes	No
Do you have a set of papers that has been waiting to be graded for a week or more?	_____	_____
Do you frequently finish jobs just before the deadline?	_____	_____
Are you regularly late handing in grades, reports, and so on?	_____	_____
Do your students usually have to wait a week or more to receive their papers back?	_____	_____
Do weeks pass before you respond to your mail?	_____	_____
Does your principal regularly remind you that a deadline has passed?	_____	_____
Do you find it difficult to get started on the big projects?	_____	_____
Do you frequently tell people you work better under pressure?	_____	_____
Do you frequently feel guilty because you have not completed a task?	_____	_____
Do you have difficulty getting jobs completed because they may not be perfect?	_____	_____

Count the number of "yes" responses. Compare your score with the following scale:

0–3   *Early starter:* By doing things today, you are free to do them again tomorrow if you choose.

4–7   *Amateur procrastinator:* Some potential problem areas may create stress for you and annoyance in those around you.

8–10   *Professional procrastinator:* Putting things off until the last minute is a way of life.

Which of the following are you most likely to procrastinate?

✓ Grading papers
✓ Completing report cards
✓ Meeting with parents
✓ Writing letters
✓ Returning phone calls
✓ Writing lesson plans
✓ Making important decisions
✓ Planning a speech
✓ Meeting with your principal
✓ Writing a grant request
✓ Applying for a new position
✓ Confronting a colleague
✓ Cleaning off your desk
✓ Buying presents

If you confess to occasionally experiencing stress, guilt, and anxiety from procrastination, you may be ready for a change. If procrastination is a way of life for you, the following suggestions may help; but be patient. You will not undo a lifetime of learning in a day, a week, or even a month. Not only new ways of behaving but possibly new ways of viewing yourself may be needed.

Identify the task you would like to quit procrastinating and answer the following questions:

1. What do you gain from procrastinating this activity?
2. What do you fear might happen if you attempt this activity?
3. What do you lose by putting off this task? What price do you pay?
4. What are the positive consequences that would result from doing this particular activity?
5. What do you tell yourself to justify your procrastination?

Attacking Procrastination

The easiest thing to procrastinate is doing something about procrastination. You may be tempted to allow short-term avoidance to overpower the longer-term advantages. If you have become a slave to deadlines, immobilized by the big and small projects you face, it may be time to combat procrastination. In the previous activity, you had an opportunity to analyze the motivation and costs of one problem area. Using those insights, you can develop a plan of attack.

It is best to pick one area in which you find procrastination most annoying (for example, grading exams,

Procrastination is the art of keeping up with yesterday.

—Don Marquis,
Archy and Mehitabel

answering letters, filing papers). Begin small and progress as you experience success. Attempting to eliminate all procrastination from your life at once is much like dieting while trying to stop smoking. You are setting yourself up for frustration and failure. Be patient.

Adhere to the following guidelines to defeat procrastination:

✓ Establish your own deadlines, and announce them to others involved. Be realistic in setting a timetable.

✓ Break the project into smaller parts. Chip away at it in small bites. Don't wait for that big chunk of time.

✓ Set a definite beginning point. You must break the inertia of inactivity. If getting started is especially troublesome, set a timer for ten or fifteen minutes. Commit yourself to doing something on the project until the timer rings. Then you can decide whether to stop or continue. Chances are you will gain momentum and continue after the timer stops. If not, try another ten minutes later in the day.

✓ Do the most important things first. Avoid the distractions of the trivial and routine tasks when a higher-priority job needs to be done. Examining each task in light of your goals will help you set priorities.

✓ Reward yourself for completing parts of a major task. It may be something as simple as a ten-minute walk, a soft drink, or a social phone call. Contract with yourself for a big reward for completing important tasks. A night on the town, sleeping late on a weekend, or a purchase you have been wanting to make may help motivate you to complete the job. Be nice to yourself.

✓ Avoid perfectionism. Excellence is a sufficient level of performance for most things in life; and for many tasks (doing the dishes, pursuing a new sport or hobby, dusting the lampshades), adequacy is all that is necessary. Give yourself permission to be less than perfect. You might double the amount of time spent typing a test, attempting to get the spacing and typing perfectly. Could you spend that extra time in another activity that will better benefit your students or yourself? Probably so.

Nothing is so fatiguing as the eternal hanging on of an uncompleted task.

—William James,
Letters of William James

Procrastination is a learned habit and can be supplanted with a more constructive habit, giving you greater control over your life. If procrastination has limited your achievements, do something about it *now!*

Tips for Getting Organized

Get as organized as you need to be to do your job well and no more. Some people become obsessed with the idea of organization to the point that it becomes an impediment to efficiency.

Know What You Want

People without goals in life are much like the airline pilot who radios, "We're making good time, but we're lost." You can be rushing through the pathway of life at ninety miles an hour; but if you don't know where you are headed, you might end up someplace you don't want to be.

Both in and out of the classroom, the very best teachers and the happiest people have a clear sense of purpose. On the grander scale, they have a dream, a vision, a view of their world as they would like to see it become. But a goal requires three additional ingredients to become reality:

1. A plan for realizing that goal
2. A passion and commitment to devote one's personal time and energy to attaining the goal
3. A realistic deadline that holds one accountable

Plan for Success

Imagine trying to build a house without a blueprint. Just go with the flow. Do what you feel like doing on the spur of the moment. "Today let's do drywall. Tomorrow we will do the plumbing and electricity." What a mess we would make of the project.

Whether teaching a lesson or building a house, a good plan helps us get things done effectively, efficiently, and correctly. A good plan stimulates creativity. Plan the process of making decisions about what to do, when to do it, and how to do it.

Save a few minutes Friday afternoon for making general plans for the following week. You can fill in details later, but the perspective of what tasks need to be done the next week will likely be fresher on Friday. It will also highlight additional information or resources you'll need to get in order to complete the planning process.

Strive to plan at least a week in advance. Include in the lesson-planning process handouts to copy, supplies to gather, and audiovisuals to request. Anticipate the potential obstacles that could occur. For example, if you plan to take a class outside for a particular activity, have a backup strategy in case of inclement weather.

Discover Your Prime Time

Are you an early bird or a night owl? When are you most creative? Most energetic? Most adults' peak mental time is in the morning, though there certainly are exceptions.

Don't waste your most creative time doing menial tasks like photocopying, stapling, cleaning, filing, or grading objective tests. Safeguard those precious hours when you are at your intellectual peak to do the most cognitively challenging tasks: writing, planning, or creating.

Of course, you have to use common sense. You can't very well tell your principal that you're not a morning person, so you don't want classes before 11:00 A.M. We all have to adapt to reality. Just resolve not to waste your most valuable creative time doing the less intellectually challenging tasks.

Keep a Personal Calendar

The single most valuable time management tool is a daily calendar. It doesn't matter which kind you use, as long as it meets your needs.

Teachers may select from a broad range of calendars. Most teachers prefer to use academic year calendars that run from July 1 to June 30, minimizing the need to carry two calendars around during the first half of the school year. My preference has always been for calendars that provide one full five-by-seven-inch page for each day of the year. These provide ample room to jot notes to oneself, keep to-do lists, and record any special appointments.

Many teachers now carry laptop computers or personal digital assistants (PDAs or handheld organizers) back and forth between home and work. A number of excellent calendar software programs provide the flexibility of interfacing with one's e-mail server, address book, to-do list, memo book, and other databases. These programs' reminder option is especially valuable in helping users keep abreast of important upcoming events. Many of these programs are available as freeware (see teachnology.com/downloads/time/ for a good selection).

At the end of each day, review your calendar to help plan your activities for the following day. Sticky notes can be used to make daily to-do lists to attach to paper calendars. Many of the software calendars provide a similar feature, often color coded to help with setting priorities.

Many teachers use their calendars to record professional expenses (meals, mileage, lodging, and so on) that might be tax deductible.

Lead a Balanced Life

There was a time, early in my career, when I was teaching five preparations, coaching three sports, taking graduate classes in the evening, and trying to help raise two-year-old twins. Life seemed like a race between vacations. "Just wait until Thanksgiving, Christmas, spring break, ah, summer." Catching up seemed an impossible dream.

Then one day I had a tremendous emotional insight: "What if Easter doesn't come!" It was an early midlife crisis, for the first time confronting the limit of my own mortality. After a period of reflection, reading, and talking with some close friends, I came to a little different philosophy of life.

It may sound as corny as it comes, but it is the best I have been able to figure out. My life philosophy now contains two pieces.

First, lighten up a little! Grab a little gusto. Live each day as though it might be the last. There are no guarantees. Live a little more in the present and not so much on delayed gratification—working hard today for the pot of gold at the end of the rainbow.

But we can't hedonistically live only for today. For like the squirrel, we must put away some nuts for the winter, just in case we are around. Hence, the second part of my guiding philosophy is a commitment to do at least one thing each day that will make for a better tomorrow—for myself, my family, and my community.

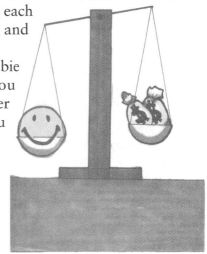

I once saw a television interview of famed ragtime musician Eubie Blake, on the occasion of his hundredth birthday. He said, "You know, if I had known I was going to live so long, I'd a taken better care of myself." At the age of one hundred! You never know, you might just make it. Do stop and smell the roses along the way.

A good place to begin is by resolving to save one hour a day to do something you really want to do. I know it won't always be possible or easy. It may mean getting up a half hour earlier or turning the television off for an hour.

Find Time for a Really Important Task

No matter how well organized we may be, unanticipated tasks occasionally demand our attention. It may be a report requested by an administrator, a favor for a friend, a school or personal crisis, or simply something important we just didn't have time to get done earlier.

The best advice is this: do not go to the faculty lounge! Social interruptions are inevitable. Here are a few tips teachers have found helpful in finding those few extra hours or minutes to accomplish a big chore that they must get done:

✓ Find a hideaway. During your planning period, find a place where you can work without interruption. This might be another teacher's empty classroom, the furnace room, or the bleachers on the football field. Let the secretary know where you can be found in case of an emergency.

✓ Close your classroom or office door. You will be less likely to be interrupted if you are not readily visible.

✓ If interrupted, be assertive. Let the person know you really have to get an important task done and agree to meet later if the other person desires.

✓ Arrive at school early. One can accomplish twice as much in the uninterrupted morning hours than once the building is full of people.

✓ Break a big task into several small chunks and chip away at it throughout the day or week. You may not be able to complete the whole job in five, ten, or fifteen minutes; but you can do something to move it along. Make a phone call, jot down one idea, write one paragraph, or grade two essays. Learn to think of big jobs as really just a bunch of little tasks that must be done one at a time. You will feel less overwhelmed and more in control of your time.

Been to a Good Meeting Lately?

In my workshops on effective use of school time, teachers continually list attending meetings as one of their greatest time robbers. Most teachers view meetings as a necessary evil but usually don't expect them to be very productive. For better or worse, meetings are an essential part of every educator's job. This includes the myriad of committees, task forces, staff meetings, parent-teacher consultations, planning sessions, case conferences, and open discussions that consume a large portion of a teacher's calendar.

Not all meetings are a waste of time; some are productive, creative, energizing, informative, or morale boosting. Such outcomes do not occur by chance but because specific events happened that assured success. With some basic training in effective communication skills, problem solving, and group dynamics, administrators and teachers can collaborate to make meetings productive.

Look for Alternatives to a Meeting

The easiest way to cut down on meeting time is to keep the number of meetings to a minimum. Too often educators attend or call meetings when the issues at hand could have been handled expeditiously in another fashion. If sharing information is the sole purpose of the meetings, consider using a memo, e-mail, or telephone call, saving both time and money.

A democratic value system and sensitivity to others' viewpoints can entice teachers into the paralysis of analysis, the inability to make even minor decisions without eliciting everyone's opinion. Decisions that affect the others' lives or are costly must be considered carefully, yet in many cases it would be just as effective to make a decision yourself or ask someone else to decide.

Standing committees that have a regular meeting date should cancel their meetings if the business at hand does not require a meeting. Many organizations have successfully adapted the Delphi technique, in which a committee functions largely by written communication and surveys.

Have an Agenda

Although spontaneity has its role in life, that generally is not the best way to run a meeting. An agenda will help focus the attention of a meeting's participants. Distribute the written agenda a day or two before the meeting if possible. Include not only an outline of topics but also questions to be considered or background information that participants should know before the meeting. Invite advance preparation.

The agenda should reflect clear-cut goals for the meeting. Is it to share information, solve a problem, seek advice, or sell an idea? Clear-cut tasks convey a businesslike atmosphere and a respect for other people's time.

Too often 80 percent of the meeting time is devoted to the items constituting only 20 percent importance. Schedule discussion of the most important items first, lest they be hastily decided at the end of the meeting. Limit discussion time on less important items.

Guard against an overly ambitious agenda. A crowded agenda decreases the group's effectiveness, leaves participants frustrated, and wastes time.

Begin on Time

Estimate how much time you have spent in the past year waiting for meetings to begin. Could that time have been better spent on other instructional-related tasks? If so, resolve to reduce your waiting time in the future. The world can be divided into two groups of people: those who are early for everything and those who are habitually late. Waiting for all of the latecomers to arrive punishes those who are punctual.

If people expect a meeting to begin late, the normally punctual people begin arriving after the scheduled starting time. The absurdity of this is that the habitually late people must now come even later to preserve their reputations. Convey the expectation that the meeting will begin on time and then make sure it does. If you are not in charge of the meeting, suggest to the chairperson that the meeting begin. Those who arrived promptly will applaud you, and after a few such instances, even the habitual latecomers are more likely to arrive on time.

Send out the notice and agenda for the meeting stating the beginning and ending times. Try scheduling meetings to begin at off-hour times, such as 2:40 or 11:10. This conveys a more specific time than 2:00, which often gets interpreted as "twoish."

Include Only Necessary People

Do you frequently sit through meetings wondering why you are there? Too often meetings are called with little attention to who really needs to be there. Large-group meetings become a series of small-group discussions, involving only a few participants, while the others sit idly observing them.

Invite only those persons whose presence is directly related to the meeting's goals. If someone's input is needed for one item on the agenda, have that person attend only that part of the meeting. This is a sound practice for two reasons. It limits the size of the group, and people may spend their time on tasks of higher priority. Unless the purpose of the meeting is primarily to share information or persuade, efficiency greatly diminishes once more than ten or twelve people are included.

Attend only those meetings at which your presence is essential. If your input is needed for only a portion of the agenda, attend only that segment. If all else fails and you must attend a meeting in which you have little stake, take something to do. Work on your to-do list or outline your correspondence.

Select a Conducive Environment

Some forethought as to the meeting place can assure a more inviting atmosphere. The major criterion should be to have a place where interruptions can be kept to a minimum. Repeated interruptions may greatly impede a group's progress, whether it is a counseling group or a formal meeting. Not only does the group lose the time the distraction takes up, but it also loses momentum, requiring the group to refocus its attention.

Seek a location that avoids traffic flow. Close the door. This communicates that you value the meeting and plan to give it your full attention. If you are fortunate enough to have a secretary, inform him or her to interrupt only for emergencies.

Group meetings should institute a policy of not allowing cell phones. The real estate office where my wife works instituted a $20 fine for any cell phone ringing during the weekly staff meeting.

Give consideration to the physical attributes of your meeting site. Is the temperature comfortable? Most people find a temperature of about sixty-eight degrees most conducive to mental activity. Rearrange the chairs to fit the meeting's purpose. Move empty chairs out of the way. If you seek interaction, form a circle. Follow the lead of fast-food restaurants and avoid overly comfortable chairs; this can lead to inertia—a body at rest tends to remain at rest.

Indeed, for some brief, informal meetings, you may choose not to have chairs at all. Stand. It will keep interaction brief and to the point. Why have a twenty-minute session if you have a five-minute task? What else could you be doing with that time that might have a greater payoff for you, your students, and the school?

Keep the Meeting on Task

If I were king or superintendent, whichever is higher, I would mandate that every meeting room throughout the land must have a clock whose face shows not the tra-

ditional numerals reflecting the hours but the cumulative salary of every person sitting in that room. Thus, everyone would clearly recognize that a ten-minute digression on last week's football game cost this organization $180.

Time is money, at least when it comes to calling professional meetings. Whenever someone decides to call a meeting of five or ten paid staff members, he or she has made a decision to allocate that portion of the organization's resources. A teacher in a meeting cannot at the same time be teaching, tutoring, or planning a lesson. In some instances the organization and the student are better served by the meeting, but in others it is a misplaced priority. Time is finite; therefore, it is the educator's most precious resource. Choose well where to invest it.

Use your communication skills to keep meetings on task and follow a predetermined agenda. If someone begins to digress, inject gate-keeping questions such as "What do we need to decide today?" or "What are our options?" to refocus the group's attention. Summarize significant points, paraphrase crucial points, and confront discrepancies in the discussion. Educators have at their disposal a variety of effective communication techniques that they can use to play a valuable leadership role in any group, even when the educator is not the designated chairperson. A teacher's training in group dynamics should be used to help with task groups. Observe the group process and intervene when necessary to invite full participation. Although consensus in every group decision is not essential, you can intervene to assure that all viewpoints are aired. Solicit the contributions of silent members. Be especially sensitive to the nonverbal or nonparticipating people and tactfully but assertively quell the overly dominant member.

Remain sensitive to the hidden agendas that participants may bring to the meeting. Some observers believe that every meeting occurs at two levels. Hidden conflicts unrelated to the meeting agenda can greatly influence the group process. Remember that the spoken reasons are not always the real reasons for or against an issue.

Record Progress

Keeping a written account of the discussion is essential, especially in problem-solving groups. At the minimum, one person should take informal notes, to serve as the group memory. Decision making can proceed in a more orderly way if a visual display of the process is available. This may take the form of writing lists on newsprint or the chalkboard. Seeing one idea written may stimulate another.

Making a storyboard on note cards or using flowcharts or the diagrams from the Program and Evaluation Review Technique (PERT) have proven to be valuable techniques for recording and stimulating group problem solving. A planning process, PERT was adapted by a NASA project to help manage large projects, like putting a man on the moon. PERT charts (sometimes called network diagrams) are similar to flowcharts but read from left to right, with the final goal appearing in the node (or box) farthest to the right. (For more about PERT diagrams, see NASA's Web site at appl.nasa.gov/ask/issues/11/practices.) Such written stimuli are especially valuable if the group must continue the meeting at a later time.

Someone should be assigned to summarize the decisions made, either in formal minutes or in a brief memorandum to all the participants. It is also helpful to include a list of any responsibilities assigned to specific members for follow-up action. If the group is meeting again, include the meeting time and agenda.

End on Time

Remember Parkinson's Law: "Work expands to fill the time available." Avoid open-ended meetings except in genuine emergencies. Participants should agree on a specific ending time at the beginning. Everyone is more likely to stay on task if they know that the meeting will conclude at a specific time. One technique for forcing meetings to end on time is to schedule your meetings back-to-back. At the beginning indicate that you have another meeting scheduled and the time it must begin. As time approaches for the next meeting, announce that you have another appointment or meeting and must be excused.

If your group plans to meet again, try to set the time for your next meeting before this meeting adjourns. It will be a lot easier than trying to coordinate each member's schedule later.

Two heads can be better than one. When channeled constructively, the group process can be a source of valuable creativity and may even increase morale and the sense of community. The group process cannot be left to chance, however. The specific skills described here can assure that your meetings are more likely to be productive and perhaps even fun.

Scrounging for Supplies

Are there activities you would like to try in your class but can't because there aren't funds for the necessary supplies? Cutbacks and tight budgets have led to rationing of paper and chalk in many schools, with little money available for teaching materials. Yet some teachers have a knack for gathering needed supplies at no cost. Since the earliest days of formal education, resourceful teachers have mastered the delicate art of scrounging.

Those teachers who approach their supply shortage creatively realize that much is available for the mere asking and hauling. What a merchant may consider to be useless discards may indeed be treasures in a creative teacher's hands. Here are seven suggestions for improving your skills in scrounging for supplies:

1. Be specific. Know exactly what you need and how much. This helps you identify potential donors. Emphasize the specific instructional purpose of the desired item.

2. Time your request appropriately. Avoid the rush hours, when merchants will be most preoccupied with their customers. Also try to time your inquiries to miss peak holiday business. Submit your request directly to the owner or manager when possible. A direct request made in person is more likely to be taken seriously.

3. Emphasize the educational purpose. Most citizens are aware of schools' strained finances. Your request permits them to help in a small and usually painless way. Mentioning the potential tax deduction for donated items also helps.

4. Make moderate requests. Certainly don't ask a donor to deliver merchandise. Any special labor expenses are likely to deter much generosity.

5. Use your contacts. Parents of present or past students, previous donors, vocal supporters of schools, relatives, and friends are prime prospects. A cousin of the school custodian has a connection with your school that may encourage generosity. A note sent to parents or a brief notice in the local newspaper describing your need may be successful. Make your needs known!

6. Don't fear rejection. There are many legitimate reasons why a request cannot be filled. Usually, it is because the source does not have what you are requesting. For example, if a newspaper office has just discarded all of its old newsprint, you might ask that they hold future waste newsprint for you. Try to pinpoint a specific date to check back.

7. Show appreciation. Future donations are more likely if a gift is acknowledged. A special note of thanks from the teacher is a minimum. A large gift warrants a note from the principal or letters from the class or even an acknowledgment in the school or local newspaper.

By looking at your local phone directory's Yellow Pages, you can quickly identify a great many potential donors for needed supplies. To stimulate your thinking, consider the following suggestions.

Potential Sources for Teaching Supplies

Airline	Magazines, courtesy kits
Appliance store	Large cartons, cardboard
Bank	Coin wrappers, free maps
Business	Computers, computer software, storage bins, boxes, cabinets
Carpet store	Carpet remnants, cardboard tubes
Caterer	Leftover crepe paper, party supplies
Computer store	Software, CDs, used computers
Contractor	Scrap lumber, boards, plastic pipe, bricks
Dentist	Toothbrushes, posters, pamphlets, old magazines
Department store	Holiday decorations (after season), damaged merchandise
Discotheque	Albums, CDs
Dry cleaner	Hangers, plastic bags
Electrician	Electrical wire, small pieces of conduit
Farmer	Burlap bags, grains, biological specimens, twine
Florist	Floral wrapping paper, ribbon, plants
Garage sale	Books, magazines, toys, window shades, storage bins, dishpans, books, and so on
Greenhouse	Pots, starter plants, flowers
Greeting card store	Loose colored envelopes
Hairdresser	Wigs, cosmetics
Hospital	Pill bottles, various containers, boxes, health literature, tongue depressors
Insurance company	Notepads, calendars, actuarial tables
Liquor store	Boxes, cartons
Lumber yard	Scrap boards, nail aprons, yardsticks, rulers, metal bands
Motel or hotel	Linen, soap, matches, cups
Newspaper office	Newsprint from roll ends, photos, film canisters
Nursing home	Pill bottles, boxes
Paint store	Wallpaper samplers, paint, paint mixer sticks, yardsticks, buckets

Parents	Furniture, carpeting, books, cloth, containers, clothing, greeting card fronts, old shirts for smocks, margarine containers, wallpaper remnants, yarn, and so on
Photography store	Film canisters, outdated film
Pizza parlor	Round cardboard plates, pizza boxes for storage
Plasterer	Five-gallon buckets
Plumber	Scrap plastic pipe
Post office	Outdated FBI wanted circulars, stamp posters
Printer	Paper, card stock, ink, cardboard boxes with lids
Professor	Books, journals, research supplies, computer printouts
Radio and television repair shop	Magnets, wires, electrical parts, knobs
Radio or television station	CDs, DVDs, albums, discarded film, used audiotape, slides
Real estate company	Notepads, calendars, local maps
Restaurant	Bottle corks, party supplies, straws, paper cups, coupons, containers, posters, napkins, bottles, ice cream cartons, ice cream vats
Supermarket	Styrofoam trays, egg crates, berry baskets, shelving, paper bags
Tailor	Cloth, empty thread spools
Theater	Tickets to use as prizes, movie posters, promotion photos
Tobacco shop	Cigar boxes
Travel agency	Travel posters, maps
Upholsterer	Scrap remnants, thread

Suppliers of Instructional Materials

ABC Feelings, Inc.
P.O. Box 2377
Coeur d'Alene, ID 83816
www.abcfeelings.com/
(800) 745-3170

Unique, award-winning books, posters, and kits; feelings exploration, anger management, and character-building tools

American Guidance Service
4201 Woodland Road
P.O. Box 99
Circle Pines, MN 55014-1796
www.agsnet.com/
(800) 328-2560

Instructional and guidance-related materials for all levels; tests, video-tapes, books, teaching aids, professional development materials

Carson-Dellosa
P.O. Box 35665
Greensboro, NC 27425
www.carsondellosa.com/
(800) 321-0943

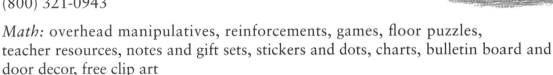

Math: overhead manipulatives, reinforcements, games, floor puzzles, teacher resources, notes and gift sets, stickers and dots, charts, bulletin board and door decor, free clip art

Continental Press
520 E. Bainbridge Street
Elizabethtown, PA 17022-2299
www.continentalpress.com/
(800) 233-0759

Instructional materials for pre-K through grade 12; instructional booklets and computer software for reading, literature, language, social studies, and early childhood

Creative Publications
5040 West 111th Street
Oak Lawn, IL 60453
www.creativepublications.com
(800) 624-0822

K–12 math and language arts; *Mathland curriculum:* manipulatives, overheads, time, counters, money, number concepts, cooperative problem solving, teacher resources, calculators, posters

Creative Teaching Press
P.O. Box 6017
Cypress, CA 90630-0017
www.creativeteaching.com/
(800) 444-4287

K–6 materials, multicultural art activities; books, pocket charts, calendars, charts, bulletin board materials, stickers, rewards, organizers, Youngheart music

Crestwood Company
6625 N. Sidney Place
Milwaukee, WI 53209-3259
www.communicationaids.com/
(414) 352-5678

Communication aids for children and adults; talking pictures and holders, communication boards, attention getters, portable communication aids and adaptations, language skill aids, adapted toys for children with special needs

Crystal Springs Books
P.O. Box 500
Peterborough, NH 03458
www.crystalsprings.com/
(800) 321-0401

Resources for K–6; whole language, multiage classrooms, developmental education, cooperative learning, inclusion, assessment and evaluation, math and science, discipline and self-esteem

Curriculum Associates, Inc.
5 Esquire Road
N. Billerica, MA 01862-0901
www.curriculumassociates.com/
(800) 225-0248 (U.S. and Canada)

Pre-K through grade 8; multicultural titles, spelling, writing, phonics, literature, software, plays, videos, activities, books (Spanish translations), study skills and test taking, test prep, ESL-bilingual: language-learning technology

Dale Seymour Publications
Pearson Learning Group
www.pearsonlearning.com/dalesey/dalesey_default.cfm
(800) 526-9907

K–8 educational materials; classroom management, manipulatives, calculators, and computers; science experiments, teaching resources, multicultural art, teaching strategies, self-esteem, cooperative learning, multicultural education, teaching the gifted

Evan-Moor
18 Lower Ragsdale Drive
Monterey, CA 93940-5746
www.evanmoor.com/store.asp
(800) 777-4362

Books: math, science, geography, writing, art, thematic units, whole language, bulletin board materials, clip art

Gamco Educational Materials
P.O. Box 1862H5
Big Spring, TX 79721-1862
www.gamco.com/
(800) 351-1404

Instructional games, transparencies, manipulatives, videos, filmstrips, cassettes, books, transparencies, software

Hubbard Scientific
401 W. Hickory Street
P.O. Box 2121
Fort Collins, CO 80522
www.shnta.com/
(970) 484-7445

Broad assortment of instructional materials for teaching science; models, videotapes, videodiscs, laboratory equipment, manipulatives, activity sets

Incentive Publications, Inc.
3835 Cleghorn Avenue
Nashville, TN 37215-2532
www.incentivepublications.com
(800) 421-2830

Books for K–8; literature, writing, thinking and life skills, multicultural language arts, drama, multicultural, science, math

Kagan Cooperative Learning
27134 Paseo Espada, Suite 303
San Juan Capistrano, CA 92675
www.coopcrativclcarning.com/
(800) 933-2667

A wide assortment of books and materials related to cooperative learning and cooperative discipline

Lakeshore Learning Materials
2695 E. Dominguez Street
P.O. Box 90749
Carson, CA 90749
www.lakeshorelearning.com/
(800) 421-5354

Arts and crafts supplies, puppets, role-playing supplies and props, classroom furniture, storage and organizer equipment, play equipment, manipulatives, teaching resources

Learning Well
P.O. Box 3759, Dept. 4
New Hyde Park, NY 11040-1042
www.learningwelled.com/
(800) 645-6564

Pre-K through grade 8; reading comprehension skills; books and software; videos, games, books

Learning Works
P.O. Box 1370
Goleta, CA 93116
www.thelearningworks.com/

Innovative books K–12: reading, creative writing, values, and feelings, creative thinking skills (gifted and talented), listening and following directions, handwriting, environment, puppetry

Mari, Inc.
1025 25th Street
Santa Monica, CA 90403
www.mariinc.com/
(800) 955-9494

K–5; study units, miniunits; reference books, whole language library, resource books; literature notes, file folder games, math workbooks, Quick Starts software guides; sticker books, puzzle pads, erasers, rubber stamps

Marsh Media
P.O. Box 8082
Shawnee Mission, KS 66208
www.marshmedia.com/
(800) 821-3303

Videos, software on health wellness, guidance, drug education, and consumer education

McGraw-Hill Children's Publishing
3195 Wilson Drive NW
Grand Rapids, MI 49544
www.mhteachers.com/
(800) 417-3261

Math, science, nature, ecology, health, history, geography, teacher resources, photo charts, giant floor puzzles, games, stickers, seals

NIMCO
117 Highway 815
P.O. Box 9
Calhoun, KY 42327-0009
www.nimcoinc.com/
(800) 962-6662

Drug and sex education materials, videos, games, posters, books, and supplies

Perfection Learning Corporation
1000 N. Second Avenue
Logan, IA 51546-1099
www.perfectionlearning.com/
(800) 831-4190 (U.S. and Canada)

Books for a literature-based classroom including audio books, big books, software, videotapes and African American, multiethnic, Asian, Spanish, and Native American fiction K–6

Phillip Roy
13064 Indian Rocks Road
Largo, FL 33774
www.philliproy.com/
(800) 255-9085

Multimedia materials for use with adult basic education, alternative education, workplace literacy, transition from school to work, critical thinking skills

Positive Promotions
222 Ashland Place
Brooklyn, NY 11217
www.positivepromotions.com/
(800) 635-2666

Safety and health-related promotional materials, calendars, health guides, monthly planners, coloring books, pens, mugs, buttons

Scholastic Professional Books
557 Broadway
New York, NY 10012-3999
teacher.scholastic.com/professional/profbooks/
(800) 325-6149

Instructor books: integrated language arts, science, social studies, math, art; transition books for new educational strategies; reference library books; teaching strategies books

Sunburst
39 Washington Avenue
P.O. Box 40
Pleasantville, NY 10570-0040
www.sunburst.com/
(800) 431-1934

Videos for K–12, games, posters, curriculum modules for grades 2–12, staff development

Tom Snyder Productions
80 Coolidge Hill Road
Watertown, MA 02172-2817
www.tomsnyder.com/
(800) 342-0236

K–12 educational software, DVDs, CD-ROMs, books, time line tools, U.S. and world geography, history, reading and writing, language arts, music

Trend Enterprises
P.O. Box 64073
St. Paul, MN 55164
www.trendenterprises.com/
(800) 328-0818

Wipe-off manipulatives, awards, classroom decorations; early childhood helpers, posters, stickers, bulletin board sets, letters

United Art and Education Supply Co.
P.O. Box 9219
Fort Wayne, IN 46899
www.unitednow.com/
(800) 322-3247
(219) 478-1121
(800) 858-3247 from Canada

Paints, brushes, crayons, markers, drawing supplies, office supplies, crafts, puzzles, classroom management resources, holiday helpers, signing helpers; musical instruments, bulletin board materials

Zaner-Bloser
2200 W. Fifth Avenue
Columbus, OH 43272-4176
www.zaner-bloser.com/
(800) 421-3018

K–8; integrated language arts, science, critical thinking, self-esteem, decision making, substance abuse prevention, handwriting, spelling

Sources of Rubber Stamps

Anima Designs
www.animadesigns.com/
(800) 570-6847

Class Act Stamps
www.classact.ca/stamps_teach-fr.shtml

Hero Arts
www.heroarts.com/

Impress Rubber Stamps
www.impressrubberstamps.com/

Mari & Me
Mostly Asian themes
www.mariandme.com
(808) 373-7269

Personalized Rubber Stamps
www.custom-rubber-stamps-express.com
(877) 612-4145

Rhapsody in Rubber
www.rhapsodyinrubber.com/
(714) 952-3856

River City Rubber Works
www.rivercityrubberworks.com/
(877) 735-2276

Rubber Stampede
www.deltacrafts.com/RubberStampede/
(800) 423-4135

Rubber Stamps of America
www.stampusa.com/store.htm
(800) 553-5031

Sellos Foreign Language Rubber Stamps
www.sellosrubberstamps.com/

Stamps Happen
www.stampshappen.com/

Student Help

Allowing students to help with many classroom tasks not only saves valuable class time but also gives them an opportunity to assume responsibility and may help them feel needed and included. It may in some instances also give students a chance to learn new skills. The best time to introduce the idea of student assistance is the first week of school when you are establishing your classroom routines. Some tasks that teachers have delegated to students include the following:

Collecting papers, books, and materials

Tutoring other students

Collecting lunch money

Running errands

Tending classroom plants

Taking inventory of books, supplies, and so on

Picking up litter in the room

Rearranging desks and furniture

Erasing or cleaning chalkboards

Videotaping class presentations

Putting away lab equipment

Greeting classroom visitors

Tending fish and other pets

Straightening the bookcase

Collating papers

Distributing papers, materials, and so on

Constructing bulletin boards

Taking attendance

Filing papers

Running audiovisual equipment

Checking completed assignments

Constructing or arranging holiday decorations

Dusting erasers

Recording brainstormed ideas on the board or newsprint

Keeping time for class activities

Setting up experiments, demonstrations

Answering the telephone

Keeping the class calendar

Making in-school deliveries

Posting assignments and special events on the board

Some teachers ask for volunteers for each task as the need arises. Others allow students to sign up for a job for a week or month. Some draw names (or assigned numbers) whenever a role needs to be filled. Occasionally, teachers award particularly attractive jobs as rewards for outstanding performance. Some teachers assign teams of students to different responsibilities. In some classrooms every student is assigned a job on a rotating basis. Here are additional suggestions:

✓ Sometimes assigning groups of students to complete specific tasks can be successful. One elementary teacher assigned pairs to each task, trained each pair in the job, and then rotated the assignments on a staggered schedule every week, so that one person of each pair moved on to a new job. The experienced partner trained the new partner in the job.

✓ It is helpful to arrange a couple of brief after-school training sessions for some of the more demanding jobs, such as running audiovisual equipment. Demonstrate what needs to be done and then give the helpers a chance to practice. When delegating responsibilities be specific in communicating your expectations. Consider your students' capabilities and interests in assigning the more difficult jobs. Another possibility is to construct a job chart listing the various functions and the person responsible. You might color code it for easier reading.

✓ Some creative teachers draw up official-looking contracts with official-sounding names, like Director of Distribution or Multimedia Technician. The students sign the contracts, which detail their responsibilities and the duration of the agreement.

✓ Construct a board with the list of duties printed on the left side. On the right side, attach clips (or wooden slots) into which you insert cards with the names of the students assigned each task. To change duties each week, just rotate the name plates. (This works well in shop and art classes for cleanup assignments.)

✓ With some particularly hostile classes, you'll probably have a difficult time getting students to volunteer as teacher helpers. Their peers would put them down. It's probably best to privately ask individual students to do particular tasks as the need arises. The less official their role, the more likely they will comply with your request.

✓ Always remember to thank students for completing their tasks. For students who are particularly helpful, write them or their parents a note, award them a certificate, or allow them some small privilege as a thoughtful way to express your appreciation.

Teacher Time Survey

Directions: After reading each question, indicate whether it is generally true for you.

Do you frequently …

		Yes	No
1.	Have to rise early to prepare that day's classes?	___	___
2.	Set deadlines for yourself?	___	___
3.	Get up late?	___	___
4.	Stop in the lounge to socialize before classes begin?	___	___
5.	Fret and agonize when interruptions outside of your control occur?	___	___
6.	Begin classes on time?	___	___
7.	Visit the lounge between classes?	___	___
8.	Allow sufficient time at the end of the period (or day) for assignments, cleanup, summary activities, and so on?	___	___
9.	Disrupt your own classroom momentum?	___	___
10.	Begin the day without interest in what you are teaching?	___	___
11.	Teach lessons for which you are unsure of what you want the students to learn?	___	___
12.	Schedule tests, movies, and seatwork primarily to occupy students while you get caught up?	___	___
13.	Relate the amount of instructional time spent on a particular objective to its importance?	___	___
14.	Procrastinate grading papers and tests?	___	___
15.	Wait more than five minutes for staff meetings to begin?	___	___
16.	Write down ideas as they occur rather than relying on memory?	___	___
17.	Anticipate problems and alternative solutions to them?	___	___
18.	Handle extracurricular activities during the academic hours?	___	___
19.	Make decisions systematically rather than muddling through?	___	___
20.	Spend time complaining to peers?	___	___
21.	Run out of prepared lesson material before the period or day is over?	___	___
22.	Find yourself going to the office to duplicate materials more than once per day?	___	___
23.	Bring up unscheduled business at faculty meetings?	___	___
24.	Set reasonable limits on parent conferences?	___	___
25.	Use student volunteers to help with routine tasks of which they are capable?	___	___
26.	Copy information from one form to another?	___	___
27.	Use parent volunteers whenever possible to assist in instructional activities?	___	___

Teacher Time Survey *(continued)*

28. Spend instructional time dealing with disruptive behavior? ____ ____
29. Prevent duplicated effort by systematically filing and saving curricular materials, lesson plans, tests, and so on? ____ ____
30. Arrive late for meetings? ____ ____
31. Participate in a regular schedule of physical fitness? ____ ____
32. Get a sufficient amount of rest each night to begin each day fresh? ____ ____
33. Think of a creative idea, only to forget it later? ____ ____
34. Do work for which others are paid? ____ ____
35. Have a balance of interests including leisure activities apart from your teaching? ____ ____
36. Choose to do menial tasks, like stapling papers, as opposed to creative, productive tasks like designing new instructional strategies? ____ ____
37. Strive to handle each piece of paper only once? ____ ____
38. Set priorities each day for the things you have to do? ____ ____
39. Have to repeat directions to students? ____ ____
40. Lose material because of a poorly organized, cluttered desk? ____ ____
41. Fail to make assignments clear and specific? ____ ____
42. Attend classes or workshops to develop new teaching ideas? ____ ____
43. Maintain contingency lesson plans in case of emergencies, sickness, and so on? ____ ____
44. Share ideas with colleagues? ____ ____
45. Review your long-term professional goals? ____ ____
46. Have difficulty saying no to requests for your time? ____ ____
47. Fall prey to perfectionism? ____ ____
48. Use vacation days and weekends to catch up? ____ ____
49. Begin class late? ____ ____
50. Make planning time a top priority? ____ ____

Scoring instructions: Give yourself one point for each of the following items to which you responded "yes": 2, 6, 8, 16, 17, 19, 24, 25, 27, 29, 31, 32, 35, 37, 38, 42, 43, 44, 45, and 50. Give yourself one point for each of the following items to which you responded "no": 1, 3, 4, 5, 7, 9, 10, 11, 12, 13, 14, 15, 18, 20, 21, 22, 23, 26, 28, 30, 33, 34, 36, 39, 40, 41, 46, 47, 48, and 49.

Total the number of points and find your score on the following scale:

40–50   *Peak performer:* You are getting a high return on your investment of time and energy.
30–39   *Striver:* You are probably pretty effective but still have a few inefficiencies.
20–29   *Plodder:* You're making your job tougher than it needs to be.
0–19   *Struggler:* How do you get anything done? Serious time management problems impede your effectiveness.

School Interruption Survey

Directions: Using the scales under the subheadings, indicate when, how frequently, and how disruptive each of these interruptions is for you.

When	How Frequently	How Disruptive
BS = Before school	0 = Never	0 = Not at all
AS = After school	1 = Seldom	1 = A little
P = During planning period	2 = Occasionally	2 = Somewhat
C = During class time	3 = Quite frequently	3 = Quite
		4 = Constantly

Interruptions	When	How Frequently	How Disruptive
Messengers from:			
Principal's office	_____	_____	_____
Guidance office	_____	_____	_____
Other teachers	_____	_____	_____
The principal	_____	_____	_____
Former students	_____	_____	_____
Custodian	_____	_____	_____
Parents	_____	_____	_____
Other teachers	_____	_____	_____
Outside observers, visitors	_____	_____	_____
Aide or volunteer helper	_____	_____	_____
Classroom behavior disturbance	_____	_____	_____
Student(s) leaving class	_____	_____	_____
Student(s) arriving late	_____	_____	_____
Assemblies	_____	_____	_____
Standardized tests	_____	_____	_____
P.A. announcements	_____	_____	_____
Audiovisual equipment breakdowns	_____	_____	_____
Telephone calls	_____	_____	_____
Hallway traffic	_____	_____	_____
Noise from other classrooms	_____	_____	_____
Outdoor distractions:			
Weather events	_____	_____	_____
Animals	_____	_____	_____
People	_____	_____	_____
Street traffic	_____	_____	_____
Airplanes	_____	_____	_____
Sirens	_____	_____	_____
Other noise	_____	_____	_____
Your actions:			
Hunting for lost items	_____	_____	_____
Changing topics	_____	_____	_____
Going back to previous topic	_____	_____	_____
Publicly reprimanding student	_____	_____	_____

Place an asterisk (*) in front of the three interruptions you would most like to eliminate.

Attendance Record

Date _____

Teacher _____ Period _____

Name	Absent	Excused	Comments

Things to Do

Date _____

Today's Schedule		Activity	Priority	Done
7:00				
7:30				
8:00				
8:30				
9:00				
9:30				
10:00				
10:30				
11:00				
11:30				
12:00				
12:30				
1:00				
1:30				
2:00				
2:30				
3:00				
3:30				
4:00				
4:30				
5:00				

Evening:

Memo

Please do not disturb!

Testing in progress

Restroom Pass

Good for one five-minute visit to the restroom.

For emergency use only.

Restroom Pass

Good for one five-minute visit to the restroom.

For emergency use only.

Restroom Pass

Good for one five-minute visit to the restroom.

For emergency use only.

Hall Pass

Name _____ Date _____

From _____ To _____

Period _____

Reason for Pass:
- _____ Get a drink
- _____ Main office
- _____ To locker
- _____ Run errand
- _____ Tardy, please excuse
- _____ To see Mr/Ms
- _____ Guidance office
- _____ Restroom
- _____ Telephone
- _____ Do make-up work
- _____ To nurse

Teacher _____

Hall Pass

Name _____ Date _____

From _____ To _____

Period _____

Reason for Pass:
- _____ Get a drink
- _____ Main office
- _____ To locker
- _____ Run errand
- _____ Tardy, please excuse
- _____ To see Mr/Ms
- _____ Guidance office
- _____ Restroom
- _____ Telephone
- _____ Do make-up work
- _____ To nurse

Teacher _____

Hall Pass

Name _____ Date _____

From _____ To _____

Period _____

Reason for Pass:
- _____ Get a drink
- _____ Main office
- _____ To locker
- _____ Run errand
- _____ Tardy, please excuse
- _____ To see Mr/Ms
- _____ Guidance office
- _____ Restroom
- _____ Telephone
- _____ Do make-up work
- _____ To nurse

Teacher _____

Hall Pass

Name _____ Date _____

From _____ To _____

Period _____

Reason for Pass:
- _____ Get a drink
- _____ Main office
- _____ To locker
- _____ Run errand
- _____ Tardy, please excuse
- _____ To see Mr/Ms
- _____ Guidance office
- _____ Restroom
- _____ Telephone
- _____ Do make-up work
- _____ To nurse

Teacher _____

Teacher Time Log

Teacher _____ Date _____

Time	Activity	Importance	Comments

Things to Do

Date _____

Today's Schedule	Activity	Priority	Done
7:00			
7:30			
8:00			
8:30			
9:00			
9:30			
10:00			
10:30			
11:00			
11:30			
12:00			
12:30			
1:00			
1:30			
2:00			
2:30			
3:00			
3:30			
4:00			
4:30			
5:00			

Evening:

Memo:

Telephone Log

Date	Name	Phone	Comments

Weekly Schedule

Dates _____

Time	Monday	Tuesday	Wednesday	Thursday	Friday

Book Sign-out Record

Teacher _____

Name	Book Title	Date Out	Date In

End-of-Year Checklist

_____ Turn in grades.

_____ Collect any book damage fees.

_____ Select and turn in any books in need of repair.

_____ Take home plants and animals.

_____ Store textbooks.

_____ Make a list of needed supplies for next fall.

_____ Submit list of room repairs needed.

_____ Submit items to file in students' cumulative folders.

_____ Order textbooks for next year.

_____ Back up all critical computer files.

_____ Take home a backup disk of crucial files.

_____ Delete outdated e-mails.

_____ Run an antivirus program on your computers.

_____ Delete unneeded documents and programs from computers.

_____ Unplug all computers and peripherals.

_____ Inventory all hardware and peripherals.

_____ Cover computers and printers with cloths to shield from dust.

_____ Return all library books.

_____ Return all audiovisual equipment to media center.

_____ Take home any files and materials needed to plan for next year.

_____ Secure any confidential files.

_____ Organize and file any papers and folders to save.

_____ Send thank-you notes to volunteers, support staff, and others.

_____ Throw out papers and materials no longer needed.

_____ Complete any required paperwork for the principal.

_____ Pack and label any items to be moved.

_____ Jot down successful teaching ideas to use next year.

_____ Turn in keys if required.

_____ Celebrate!

Chapter Seven

Helpful Teaching Resources

The Internet as a Learning Resource

Since 1990 approximately two billion dollars have been spent to put an additional two million computers in America's schools. According to a 2003 U.S. Census Bureau report, over 13.6 million computers are available for classroom use in the nation's elementary and secondary schools, providing one computer for every four students. The advent of cyberspace and the explosive expansion of the information superhighway have the potential to profoundly influence American education. Though they will never replace effective teachers, in the coming decade computers will play an increasingly dramatic role in reshaping teaching.

Schools throughout the nation, indeed the world, are plugging into the Internet. The global classroom is fast becoming a reality. Thousands of classrooms already have access to the Internet, and many more are joining each month. A number of states have already made a commitment to connecting every school to the Internet.

The Internet is a worldwide collection of computer networks connecting millions of computers to one another. By the end of 2003, the search engine Google indexed almost 3.5 billion text documents, which doesn't include images and multimedia files. The Internet is an enormous learning resource of almost unimaginable potential for enhancing education. By the beginning of 2004, a Pew Foundation survey found that 63 percent of U.S. adults were Internet users.

Many teachers and students have already discovered exciting, creative, and productive applications of this technological revolution. Those who do not obtain access to the Internet will surely be at a disadvantage. The Internet holds tremendous promise for use in all aspects of education: administration, instruction, professional development, and community involvement. Students in the most remote schools in the nation can soon have the world at their fingertips.

Professional development opportunities abound with the Internet. Every day teachers can interact with others teaching the same subjects and facing the same problems. Collaboration with teachers halfway around the world can be facilitated. Discussion groups already exist for virtually every topic being taught in school. Via e-mail, teachers have direct access to top experts in virtually every field. The potential for using the Internet as a tool to enrich global and cultural awareness is unlimited.

Millions of files are open to your use as teaching resources, including guides and images for use in the classroom. Students can directly communicate with students from other countries and states.

Here is just a sampling of what you can find on the Internet:

✓ The Library of Congress offers photographic and sound collections from both the American Memory Project and the African-American Culture and History online exhibit, as well as access to LOCIS (the Library of Congress Information System). Access to the Library of Congress catalog is also available (locis.loc.gov).

✓ EdWeb Project (www.edwebproject.org/) is an online tutorial for K–12 educators concerned with the use of telecommunications in teaching. The site provides success stories of computers in the classroom.

✓ Opportunities exist for students to engage in cross-cultural language exchanges with French, Russian, Spanish, Japanese, or German students. For example, see Intercultural E-mail Classroom Connections at www.iecc.org/.

✓ Global Lab (globallab.terc.edu/) permits students around the world to share ecological data over the Internet. Students collaborate on scientific investigations, using a local study site for authentic, hands-on, integrated science investigations.

✓ An assortment of electronic publications—journals, books, newsletters, newspapers, and digests—is available through the Internet. The full text of these publications is available for online reading or retrieval as portable document format (PDF) files. Many are listed at the end of this chapter and in Chapter Six.

✓ The daily CNN Newsroom (www.turnerlearning.com/newsroom/) curriculum guide is a valuable source of teaching ideas. CNN Student News provides schools with a thirty-minute broadcast program and a supporting Web site filled with interesting curriculum materials related to current events.

✓ The Educator's Reference Desk (www.eduref.org/) provides a wide assortment of information to educators. The site houses over two thousand lesson plans and more than three thousand links to online education information.

✓ Thomas (thomas.loc.gov), the Internet link to documents from the House of Representatives and Senate, provides full texts of the *Congressional Record* and information on pending legislation.

✓ Log into NASA's SpaceLink (spacelink.nasa.gov/), a searchable database of educational materials and information related to NASA Aeronautics and Space Research.

✓ Images can be downloaded from the National Oceanic and Atmospheric Administration, National Climate Research Center, or the National Weather Service (www.nws.noaa.gov) to study weather patterns. Global weather changes can be observed almost as they are occurring.

✓ World War II Resources (www.ibiblio.org/pha/) houses hundreds of primary source materials regarding all aspects of the war.

✓ The Perry-Castañeda Library Map Collection (www.lib. utexas.edu/maps/index.html) at the University of Texas at Austin holds an extensive collection of maps from every area of the world. Many items in the collection can be downloaded as JPEG files.

✓ Daily White House press releases and briefings are available online at www.whitehouse.gov.

✓ A computerized cadaver is available through the Visible Human Project at the National Library of Medicine. Magnetic resonance imaging and computerized tomography were used to scan nineteen hundred slices of the corpse of a 205-pound man. Portions of this database may be viewed at www.nlm.nih.gov/.

E-mail

E-mail is the most frequent use of computer networks. In November 2003 an estimated 513 million e-mail users worldwide were sending and receiving over fifty-seven billion e-mail messages each day.

Any Internet user can send text messages to any other computer user with an Internet address. A variety of directories can help locate another user's Internet address (one directory is Switchboard at switchboard.com). Software such as Eudora or Outlook Express make sending and receiving e-mail messages much easier. You can also attach files to your messages. Messages are stored in a mailbox or holding file until you log in and read your messages.

Here are just a few of e-mail's educational applications:

✓ Some students practice their new foreign language skills by communicating with native students speaking that language.

✓ Anyone can send messages to the president or vice president through e-mail (president@whitehouse.gov or vpresident@whitehouse.gov).

✓ Often the top experts in any field of study can be contacted by e-mail.

✓ Many schools use electronic pen-pal connections to learn more about other cultures.

Electronic Discussion Groups

Thousands of e-mail discussion groups cover almost every conceivable topic, including scores of groups related to education. To participate in discussions, a user must first subscribe to the listserv. The process may vary somewhat, but generally one sends an e-mail to the subscription address with the message "subscribe NAME OF GROUP First name Last name." For example: "subscribe MIDDLE-L Janet Smith" (without the quotes) would get Janet Smith subscribed to the Middle-L discussion group.

Several excellent Web sites catalog the thousands of discussion groups. These are among the most comprehensive directories:

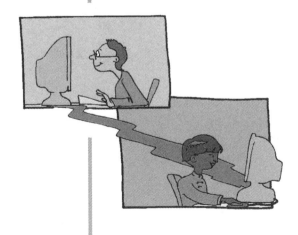

Classroom Connect
www.classroom.com/community/email/

EdWeb K–12 Resource Guide
http://www.edwebproject.org/lists.html

K12Net
www.ggw.org/freenet/k/K12Net/

Liszt Directory of Listservs and Usenet Groups
www.liszt.com

TeacherNet
teachers.net/mailrings/

USENET Discussion Groups
www.edwebproject.org/usenets.html

Yahoo Groups
groups.yahoo.com/

Some Popular Online Education Discussion Groups

Title	Topic	Subscription E-mail Address
ACSOFT-L	Educational software	listserv@wuvmd.wustl.edu
ADHD	Attention deficit hyperactive disorder	CatEyes627-subscribe@topica.com
ADMIN	Educational administration	listproc@bgu.edu
BGEDU-L	Educational reform	bgedu-1@ukcc.uky.edu
BIOPI-L	Teaching biology	listserv@ksuvm.ksu.edu.
BLUEWEBN	List of top education sites	majordomo@lists.sdsu.edu
CHATBACK	Special education	listserv@sjuvm.stjohns.edu
ECENET-L	Early childhood education	listserv@listserv.uiuc.edu
ED1VIDCONF	Videoconferencing in teaching	listserver@pacbell.com
EDUTEL	Educational technology	listserv@vm.its.rpi.edu
EFFSCHPRAC	Effective school practices	mailserv@oregon.uoregon.edu
ELED-L	Elementary education	listserv@ksuvm.ksu.edu
E-PALS	E-mail buddies for classes	E_Pals-subscribe@topica.com
FLTEACH	Teaching foreign languages	listserv@ubvm.cc.buffalo.edu
FTT	Free teacher tools	ftt-subscribe@topica.com
HILITES	Online collaboration	gsn-hilites-list-subscribe@topica.com
INTER-L	Internet in education	listproc2@bgu.edu
GEOGED	Geography education	listserv@ukcc.uky.edu
K12MATH	Math instruction	k12math@k12groups.org
L-ACLRNG	Active and collaborative learning	listserv@lists.psu.edu
MEMO-NET	Educational media	listserv@vax1.mankato.msus.edu
MIDDLE-L	Middle-level education	listserv@postoffice.cso.uiuc.edu
MULT-ED	Multicultural education	listproc@gmu.edu
PHYSHARE	Teaching high school physics	listserv@lists.psu.edu
PROJECTS-L	Project-based learning	listserv@listserv.uiuc.edu
TAG-L	Talented and gifted education	listserv@listserv.nodak.edu
TEACHEFT	Teacher effectiveness	listserv@wcupa.edu
TEACH-LING	Teaching linguistics	listproc@lists.nyu.edu
TEACHMEDIA	Teaching multimedia	teachmedia-subscribe@topica.com
TECHED	Technology education	teched-subscribe@topica.com
VOCNET	Vocational education	listserv@cmsa.berkeley.edu

Online Resources for Beginning Teachers

Advice for first-year teachers
Education World
www.education-world.com/a_curr/curr152.shtml

Beginning teachers' resources
Los Angeles County Office of Education
lacoe.edu/documentation/places/newteachers.html

Beginning teacher's toolbox
Inspiring Teachers
www.inspiringteachers.com/

First Years e-mail list for student and beginning teachers
D & W's Teacher Spot
www.ametro.net/~teachers/home.html

Ideas for new teachers and education students
ADPRIMA
www.adprima.com/ideamenu.htm

New teachers' place
Teacher Focus
www.teacherfocus.com

Teacher tap
ICATS: Integrating Teaching and Technology
www.eduscapes.com/tap/

What to expect your first year of teaching
U.S. Department of Education
www.ed.gov/pubs/FirstYear/foreword.html

Online Lesson Plan Archives

Boggle's World
bogglesworld.com

Lessons for teachers of elementary and middle school English

Collaborative Lesson Archive, University of Illinois
ccb.atmos.uiuc.edu

Browse lessons by grade level or by subject.

Cool Teaching Lessons and Units
www.coollessons.org/coolunits.htm

Emphasizes hands-on learning projects

Educator's Network
www.theeducatorsnetwork.com/

A huge treasury of teacher resources and tools

Educator's Reference Desk
(formerly AskERIC Education Information)
www.eduref.org/

Over two thousand unique lesson plans submitted by teachers

Federal Resources for Educational Excellence
www.ed.gov/free/

Teaching and learning resources from thirty federal agencies

Gateway to Educational Materials
www.thegateway.org/

Thousands of educational materials, including lesson plans, projects, and activities

Lesson Plans Page
LessonPlansPage.com/

Over two thousand free lessons

Math and science lessons, The Eisenhower National Clearinghouse for
Mathematics and Science Education
www.enc.org/

Teaching units, activity books, and lab manuals

Mathematics lesson plans, National Council of Teachers of Mathematics
illuminations.nctm.org/index.html

Internet resources for teaching math

New York Times Lesson Plans Archive (grades 6–12)
www.nytimes.com/learning/teachers/lessons/archive.html

Search by subject or grade.

Science NetLinks
www.sciencenetlinks.com/matrix.cfm

Outstanding science lessons

Online Collaborative Learning Resources

Center for Improved Engineering and Science Education
k12science.ati.stevens-tech.edu/collabprojs.html

Hands-on math and science projects

Connectivity Programs Online Collaborative Projects
www.projectharmony.org

Projects promoting multicultural awareness, knowledge, and perspective

EPal Classroom Exchange
www.epals.com/newsletters/august2002/

Claims to be the largest online classroom community; students from 191 countries participate in ePal programs.

Global SchoolNet Foundation
www.globalschoolnet.org

Lists over 750 online collaborative learning projects

Online Collaborative Education Projects
www.globalclassroom.org/collaboration/

Projects connect students around the world.

OzProjects
ozprojects.edna.edu.au/

This Australian site promotes international online curriculum projects.

Schools Online
www.schoolsonline.org/whatwedo/

Projects emphasize cross-cultural dialogue.

SchoolWorld Internet Education
www.schoolworld.asn.au/projects.html

This group has provided free educational resources and services to over fifty thousand schools in eighty-three countries.

Online Collaborative Learning Projects

Widespread access to the Internet in classrooms has made possible collaborative learning activities with students across town or around the globe. Online collaborative projects engage and motivate students, challenging them to solve hands-on, real-world problems. Here are a few useful Web sites for getting started in online collaborative learning:

Kids Video Collaboration Project
www.schoolsonline.org/whatwedo/cprojects.htm

Students from around the world make and exchange video postcards, featuring three aspects of their countries' environment: preservation, waste management, and national parks.

Hooked on Books
www.kidlink.org/KIDPROJ/Books/

The Hooked on Books project inspires middle school students to read books, reflect, and share their favorites with other students—in their class, within their country, and from other nations.

Looking for Dark Skies
www.millennium.scps.k12.fl.us/mailform700/darkskieshome.html

Middle school and high school students around the world are participating in Looking for Dark Skies, which explores light pollution by promoting research and mapping of nighttime skies and ambient light levels. Students from locations around the globe exchange their data and create Web sites discussing lighting laws, health and environmental impacts, and responsible outdoor lighting.

Nonprofit Prophets
www.kn.sbc.com/wired/prophets/

This community action project challenges student teams to explore problems that they select and to create a Web site to teach others about the issues.

Rock Swap
www.fi.edu/fellows/payton/rocks/collab.htm

This online collaborative project requires students to collect and identify rocks. Students exchange golf ball–sized rocks with other students participating in the global learning experience.

The Way We Are
www.epals.com/projects/thewayweare

Classrooms from many nations become acquainted through this online twinning project. Students exchange views by e-mail on school life, environmental issues, human rights, and their social lives. The program is available in both French and English.

Youth in Action
www.teaching.com/act/

This project encourages students to select significant social and environmental issues for exploration and to take action in the form of contacting the media, signing petitions, or conducting surveys. A variety of discussion forums encourage students to exchange views with young folks from around the world.

Educational Search Engines

Ask Jeeves for Kids
www.ajkids.com/

Kid-friendly filtered search engine

The Awesome Library
www.neat-schoolhouse.org/searche.html

Includes the top 5 percent of education resource sites

KidsClick!
sunsite.berkeley.edu/KidsClick!/

Web search engine created by librarians

OneKey, The Kid Safe Search Engine
www.onekey.com/

Accesses Google's kids' search engine

SurfSafely.com
www.surfsafely.com/

Allows schools to configure browser controls to set appropriate viewing levels

Useful Online Databases

A vast array of easily accessible databases may be found on the Internet. Creative teachers incorporate online research of these treasures into their lessons.

Smithsonian Institution: The Smithsonian Institution (www.si.edu/) provides an assortment of information and pictures on the Internet. Teachers and students may access hundreds of stimulating online exhibits.

Access to Libraries: Teachers and students can access online library catalogs and databases at virtually every major library in the United States, including the Library of Congress, and many in other nations. Databases such as ERIC, the world's largest collection of information about education, can be accessed. For example, Harvard's libraries can be accessed at lib.harvard.edu/ and Stanford University's libraries at www-sul.stanford.edu/.

Song Lyrics: The Lyrics Connection (www.lyricsconnection.com/index.html) provides a search function to locate song lyrics, biographies, and discographies. The Digital Tradition (www.mudcat.org/) is an Internet archive containing the lyrics and music to thousands of folk songs and children's songs.

Tutorials and Lessons: Workshops and courses are available over the Internet. Thousands of learners can participate simultaneously in a broad and rapidly expanding array of tutorial programs. Its use as a virtual classroom is likely to increase in the coming decade. The paperless classroom is not beyond imagination. The electronic town hall meeting is fast becoming a reality. For example, Mr. Shakespeare and the Internet (shakespeare.palomar.edu) organizes anything and everything about the Bard and his works, from full-text files of his plays and sonnets to an assortment of lesson plans. Check out the Shakespeare Biography Quiz.

E-books: Project Gutenberg (promo.net/pg/) is a master depository of over six thousand e-books, full texts available over the Internet.

Facts and Figures: The *CIA World Factbook* (www.cia.gov/cia/) provides current information on the nations of the world. Access it online or download the book as a PDF file. The U.S. Census Bureau (www.census.gov/) offers a mass of data on the decennial census, as well as approximately a hundred surveys and other census analyses conducted each year. View, download, and print a vast library of maps covering virtually any U.S. address.

NASA: NASA (www.nasa.gov/home/index.html) provides the educational community a virtual library of space- and aeronautical-related files and links. Special events, missions, and intriguing NASA Web sites are featured in Spacelink's Hot Topics and Cool Picks areas.

Software and shareware: Download hundreds of freeware and shareware programs from Pass the Shareware (www.shareware.com). All programs are scanned for viruses, tested, and rated. Macintosh users can find a large depository of freeware and shareware at (macware.erehwon.org/).

Telescopes in Education: The Telescopes in Education program (tie.jpl.nasa.gov/tie/) demonstrates desktop astronomy and astrophysics to students. Two remote automatic telescope systems are available online, as well as an archive of images from the Mt. Wilson Observatory (www.mtwilson.edu/).

Tips on Getting Started on the Internet

Exploring the Internet has become an easy process. User-friendly search engines and more sophisticated browsers have made the Internet more inviting to nontechies. Two challenges face the teacher wanting to capitalize on the opportunities of cyberspace: getting access to the Internet and finding your way around the massive network of

networks. Fortunately, both tasks are getting easier by the week. With perseverance, leading-edge teachers excited at the prospects of surfing the Internet can find many treasures awaiting them.

✓ An Internet account is required for access. Most universities, colleges, and schools already are connected to the Internet; and many states have statewide networks. Access can also be gained through independent vendors. Seek a local resource person who can help you discover the options available in your area.

✓ Finding a mentor to help you learn the intricacies of Internet access and navigation will save you a lot of time and frustration. Most schools have several people who are already experimenting with the Internet. Don't be afraid to ask students for help. Many are quite advanced in their computer literacy by the time they begin school.

✓ Local universities or colleges are also good sources for help. Many offer workshops on getting started on the Internet. Some state departments of education are also providing training opportunities.

✓ A variety of books and guides are available to help you through the maze of the Internet. Some are available free and can be accessed online. Several helpful resources are listed in Helpful Books on Using the Internet; read at least one.

✓ A variety of free tutorials designed for teachers learning to use the Internet are available online. The Microsoft Insider Internet Guide (www.microsoft.com/insider/) is a good example.

✓ Don't worry about trying to learn every aspect of the Internet at once. Work on developing some comfort with one function, such as e-mail. There is a learning curve to work through. You will gradually develop additional expertise.

✓ Don't be afraid to experiment. Explore files and connections to see what is available.

✓ Be patient. Access to the Internet is becoming faster, simpler, and cheaper. The Internet is already having a profound effect on education. The early users or pathfinders will stay on the cutting edge of this exciting new technology and will play a role in defining how it is used.

✓ Set time limits on how much you will stay on the Internet. Fascination with the masses of interesting sites can consume hours of your time. It is best to save such experimenting for your leisure time. Internet addiction is one of the newest psychological disorders!

✓ Most of the excellent resources listed discuss *netiquette,* Internet etiquette. Over a million people use the Internet each day. For many it is an integral part of their jobs. Only courtesy and sensible use of the Internet will keep the system flowing smoothly.

Online Directories

Numerous online catalogs describing Internet services and resources are available, many of these on the Internet. Some of the more helpful ones include the following:

About.com, the Human Internet
about.com/

Over one million links to the finest Internet sites, covering over fifty thousand subjects, are conveniently organized into twenty-three channels.

CMC Information Services
www.december.com/cmc/info/

Also known as the December List, this contains annotated links to Web sites dealing with computer-mediated communication technology. It provides numerous links to resources on how to learn about how to use the Internet.

Kathy Schrock's Guide for Educators
school.discovery.com/schrockguide

This is a must-see site for all professional educators. Its neatly cate-gorized list of sites offers links to useful curriculum and profes-sional growth information.

KidsClick!
www.kidsclick.org/

Created by a group of librarians, this outstanding site leads users to good sites. However, it does not block them from "bad" sites. Use this in conjunction with a filter product if you are using it with children.

Librarians' Index to the Internet
lii.org/

Driven by the motto "Information you can trust," this top-notch portal selects the best of the Web, excluding purely commercial sites that offer no information. Updated weekly, this site is a good starting point for scholarly information seeking.

Yahoo
www.yahoo.com/

Yahoo is one of the oldest and largest Internet directories, offering an extensive master index to much of what is available on the World Wide Web.

Helpful Books on Using the Internet

Ackermann, E. C., & Hartman, K. (2001). *Internet and Web essentials: What you need to know.* Wilsonville, OR: Franklin, Beedle & Associates.

Fallon, T. J. (2001). *The Internet today.* Upper Saddle River, NJ: Prentice Hall.

Lehnert, W. G. (2003). *Web 101: Making the 'Net work for you* (2nd ed.). Boston: Addison-Wesley.

Levine, J. R., Levine Young, M., & Baroudi, C. (2003). *The Internet For Dummies* (9th ed.). Hoboken, NJ.

Roblyer, M. D. (2003). *Starting out on the Internet: A learning journey for teachers.* Upper Saddle River, NJ: Merrill/Prentice Hall.

Snell, N. (2002). *Sams teach yourself the Internet in twenty-four hours.* Indianapolis, IN: Sams.

Organizations Supporting Educational Use of the Internet

Educator's Reference Desk
Information Institute of Syracuse
Syracuse University
621 Skytop Road, Suite 160
Syracuse, NY 13244-5290
Internet: www.eduref.org/
E-mail: iis@iis.syr.edu

Consortium for School Networking
1112 Sixteenth Street, NW, Suite 600
Washington, DC 20036
Internet: www.cosn.org
E-mail: cosn@bitnic.bitnet

The Global SchoolNet Foundation
7040 Avenida Encinas 104-281
Carlsbad, CA 92009
Internet: www.globalschoolnet.org
E-mail: andresyv@cerf.net

The National Science Foundation
4201 Wilson Boulevard
Arlington, VA 22230
Internet: www.nsf.gov

Internet Society
12020 Sunrise Valley Drive, Suite 270
Reston, VA 22091
Internet: www.isoc.org
E-mail: isoc@nri.reston.va.us

Glossary of Internet-Related Terms

bandwidth: The amount of data that can flow through a connection at a given time. Usually measured in bits per second (bps).

broadband: High-speed data transmission. The most readily available broadband connections are through cable modems (using a cable TV line) and DSL modems (using regular telephone lines).

browser: Software that serves as an interface between the user and the World Wide Web. When a user seeks information, a browser contacts an Internet site and requests, retrieves, and displays the requested information. Microsoft Internet and Netscape Navigator are the two most popular browsers.

chatting: Communicating in real time to other network users from anywhere in the world.

database: A collection of organized information that can be searched to retrieve data of interest.

download: To transfer information or files from one computer to another.

e-mail: Electronic mail. The computer function that allows individuals to exchange personal messages via a computer network. Through e-mail any person on the Internet can communicate directly with any other person on the Internet.

firewall: Hardware and software that restricts the kinds of messages a computer sends to and receives from the rest of the Internet. Used for security purposes.

freeware: Software that is available without charge but on which the creator holds the copyright. Usually, you may acquire freeware and give it to others but may not sell it.

FAQ: Frequently asked questions. These informational files posted on many Web sites are a good starting point for information about site content.

FTP: File transfer protocol. As a noun FTP refers to the procedure by which files can be transferred from one computer to another over the Internet. Sometimes FTP is used as a verb, meaning to transfer a file via the Internet.

GIF: Graphics interface format. A software format for economically storing screen images. Used frequently in Web page design.

HTML: Hypertext markup language. The computer coding language in which World Wide Web pages are transferred.

intranet: An internal computer network designed for use within a school or other organization.

JPEG: Joint Photographic Experts Group. A compression format that shrinks the size of image files, requiring less storage space and allowing easier Internet transfer.

listserv: Software that allows an Internet user to subscribe to a particular discussion group.

login: To sign on to a computer in order to access its software. A password may also be required.

newsreader: Software that permits selection of newsgroups to monitor and select specific articles to read.

public domain: Computer software and other work that is not copyrighted. There is no restriction on the use, distribution, or modification of works in the public domain. Many computer user clubs maintain large depositories of public domain software. Many programs can also be downloaded from archives through the Internet.

shareware: Software that you may use before you decide whether to buy it. If you decide to keep it after the trial period, you are honor-bound to send a small fee to the creator. You may make copies to give others to try out but may not sell it.

spam: Junk mail. Unsolicited messages sent via e-mail or a discussion group to a large group of people. Also used as a verb to denote the sending of unsolicited junk e-mail.

TIFF: Tagged interchangeable file format. Bitmap graphics format often used for high-resolution PostScript printing. Specified as TIF for use on PCs or TIFF with Macintosh computers.

URL: Uniform resource locator. The URL is the address that defines where a resource is located on the World Wide Web.

USENET: A network of discussion groups accessible through an Internet connection's newsreader.

virus: A small software program or scripts that can negatively affect the operation of an infected computer. They are often transmitted by e-mail attachments. Antivirus programs (such as Norton AntiVirus, McAfee VirusScan, and Virex) scan incoming files for viruses before they can infect a computer.

Web site: An online document created for viewing through a Web browser. Usually written in HTML.

A menu-driven search system that creates direct links between related resources. A most useful and timesaving tool for browsing the Internet.

Computer Software for Improving Teacher Productivity

The prices listed here were accurate in the spring of 2004. They may vary with time and by vendor.

Certificate Maker
$39.95 (Macintosh, Windows)
Springboard Software, Inc.
7808 Creekridge Circle
Minneapolis, MN 55435
(612) 944-3915

Create a variety of certificates.

Class Action Gradebook
$29.00 (Macintosh, Windows)
CalEd Software
www.classactiongradebook.com/

Grade book, seating charts, proficiency reports, and more

Classmaster
$66.00 (Macintosh, Windows)
William K. Bradford Publishing Co.
www.wkbradford.com/classmast.htm

Grade weighting, attendance, individual progress reports, graphs, and reports for parents

Crossword Compiler
$45.00 (Windows)
www.crossword-compiler.com/
info@crossword-compiler.com

Make your own crossword puzzles.

Crossword Construction Kit
$29.95 (Windows)
Insight Software Solutions
www.crosswordkit.com/
(801) 927-5009

Design crossword puzzles.

Excelsior Gradebook2
$49.99 (Macintosh, Windows)
Excelsior Software, Inc.
www.gradebook.com/

Keep grades and attendance records, individual student mastery of objectives.

Gradebook Plus
$64.95 (Macintosh, Windows)
SVE & Churchill Media

www.svemedia.com/gb/
(800) 829-1900

Calculate student grades, class performance, summary reports.

Gradekeeper
$20.00 (Macintosh, Windows)
www.gradekeeper.com/

Record grades and attendance.

Grade Machine
$104.00 (Macintosh, Windows)
Misty City Software
www.mistycity.com
(800) 795-0049

Grade keeping and reports

Grade Quick!
$69.95 (Macintosh, Windows, Palm)
Jackson Software
www.jacksonsoftware.com/
(800) 850-1777

Automated electronic gradebook, attendance, progress reports

Inspiration
$54.00 (Macintosh, Windows)
Inspiration Software
www.inspiration.com/
(800) 877-4292

Electronic graphic organizer tool; draws concept maps

Lesson Plan Locker
$14.95 (Windows)
www.lessonplanlocker.com

Create and organize lesson plans.

Lesson Planner II
Price not available (Windows)
New Intelligence Inc.
www.newintel.com
(888) 745-4151

Create and print lesson plans, address lists, and mailing labels.

Making the Grade
$99.95 single user (Macintosh, Windows)
Jay Klein Productions
www.gradebusters.com/jayklein.htm
(888) 665-4046

Grade keeping, attendance records

MicroGrade
$89.95 (Macintosh, Windows)
Chariot Software Group
www.chariot.com/micrograde/index.asp
(619) 491-0021

Score assignments, calculate grades, generate performance reports.

MicroTest III
$89.00 (Macintosh, Windows)
Chariot Software Group
www.chariot.com
(619) 491-0021

Test bank holds up to fifteen thousand items; customize tests.

Puzzlemaker
$49.95 (Macintosh, Windows)
Discovery Channel School
shopping.discovery.com
(877) 900-8830

Generate twelve kinds of word and math puzzles.

School Maestro II
$39.00 (Windows)
Russ & Ryan EdWare
www.rredware.com
(989) 727-2066

Advanced gradebook software. Students and parents can access online progress reports, attendance reports, and homework assignments.

Test Maestro II
$35.00 (Windows)
Russ & Ryan EdWare
www.rredware.com
(989) 727-2066

Test bank and test generator for teachers.

Test Pro Developer
$100.00 (Windows)
Atrixware
www.atrixware.com
(609) 634-2790

Develop paper or online tests and flash cards.

ThoughtManager for Education
$39.00 (Macintosh, Windows, Palm)
Hands High Software
www.thoughtmanager.com/html/

Create and organize lesson plans, lectures, and learning activities. Record student learning with standards-based checklists and rubrics. Manage classroom activities.

WebQuiz XP
$105.00 (Windows)
SmartLite Software
www.smartlite.it

Create online quizzes, tests, and surveys.

Word Search Construction Kit
$24.95 (Windows)
Insight Software Solutions
www.crosswordkit.com/
(801) 927-5009

Design word search puzzles.

Other Books of Interest

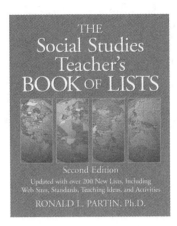

The Social Studies Teacher's Book of Lists

2nd Edition
Ronald L. Partin, Ph.D.

Paper/448 pages/2003
ISBN: 0-7879-6590-1

This unique information source and time-saver for social studies teachers provides more than 550 useful lists for developing instructional materials and planning for students from the fourth through the twelfth grades. This updated and expanded edition contains 200 new lists!

For quick access and easy use, all of these lists are organized into seven sections corresponding to seven areas of the social studies curriculum, numbered consecutively, and printed in a format that can be photocopied as many times as required for individual or group instruction.

This book is filled with illuminating facts, startling statistics, practical checklists, and relevant research findings, which will enhance social studies courses. In each section of this resource you'll find interesting and challenging information to enrich and enhance your social studies classes on topics such as:

- United States History
- World History
- American Government
- Consumer Economics
- Sociology
- Psychology
- Geography

The National Council for the Social Studies has established ten interdisciplinary thematic standards that encompass the subject areas of social studies. The lists provided in this book can augment instruction in at least one and often several of these ten thematic standards.

Ronald L. Partin, Ph.D., is a professor emeritus from the College of Education at Bowling Green State University. He lives, writes, and consults in the mountains of Western North Carolina.

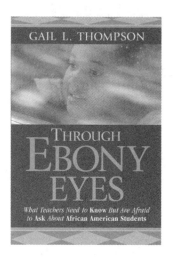

Through Ebony Eyes:
What Teachers Need to Know But Are Afraid to Ask About African American Students

Gail L. Thompson

Cloth/352 pages/2004
ISBN: 0-7879-7061-1

"For those teachers, administrators, and researchers who deal with culturally sensitive issues, *Through Ebony Eyes* is a powerful tool. Gail Thompson writes with passion and authority on teachers' beliefs and attitudes regarding African American students, and how these affect their instructional practices and achievement. Her research and observations are insightful, and her recommendations essential."

—James P. Comer, M.D., Maurice Falk Professor of
Child Psychiatry, Yale Child Study Center,
associate dean, School of Medicine

In this book, Gail L. Thompson takes on the volatile topic of the role of race in education and explores the black-white achievement gap and the cultural divide that exists between some teachers and African American students. Solidly based on research conducted with 175 educators, *Through Ebony Eyes* provides information and strategies that will help teachers increase their effectiveness with African American students. Written in conversational language, *Through Ebony Eyes* offers a wealth of examples and personal stories that clearly demonstrate the cultural differences that exist in the schools and offers a three-part, long-term professional development plan that will help teachers become more effective.

Gail L. Thompson is associate professor of education at Claremont Graduate University. Her research has focused on the schooling experiences of students of color. She is the author of *African American Teens Discuss Their Schooling Experiences* and *What African American Parents Want Educators to Know*, as well as numerous journal articles.

Other Books of Interest

Teaching with Fire:
Poetry that Sustains the Courage to Teach

Sam M. Intrator and Megan Scribner

Cloth/256 pages/2003
ISBN: 0-7879-6970-2

"*Teaching with Fire* is a glorious collection of the poetry that has restored the faith of teachers in the highest, most transcendent values of their work with children. . . . Those who want us to believe that teaching is a technocratic and robotic skill devoid of art or joy or beauty need to read this powerful collection. So, for that matter, do we all."

—Jonathan Kozol, author of
Amazing Grace and Savage Inequalities

Those of us who care about the young and their education must find ways to remember what teaching and learning are really about. We must find ways to keep our hearts alive as we serve our students. Poetry has the power to keep us vital and focused on what really matters in life and in schooling.

Teaching with Fire is a wonderful collection of eighty-eight poems from well-loved poets such as Walt Whitman, Langston Hughes, Billy Collins, Emily Dickinson, and Pablo Neruda. Each of these evocative poems is accompanied by a brief story from a teacher explaining the significance of the poem in his or her life's work. This beautiful book also includes an essay that describes how poetry can be used to grow both personally and professionally.

Teaching with Fire was written in partnership with the Center for Teacher Formation and the Bill & Melinda Gates Foundation. Royalties will be used to fund scholarship opportunities for teachers to grow and learn.

Sam M. Intrator is assistant professor of education and child study at Smith College. He is a former high school teacher and administrator and the son of two public school teachers. He is the editor of *Stories of the Courage to Teach* and author of *Tuned In and Fired Up: How Teaching Can Inspire Real Learning in the Classroom*.

Megan Scribner is a freelance writer, editor, and program evaluator who has conducted research on what sustains and empowers the lives of teachers. She is the mother of two children and PTA president of their elementary school in Takoma Park, Maryland.

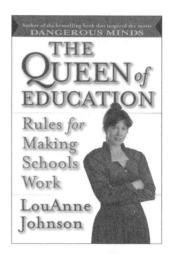

The Queen of Education:
Rules for Making Schools Work

LouAnne Johnson

Cloth/272 pages/2004
ISBN: 0-7879-7470-6

Down-to-earth advice about fixing schools from someone who's wrestled with tough kids and even tougher adults.

This book offers a vision of what school should be—from the gutsy teacher whose life and best-selling book inspired the movie *Dangerous Minds*. LouAnne Johnson is a passionate advocate for schools that are less bureaucratic and more child-centered, arguing for schools that are smaller, healthier, more humane, and more attuned to different learning styles. In doing so, she reveals little-known facts about growing problems—such as ADHD and illiteracy—that, in some cases, have some surprising remedies. For example, the misbehaving boy who simply has an undiagnosed reading problem, or the withdrawn girl who blossoms when allowed to express herself through journal writing. LouAnne is clearly fed up with an educational system that is too quick to label and write-off children who don't fit the mold. Yet, in story after story, she shows how a compassionate teacher, counselor, or parent can cut through the red tape and make a crucial difference in the life of a child. Her edicts address all aspects of schooling—from restlessness in the classroom to health risks for kids, from class size to the effects of detention. Johnson's "rules for schools" are concepts that everyone—from parent to presidential candidate—should take note of.

LouAnne Johnson (Lexington, NC), a former U.S. Navy journalist, Marine Corps officer, high school teacher, and college instructor, is also the author of several books, including the New York Times best-seller *Dangerous Minds*.

Other Books of Interest

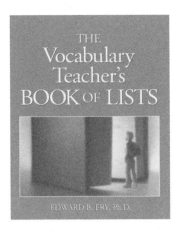

The Vocabulary Teacher's Book of Lists

Edward B. Fry, Ph.D.

Paperback/404 pages/2004
ISBN: 0-7879-7101-4

"*The Vocabulary Teacher's Book of Lists* will serve as an invaluable reference tool to any instructor involved in teaching English or designing project work. The content spans the grades from 4th up to college and is characteristic of Edward Fry's contribution to be both comprehensive and creative."

—Pat Costigan, learning consultant,
Bordentown Regional School District, New Jersey

The Vocabulary Teacher's Book of Lists provides content for literally hundreds of vocabulary improvement lessons for use by elementary, middle, and secondary school teachers, self-improving adults, homeschoolers, and students studying for the SATs and ACTs.

Replete with lists of words, books, teaching strategies, and many other useful tidbits of information related to language and literacy, this book picks up where Dr. Fry's best-selling *The Reading Teacher's Book of Lists* leaves off. Its primary focus is on vocabulary improvement for reading and writing. It contains a comprehensive section on roots and word origins; extensive lists of words used in science, psychology, and literature; along with an entire chapter on vocabulary teaching methods and options for curriculum content. Other chapters include spelling, homophones, exonyms, affixes, and specialized subject area terms. With a wide variety of levels and lengths, some lists may be appropriate for individual students as extra credit; other lists will help ESL students to master English; and yet other students will use these lists to prepare for college entrance exams.

Based upon extensive scholarship and comprehensive references, Dr. Fry's *Vocabulary Teacher's Book of Lists* bridges popular notions of vocabulary building and word-smithing with the more formal academic study of language syntax and lexicon. It is an indispensable resource for both teachers and parents aiming to improve their students' vocabulary and literacy skills.

Edward B. Fry, Ph.D., is professor emeritus of education at Rutgers University, where for twenty-four years he was director of the Reading Center. Dr. Fry is known internationally for his Readability Graph, which is used by teachers, publishers, and others to judge the difficulty of books and other materials. Fry was elected to the Reading Hall of Fame in 1993. He is the coauthor of *The Reading Teacher's Book of Lists,* now in its fourth edition, from Jossey-Bass.